DAHMANE
EROTIC SESSIONS

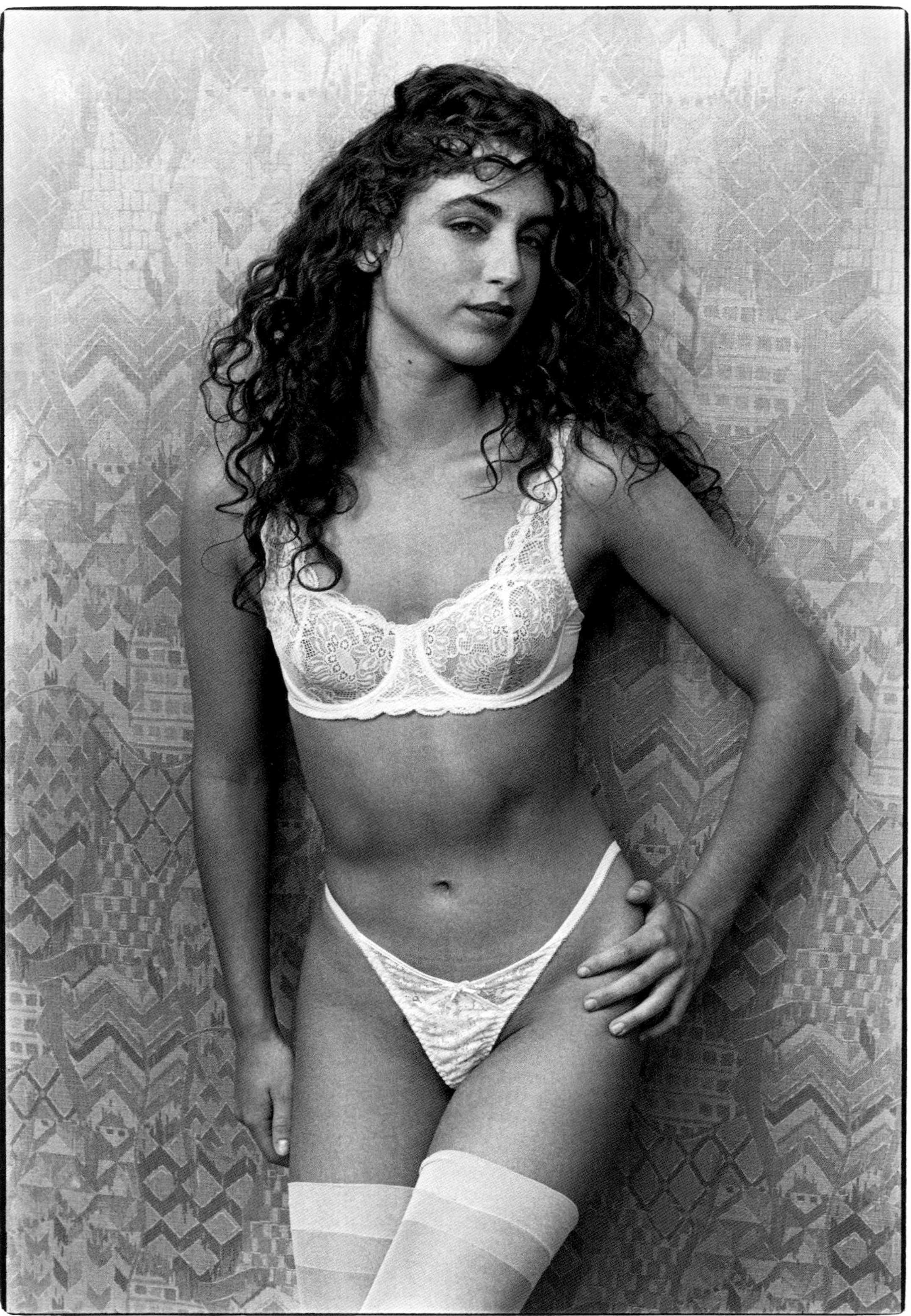

DAHMANE
EROTIC SESSIONS

SPECIAL PAPERBACK EDITION
REVISED AND ENLARGED

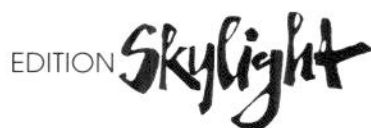

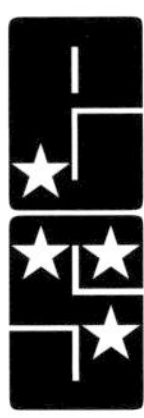

Special Paperback Edition revised and enlarged
2nd Edition 2025
1st Edition 2022
Copyright © 2022 by Edition Skylight
Original Hardback Edition published 2003

EDITION SKYLIGHT
Rosengartenstr. 13B
8608 Bubikon/Zürich
Switzerland
info@edition-skylight.com
www.edition-skylight.com

ISBN 978-3-03766-683-8

Bibliographic information published by Die Deutsche Bibliothek
Die Deutsche Bibliothek lists this publication in the
Deutsche Nationalbibliografie; detailed bibliographic data
are available in the Internet at http://dnb.ddb.de.

Printed in Bosnia and Herzegovina

Helo hieß das Mädchen mit richtigem Vornamen und bei ihr verlor ich vor recht langer Zeit meine Jungfräulichkeit. Ich war fünfzehn, wir steckten mitten in den Siebzigern, Flower Power zeigte seine ganze Kraft und stahl sich ins Bewusstsein derjenigen, die am empfänglichsten dafür waren: diese hübsche Deutsche und ich zählten zu den glühenden Anhängern. 1974 war ein entscheidendes Jahr, in dem das Gefühl der Zärtlichkeit, das mich schon in jungen Jahren erfüllte, eine, sagen wir mal … festere Beschaffenheit annahm. Ja, und dann entdeckte ich die Fotografie in Gestalt einer außergewöhnlichen neuen Bekannten meiner Eltern. Sie war Kunstfotografin, und ich verliebte mich sofort in sie. Ende der Ferien kehrte Helo an ihre Universität in Freiburg zurück. Ich hatte sie also gerade zum richtigen Zeitpunkt kennengelernt, um die Liebe zu entdekken. Die Liebe und die Fotografie, meine beiden stärksten Leidenschaften, kamen in jenem Jahr zusammen und haben seitdem nie aufgehört, sich innig zu vermischen. Abgesehen von einigen wenigen Ausnahmen, und in unterschiedlichem Ausmaß, liebte ich – und liebe noch heute – all diese Mädchen und jungen Frauen, die ich fotografiert habe. Tiefe Dankbarkeit erfüllt mich, denn sie machten mir das Geschenk, für mich zu posieren und gaben mir die Erlaubnis, unsere Fotografien in diesem Buch zu veröffentlichen. Ich hätte große Lust, die Gefühle der Zuneigung, Freundschaft und Leidenschaft, die ich mit meinen Modellen geteilt habe, sowie ihren Charakter, ihre Reize und ihre Persönlichkeit detailliert zu beschreiben, aber ich glaube, dass ich das alles viel besser in Form von Bildern machen kann …

La jeune fille qui me fit perdre ma virginité, il y a bien longtemps déjà, s'appelait Helo de son vrai prénom. J'avais quinze ans, nous nous trouvions en plein milieu des années 70, le Flower Power exprimait toute sa puissance et imprégnait les esprits les mieux disposés : nous en étions, cette belle Allemande et moi, de fervents adeptes. 1974, année capitale, où le sentiment amoureux, qui m'avait étreint depuis mon plus jeune âge, prenait enfin consistance. La photographie allait se révéler à moi sous la forme d'une extraordinaire nouvelle amie de mes parents, photographe d'art, dont je m'épris instantanément. Les vacances finies, Helo était retournée à l'université de Freiburg ; je l'avais connue à temps pour découvrir l'amour et Johne allait prendre le relais pour m'initier à la photographie.
Amour et photographie, mes deux passions essentielles, se rencontrèrent cette année-là et n'ont plus cessé depuis de se mêler intimement. À des degrés divers, j'ai aimé, parfois d'amour – et j'aime encore –, toutes les jeunes filles et les jeunes femmes que j'ai photographiées ; le merveilleux présent qu'elles m'ont fait en posant pour moi et en me permettant de publier nos photos au sein d'un livre m'emplit d'un sentiment de reconnaissance émue. L'envie ne me manquerait pas de décrire par le menu les affections, les amitiés ou les passions que j'ai partagées avec mes modèles, et aussi leurs caractères, leurs charmes, leurs personnalités, mais je crois que je sais mieux raconter tout cela en images …

Her real name was Helo and she was the young girl I lost my virginity to all those years ago. I was fifteen, we were bang in the middle of the Seventies, and Flower Power was flexing all its muscles and infiltrating the minds of those most ready for it; and we, that is, this pretty German girl and I, had become fervent followers of it. 1974 was a decisive year, in which the feeling of tenderness which had enveloped me from an early age started taking on a, shall we say… more solid consistency.
I had just discovered photography in the guise of an extraordinary new friend of my parents, an art photographer, and I fell for her at once. When the holidays were over, Helo returned to the University of Freiburg; I had got to know her just in time to discover love, and my initiation into the world of photography was continued by Johne. Love and photography, my two most profound passions, came together that year and have never stopped intermingling since. With varying intensity, and with very few exceptions, I loved – and still love – all of the girls and young women I photographed; the wonderful gift they gave me by posing for me and allowing me to publish our photographs in book form fills me with a feeling of deep gratitude. I would love to give a detailed description of the feelings of affection, friendship and passion which I shared with my models, not forgetting their characters, their charms and their personalities, but I think I can do all that much better with pictures …

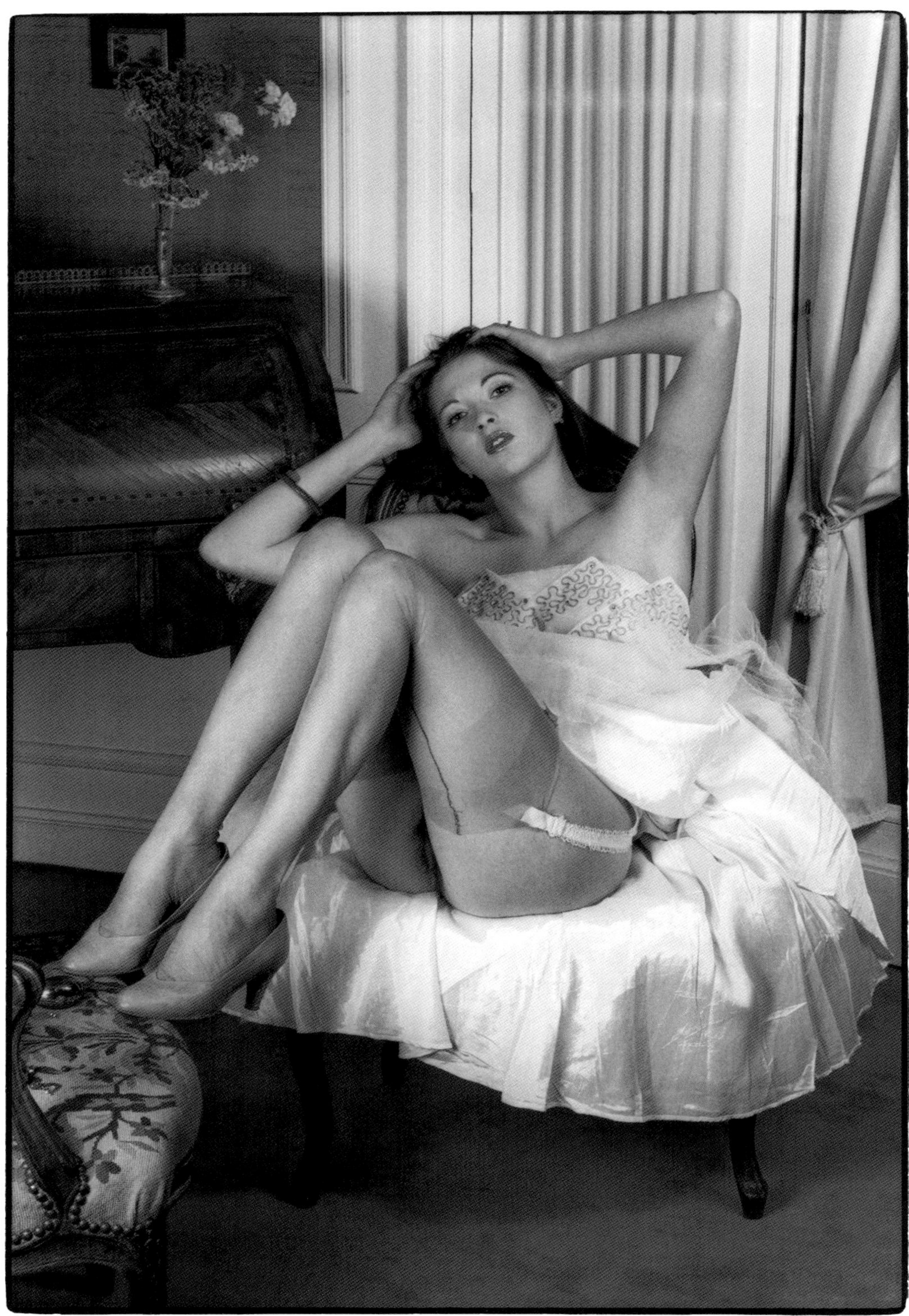

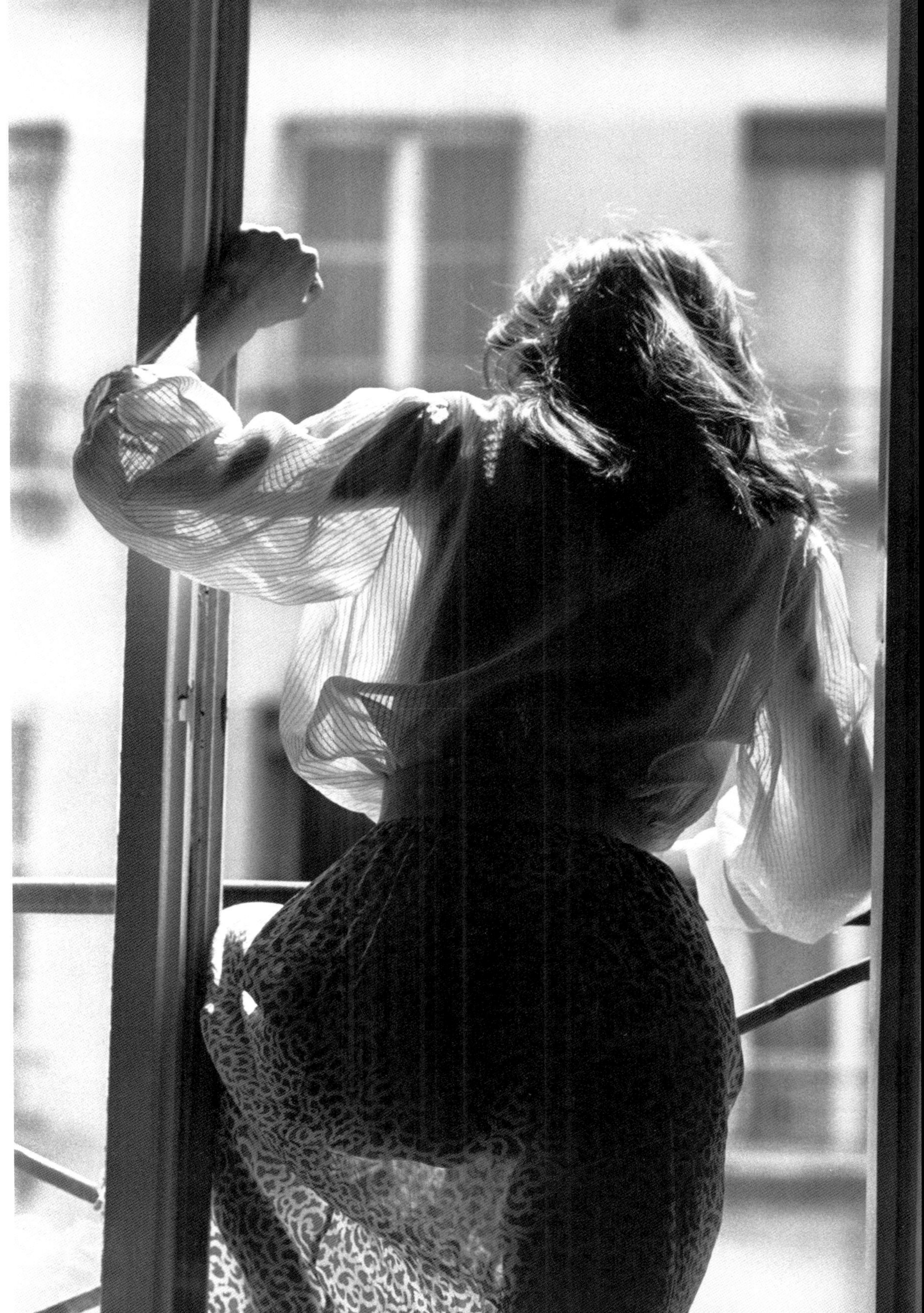

Anna
1981

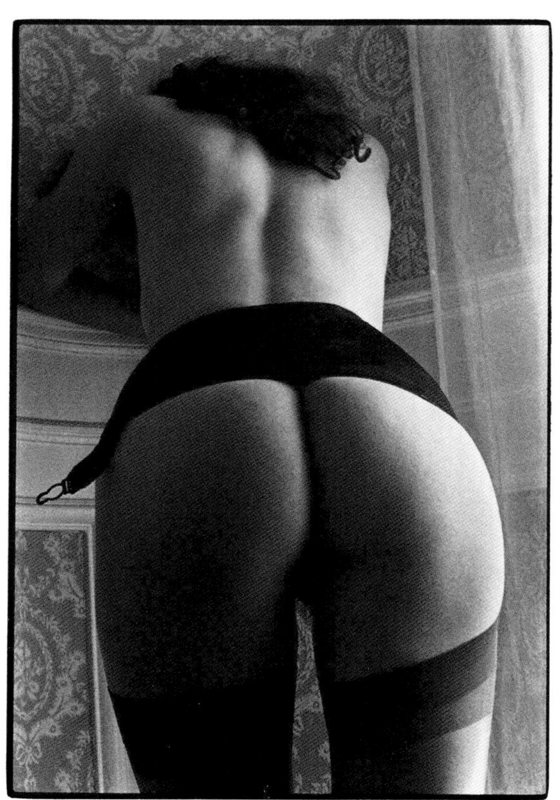

  Françoise 1976

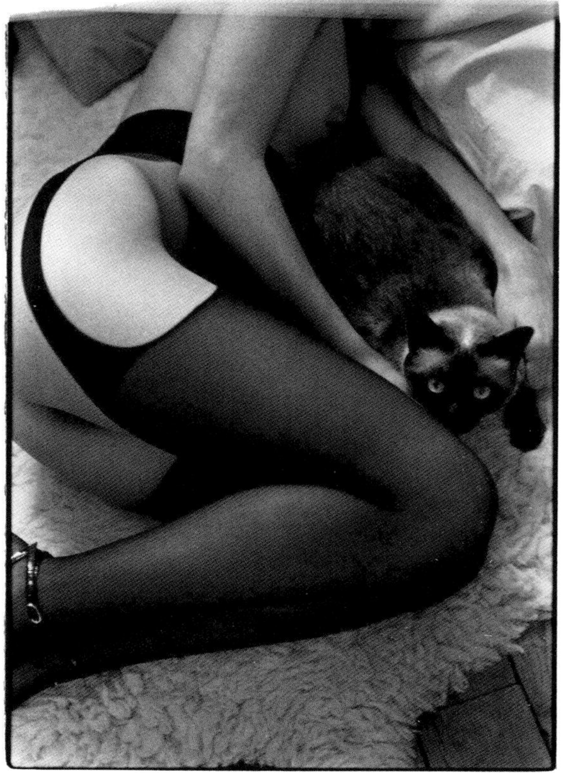

Anna 1977

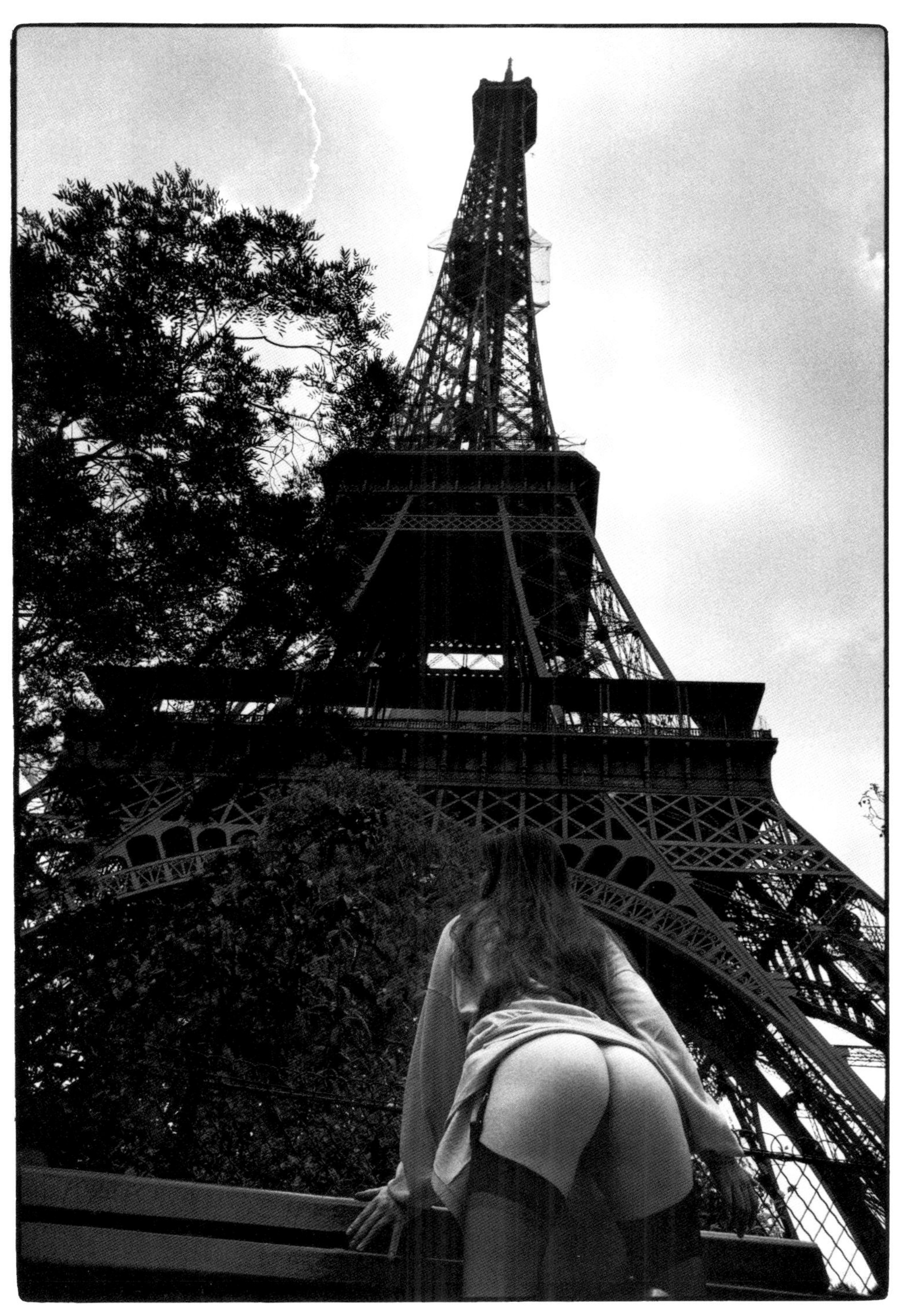

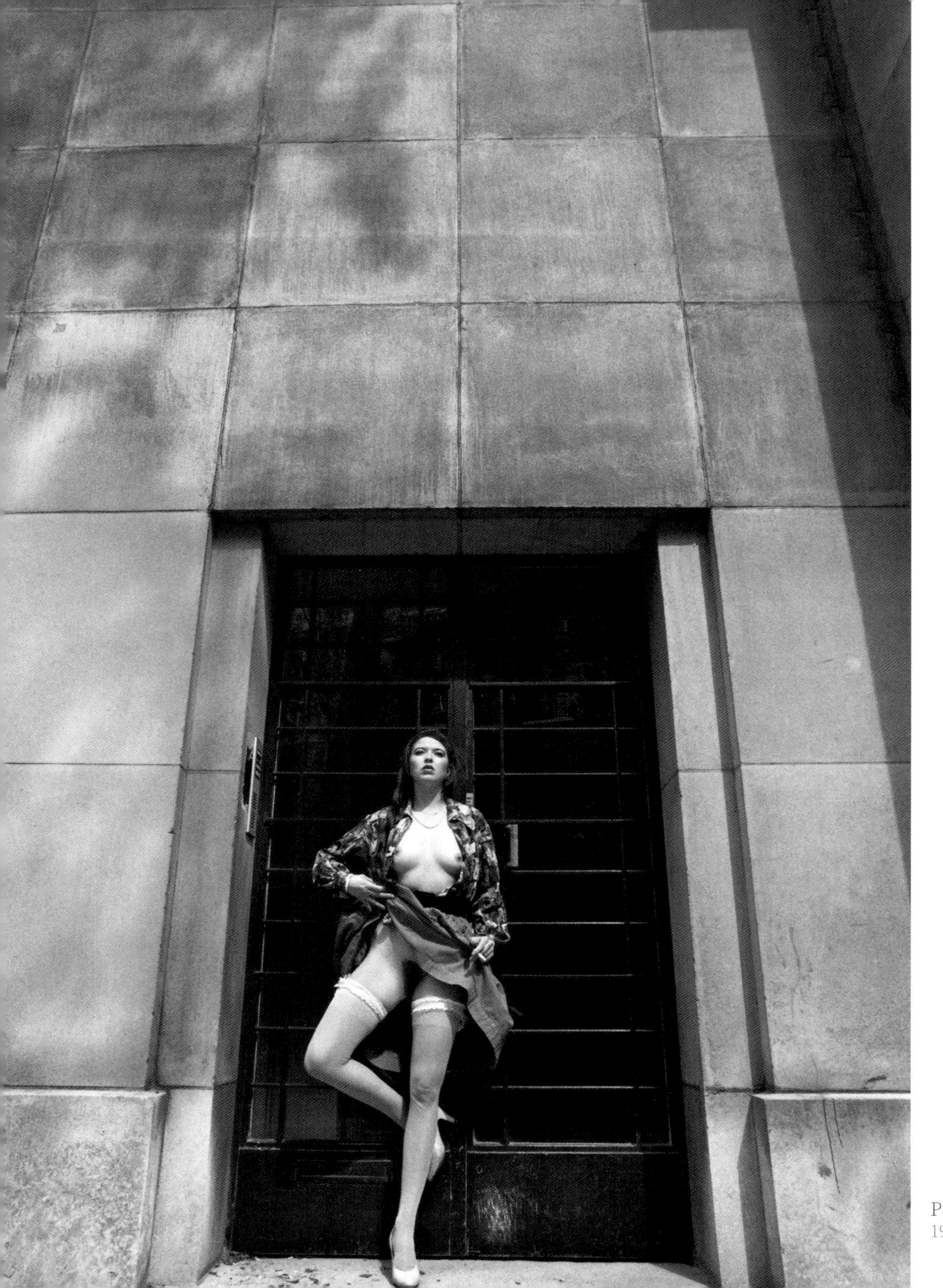

Pascale
1981

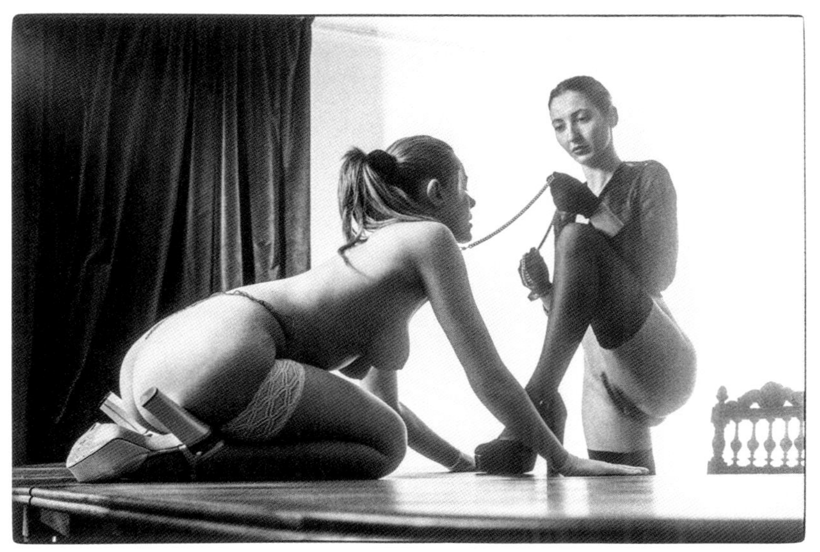

Julie & Johanna 1981

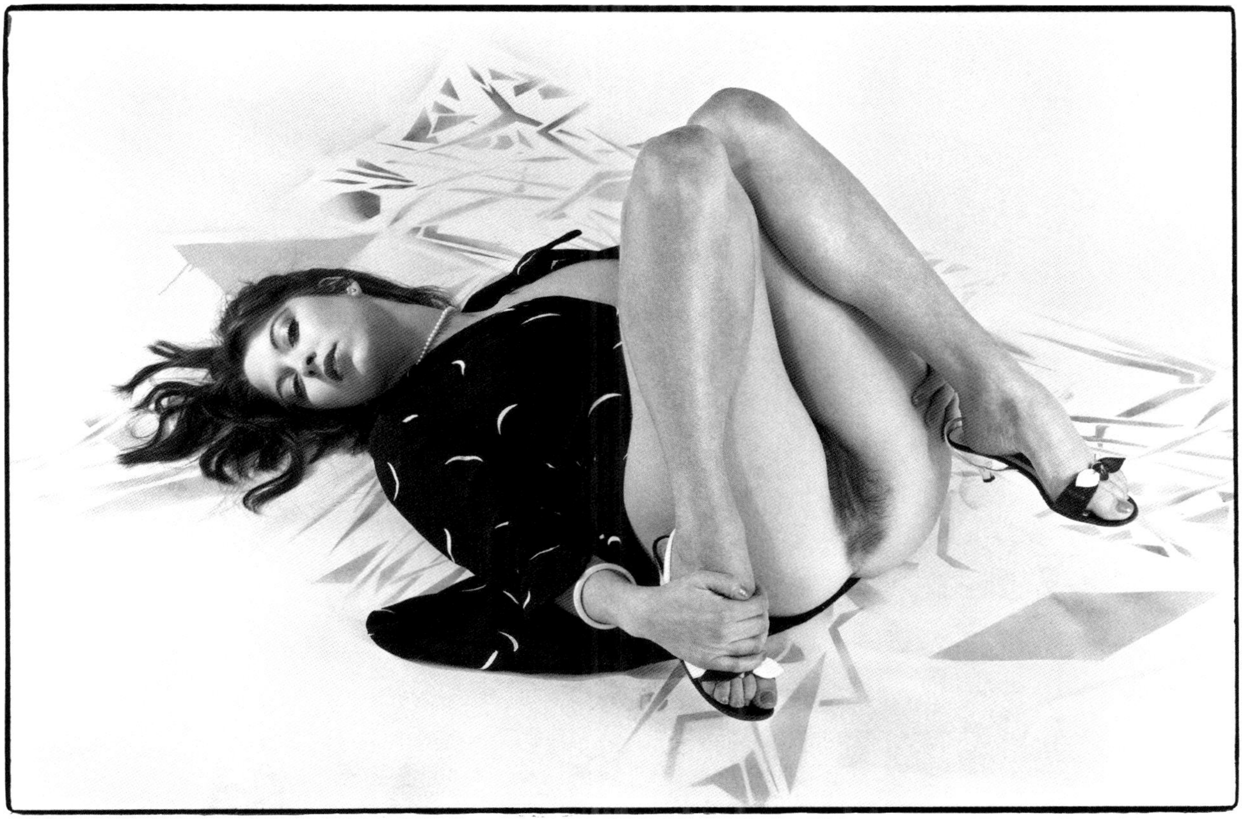

Pascale 1981   11

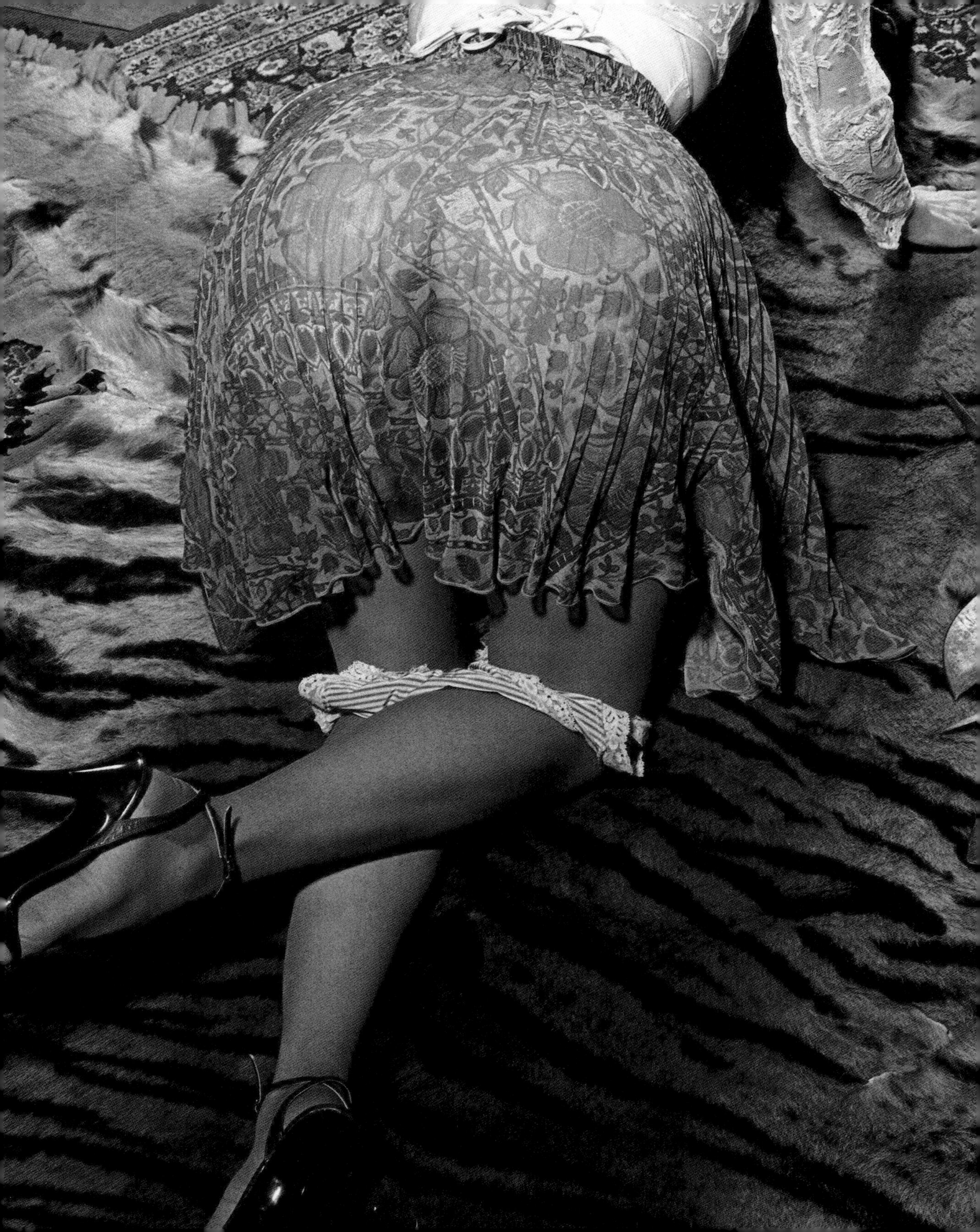

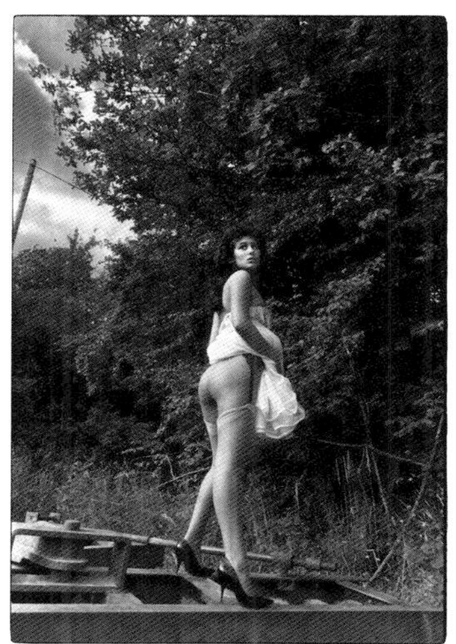

Toni 1982

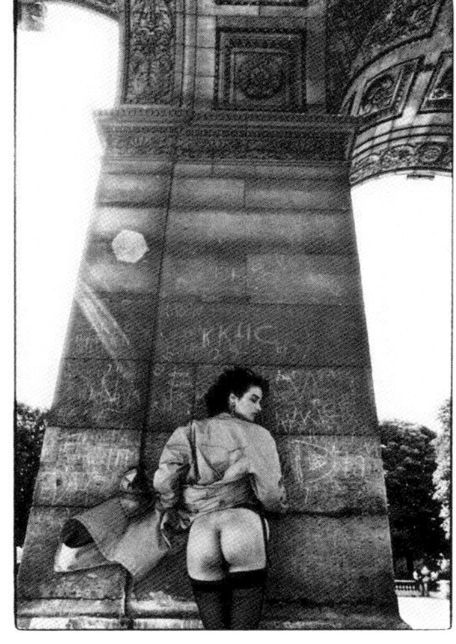

Raphaëlle 1982

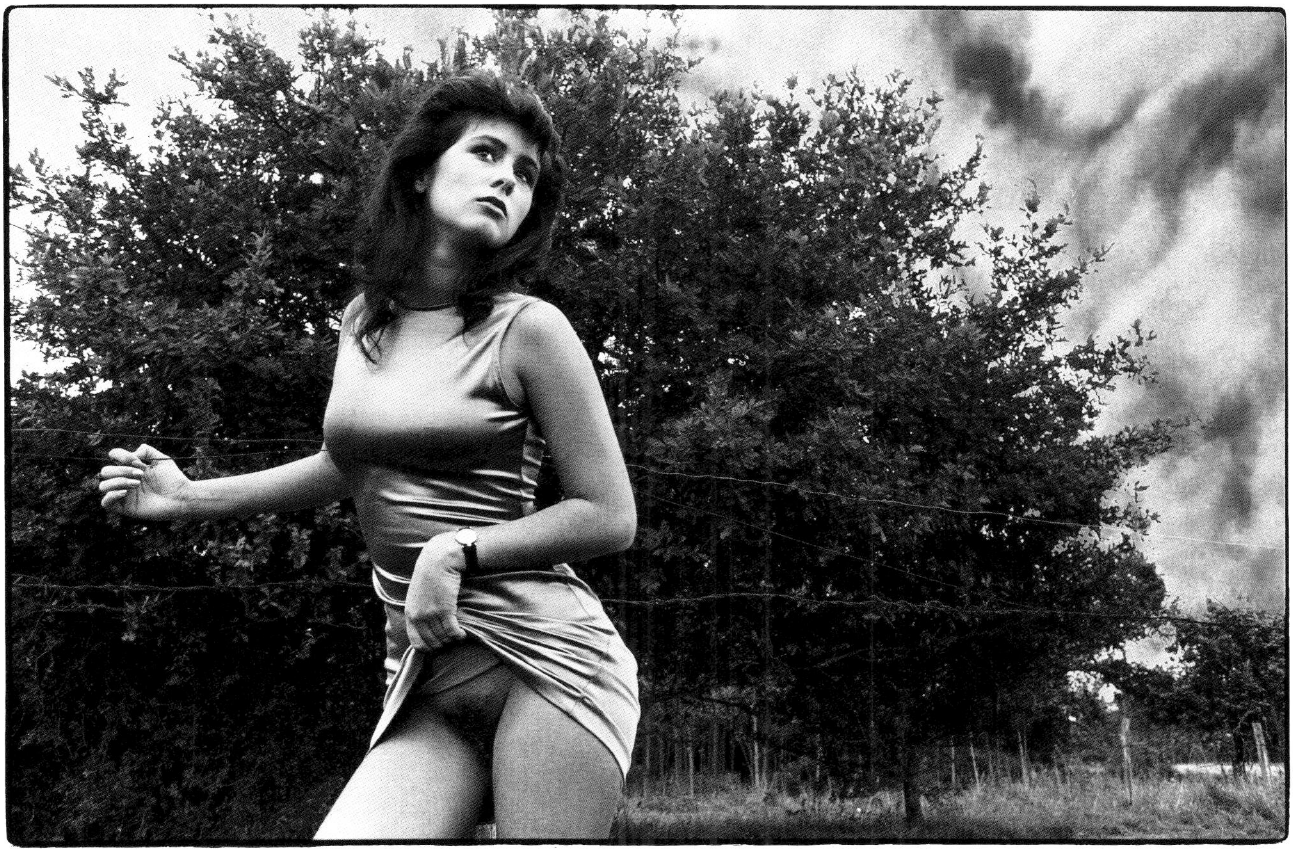

Toni 1982

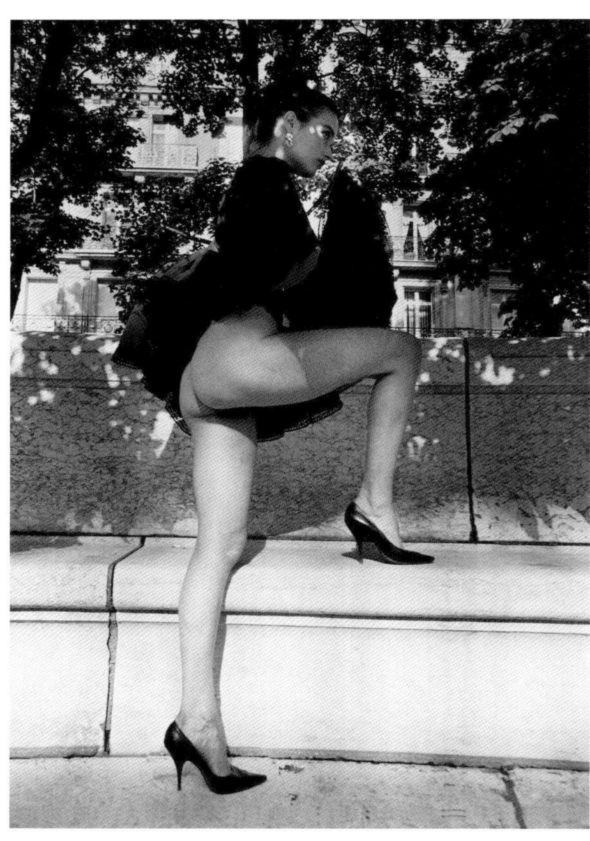

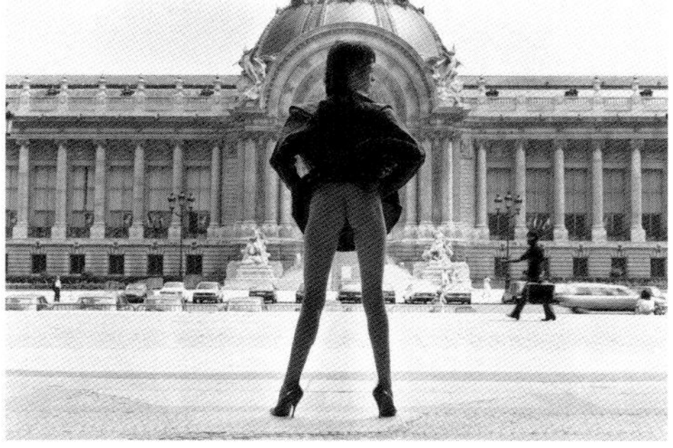

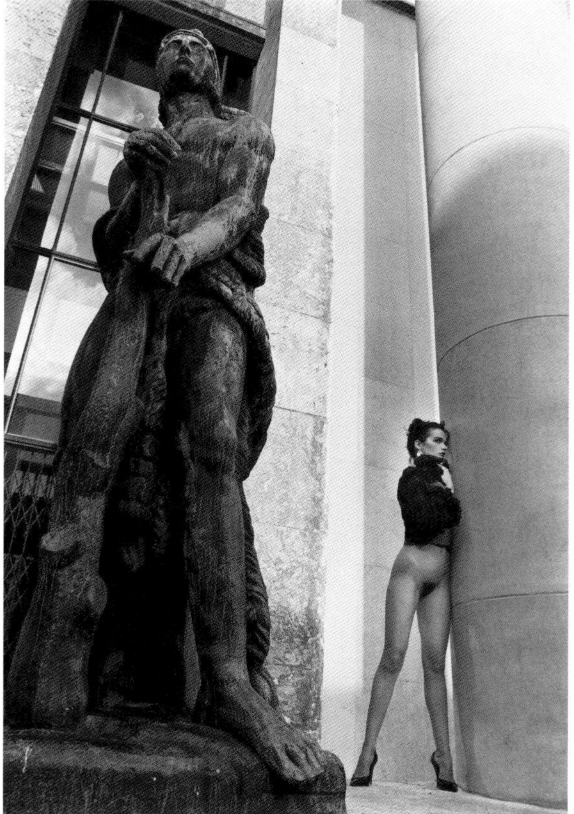

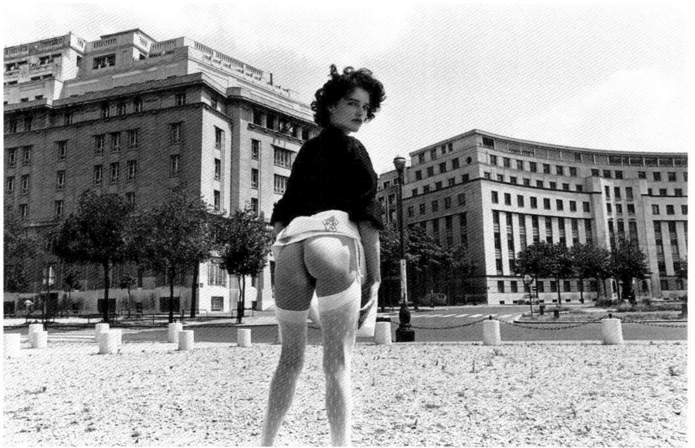

Raphaëlle 1983

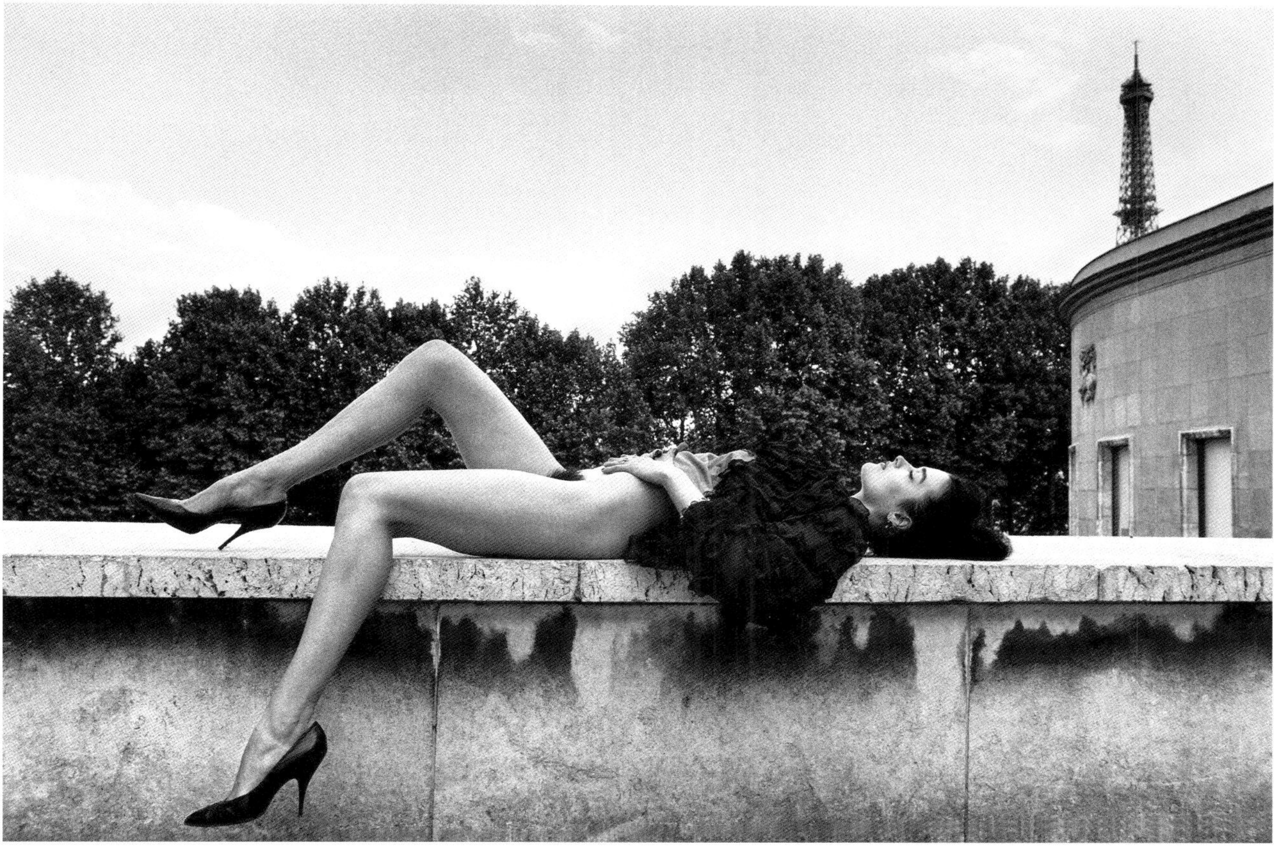

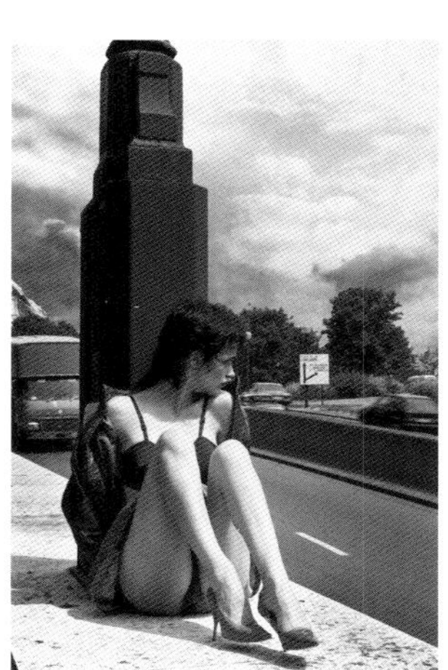

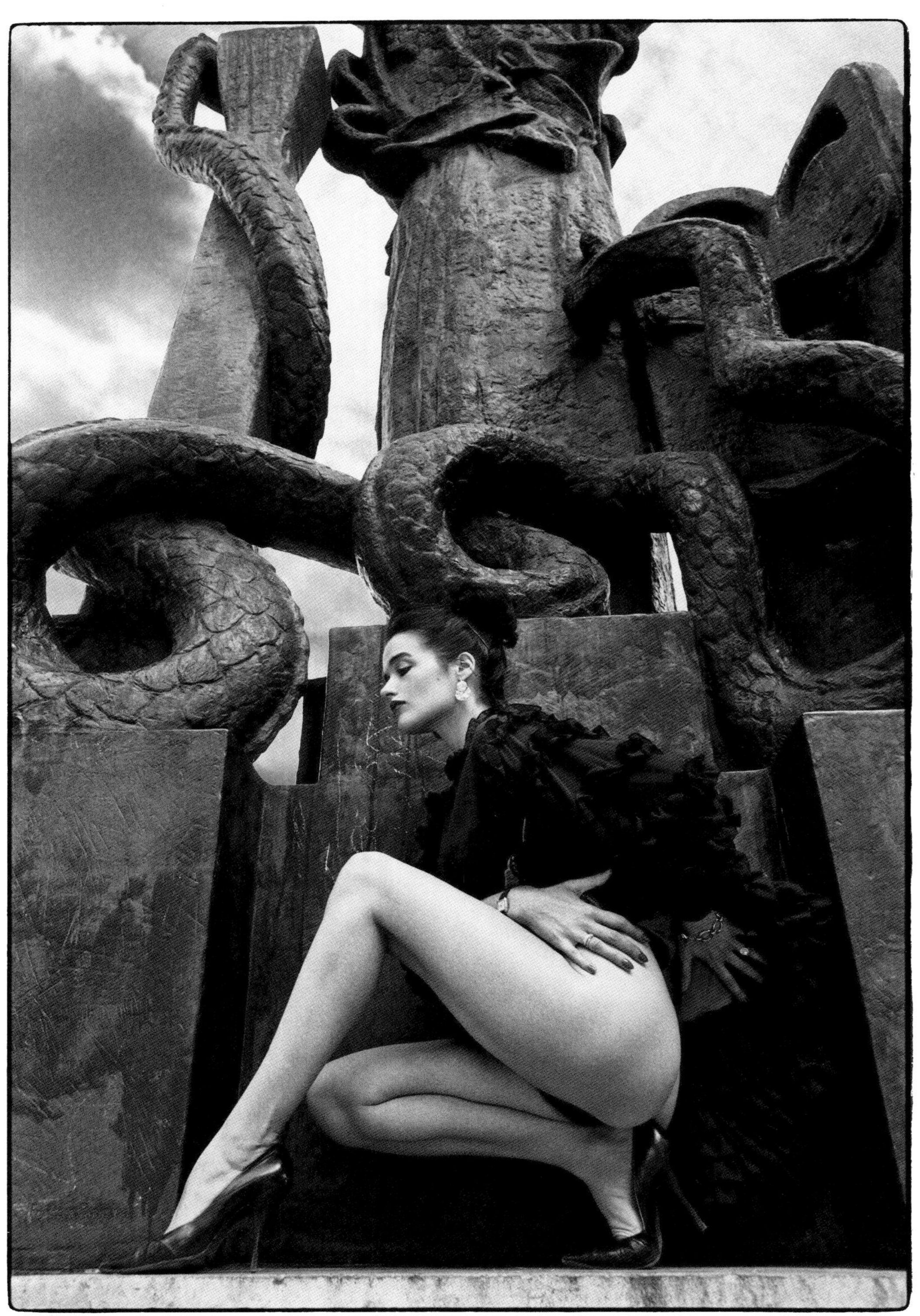

16 Raphaëlle 1982

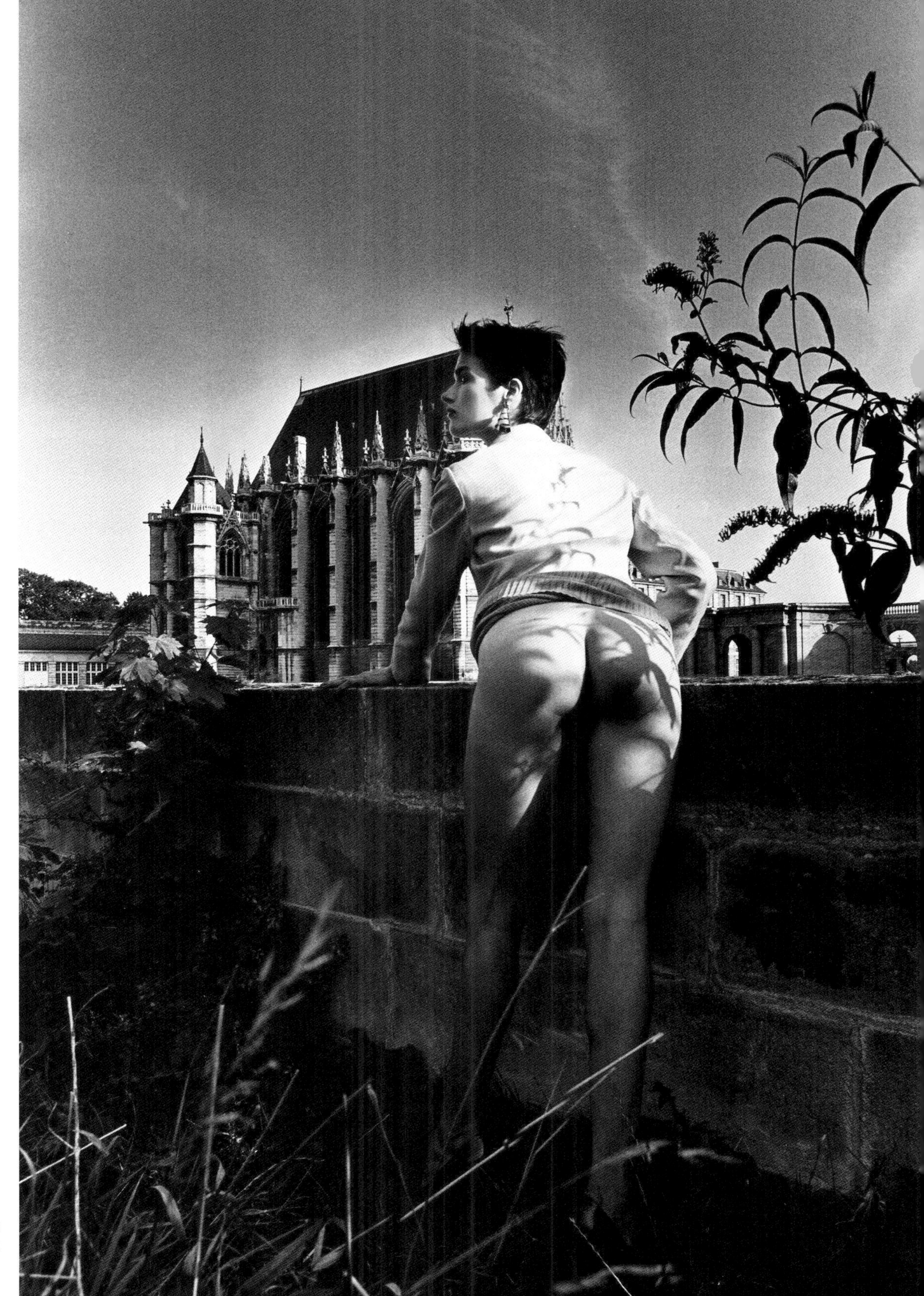

Raphaëlle
1983

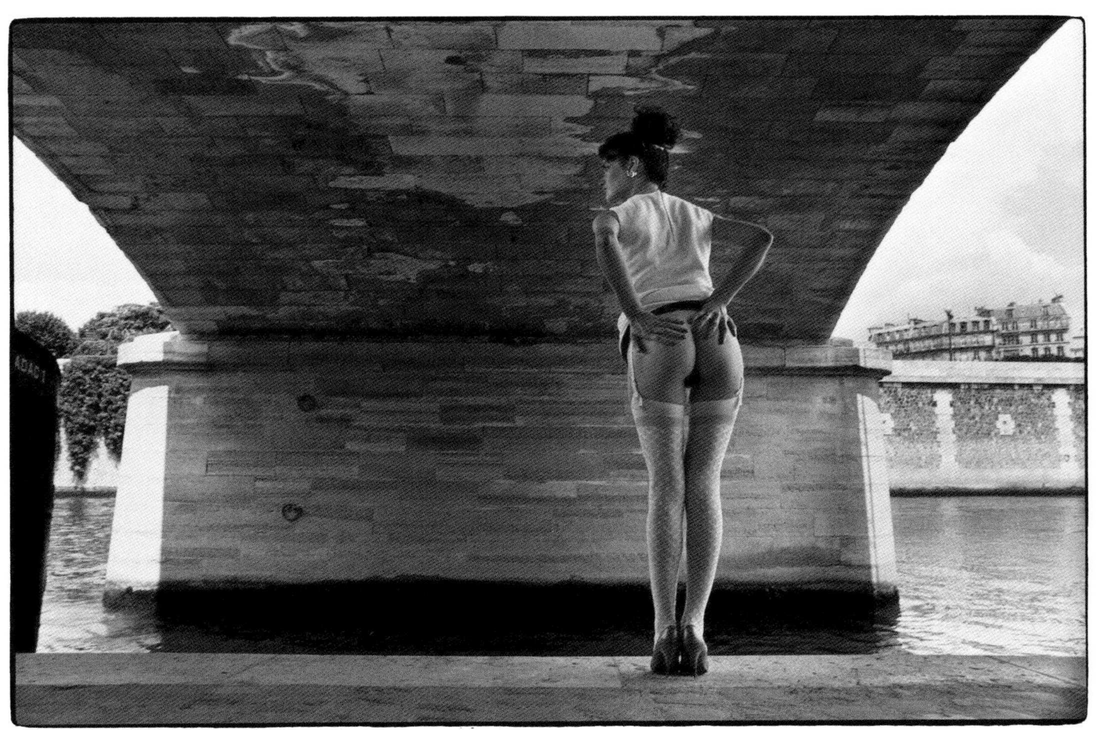

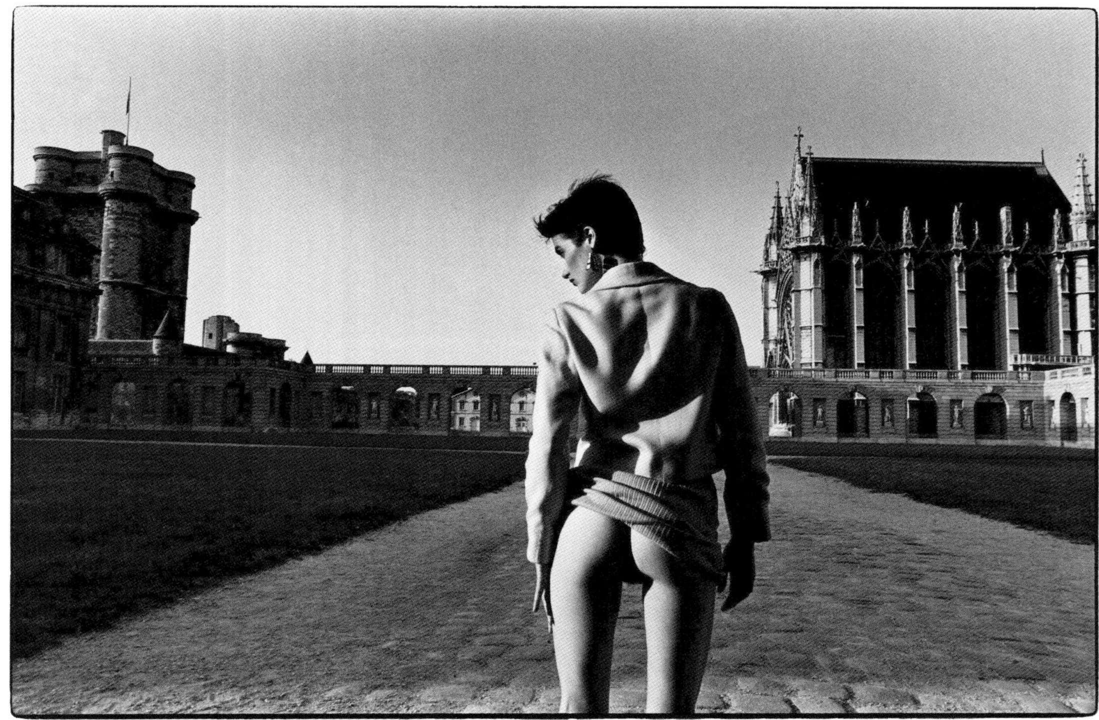

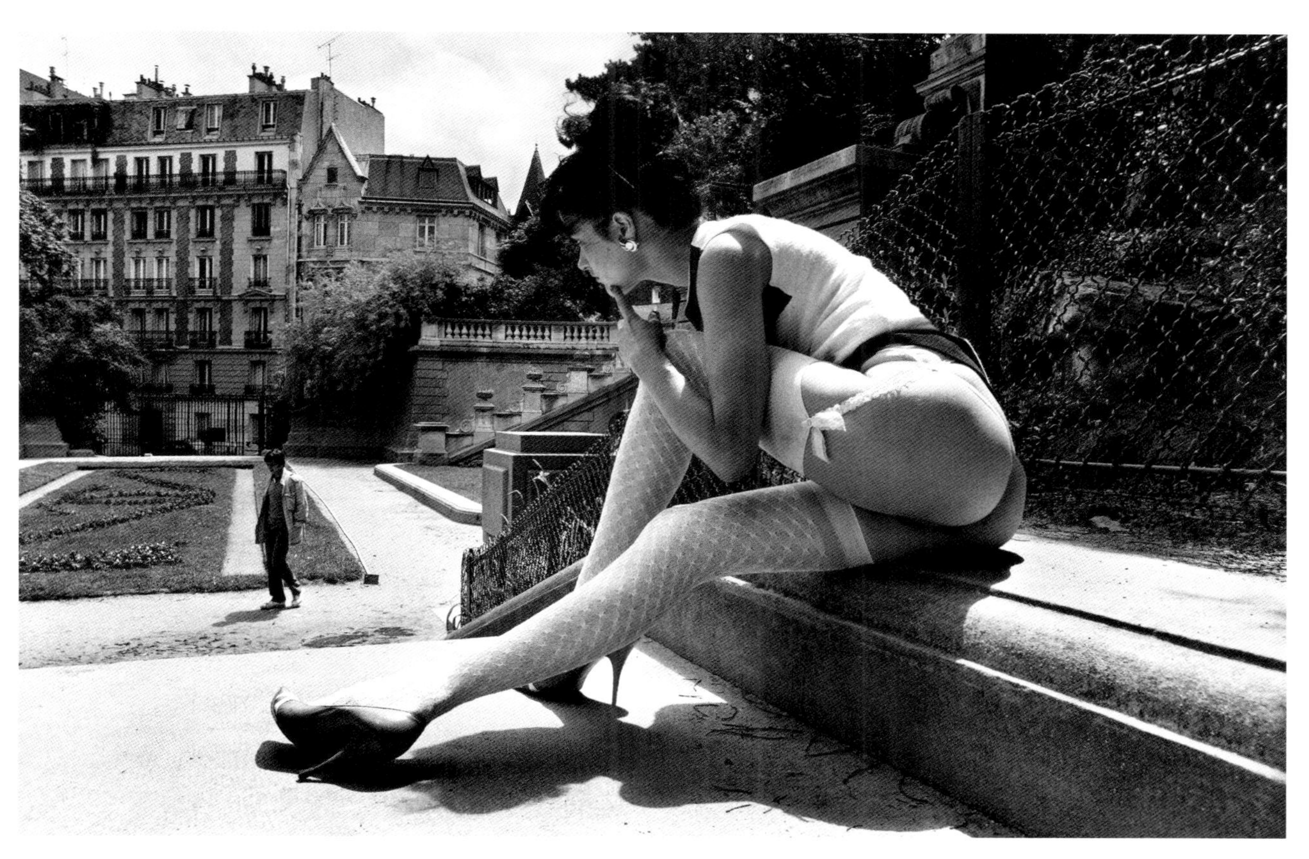

Raphaëlle 1983   19

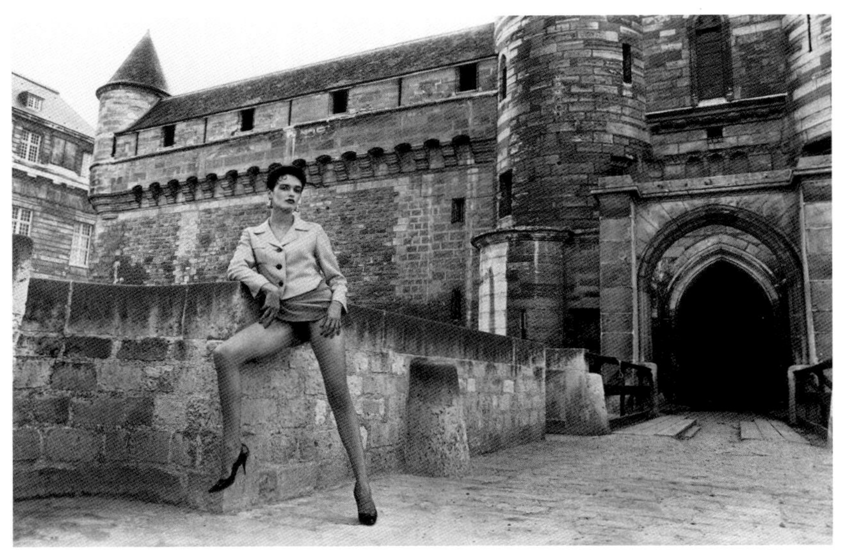

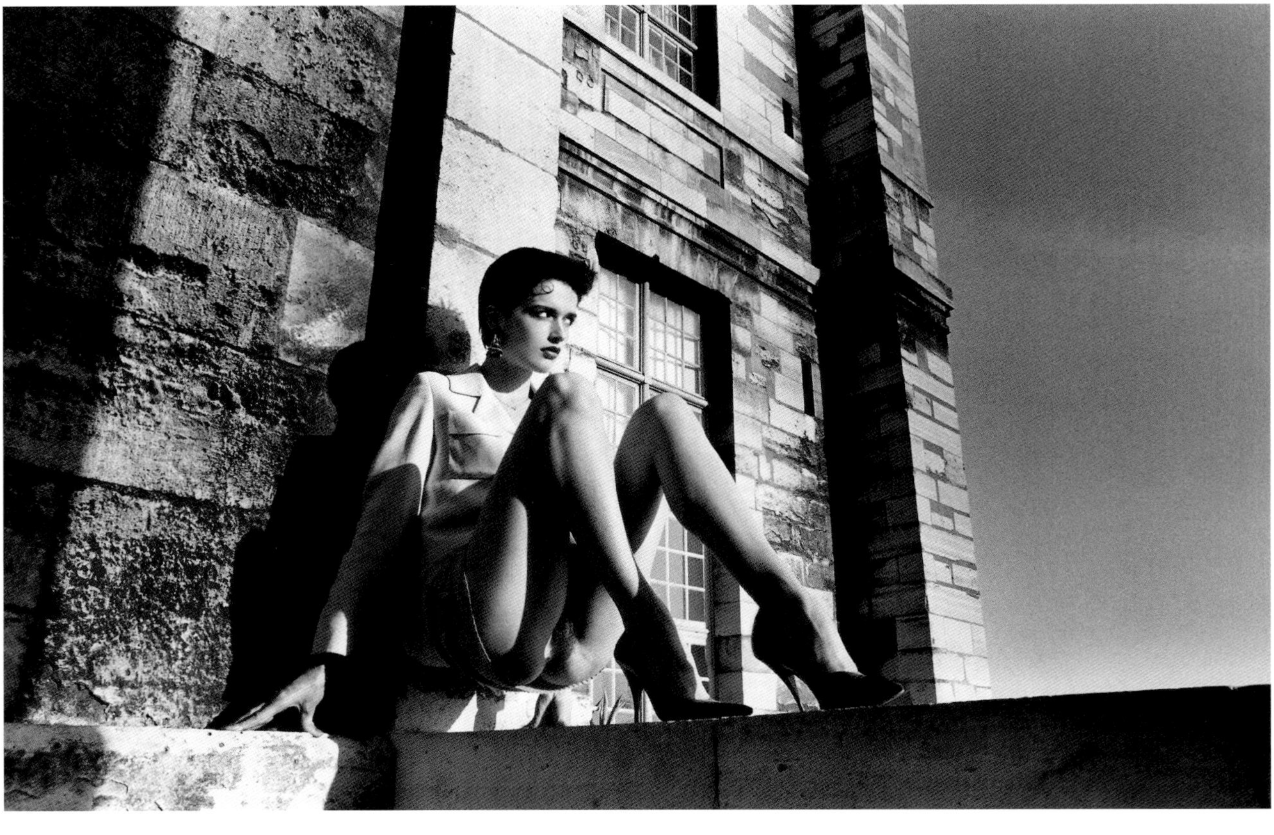

20　Raphaëlle 1983

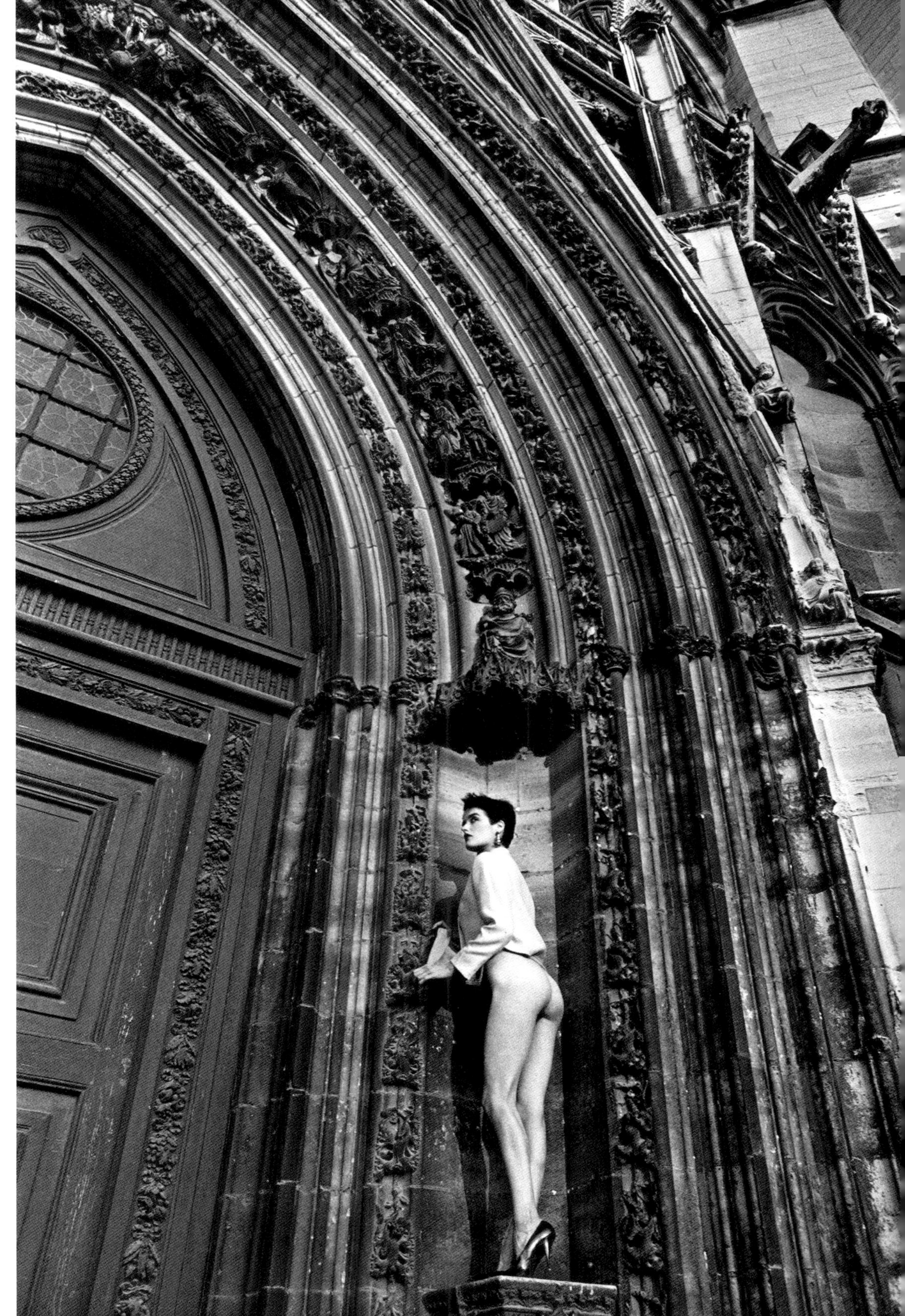

Raphaëlle
1983

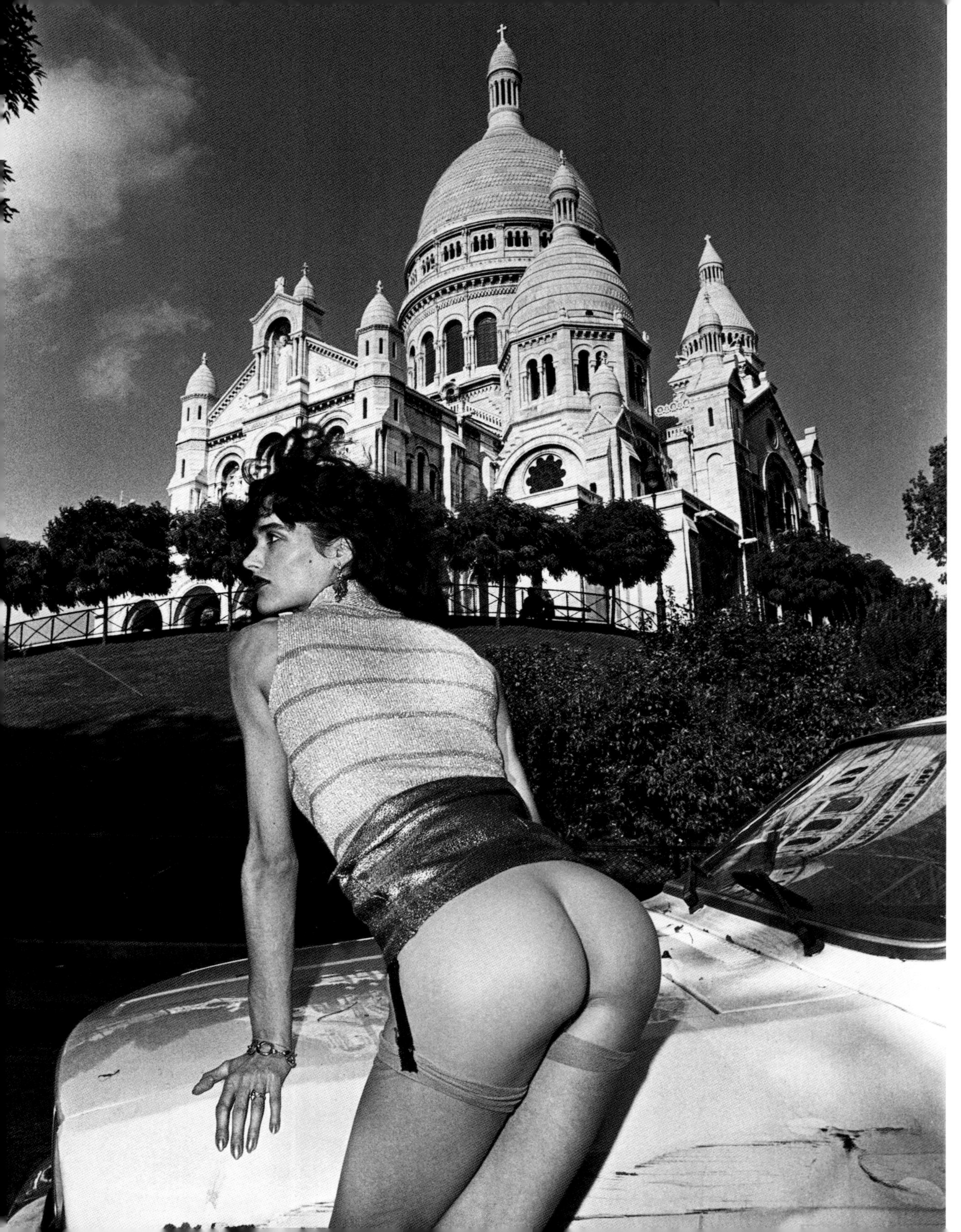

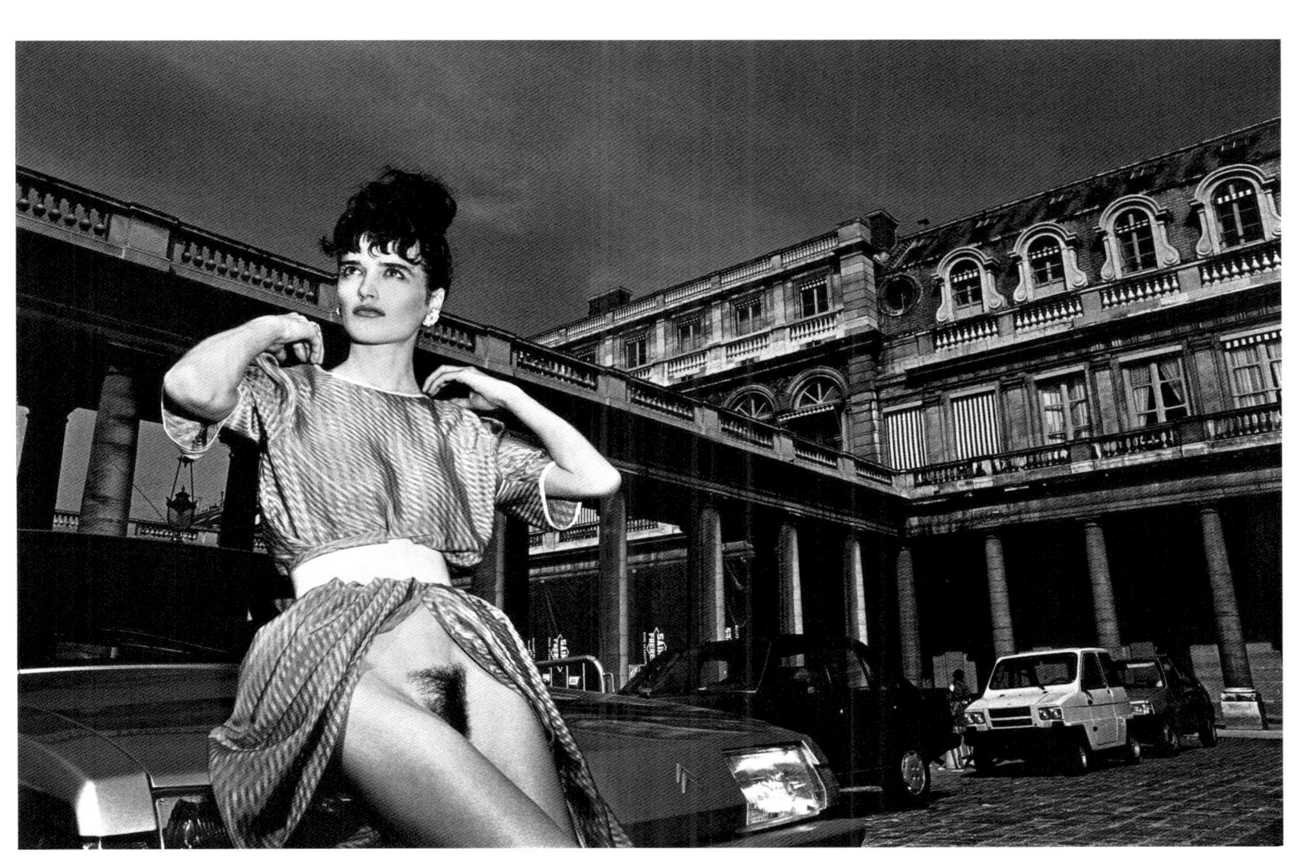

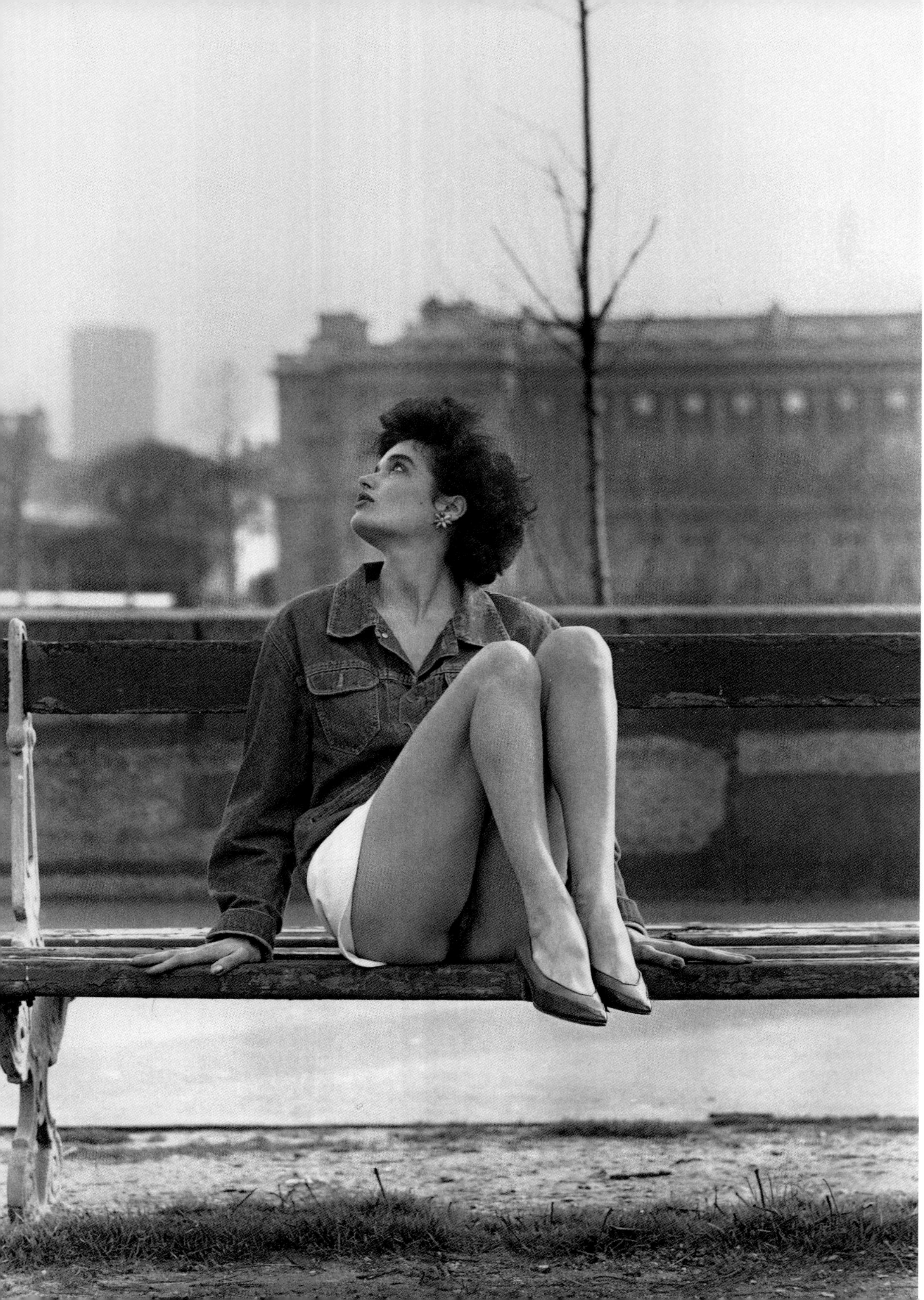

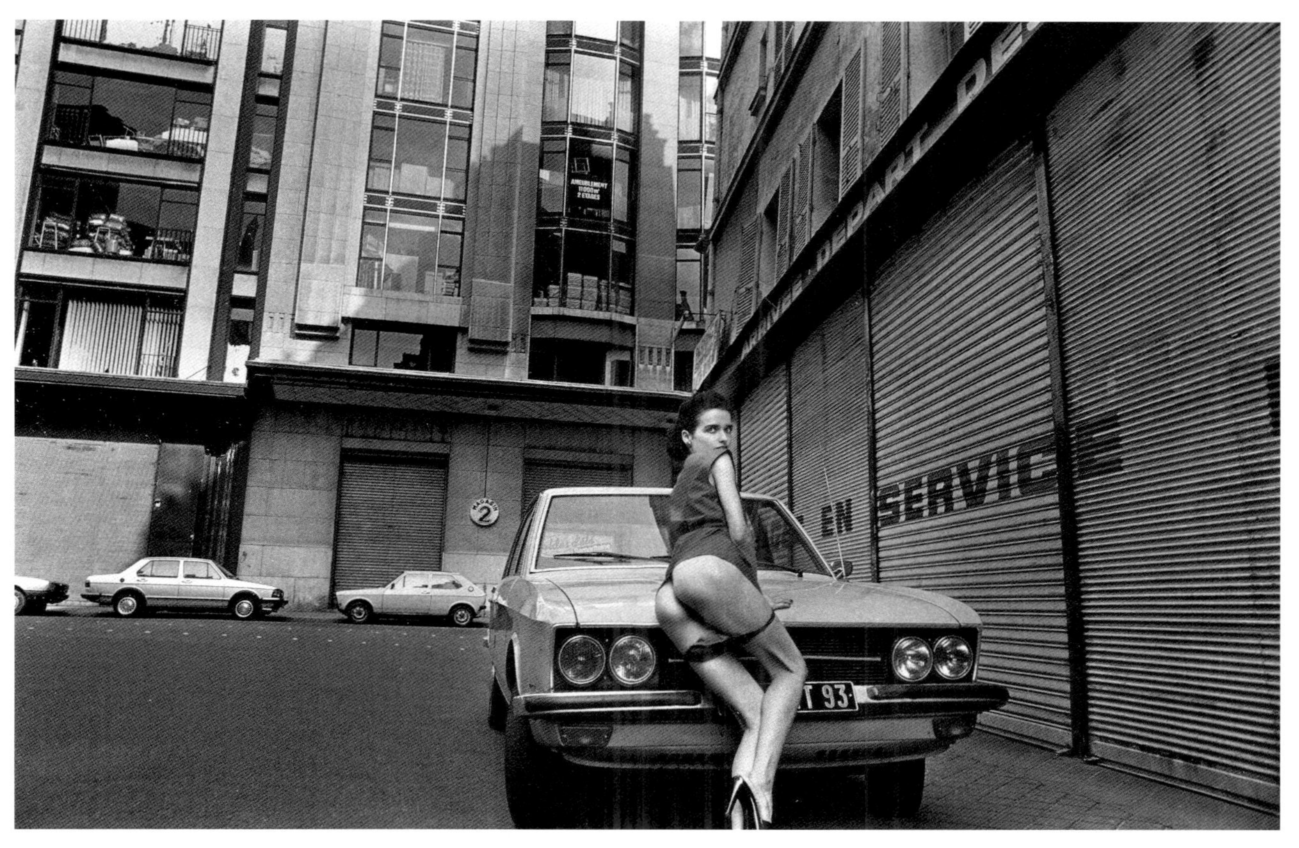
EN SERVICE
93

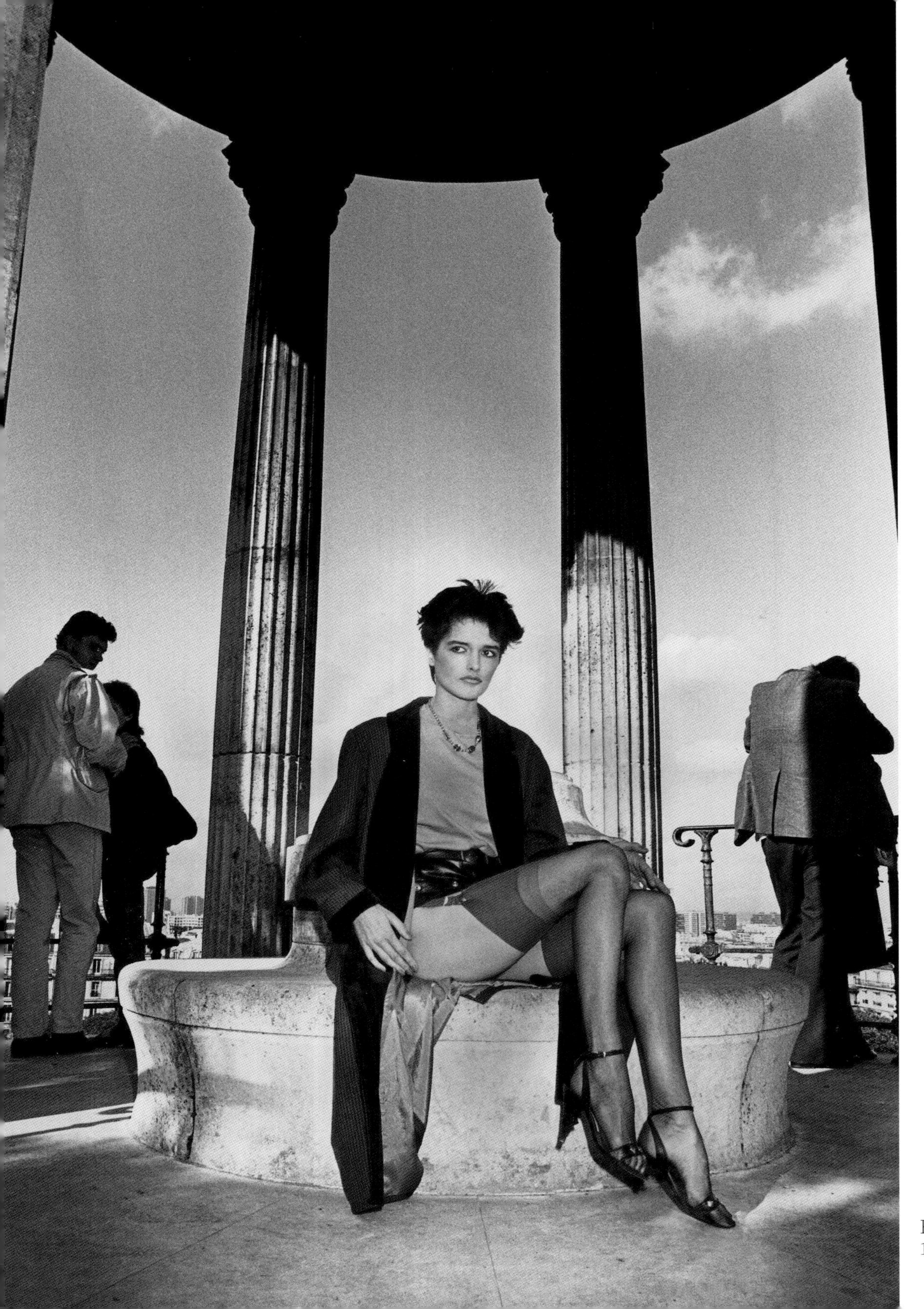

Raphaëlle
1983

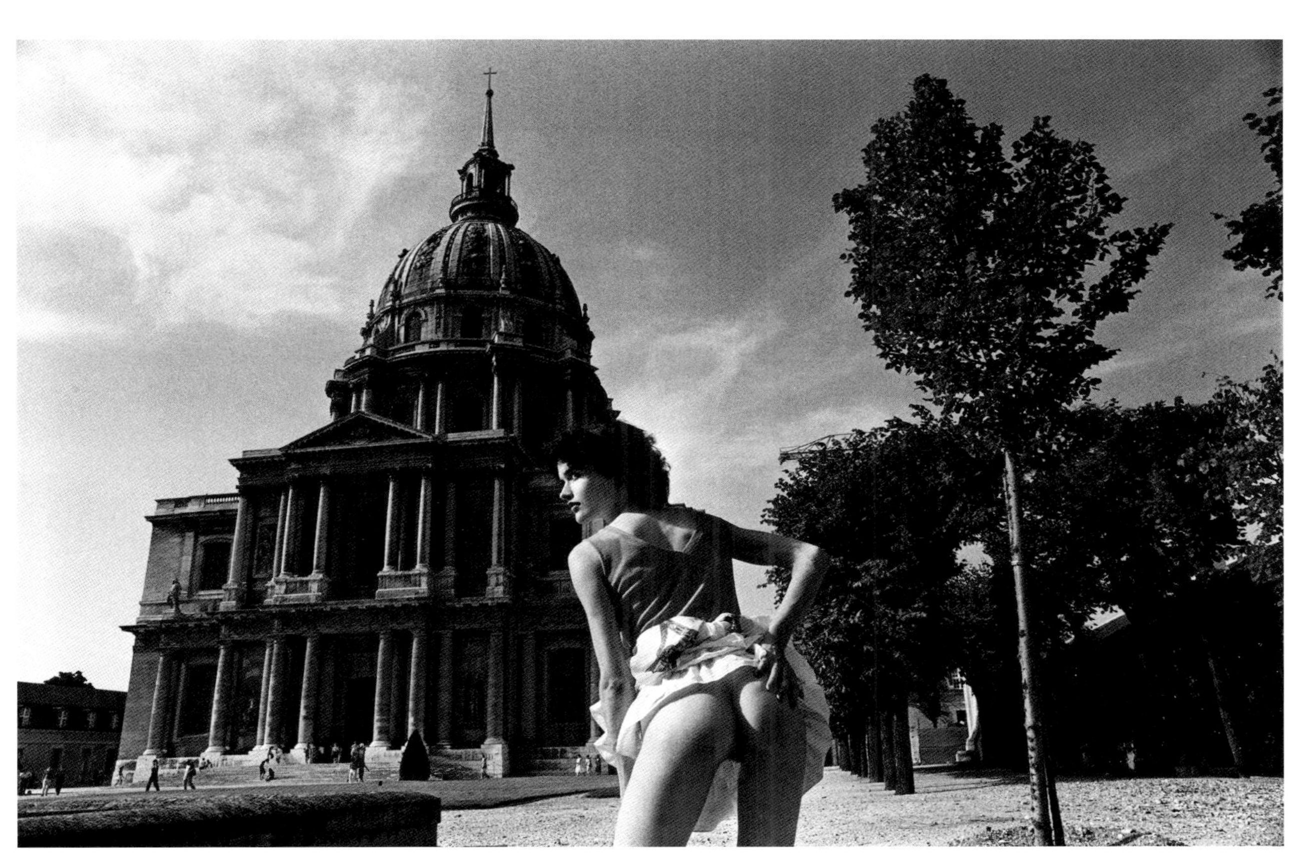

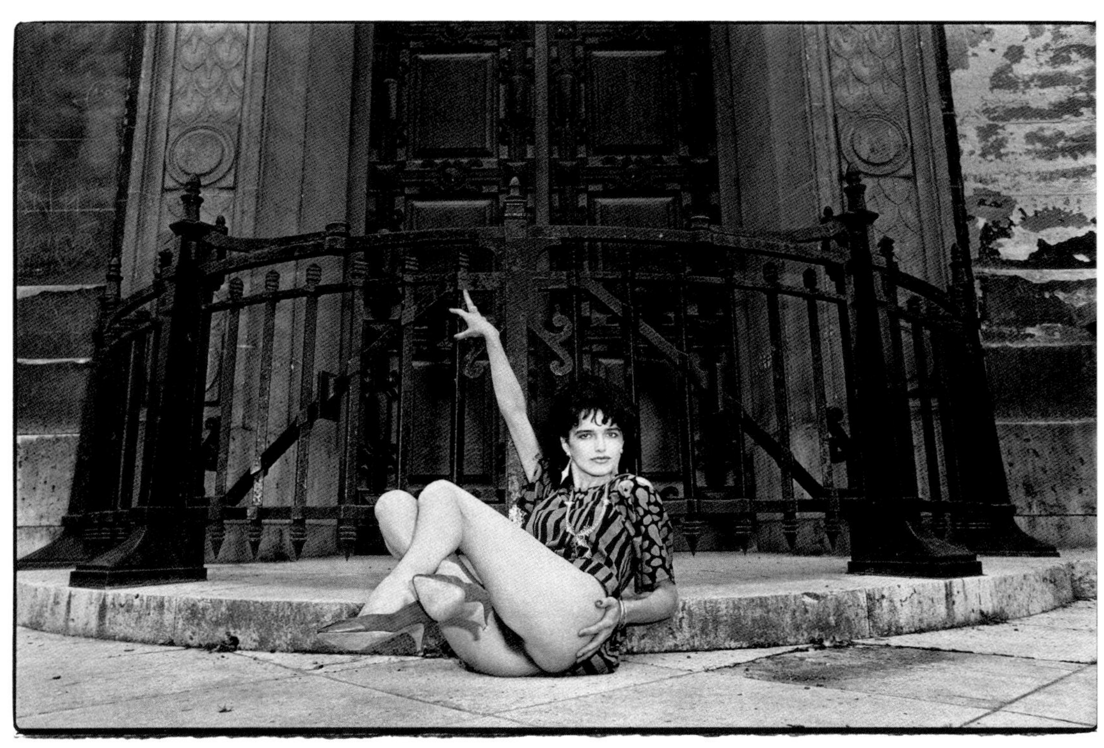

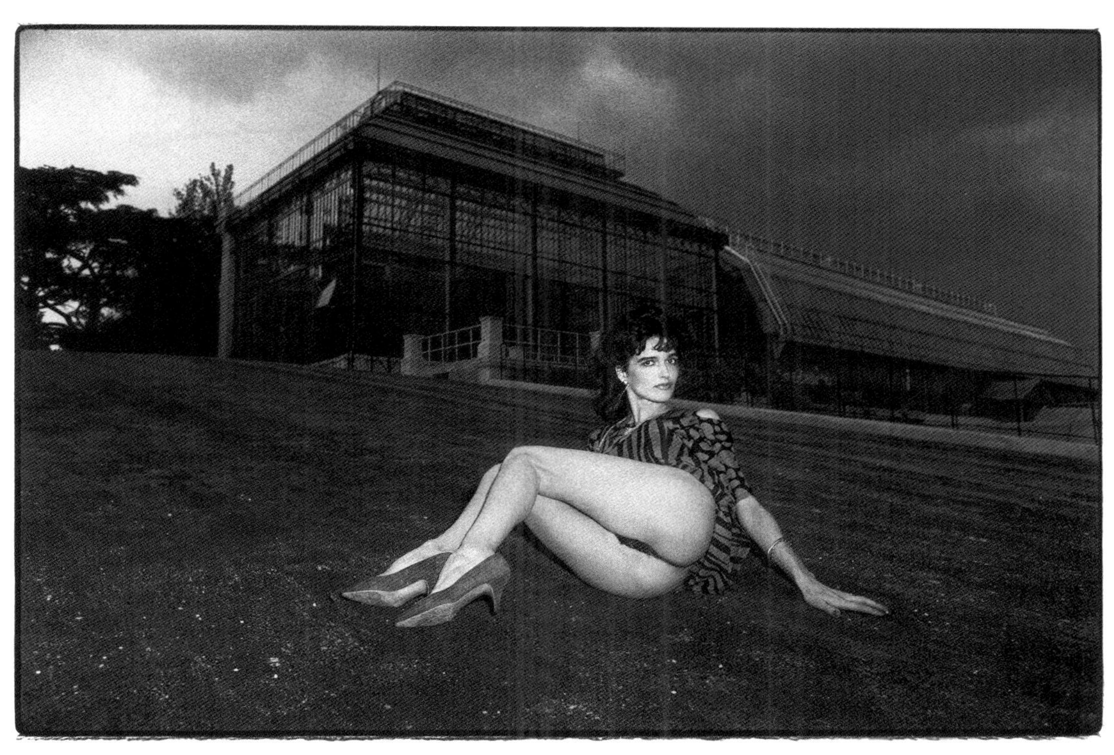

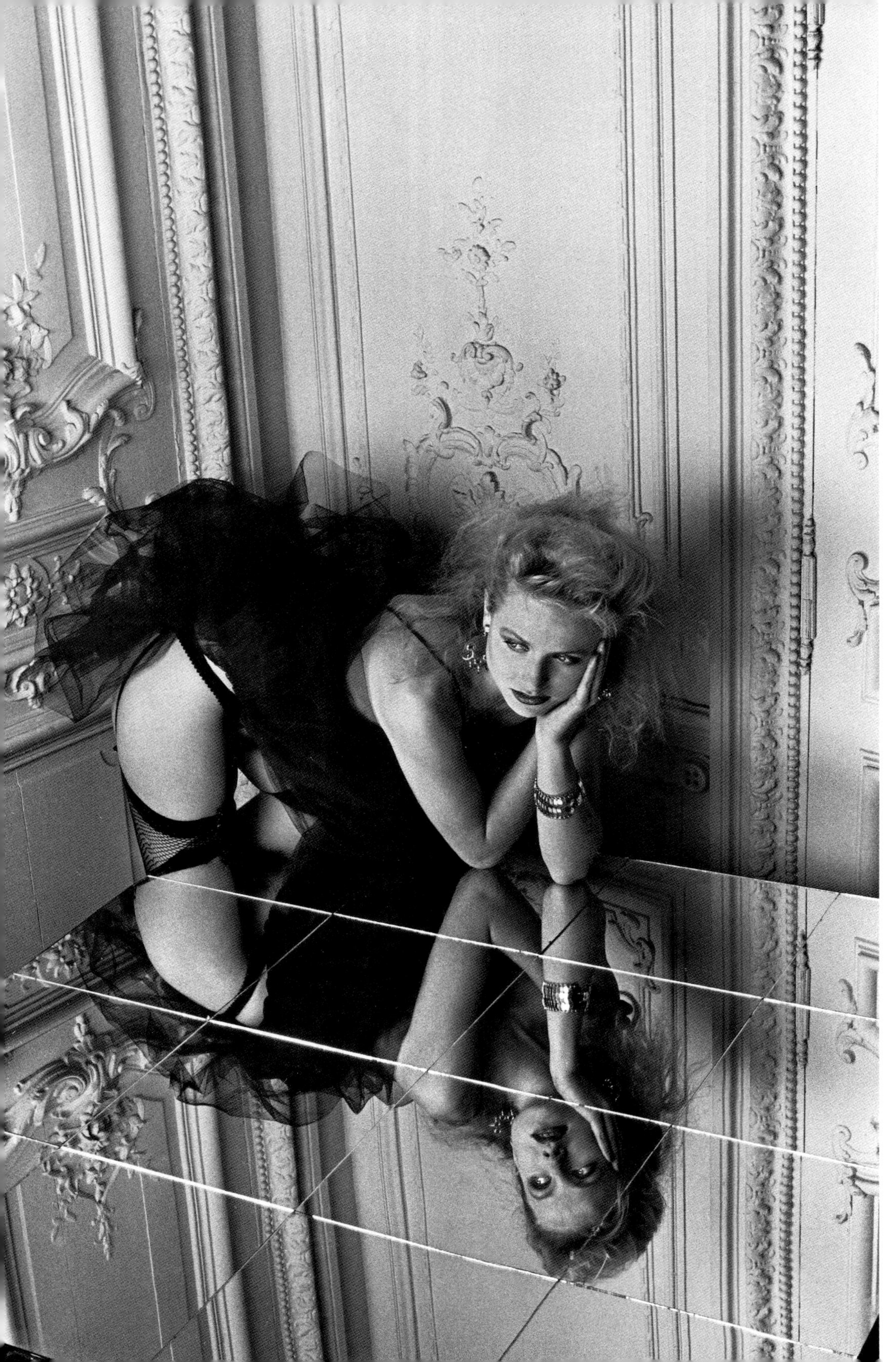

Sofie
1983

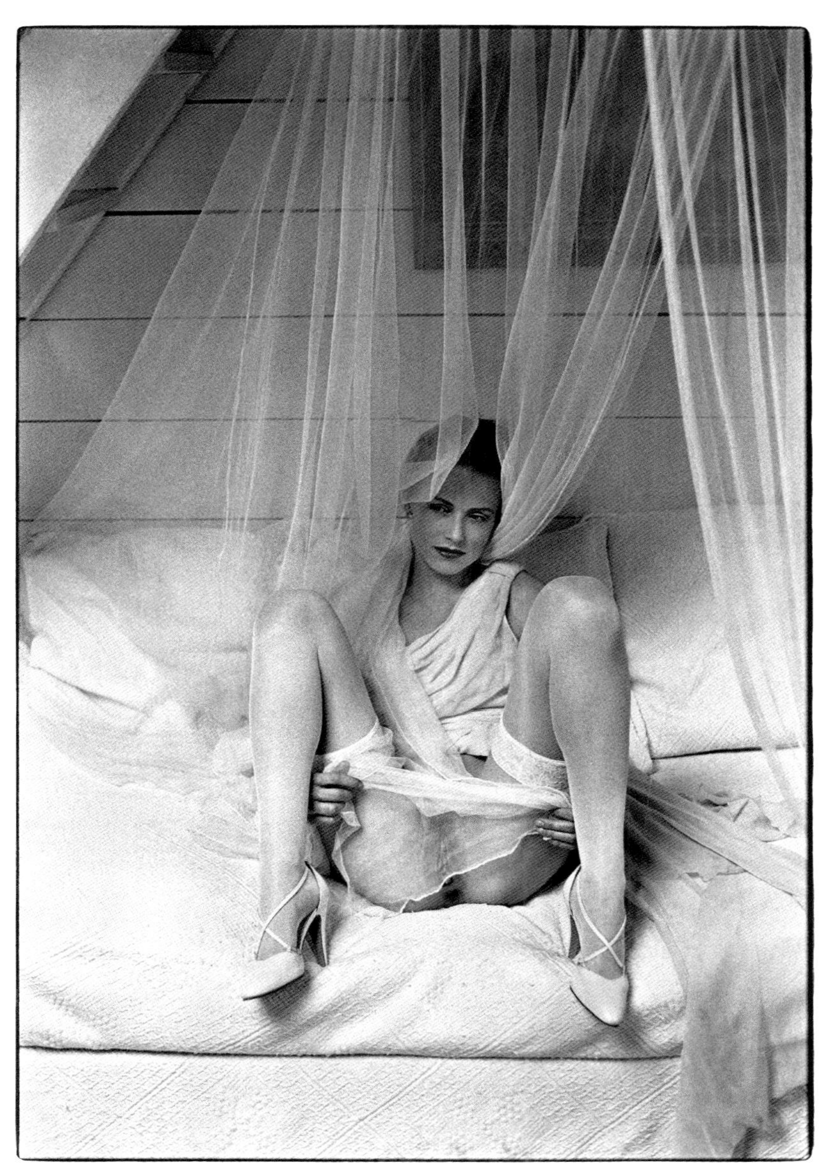

Sofie 1993   31

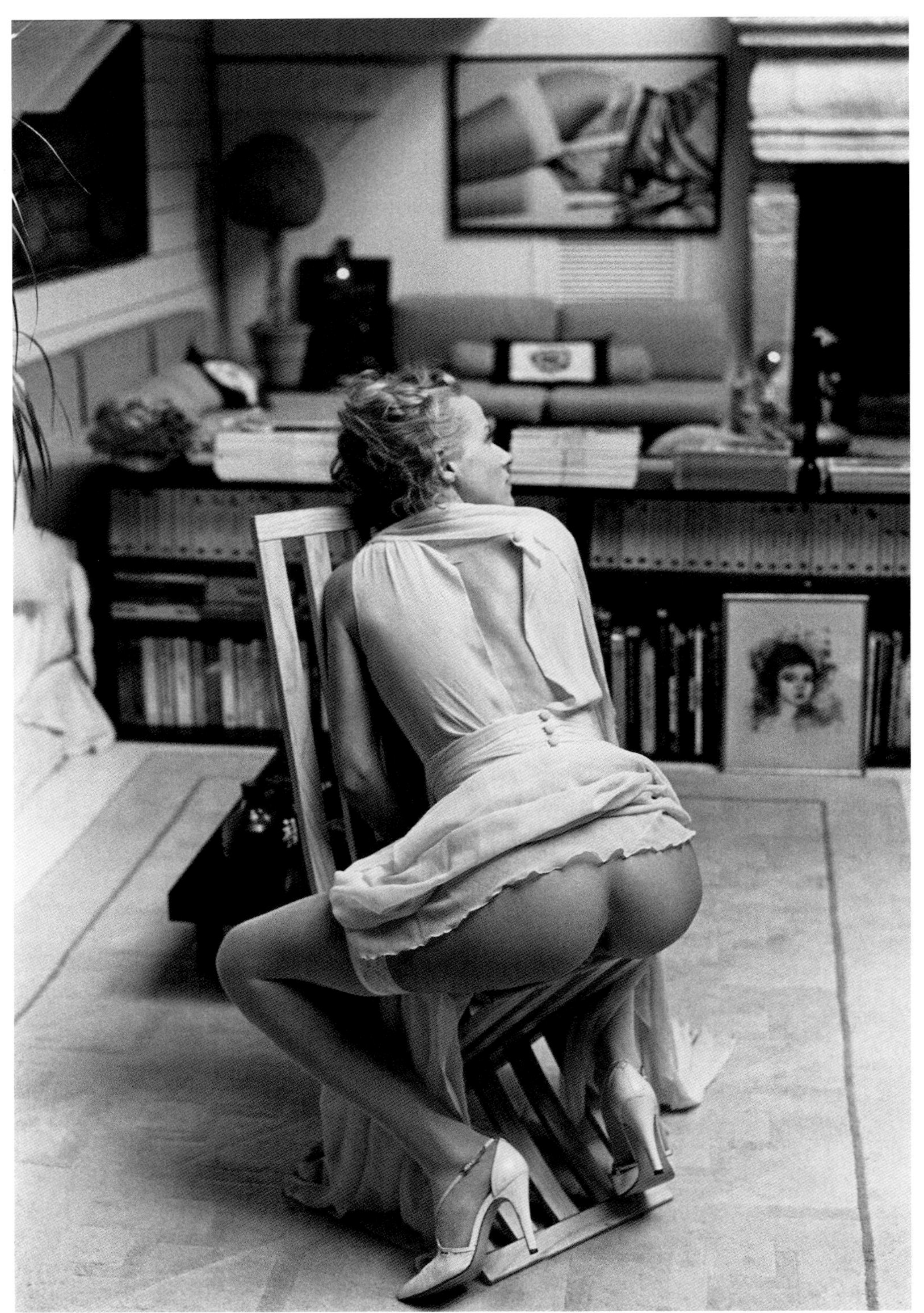

32   Sofie 1993

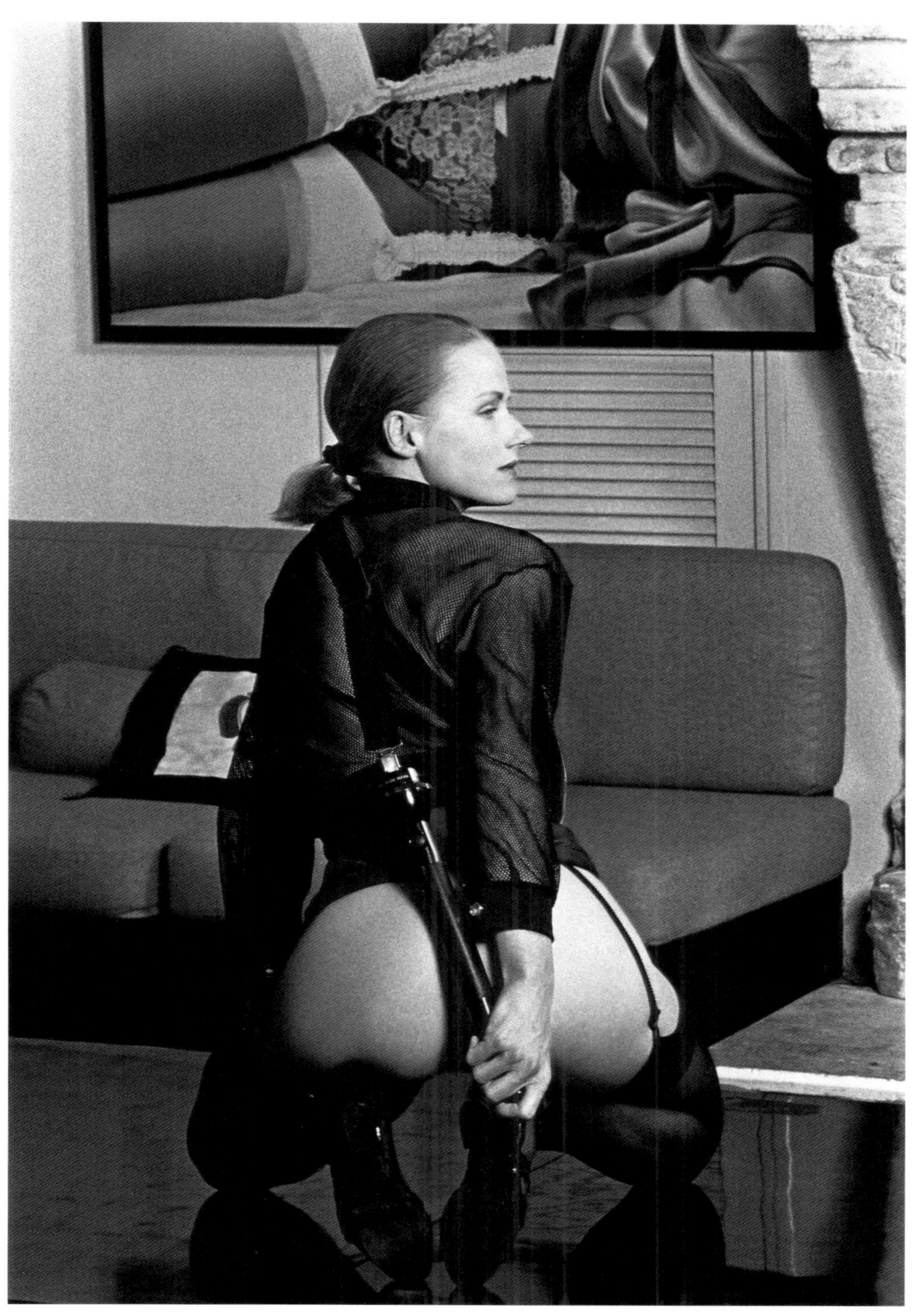

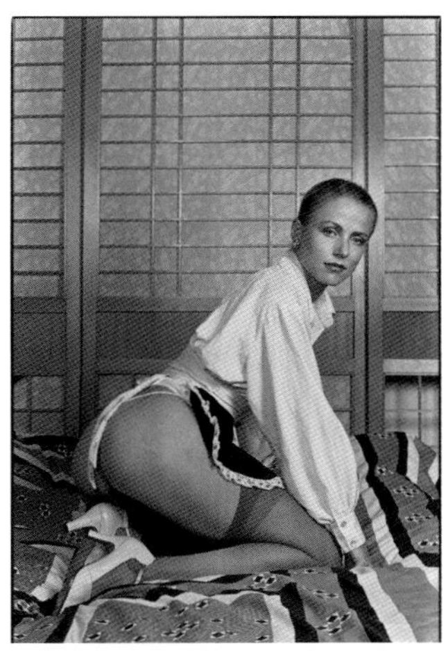

   Sofie 1993

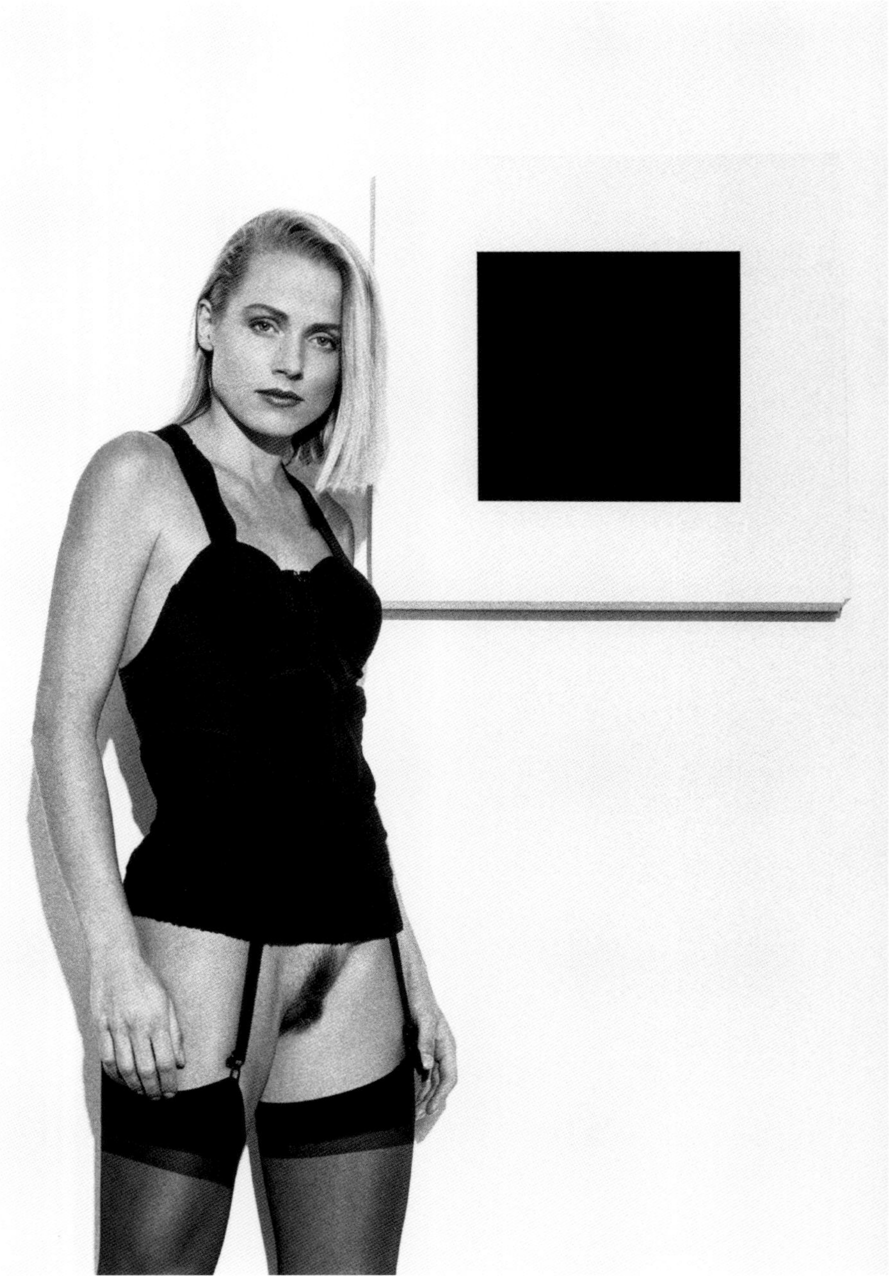

Sofie 1991

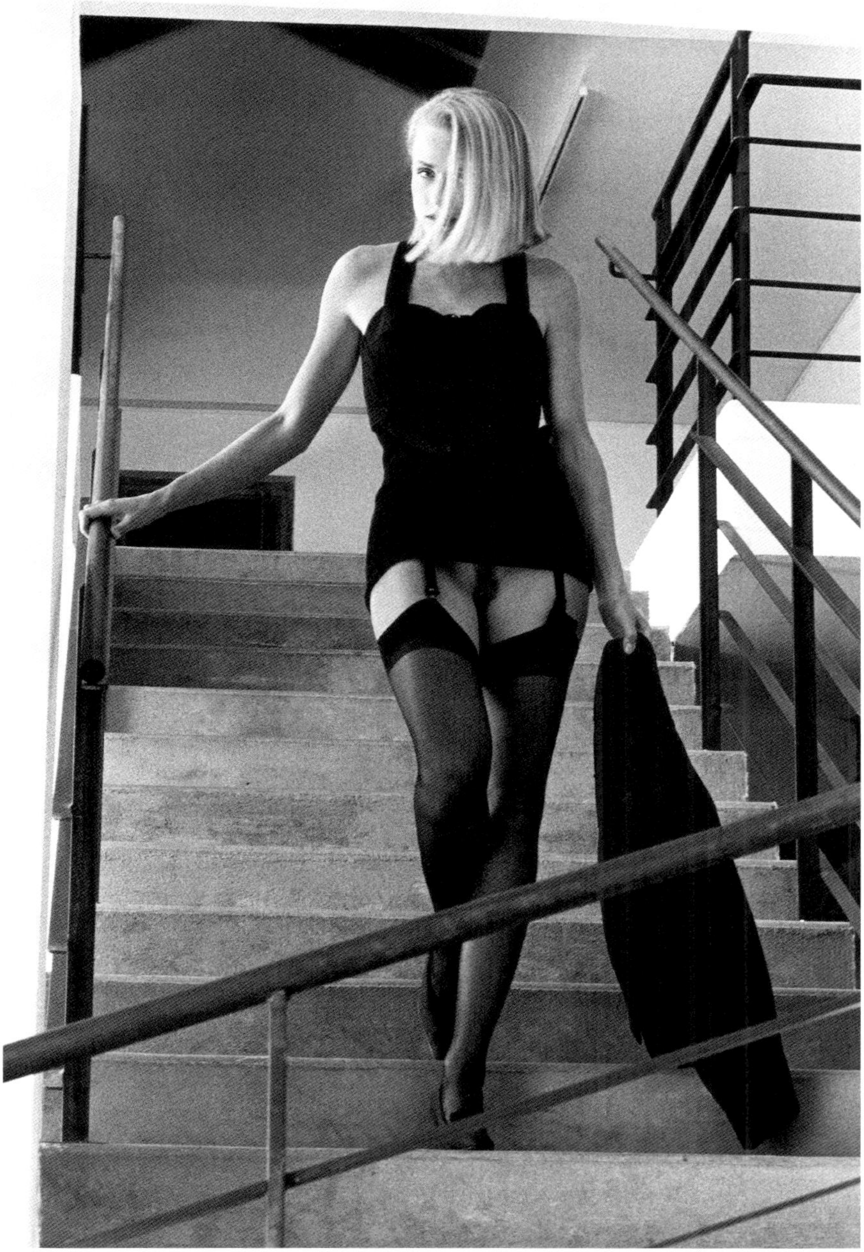

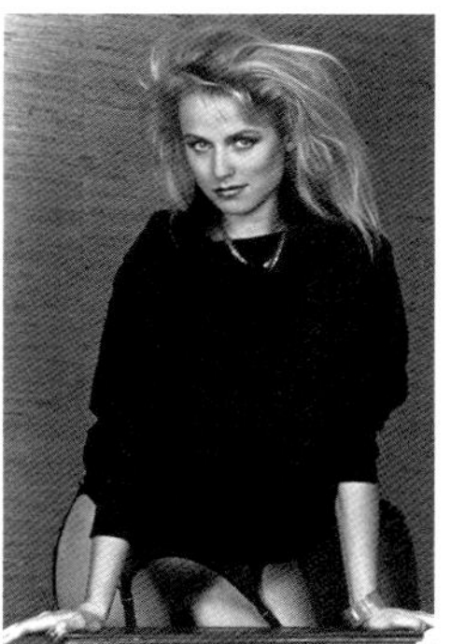

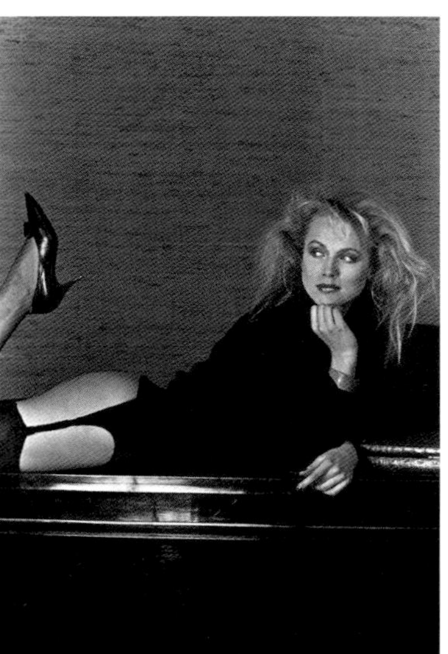

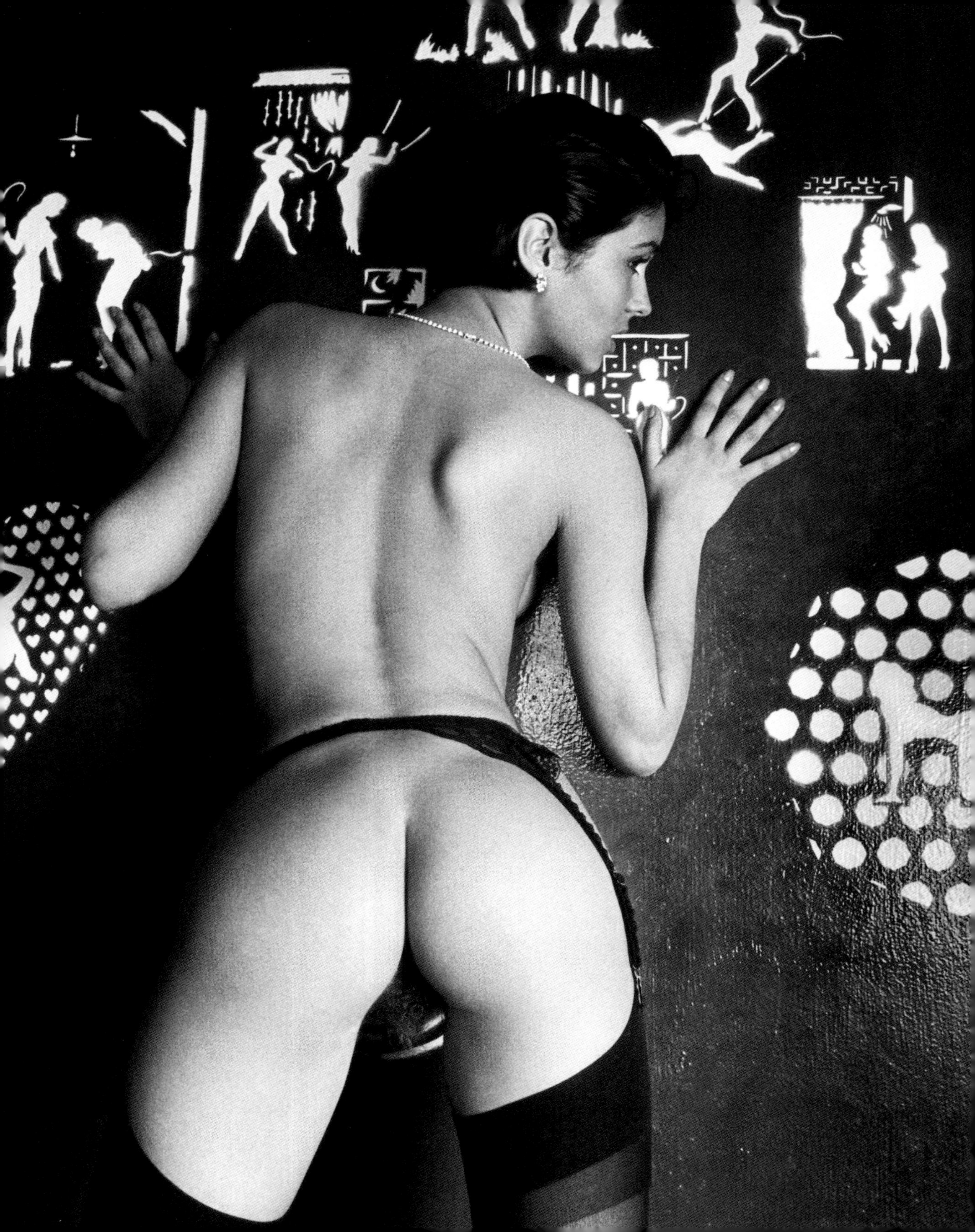

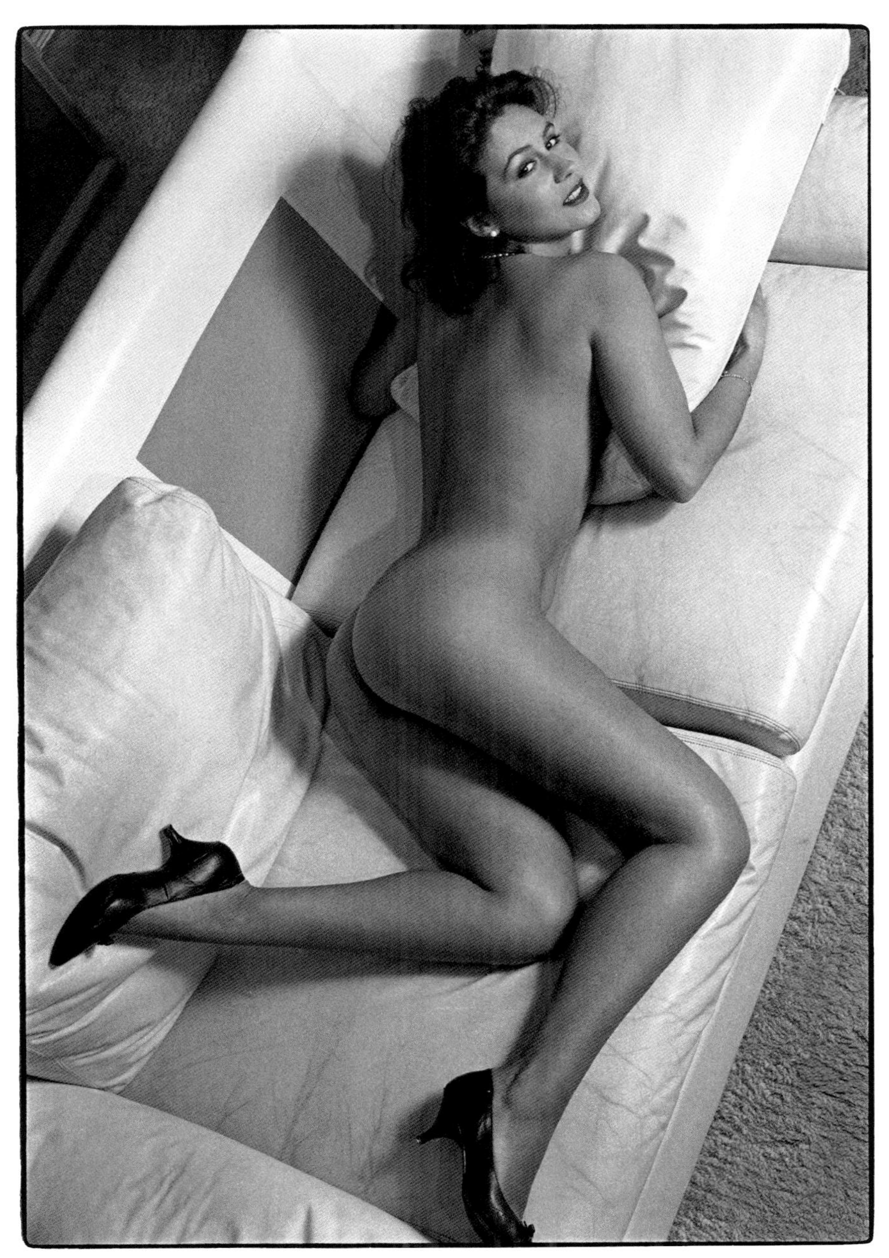

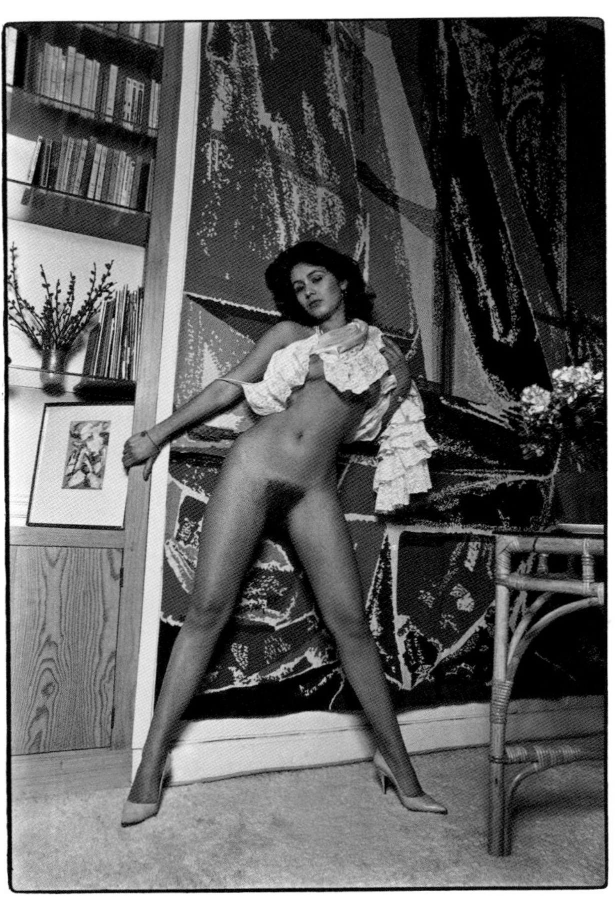 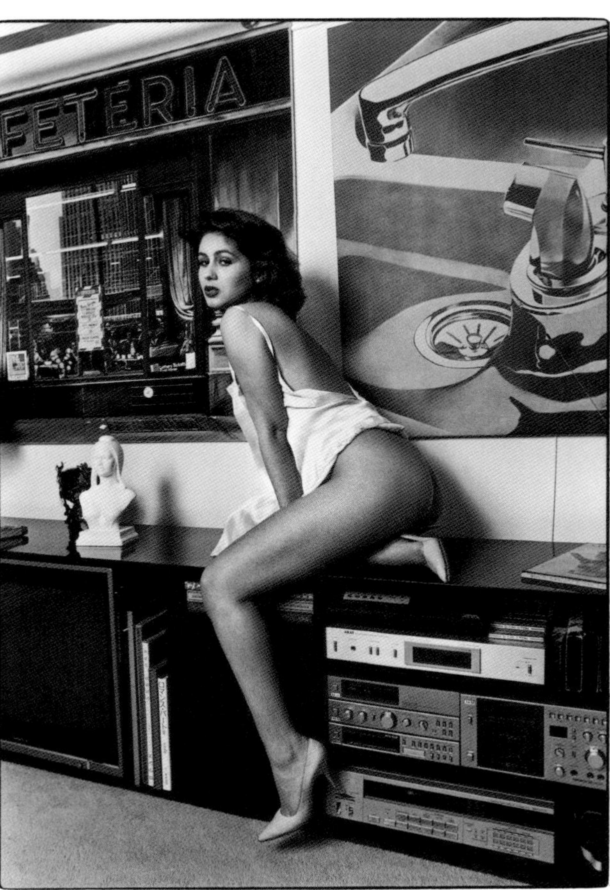
FETERIA

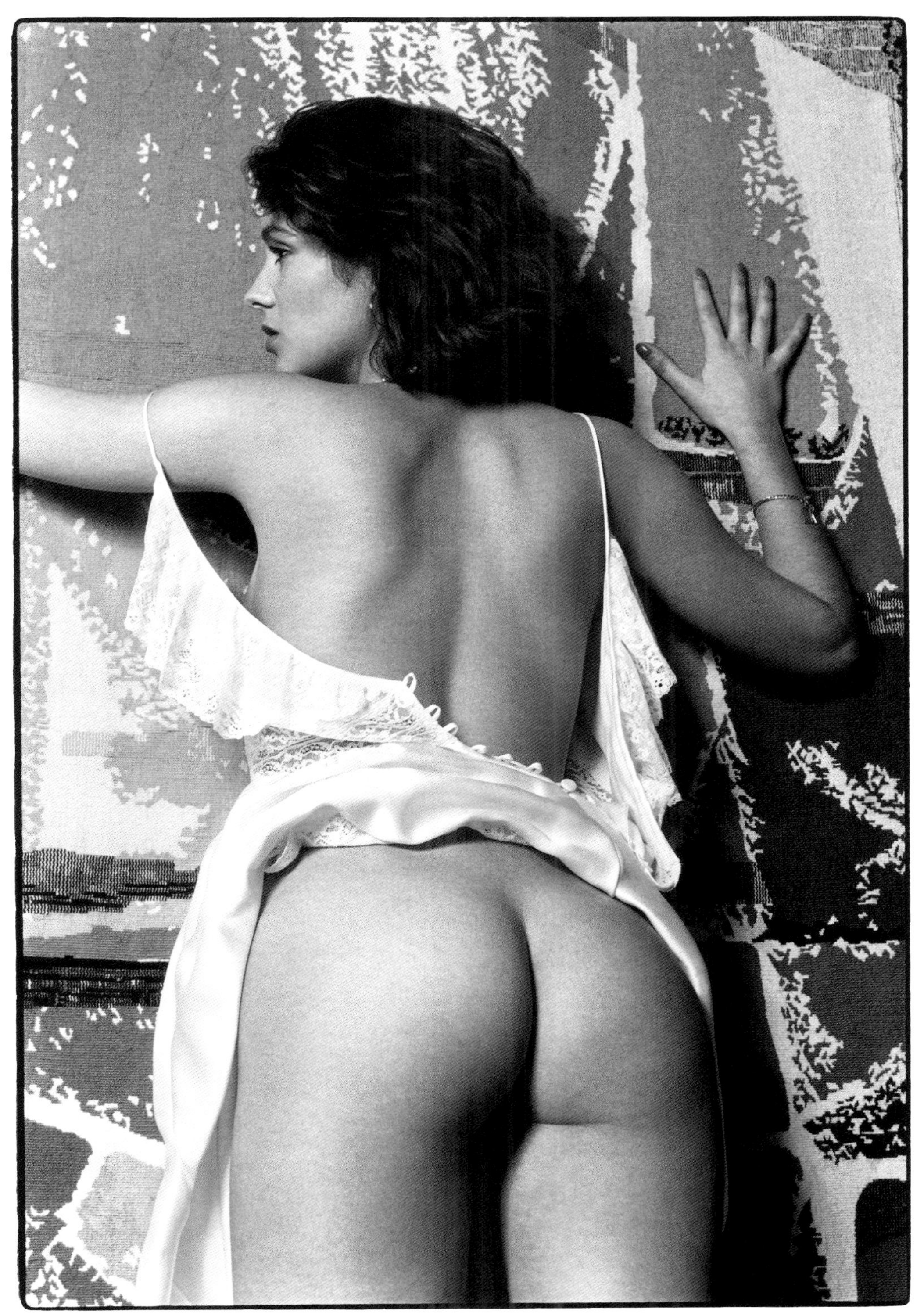

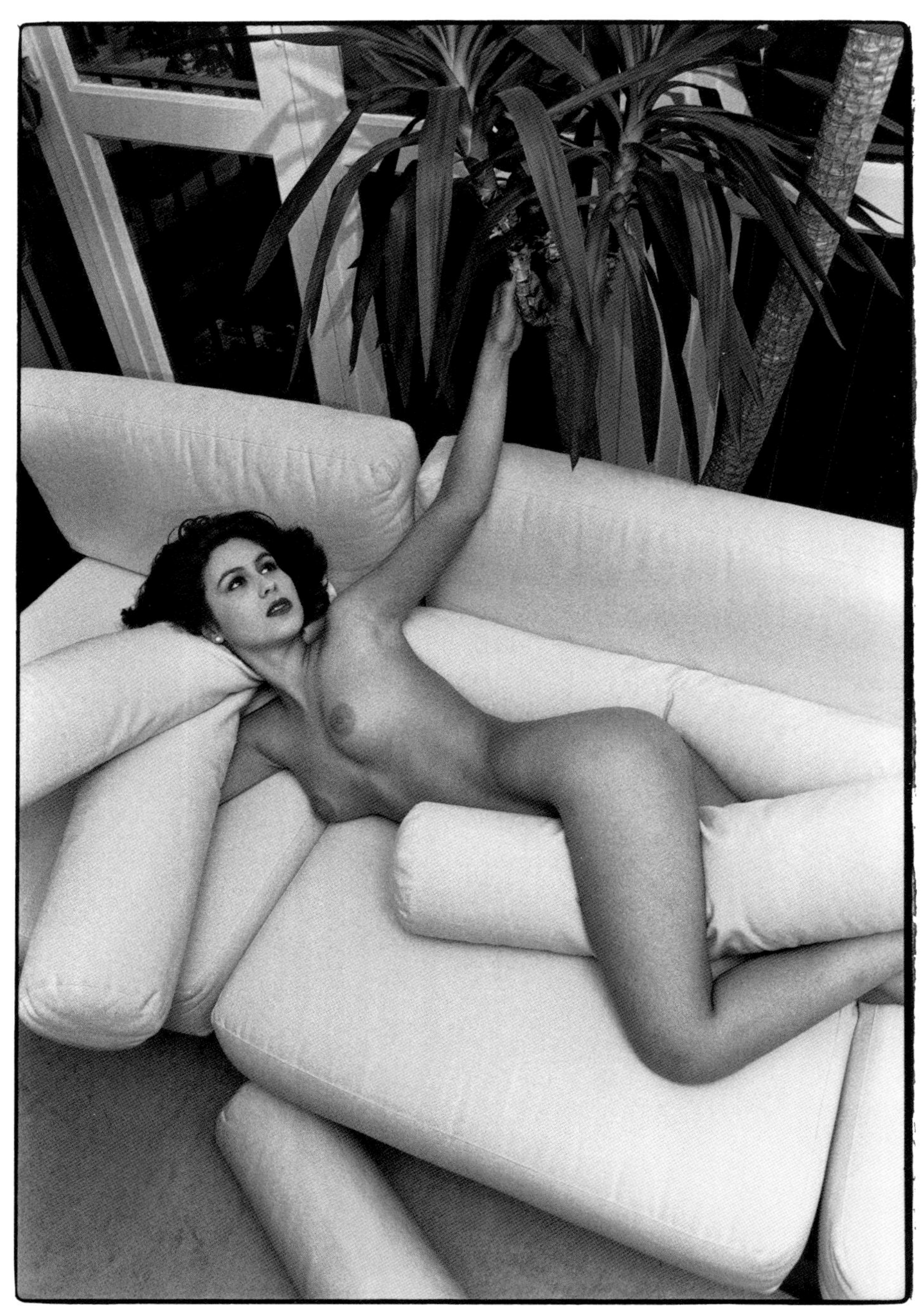

40   Toni 1985

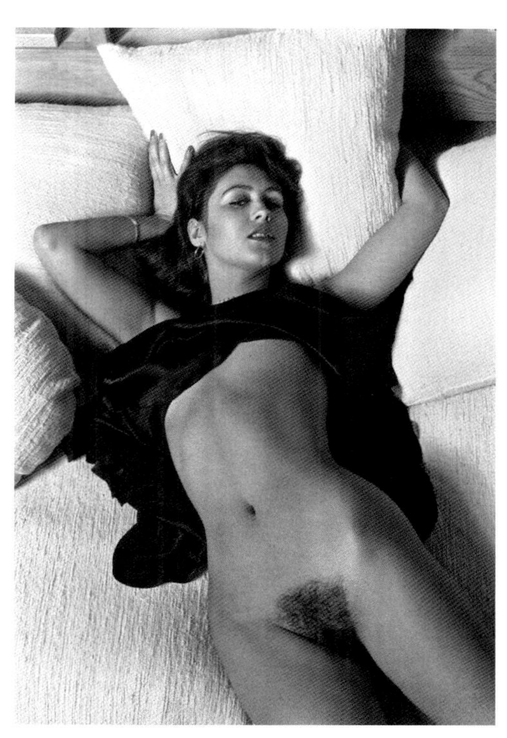

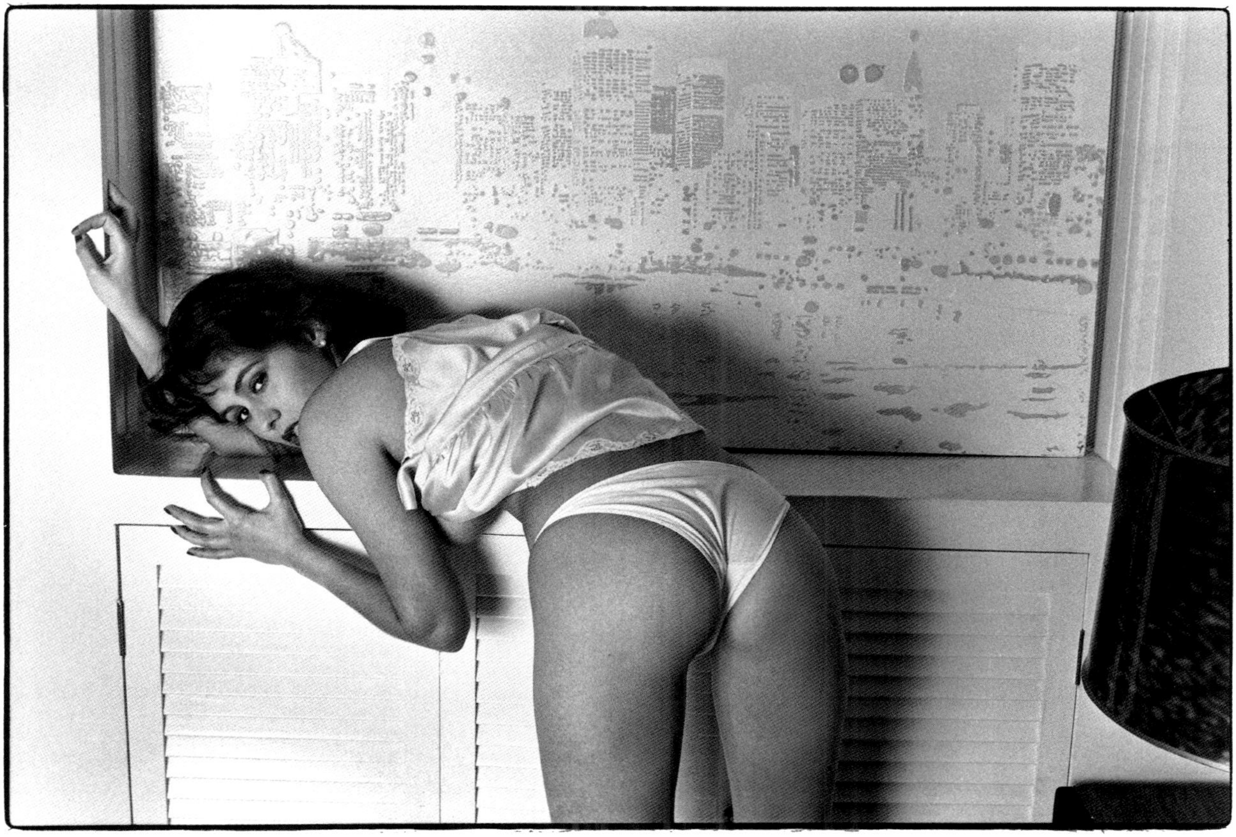

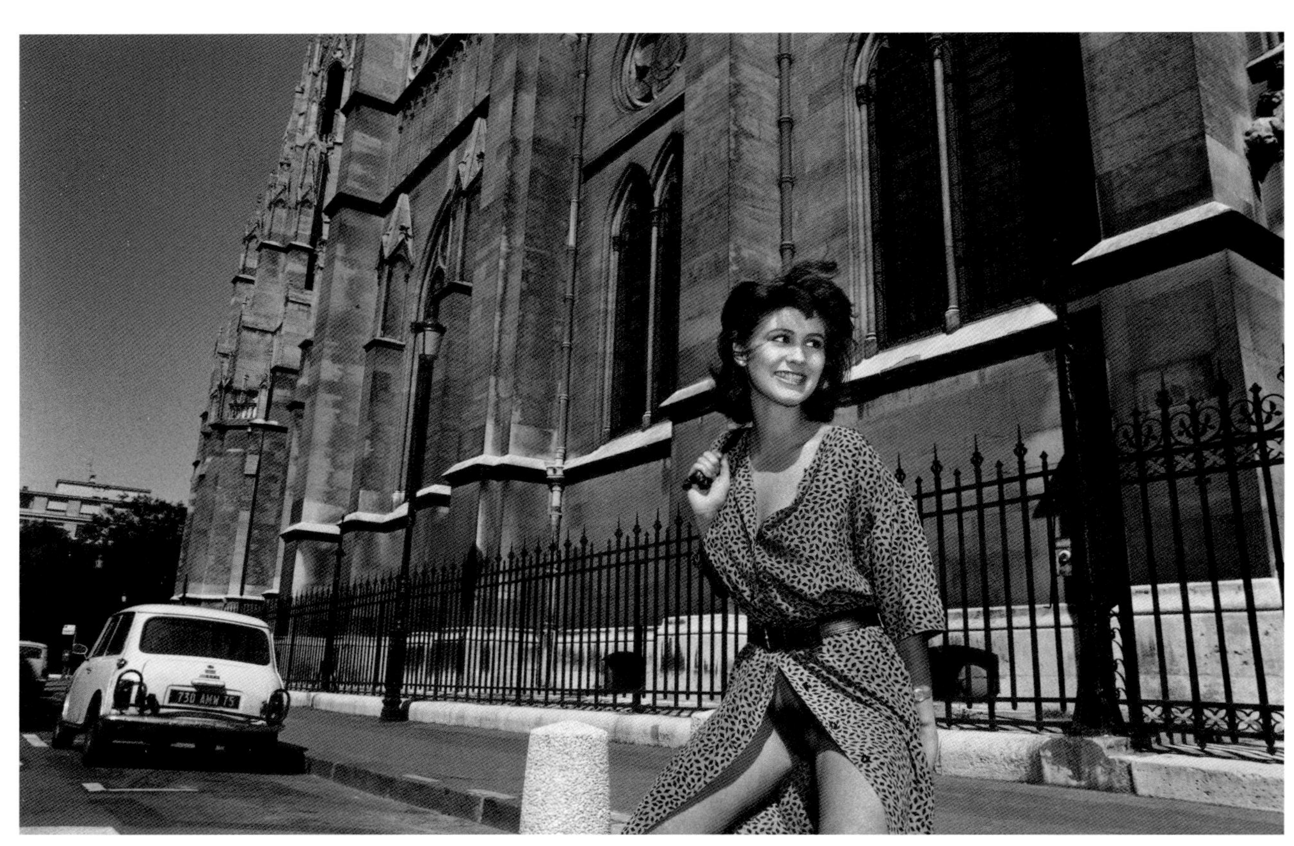

Caroline 1986 →

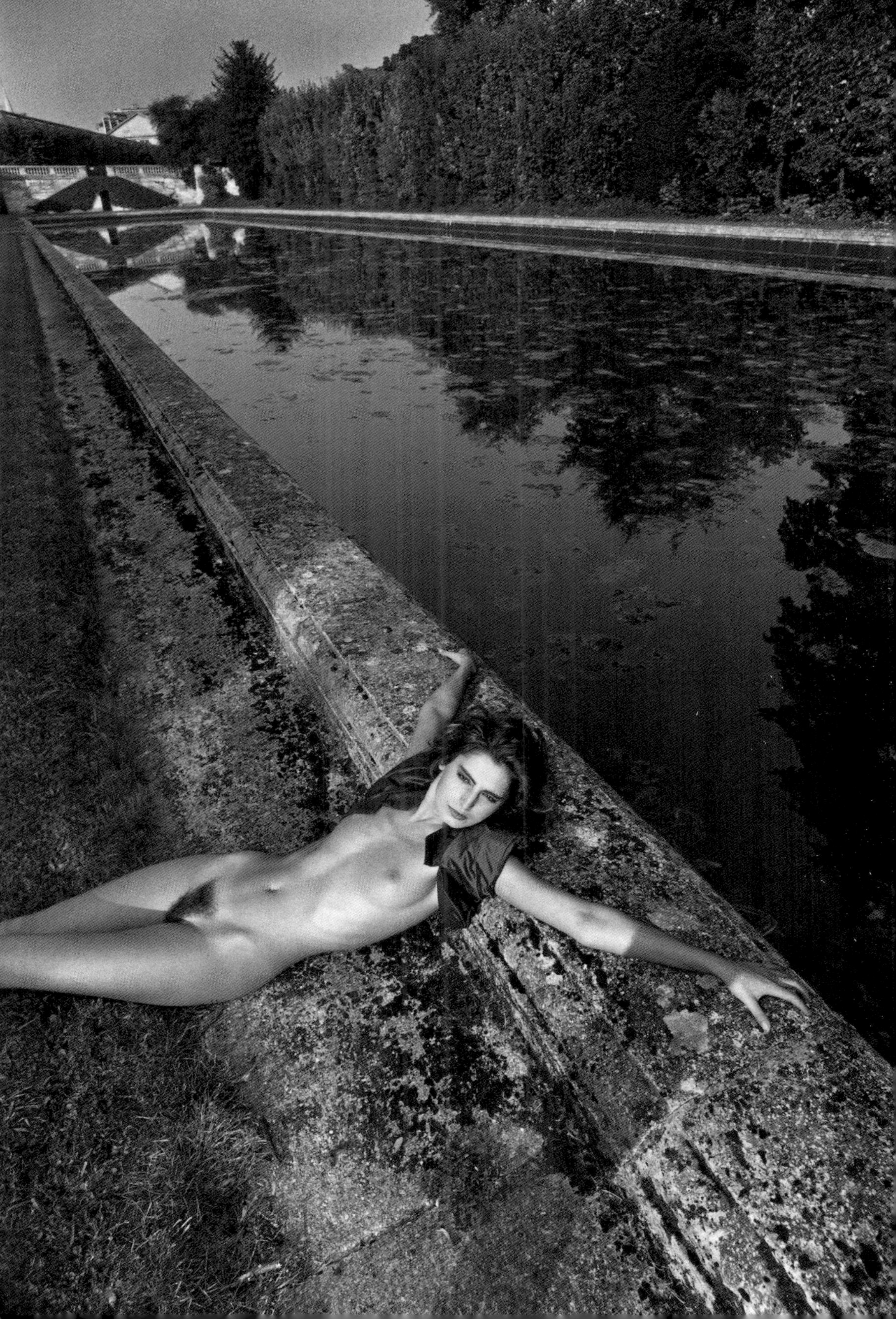

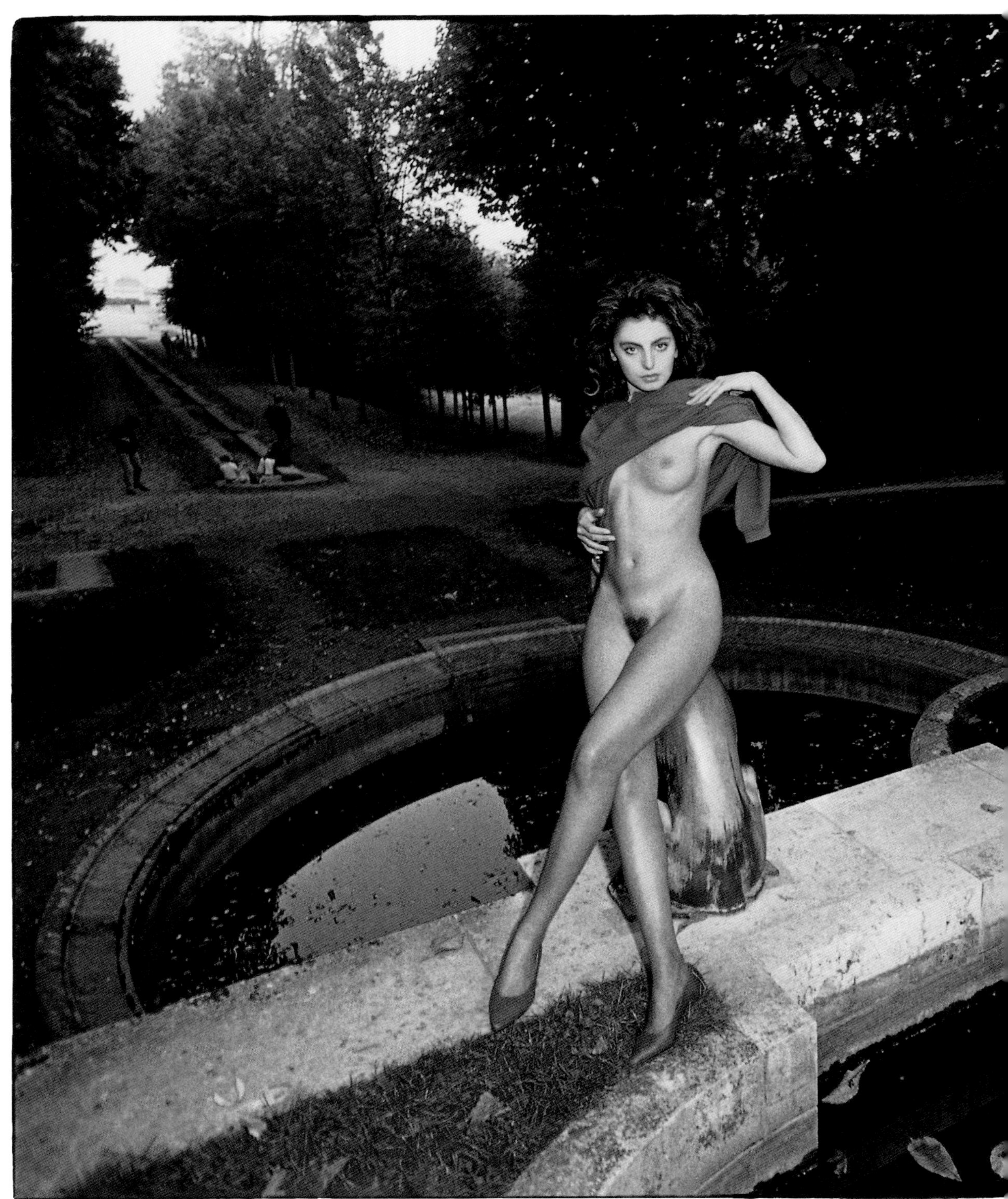

44   Caroline 1986

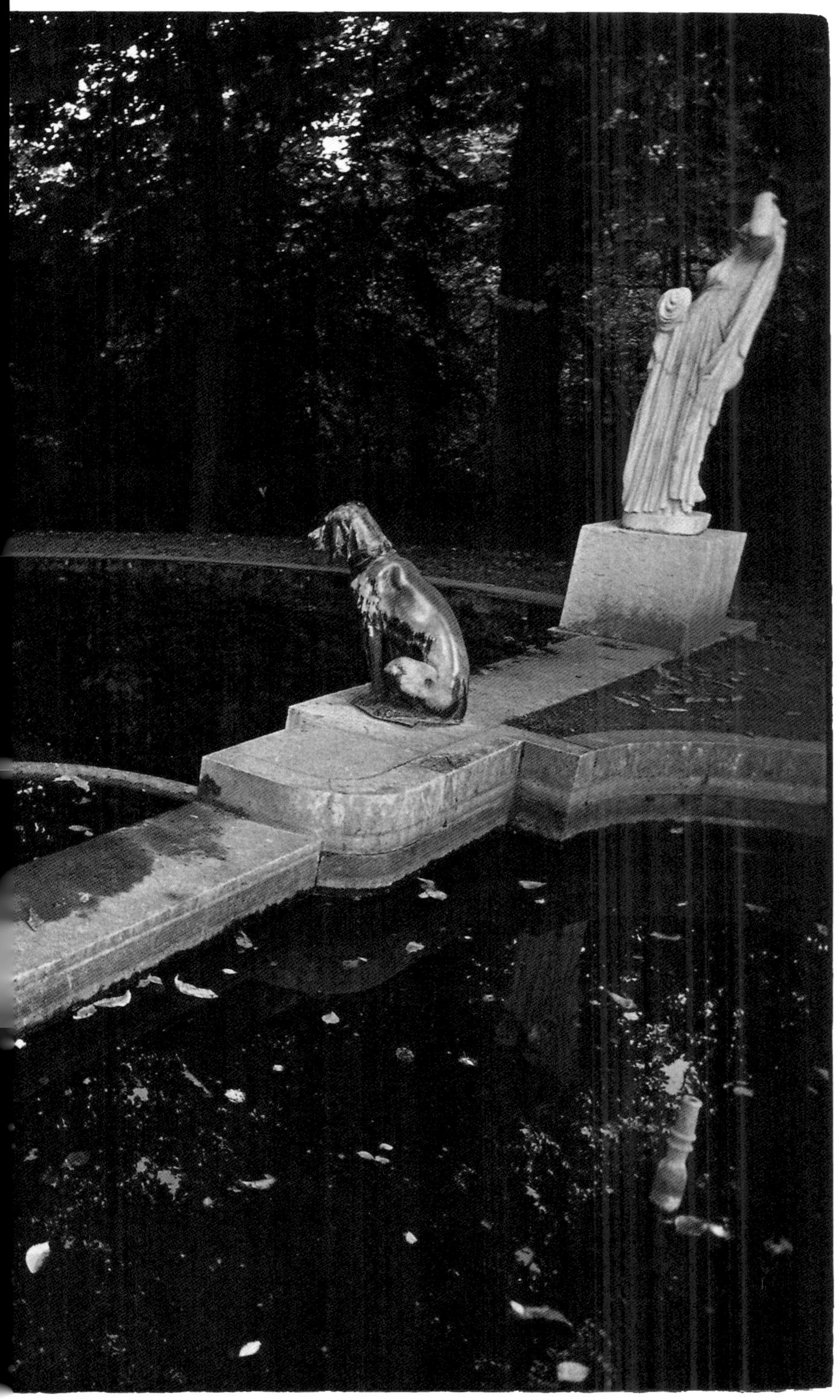

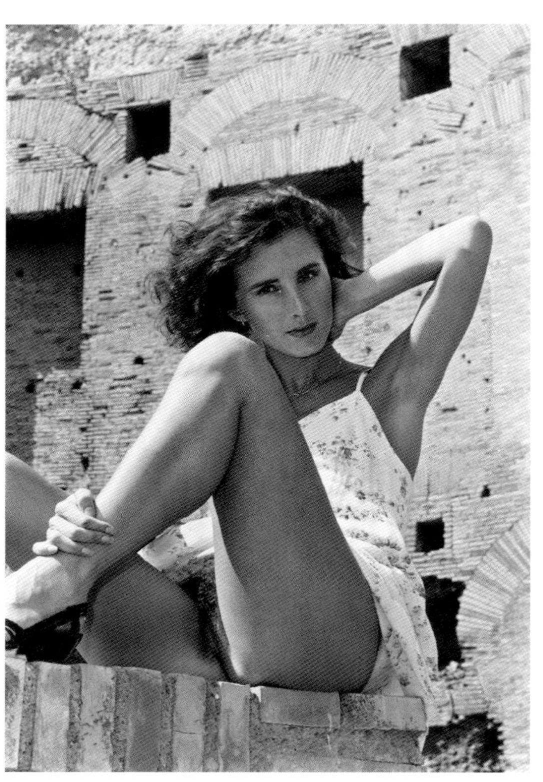
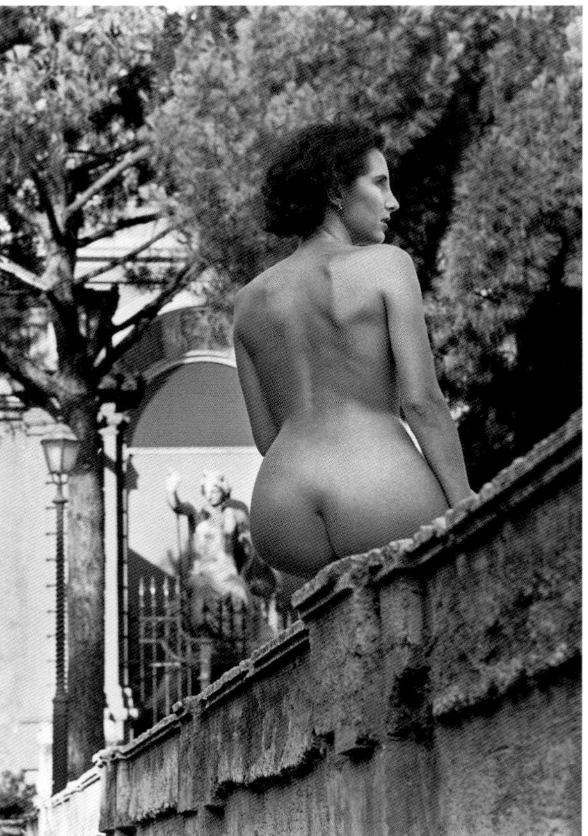
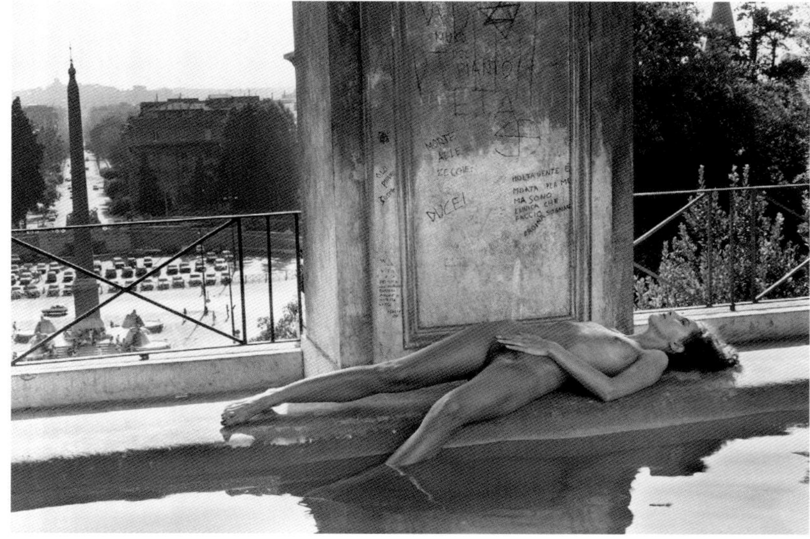

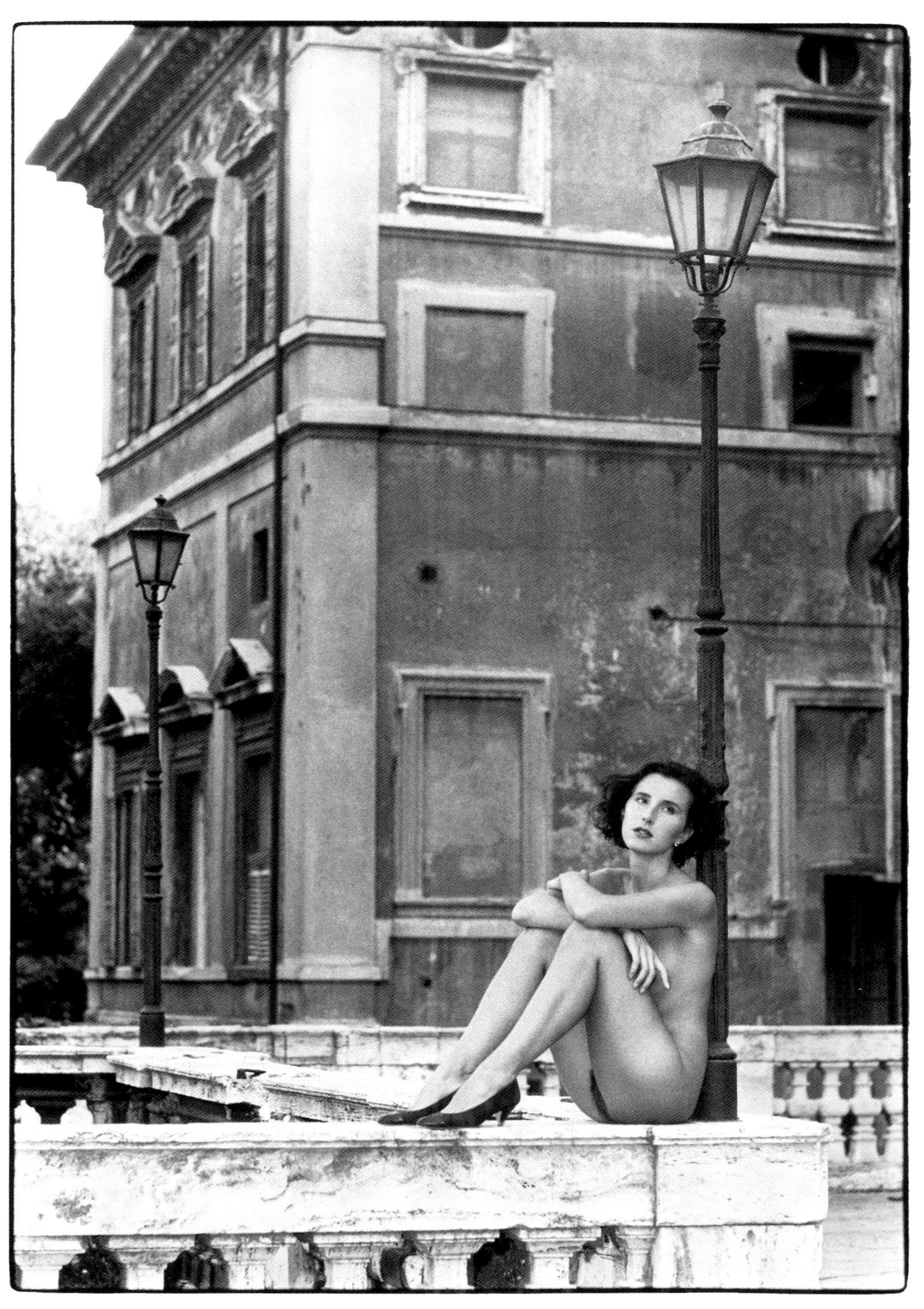

Valérie 1987   47

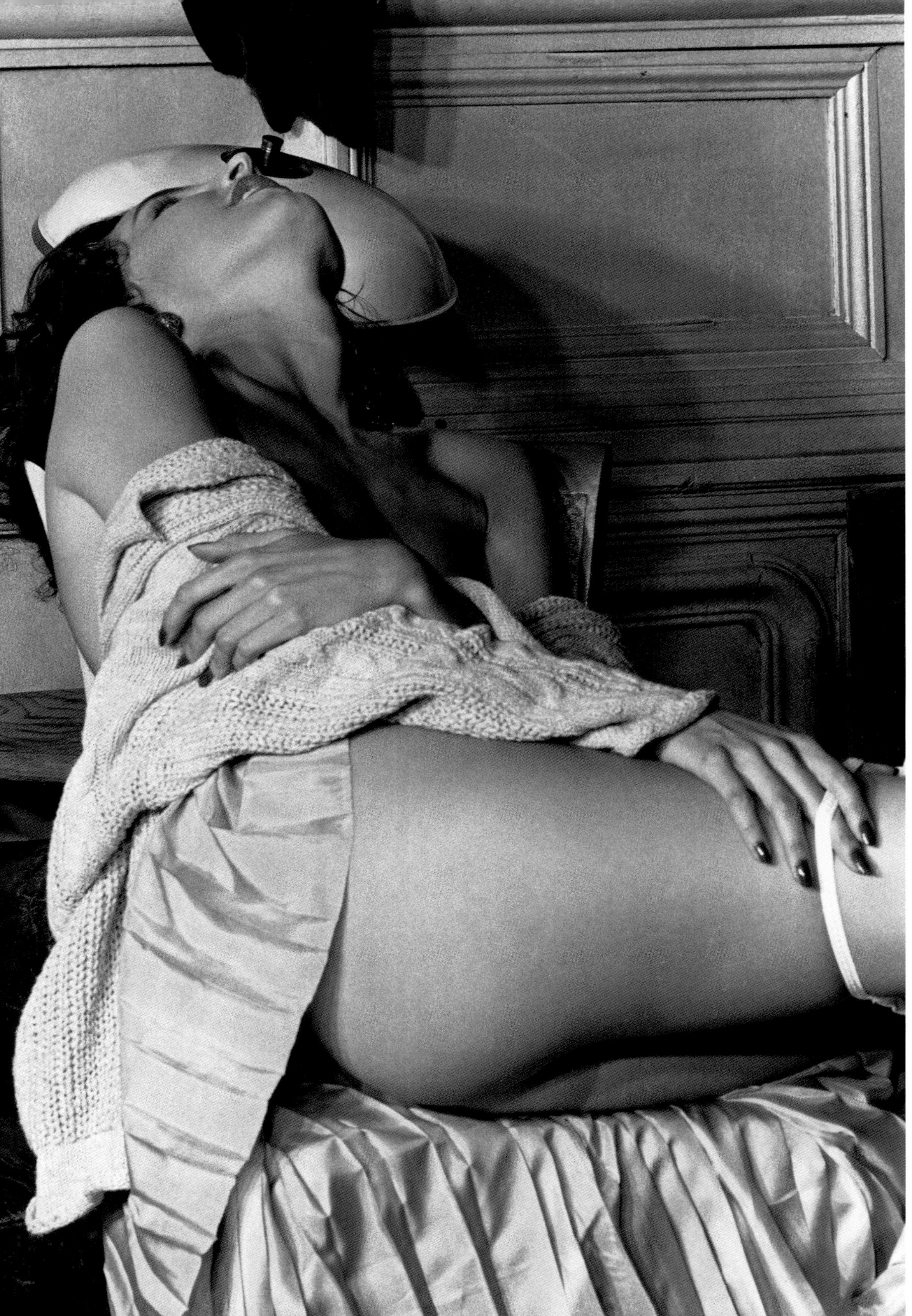

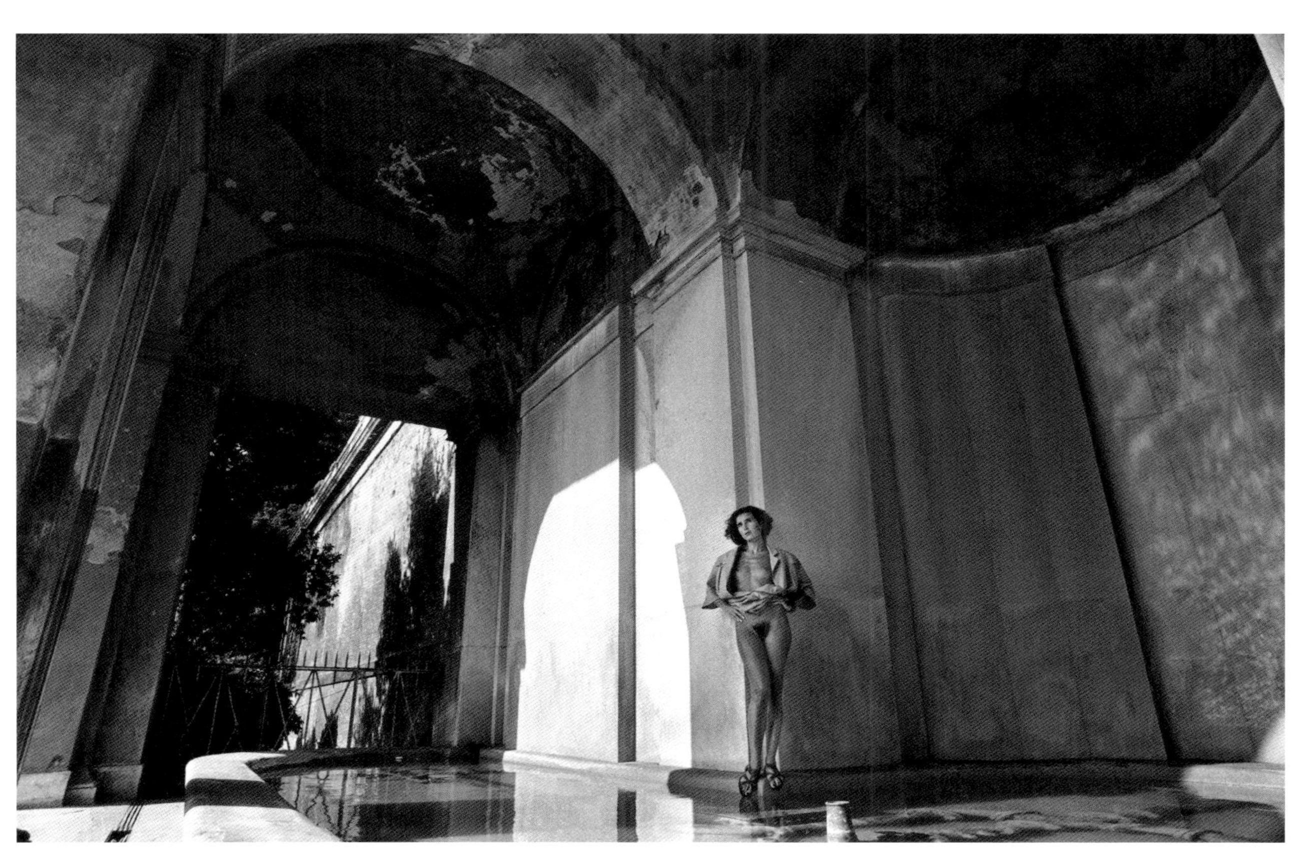

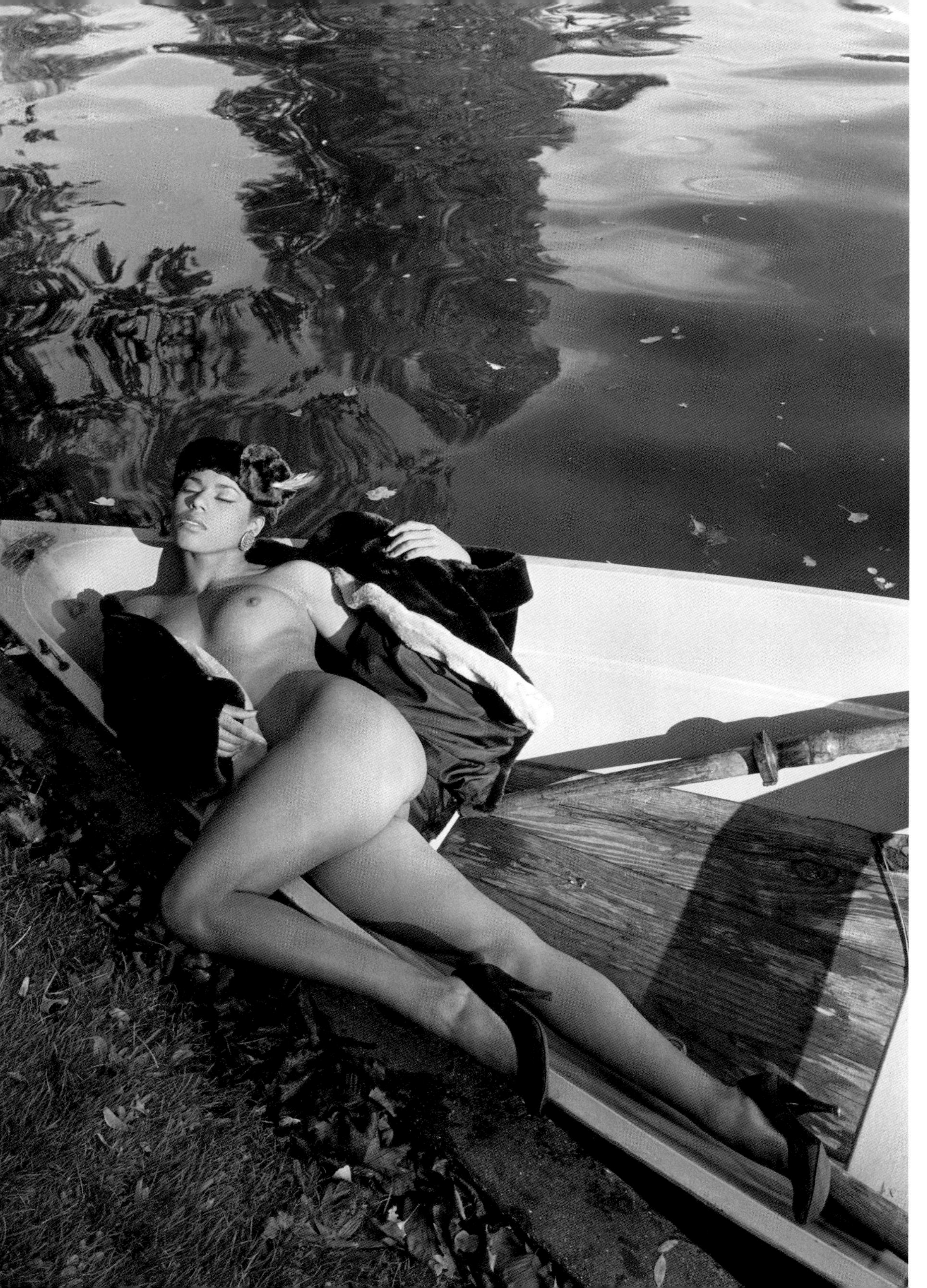

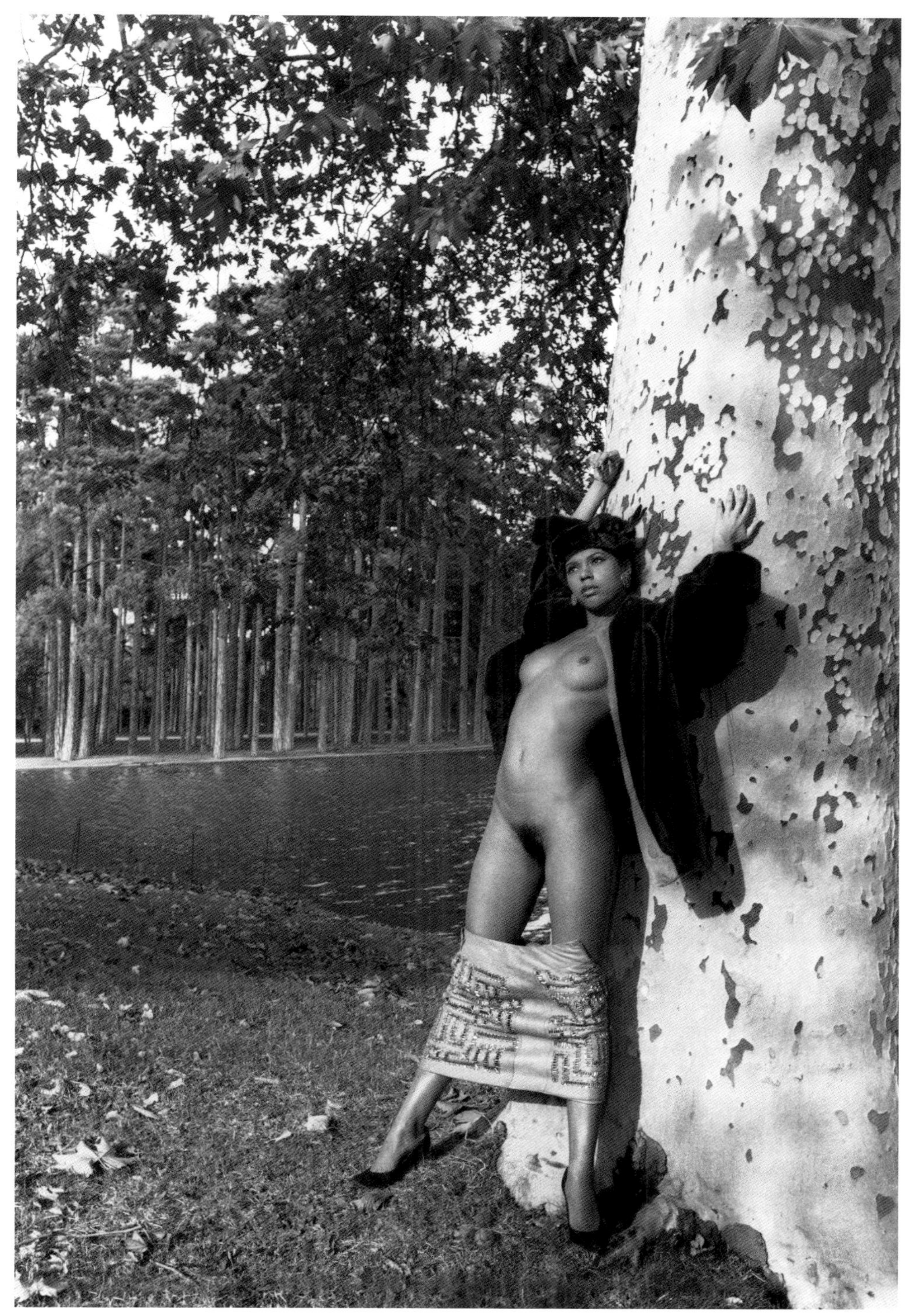

Carole 1987   51

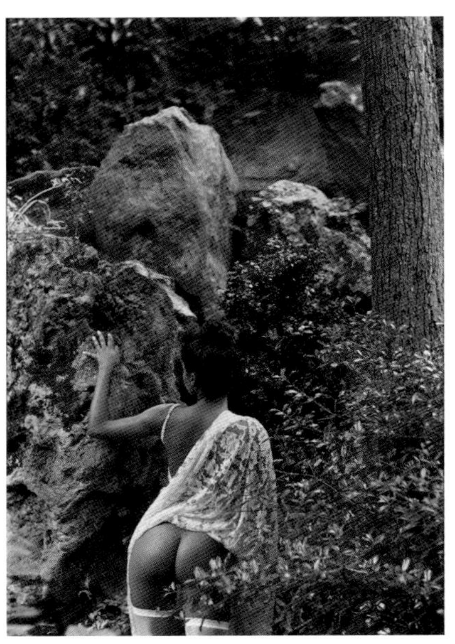 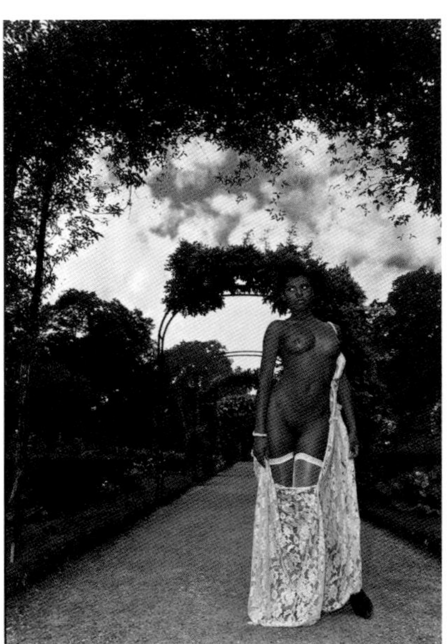 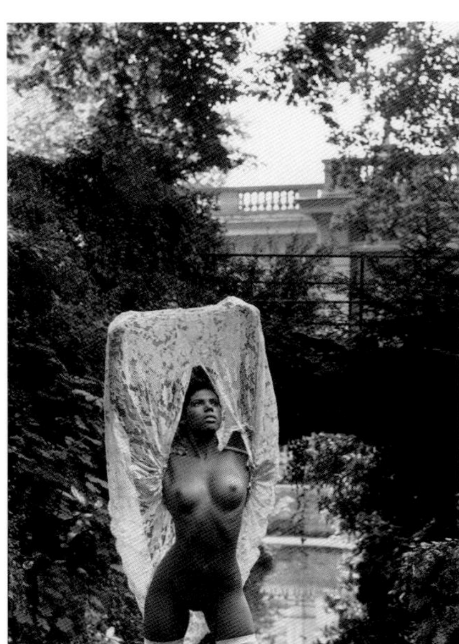

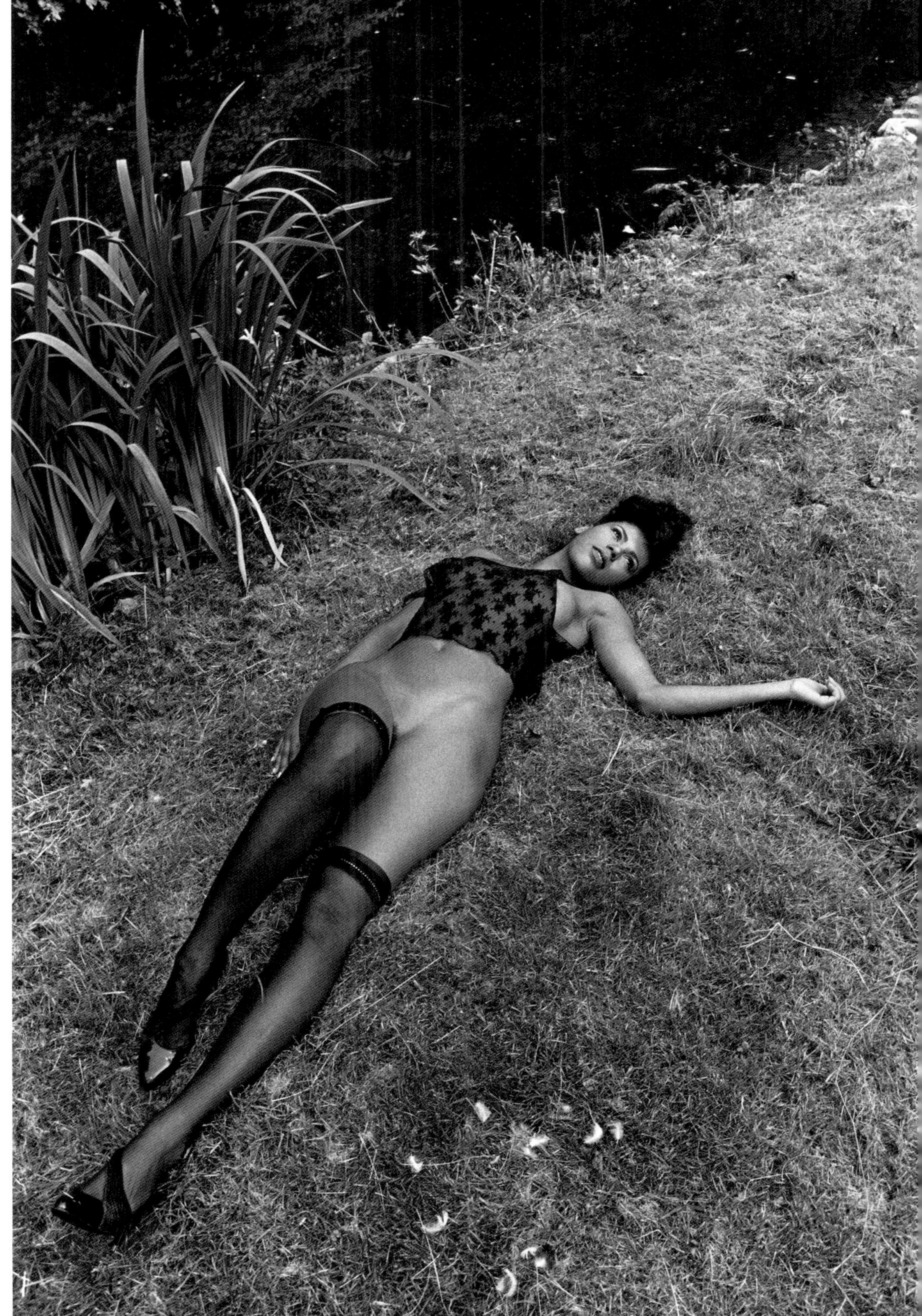

Carole
1987

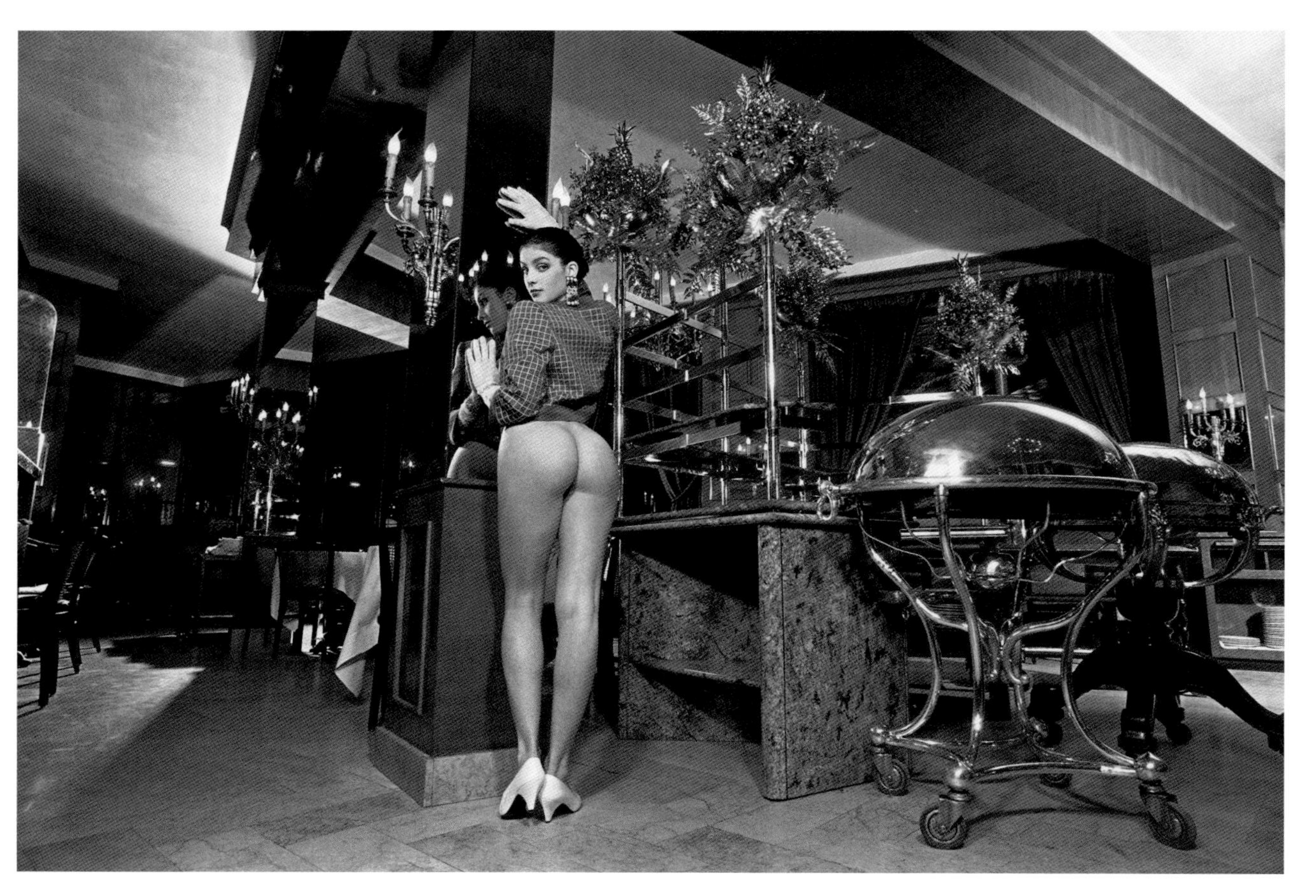

54   Coryne 1988

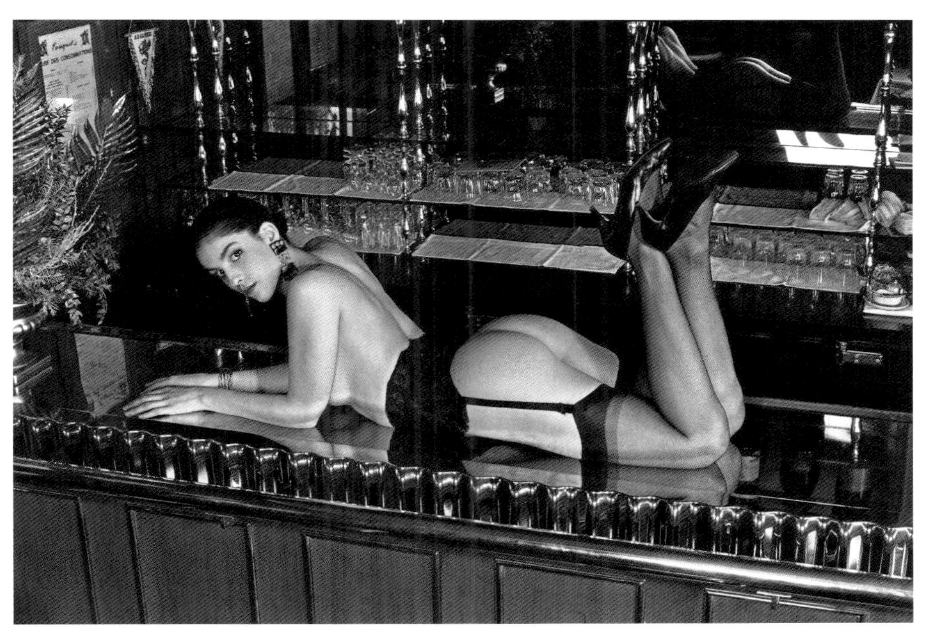

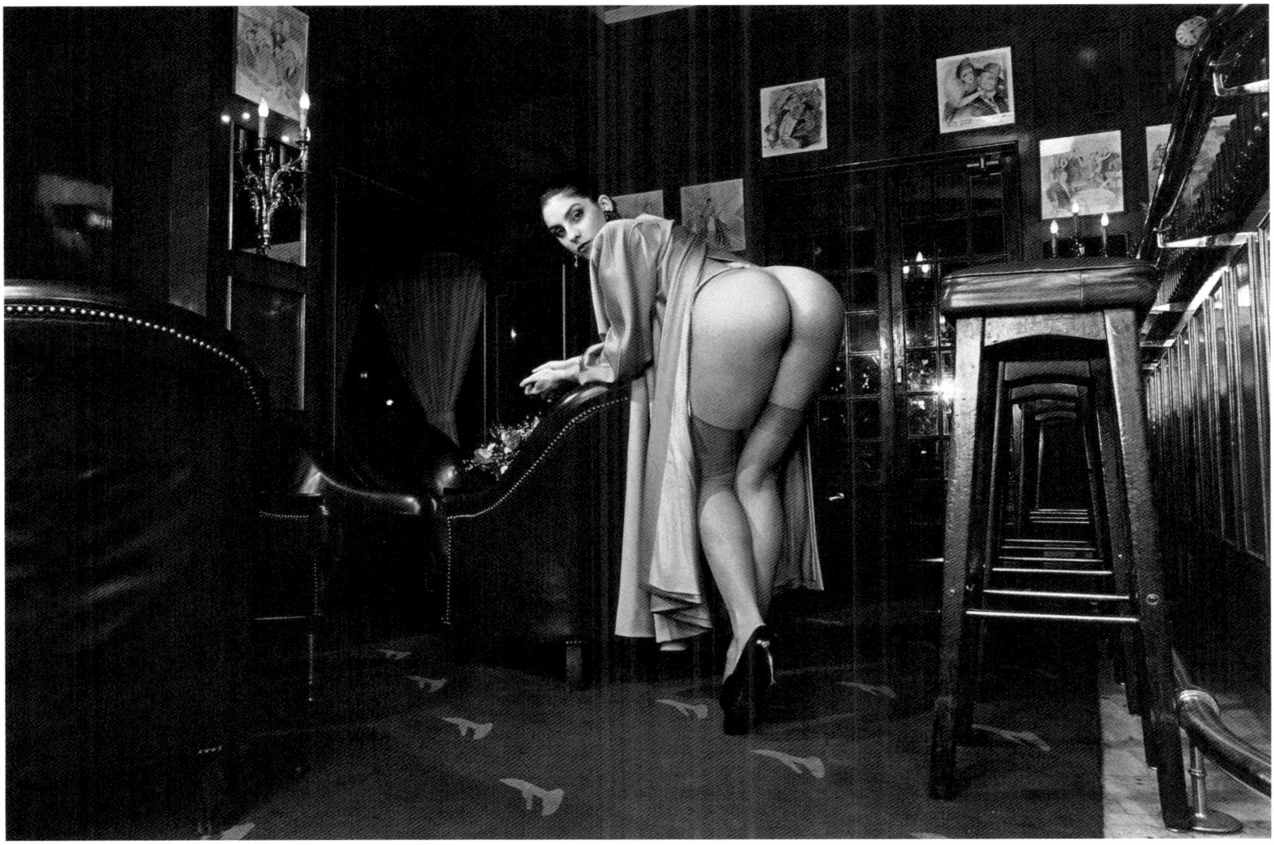

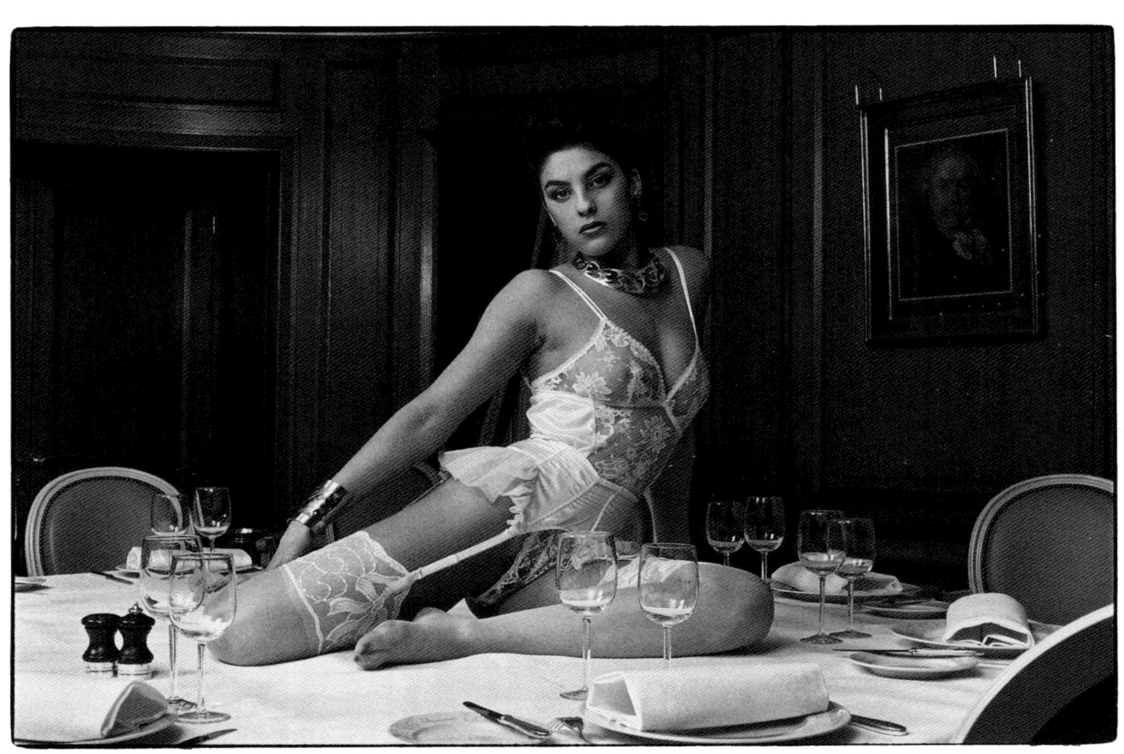

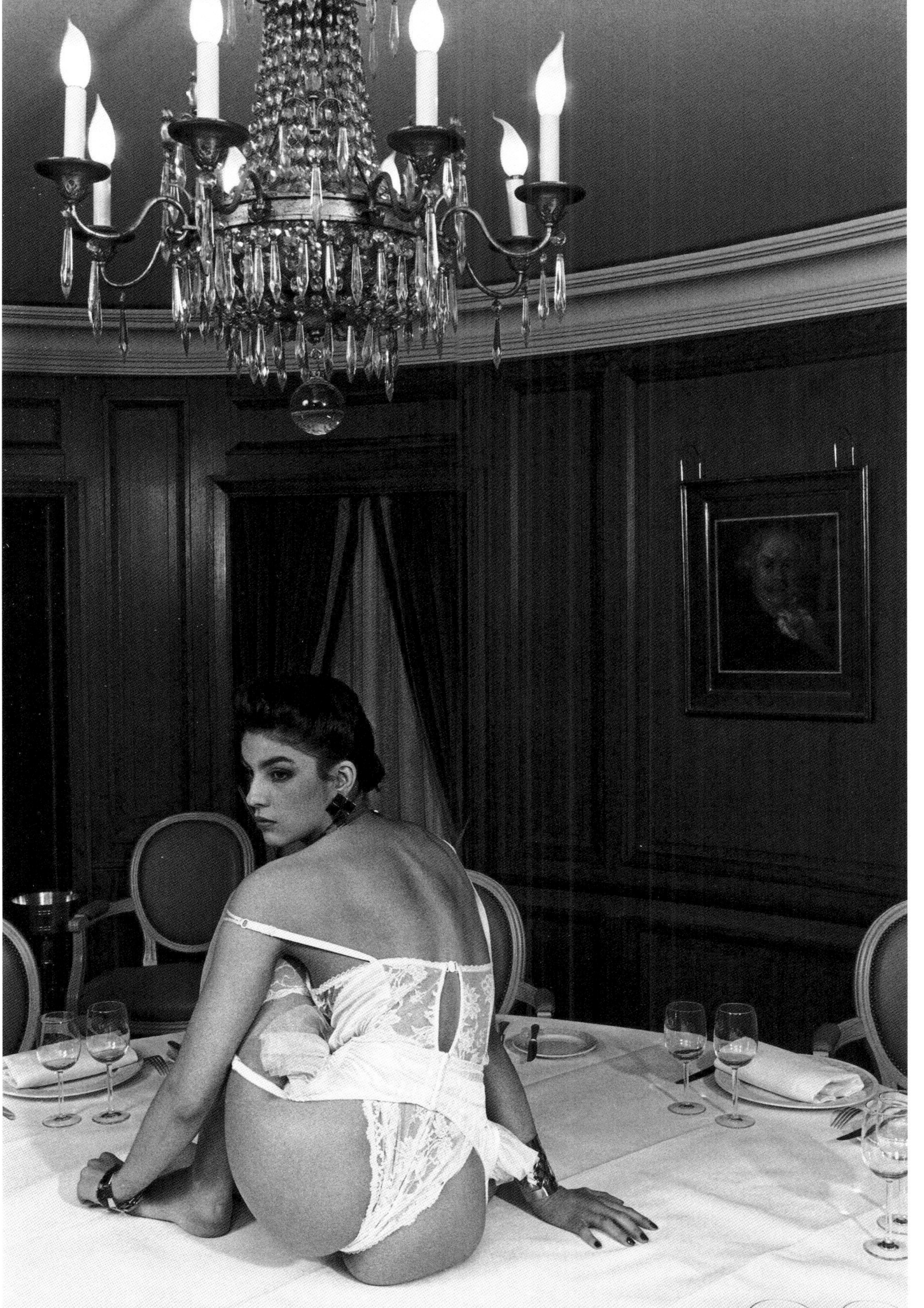

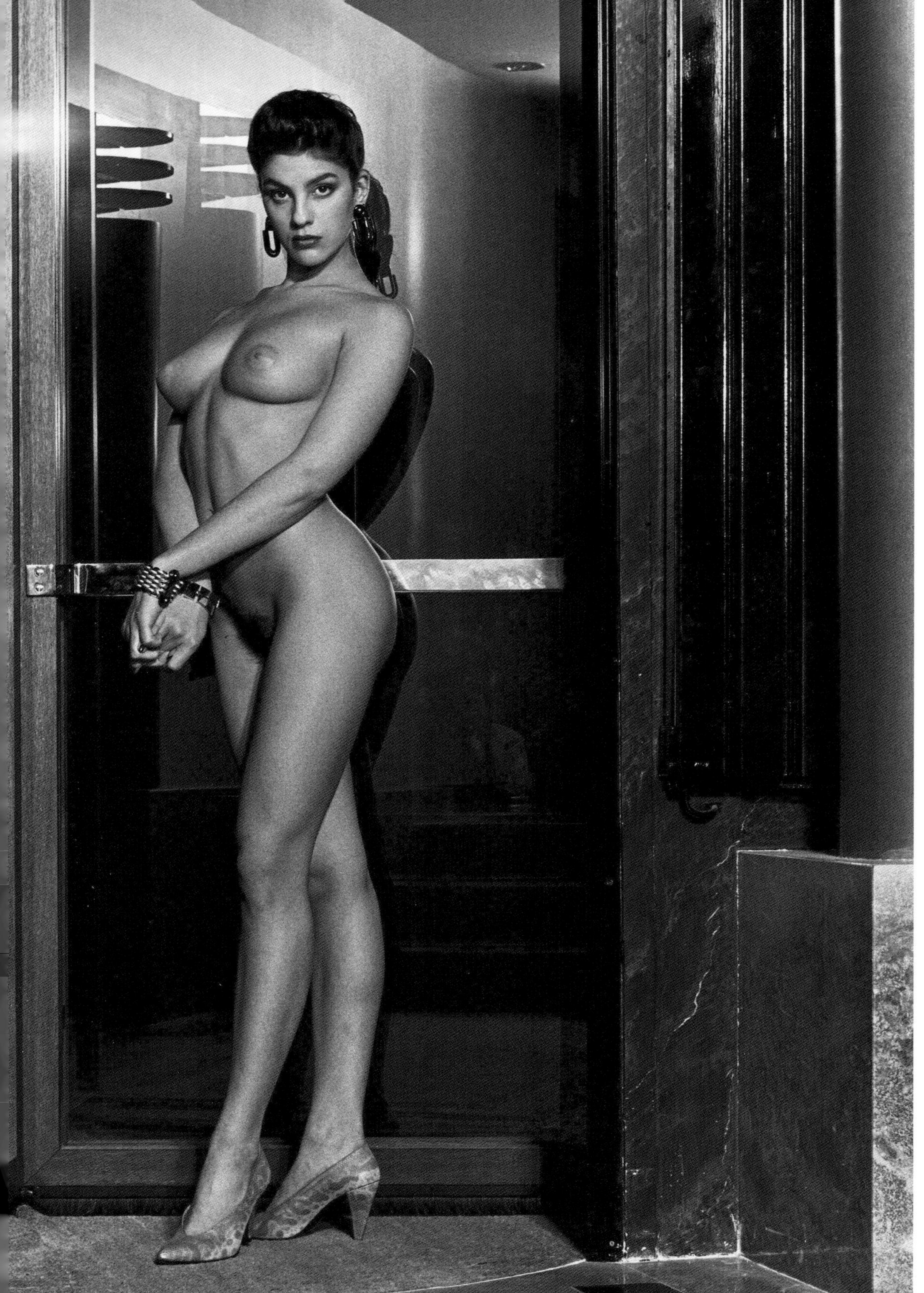

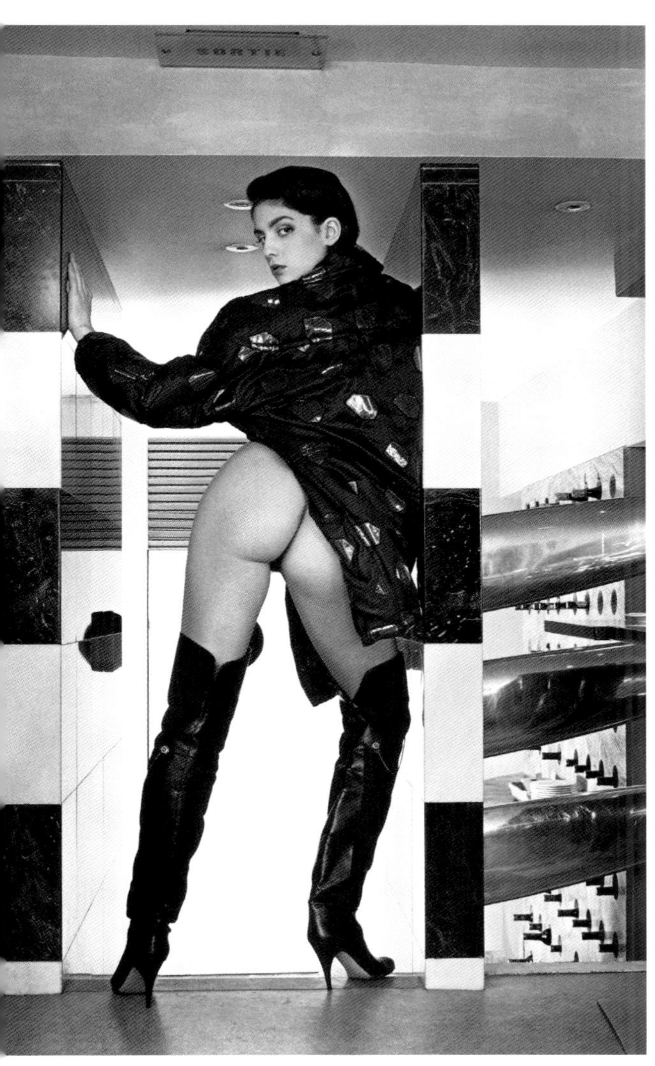
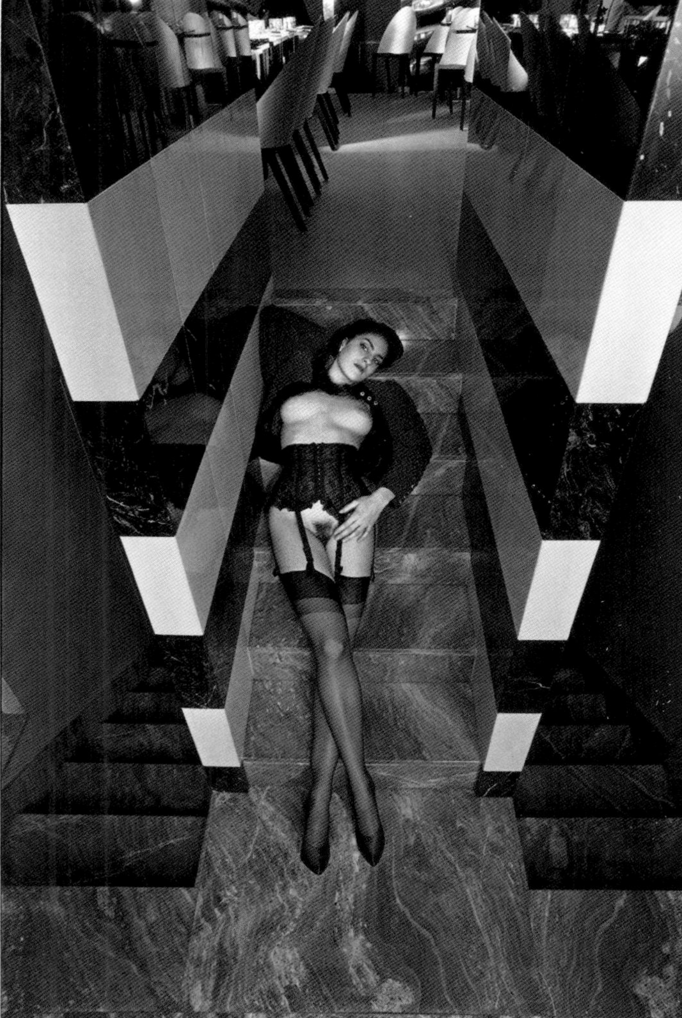

← Coryne 1988

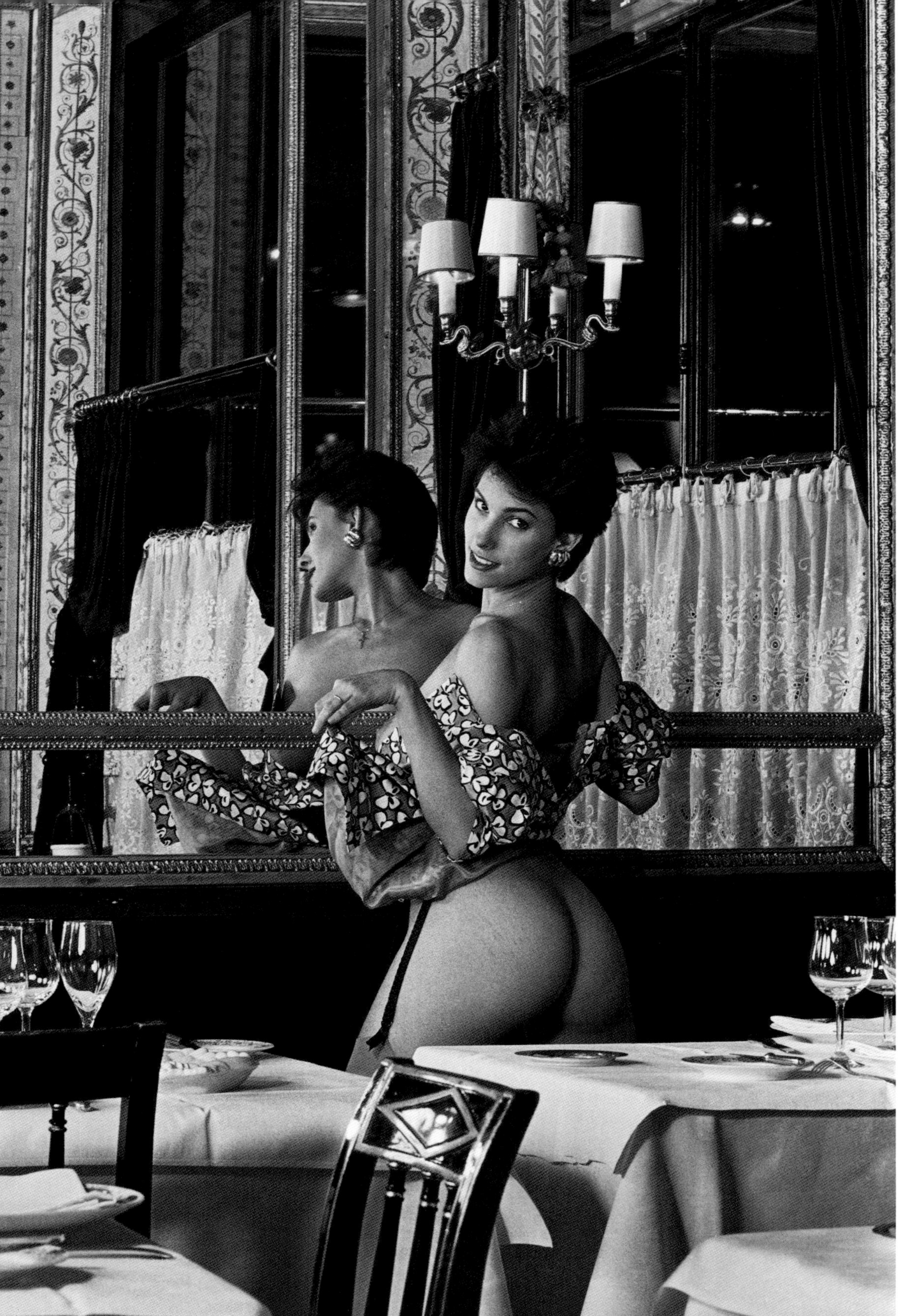

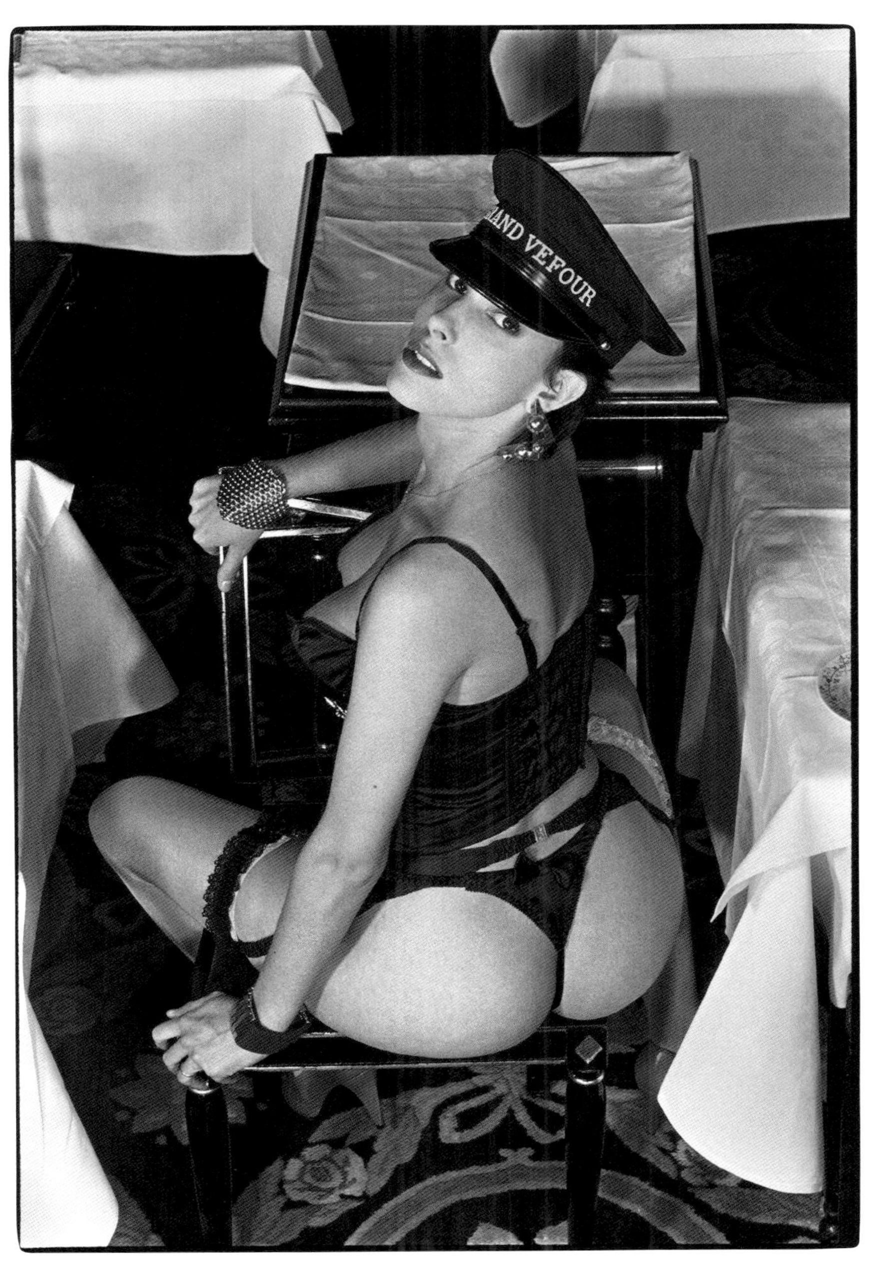
AND VEFOUR

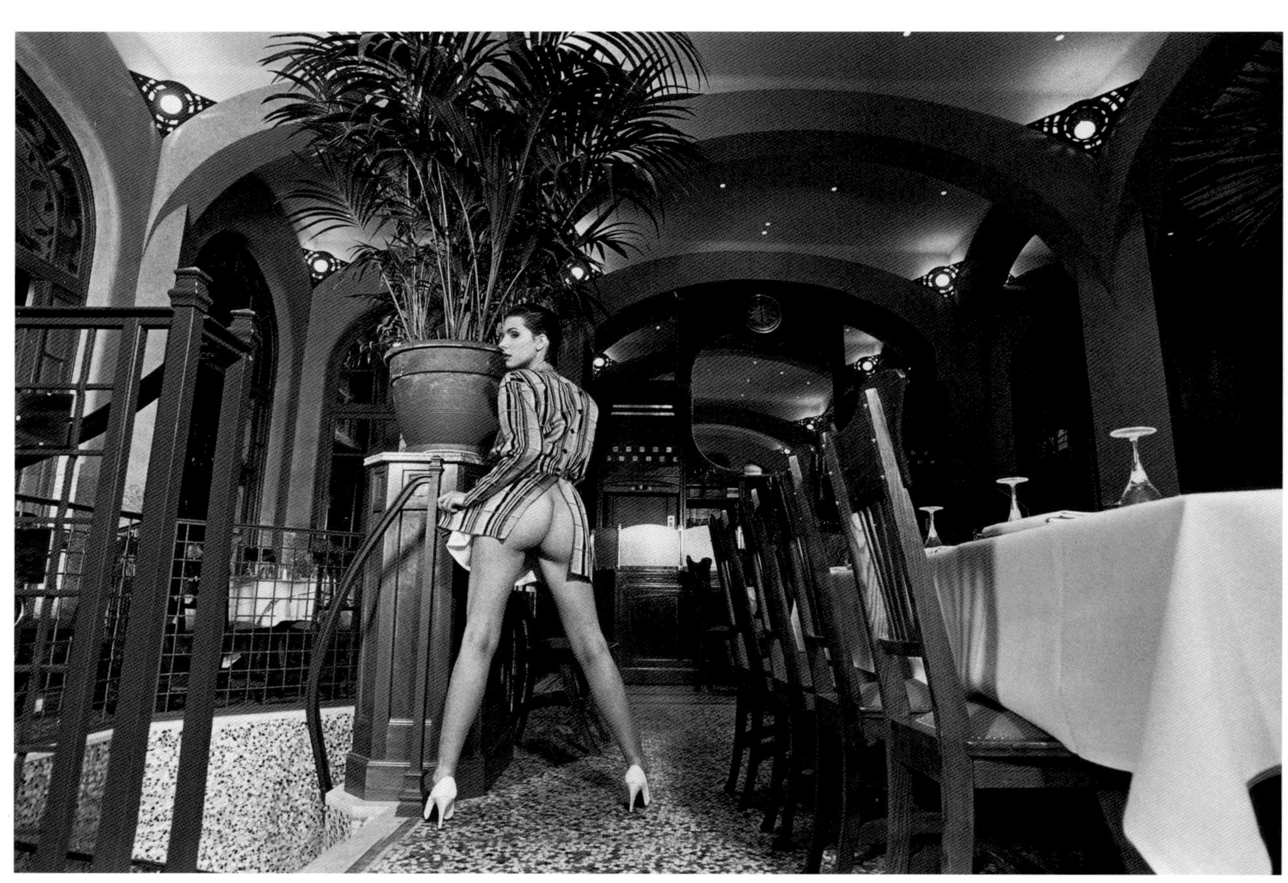

62   Laurence 1988

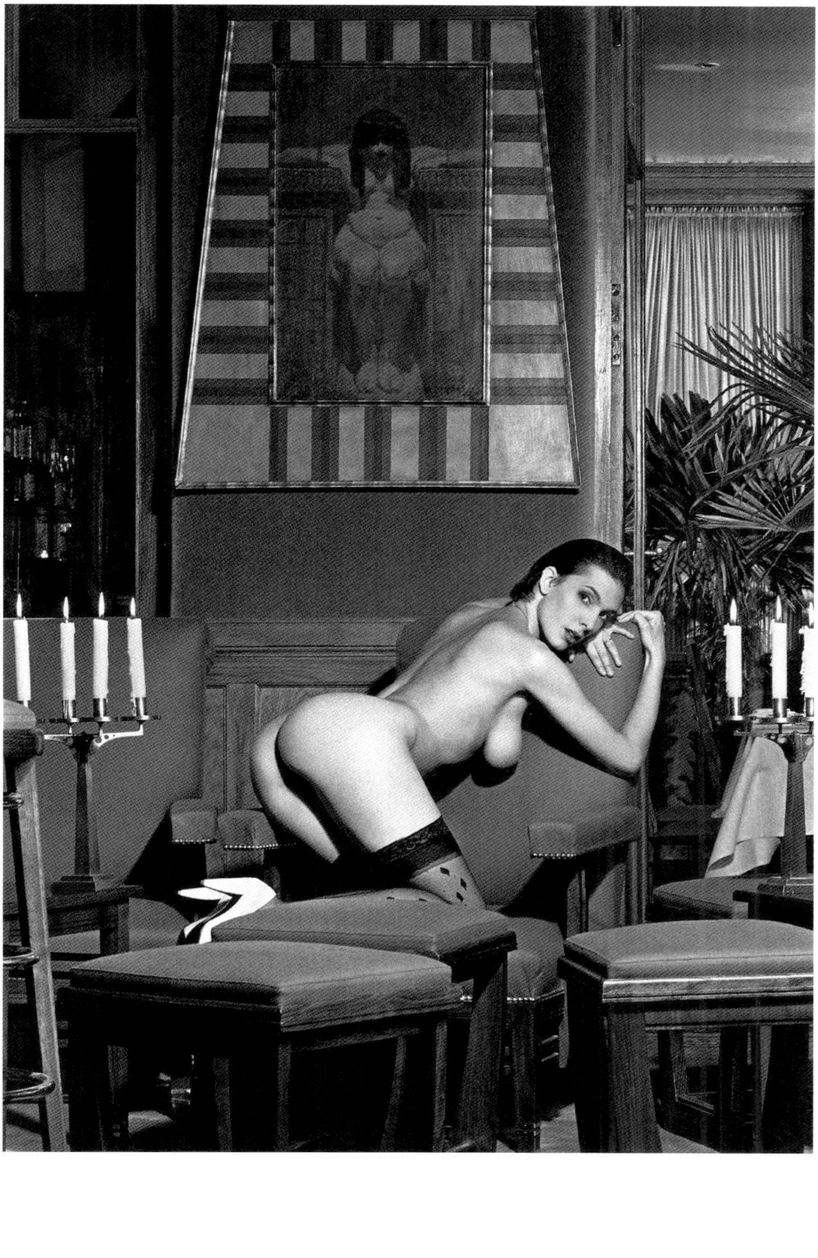

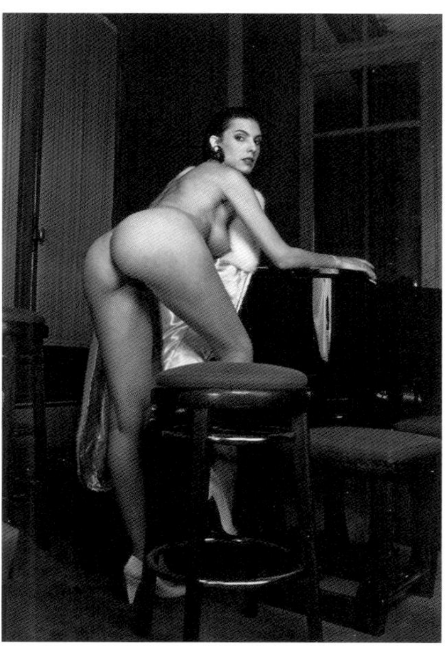

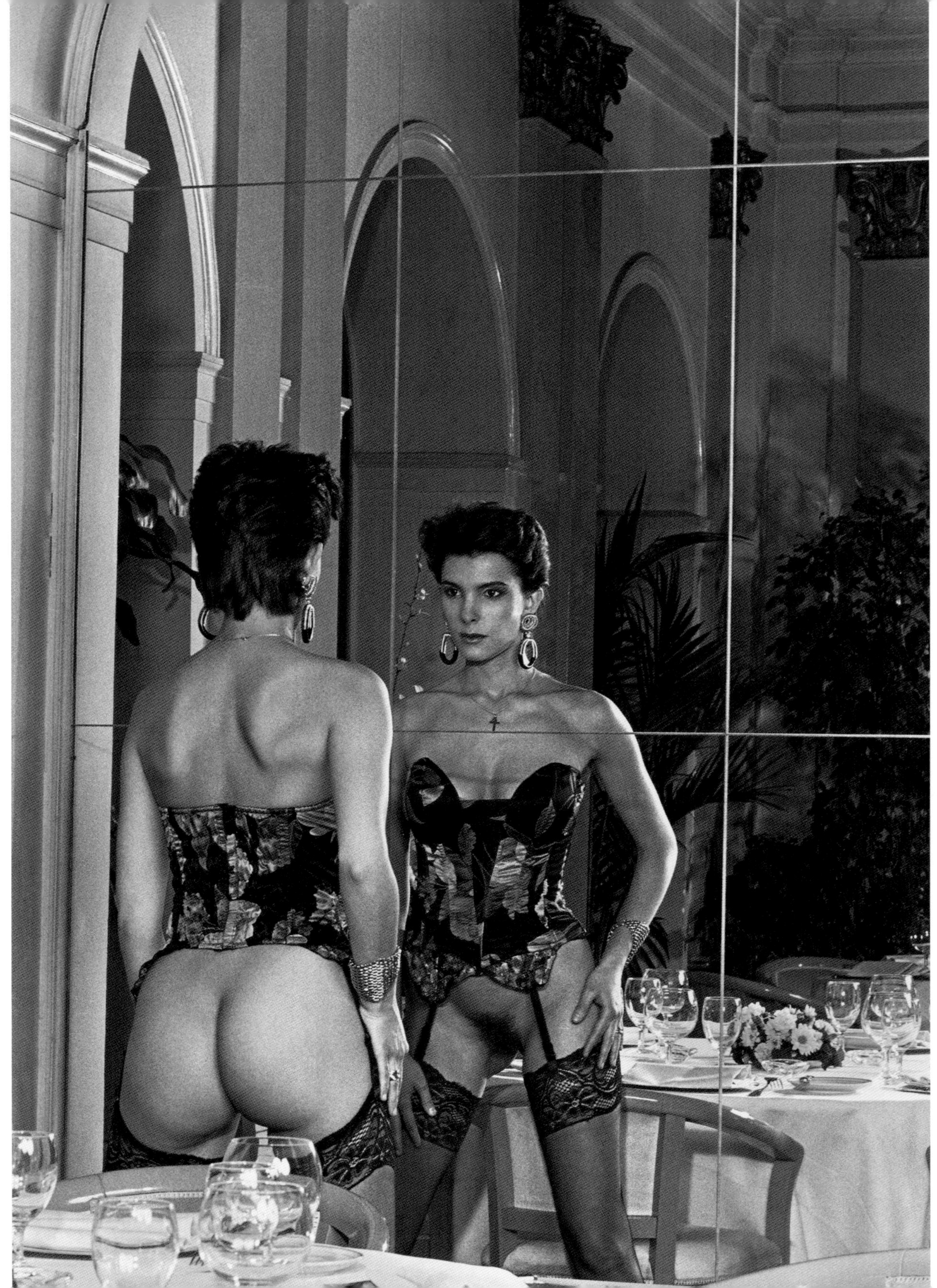

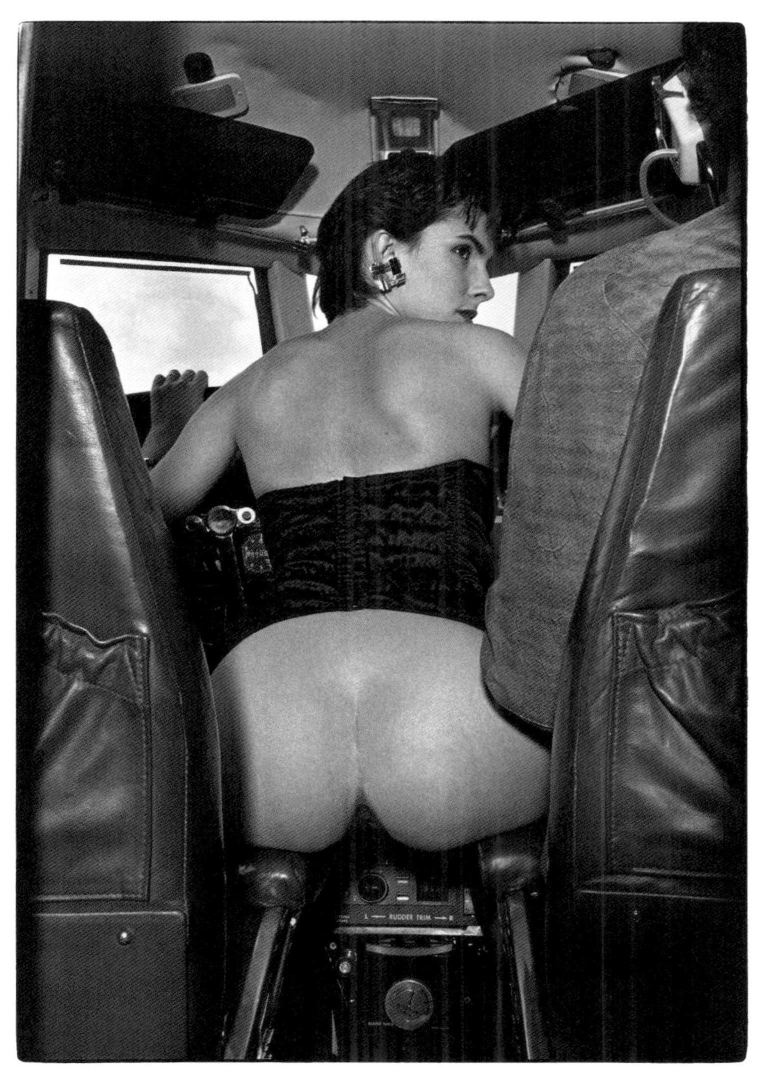

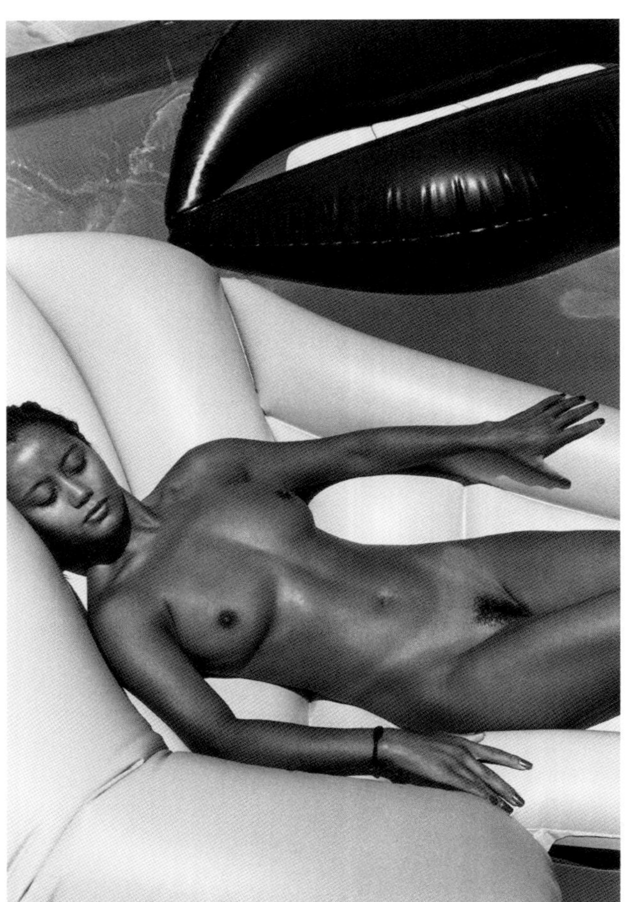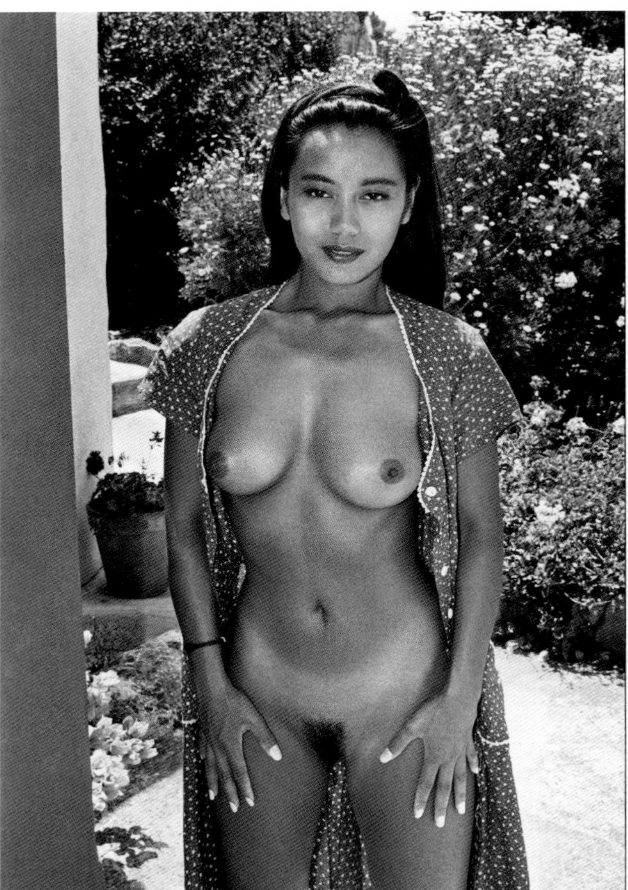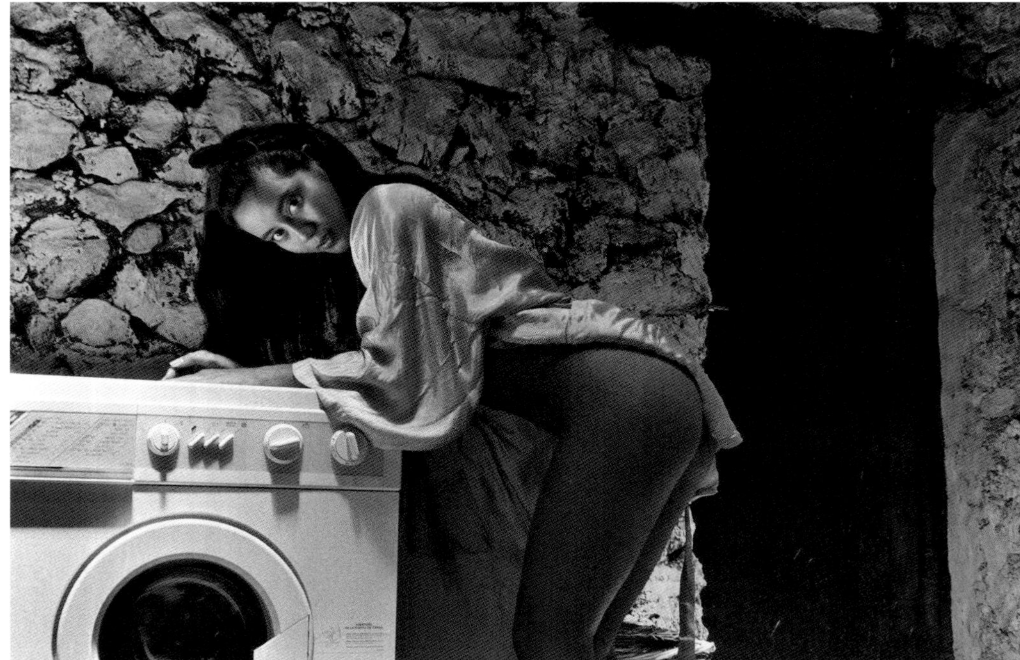

66   Laminah 1992

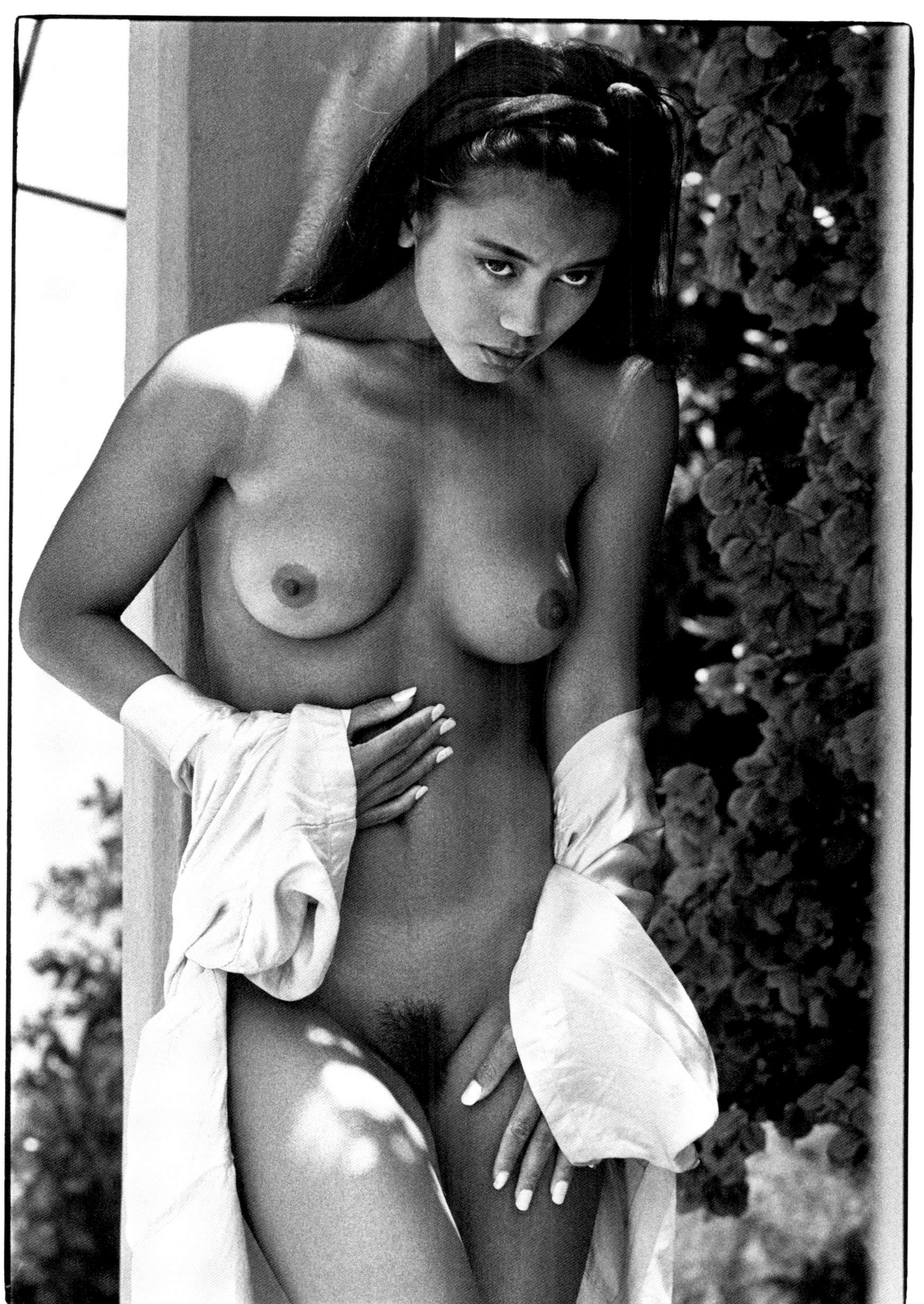

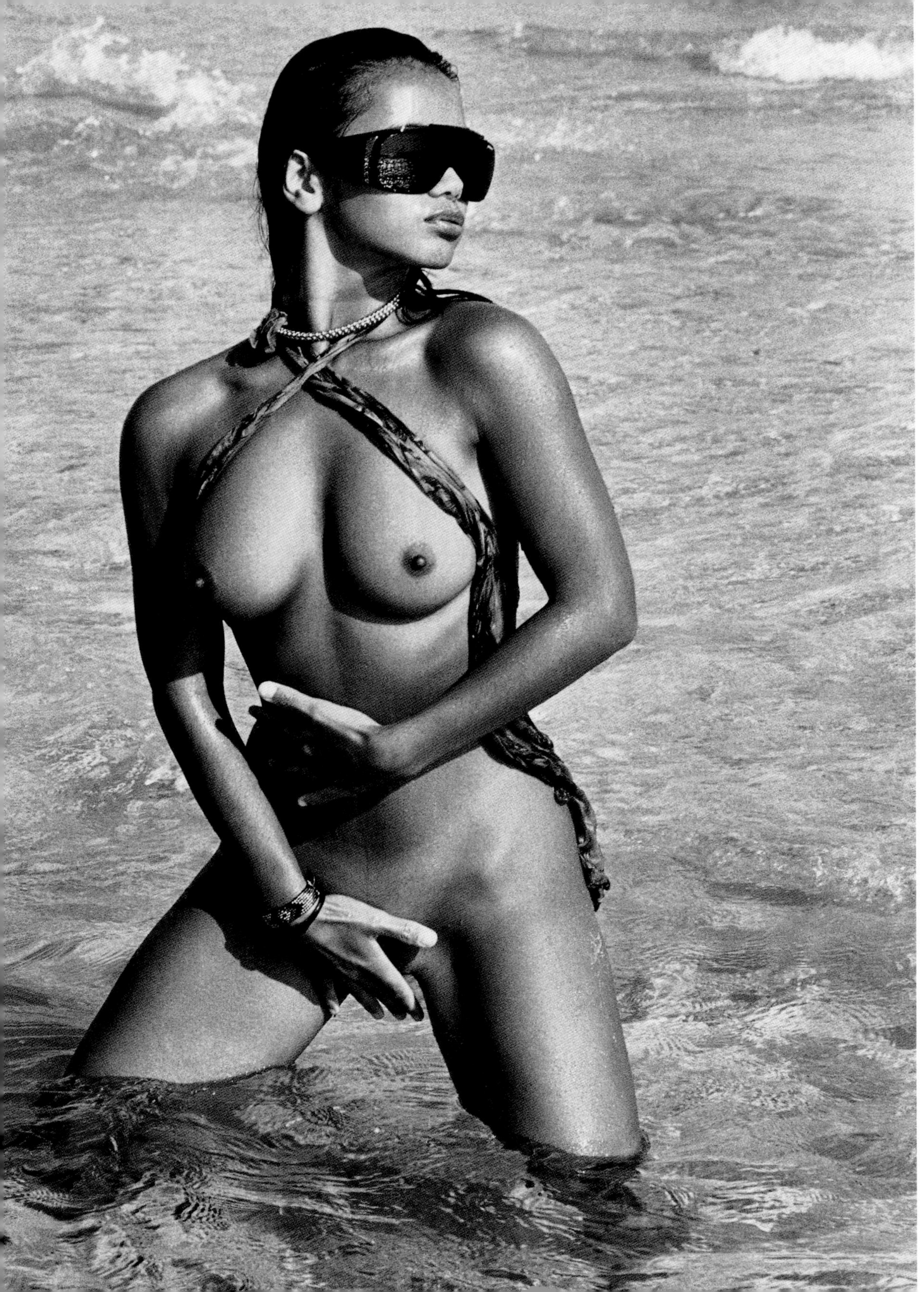

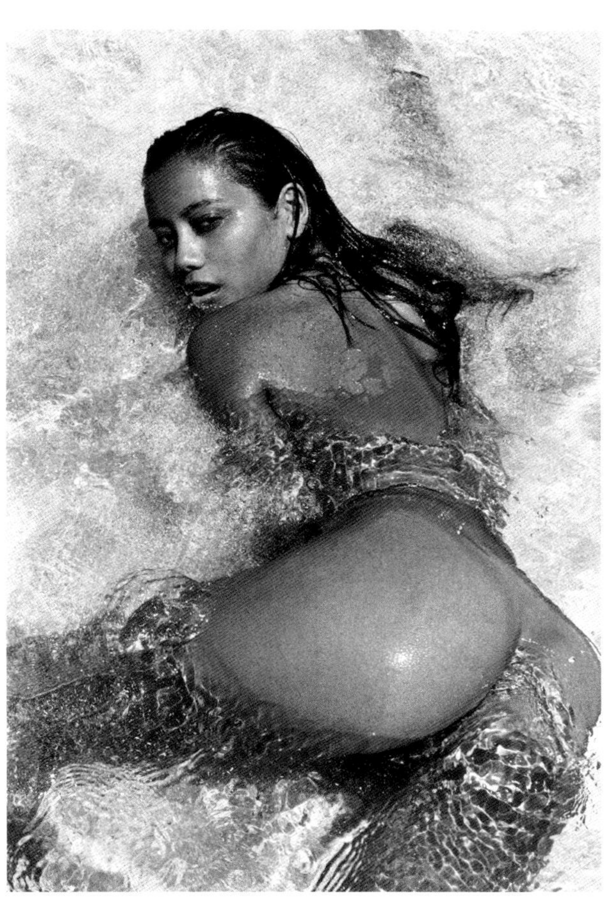

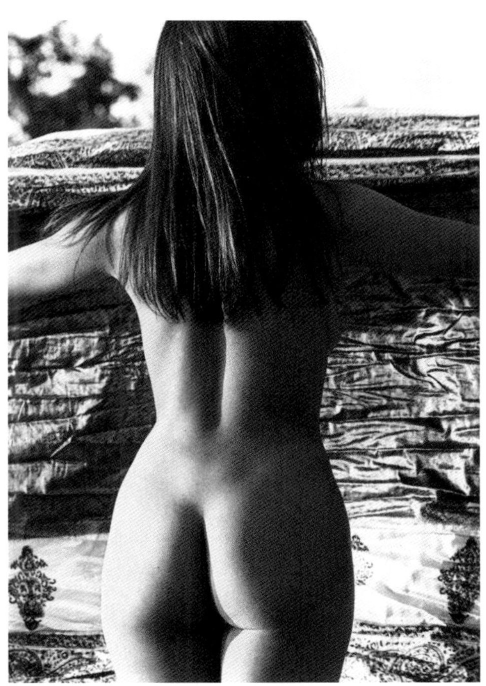

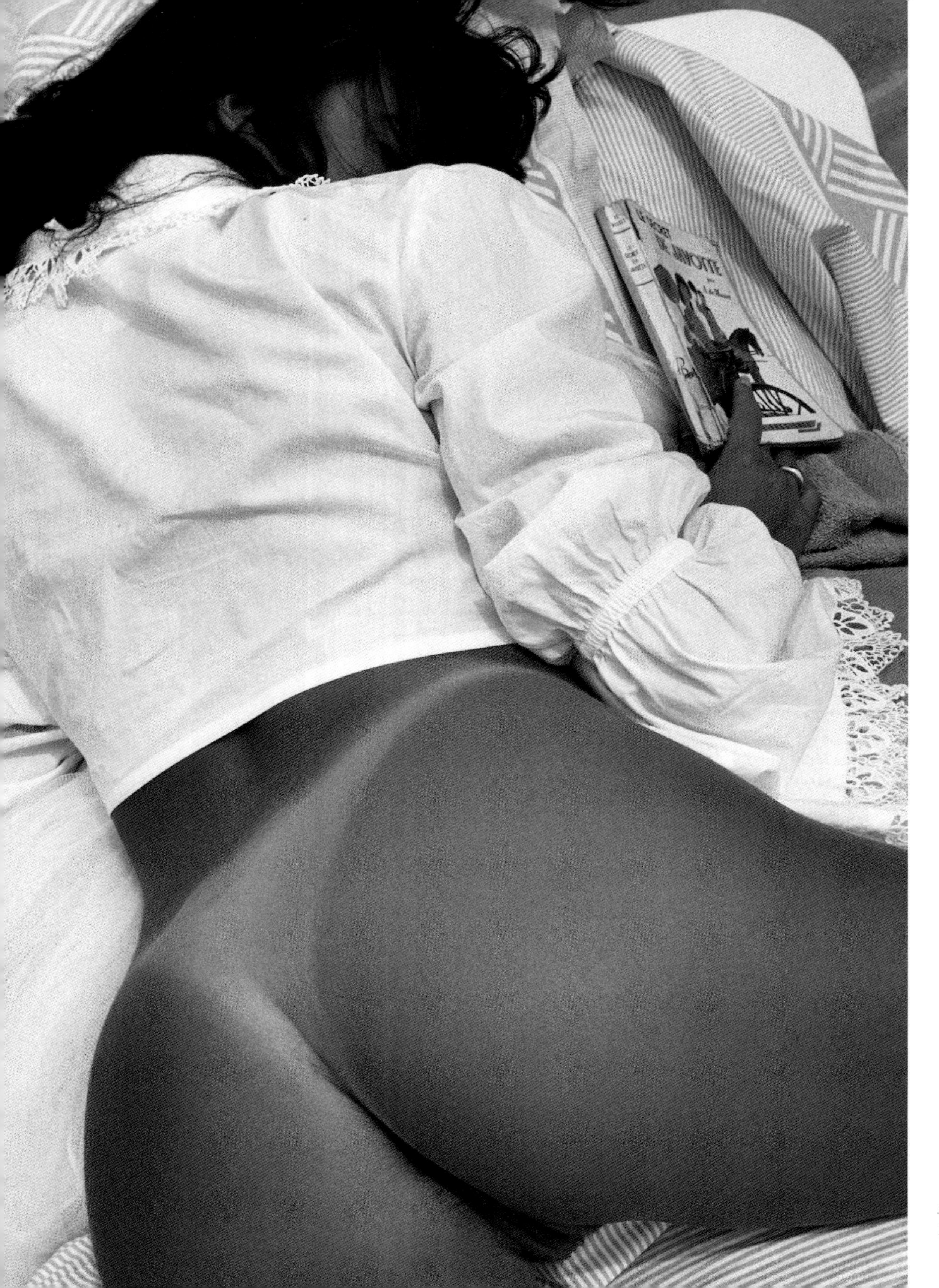

Ariane
1992

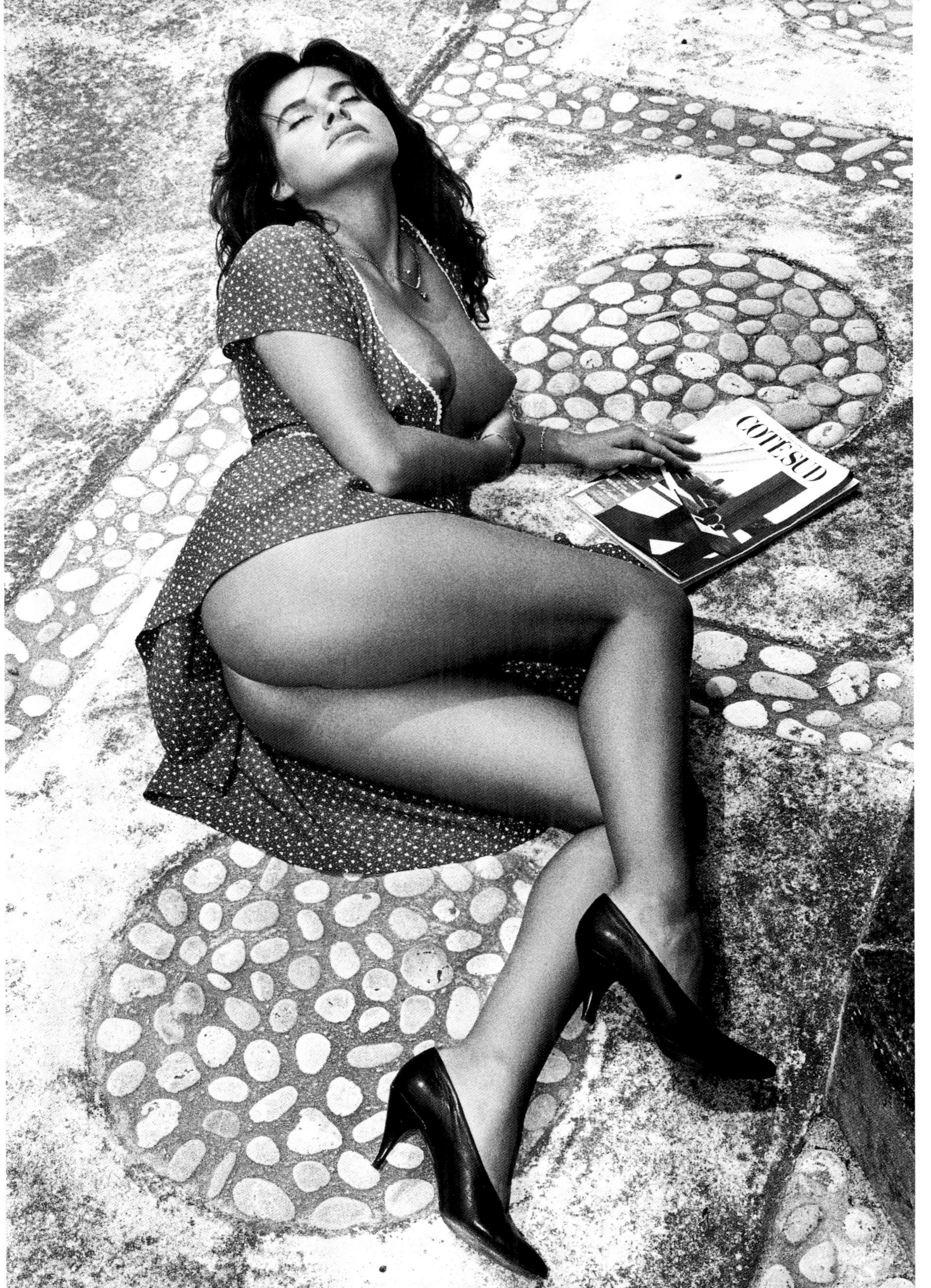
CÔTÉSUD

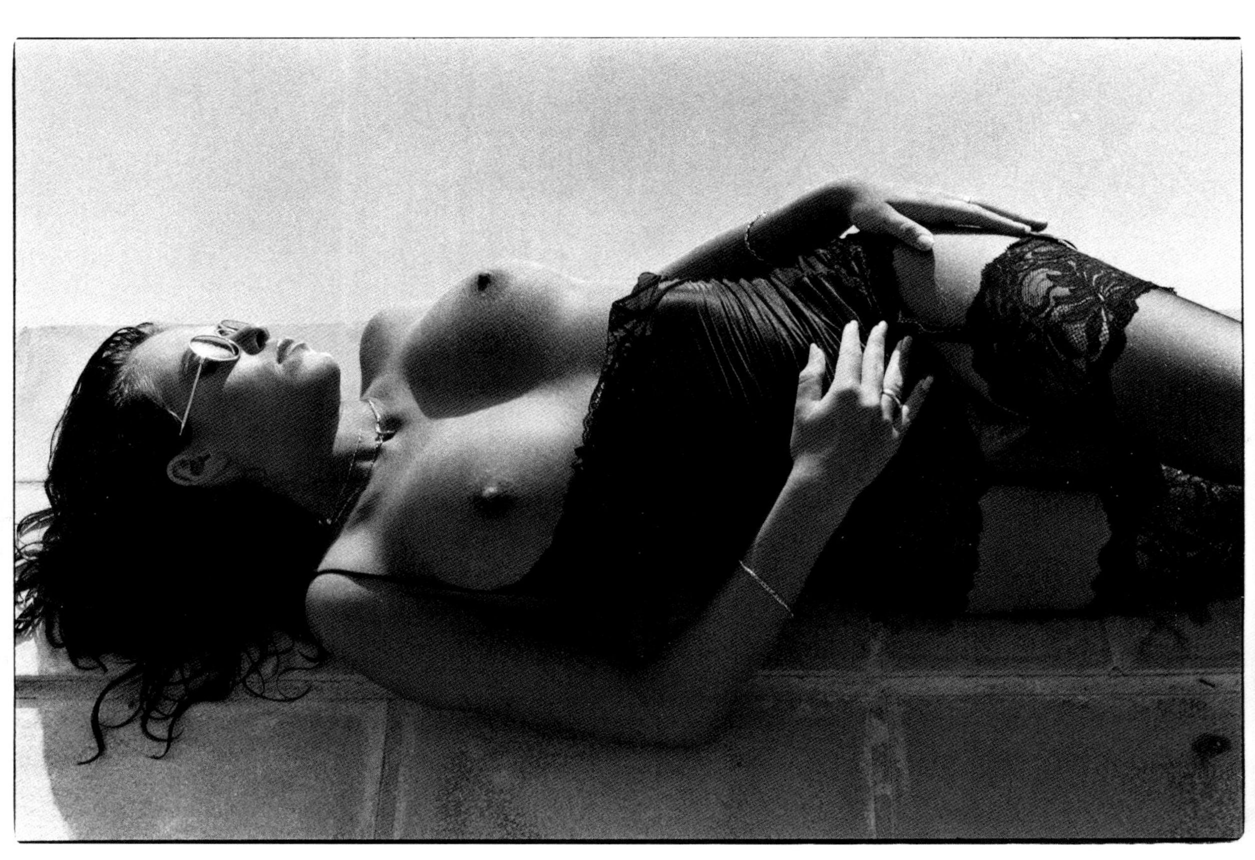

72　Ariane 1992

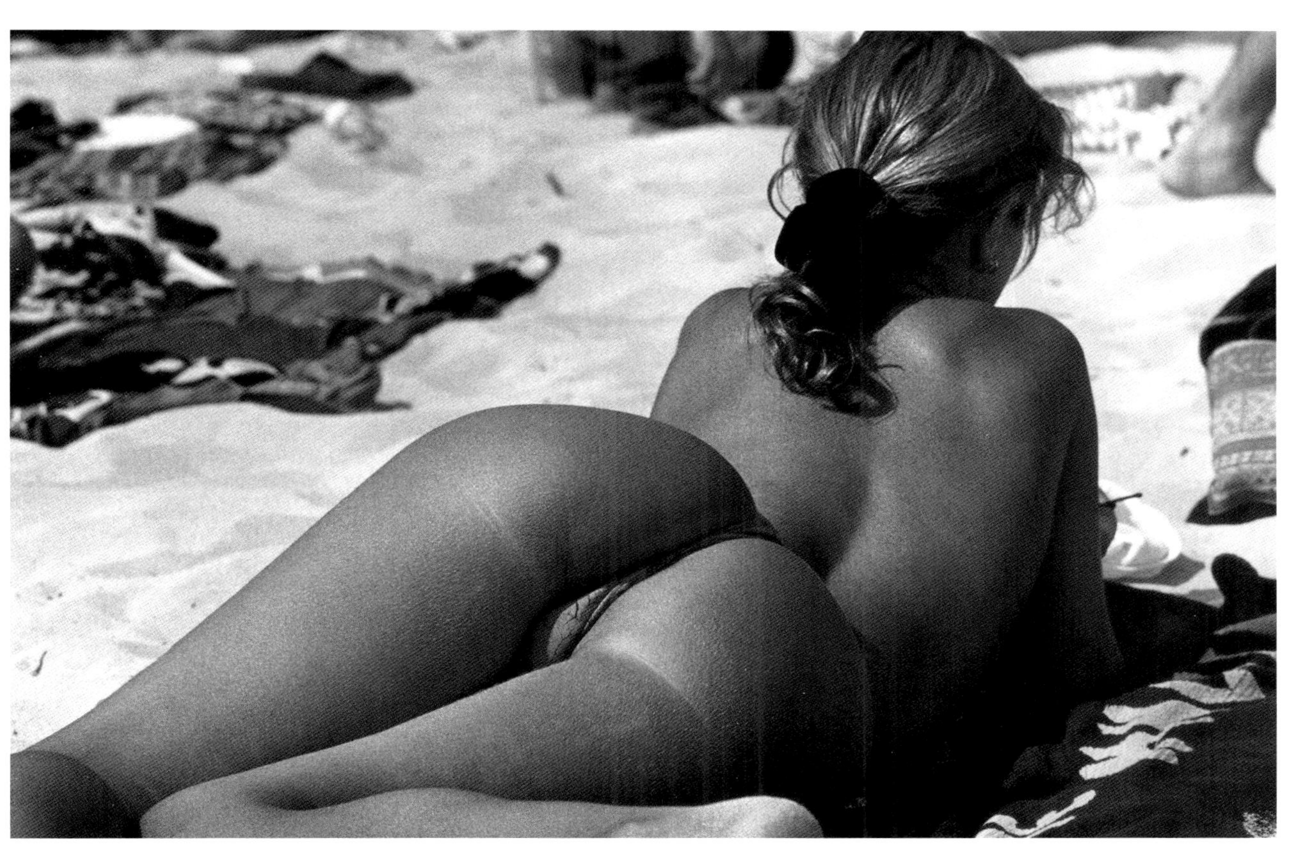

Inconnue (unkwnown person) 1992   73

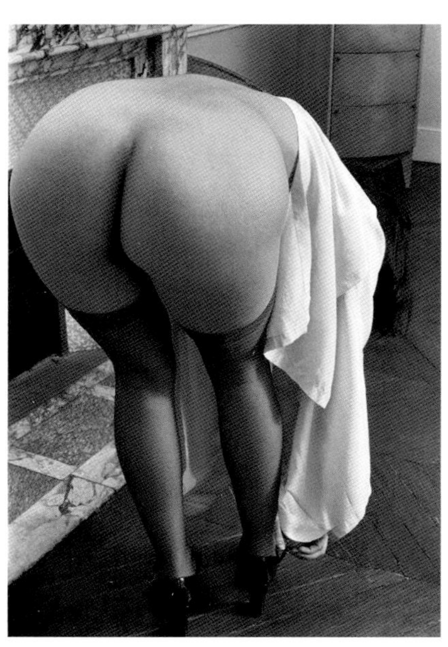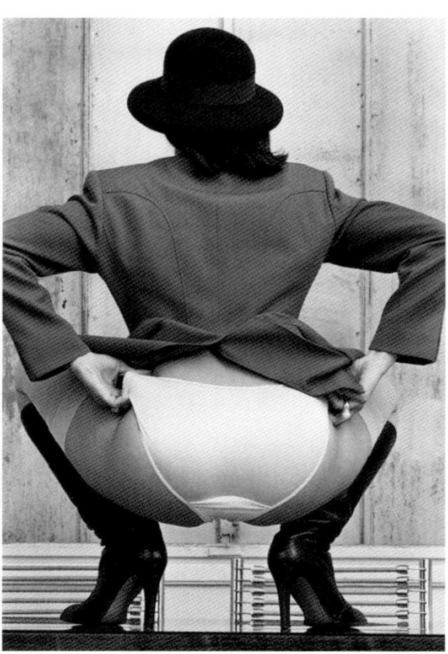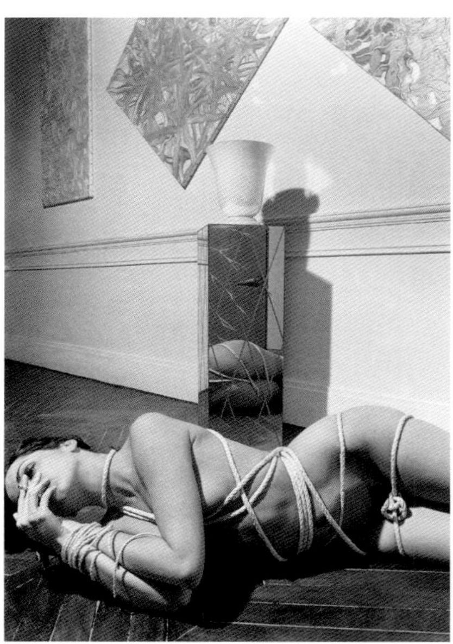

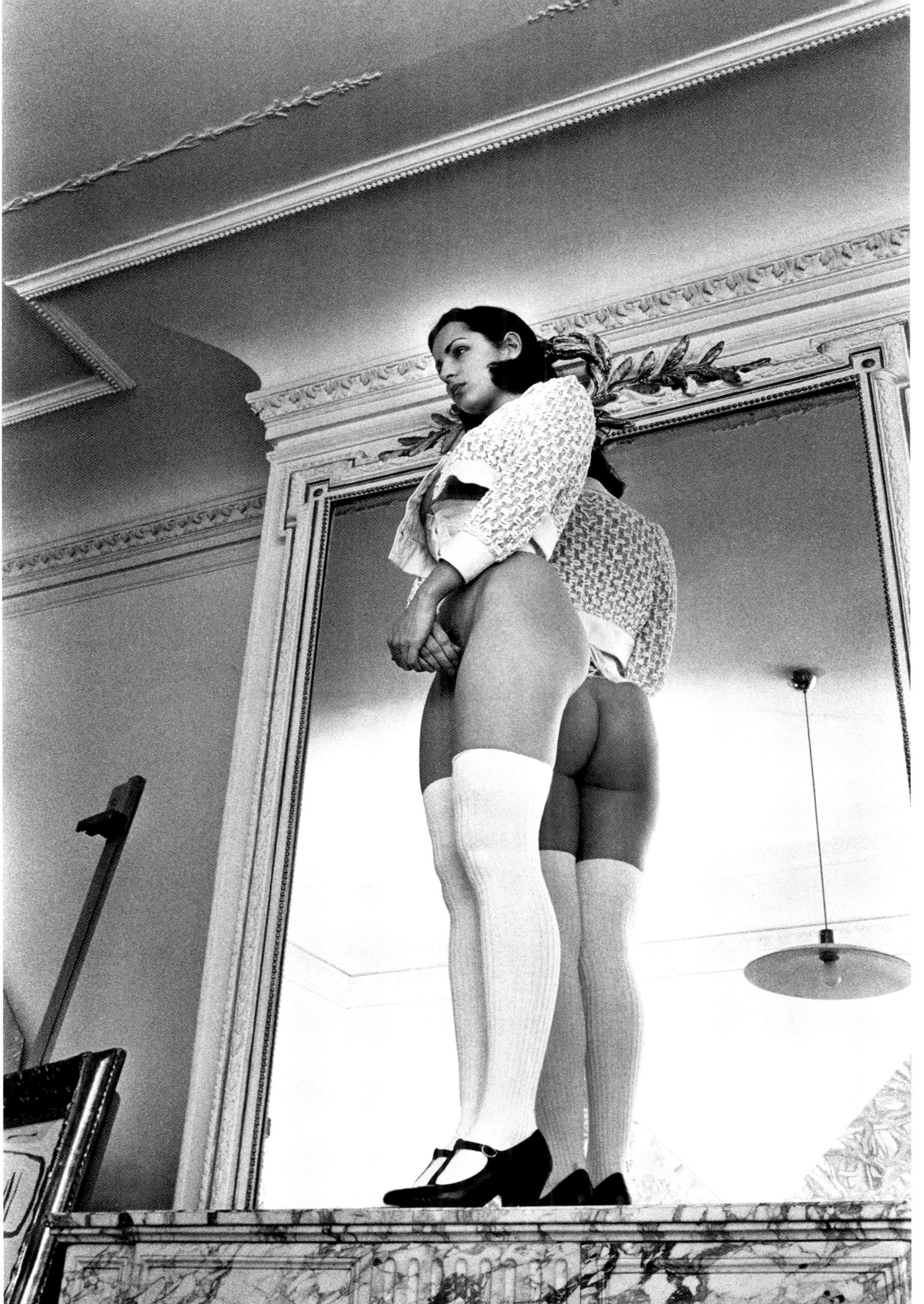

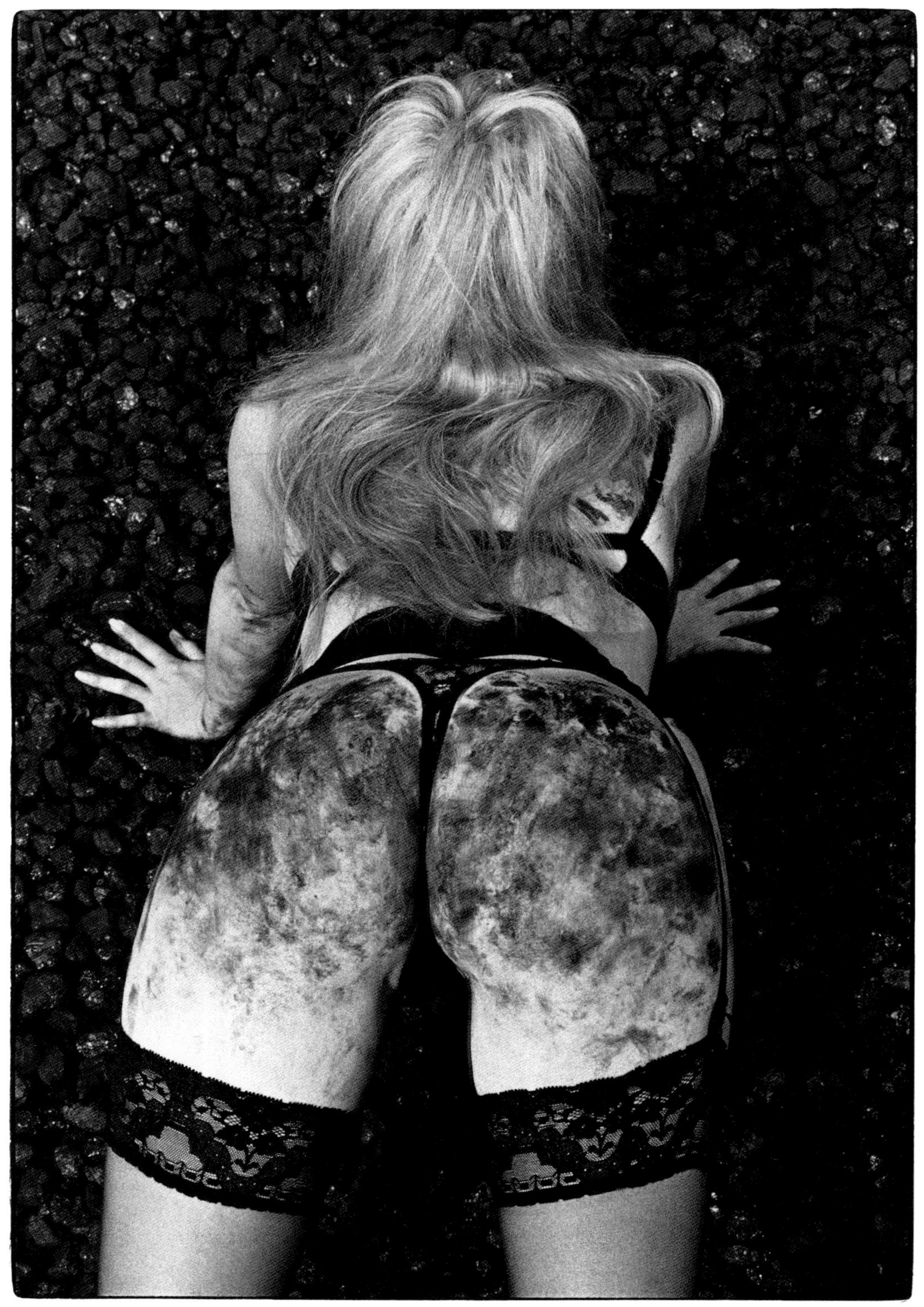

 Cat 1992

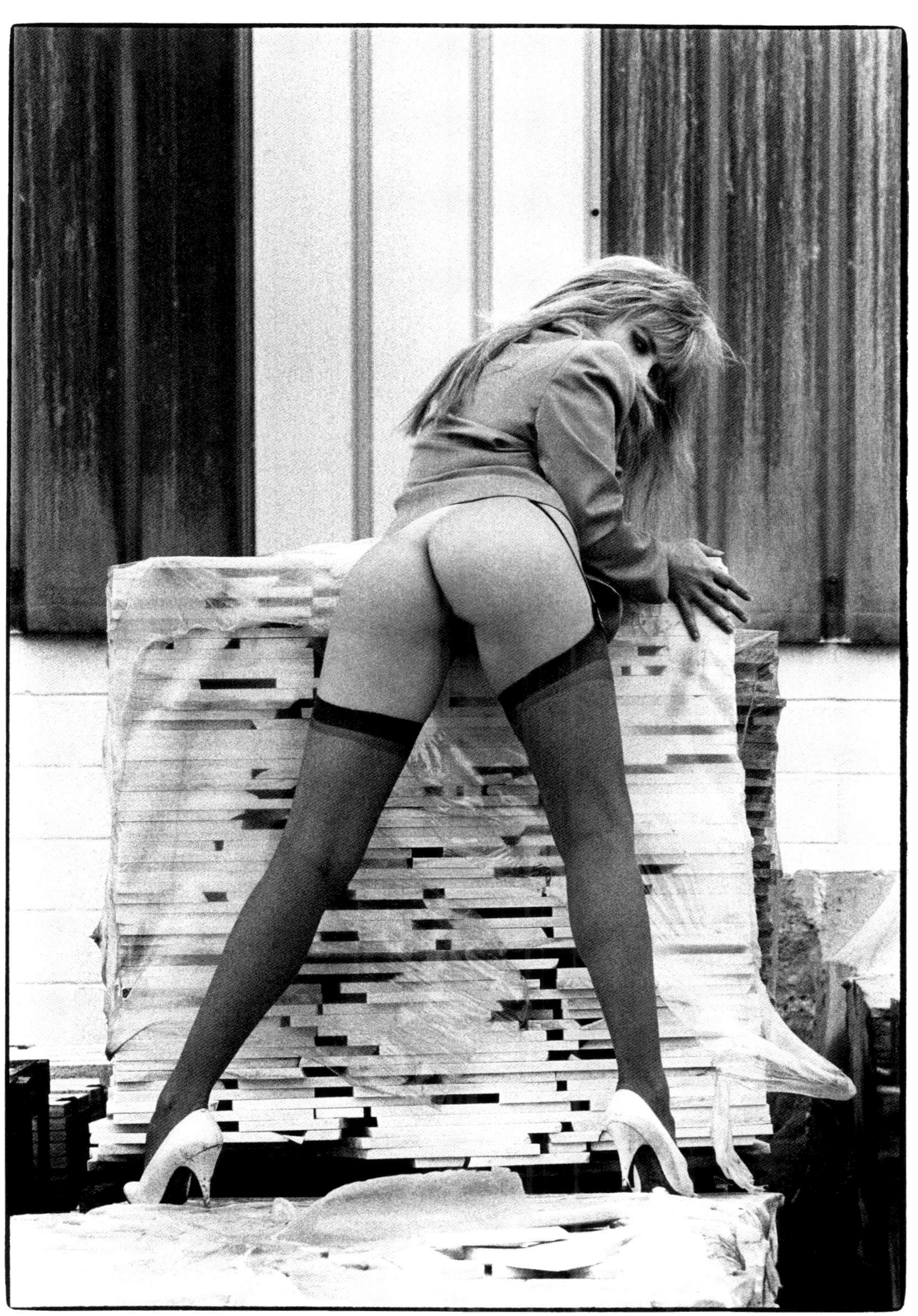

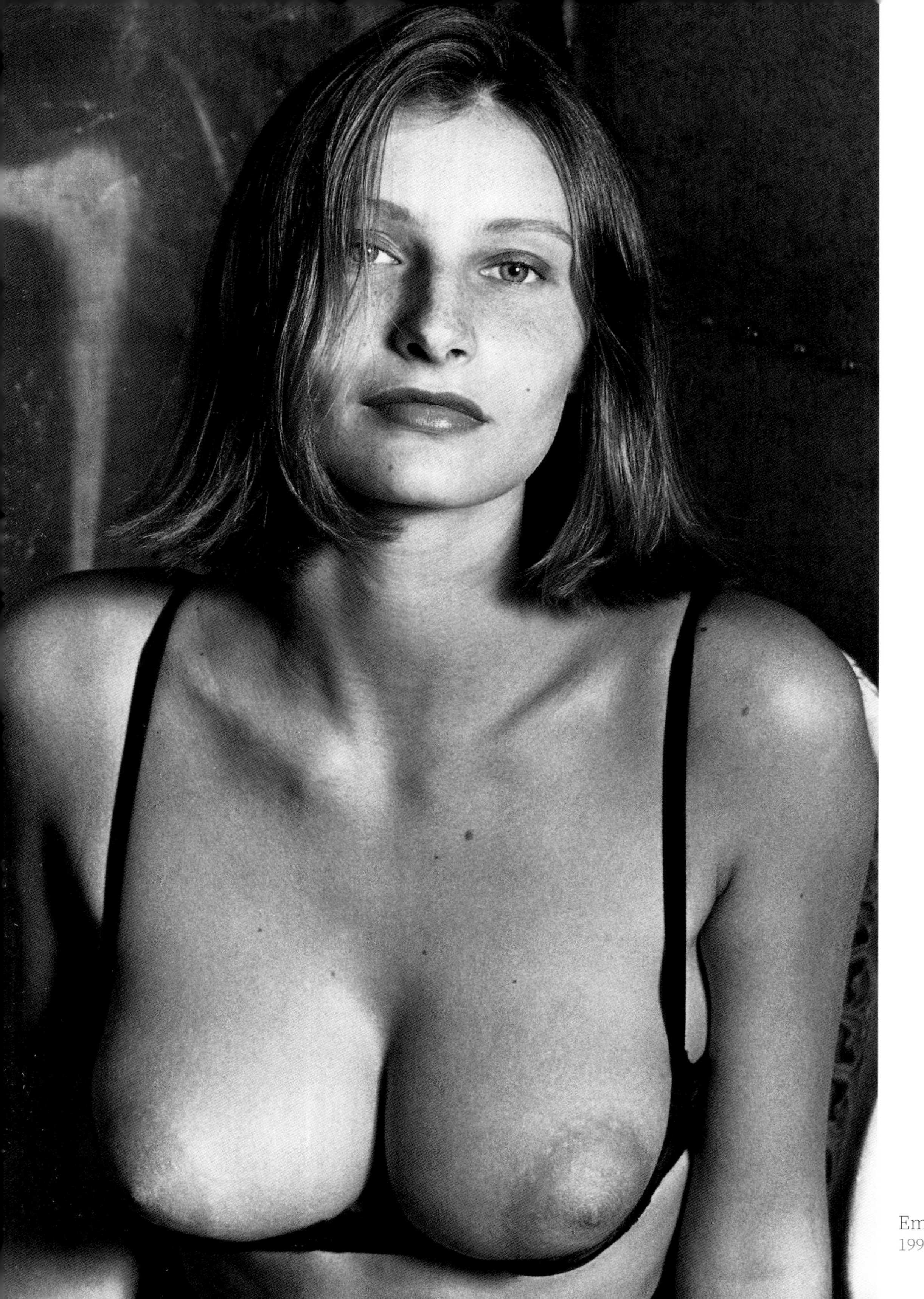

Emmanuelle
1993

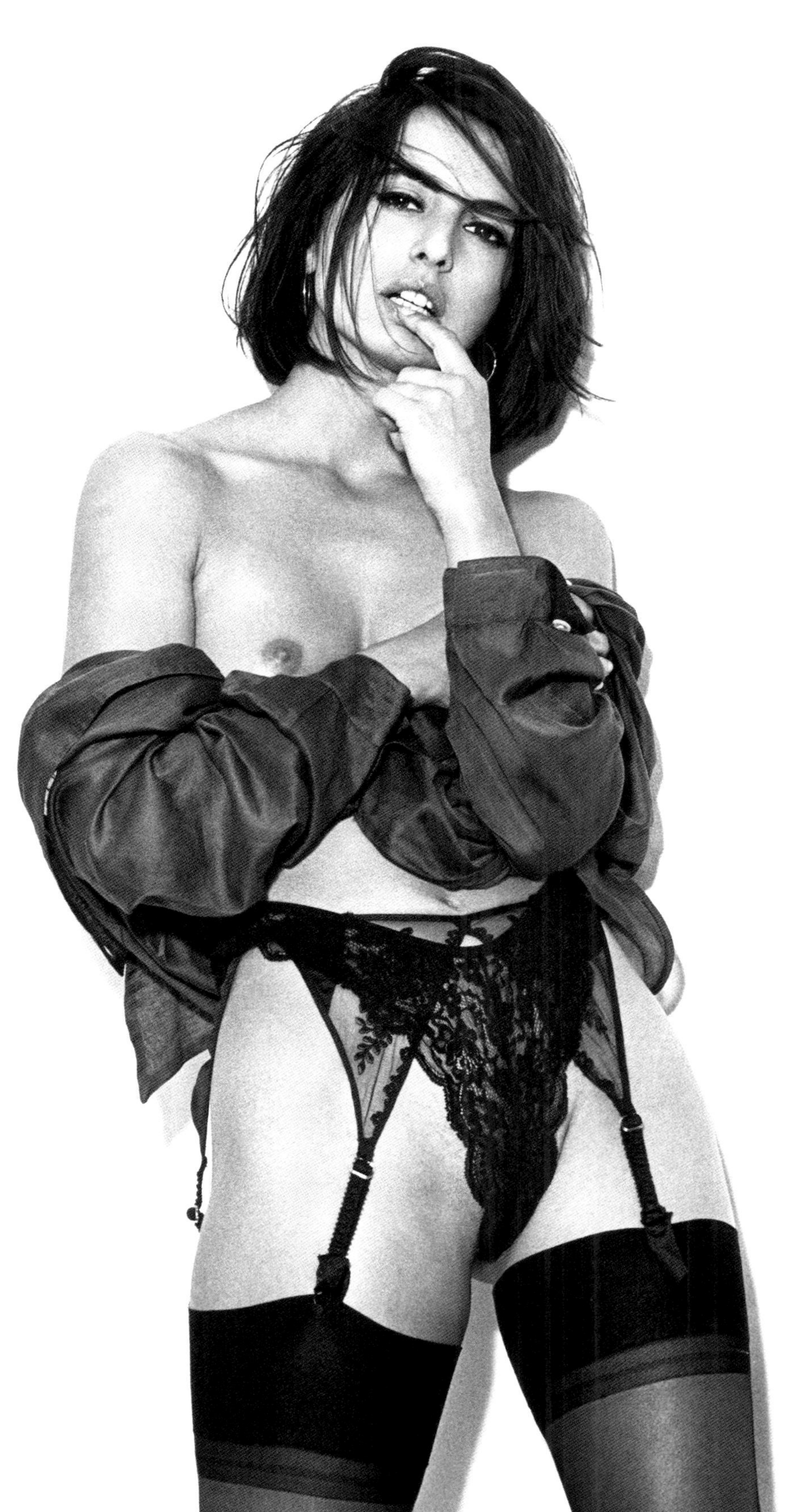

Pauline
1992   79

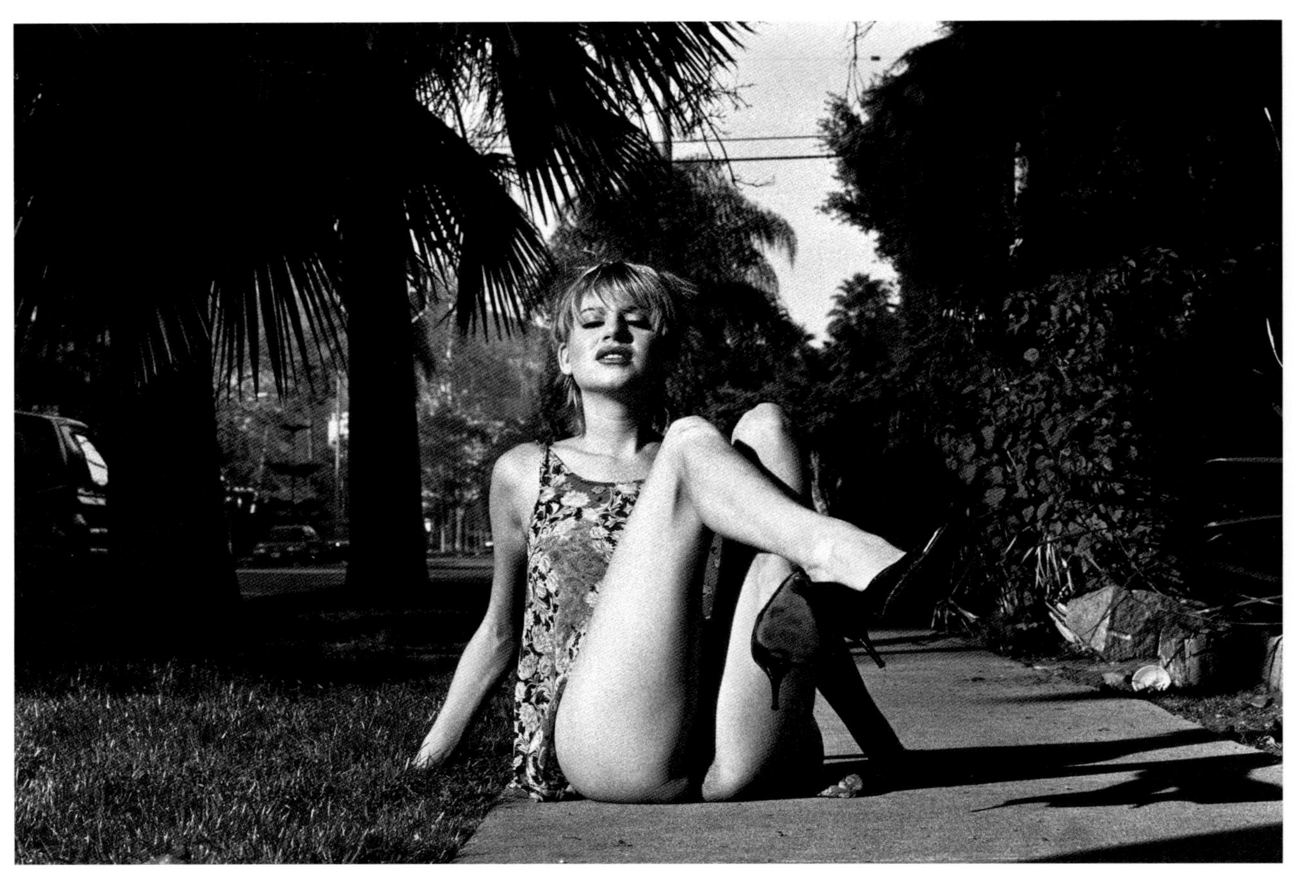

Emmanuelle 1993 →

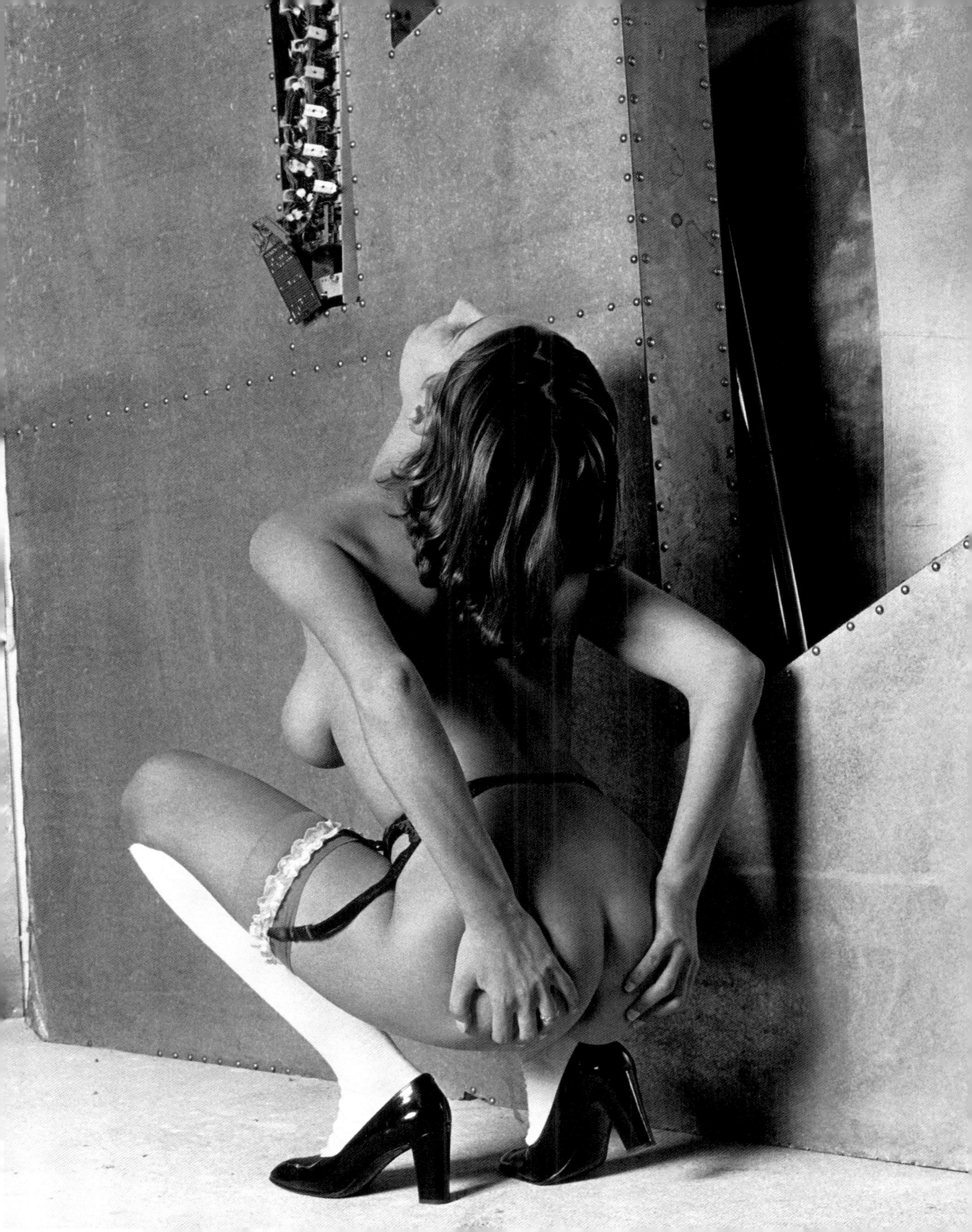

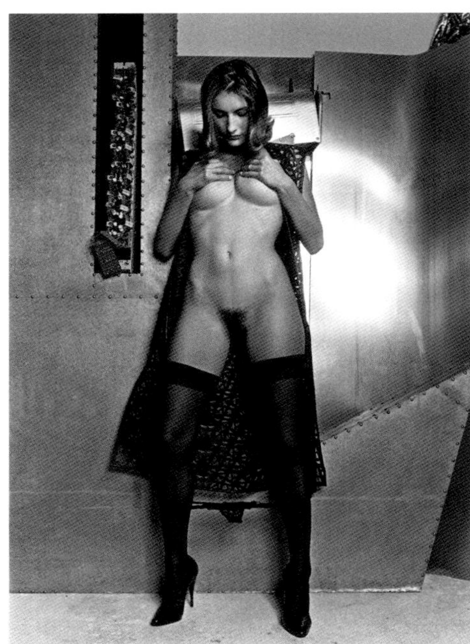
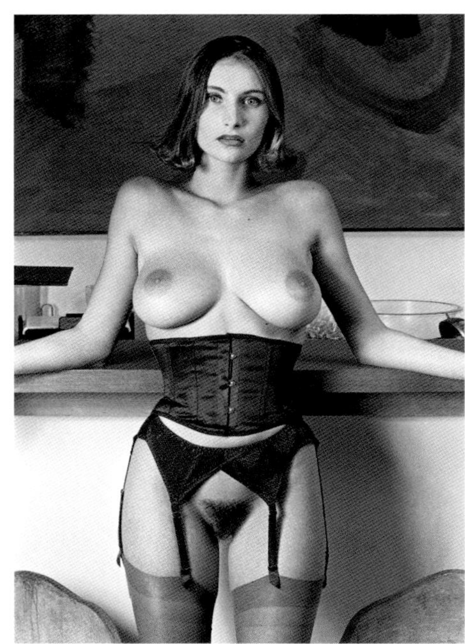
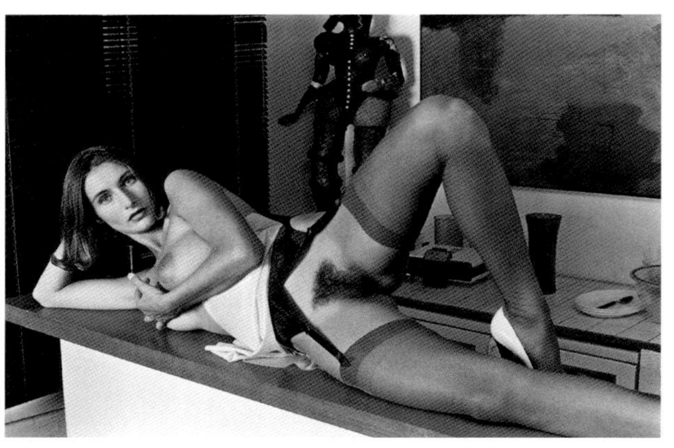
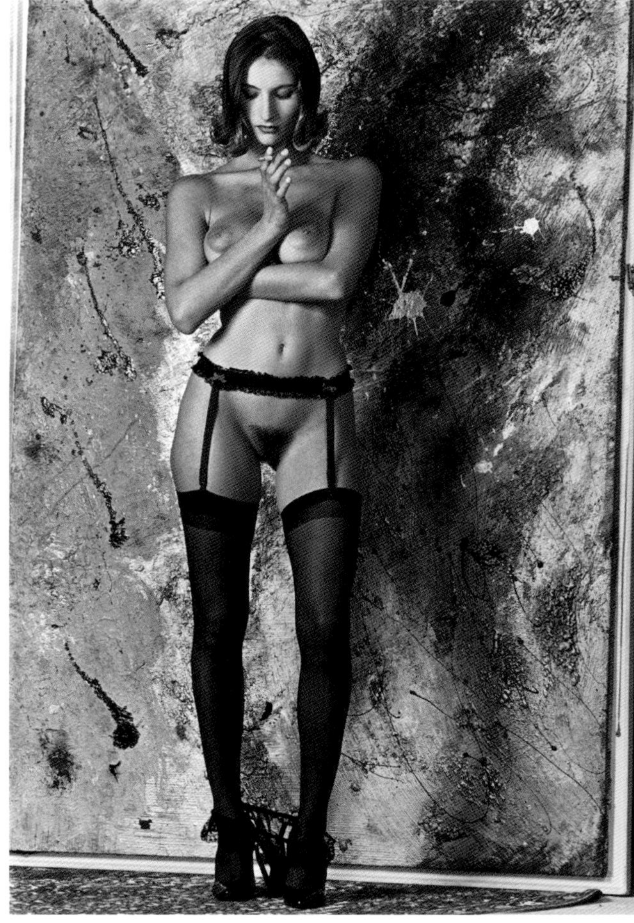

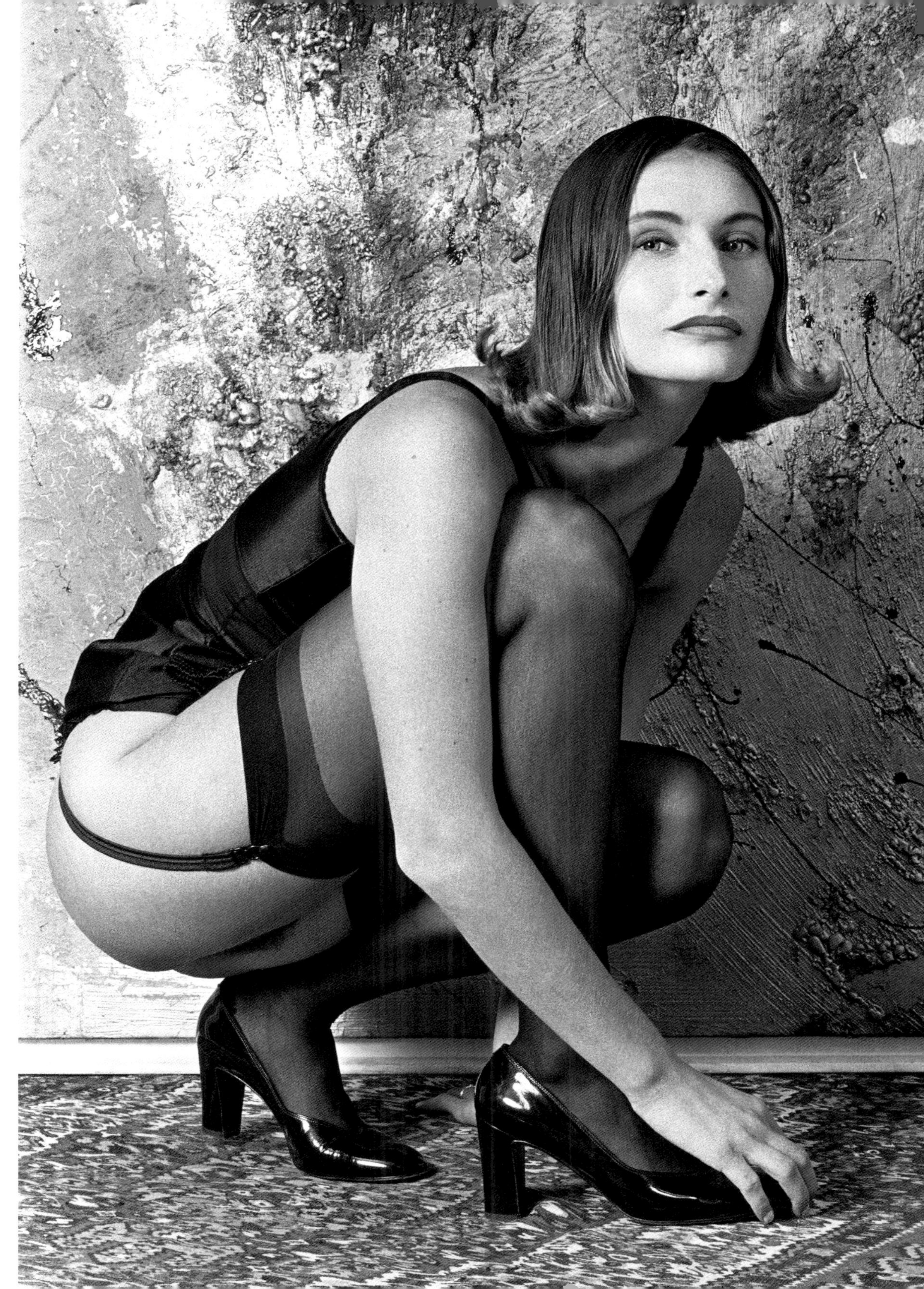

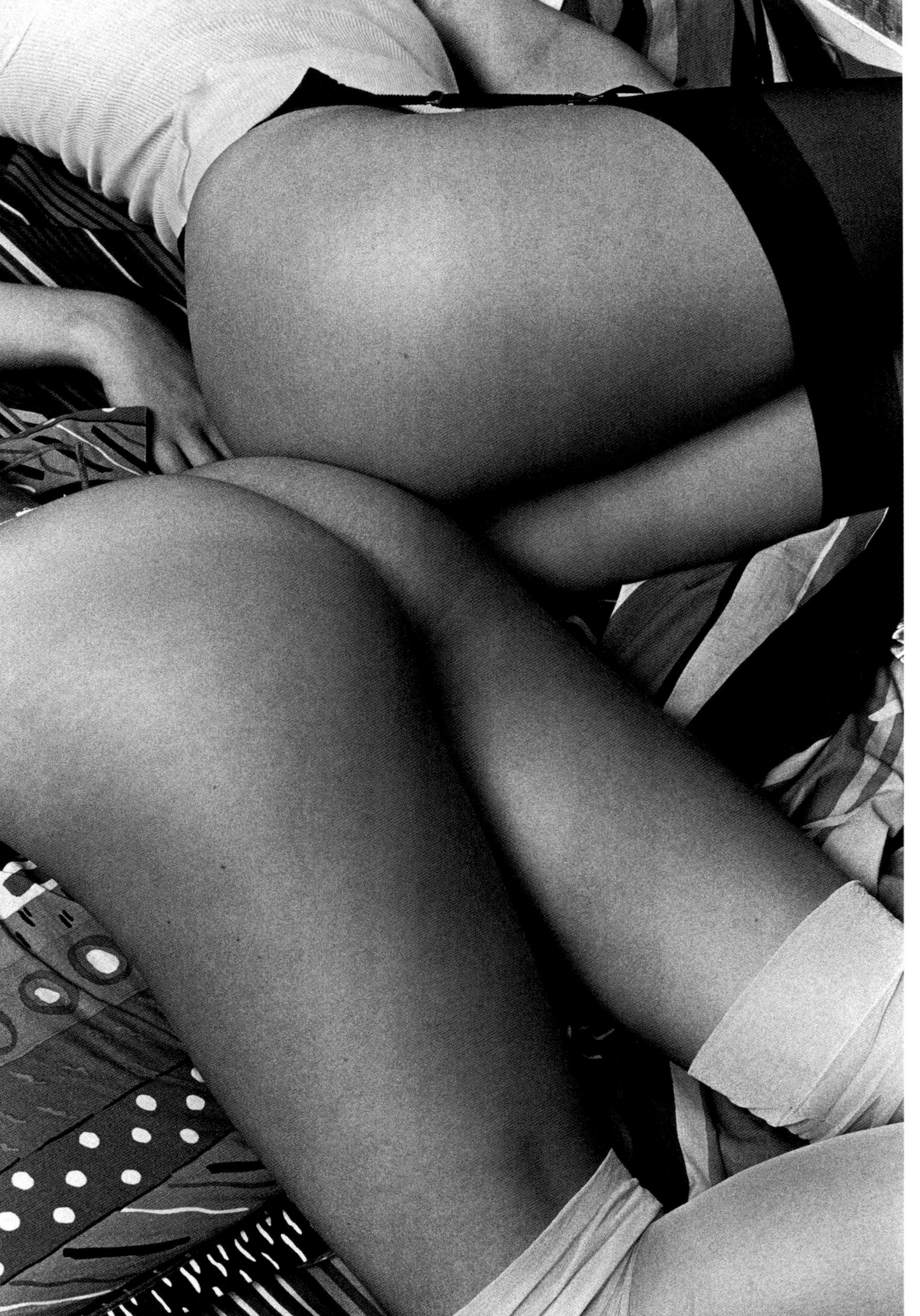

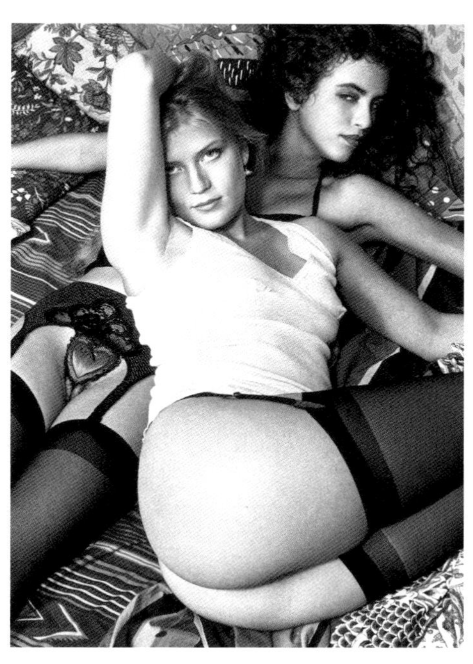

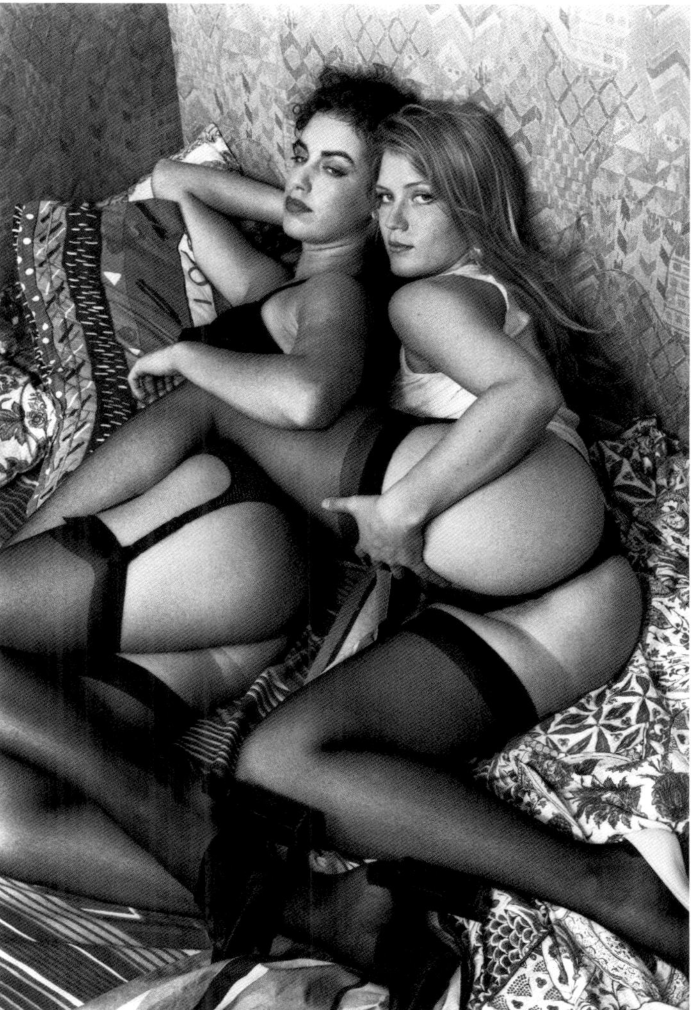

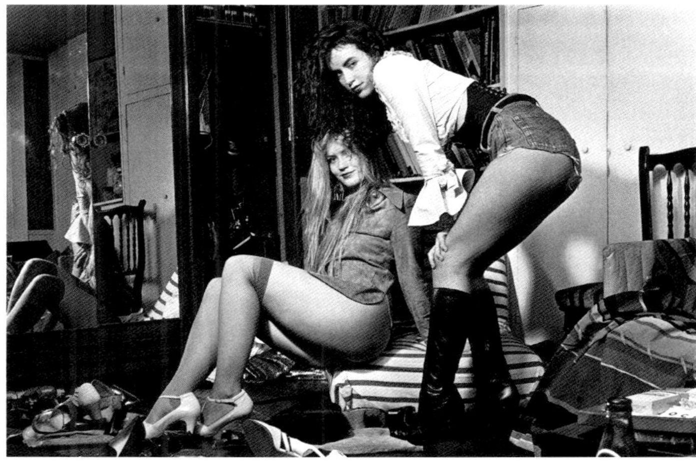

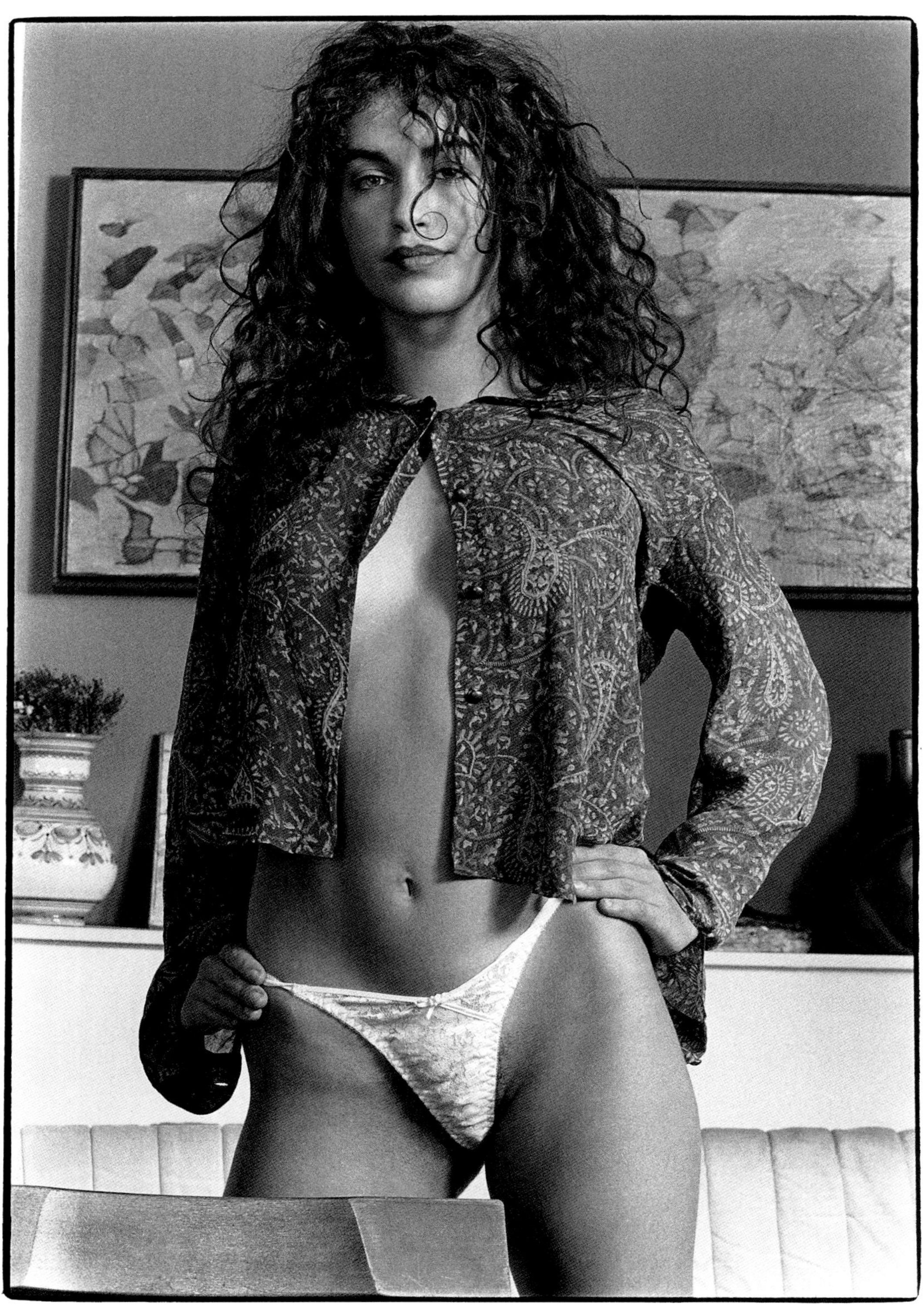

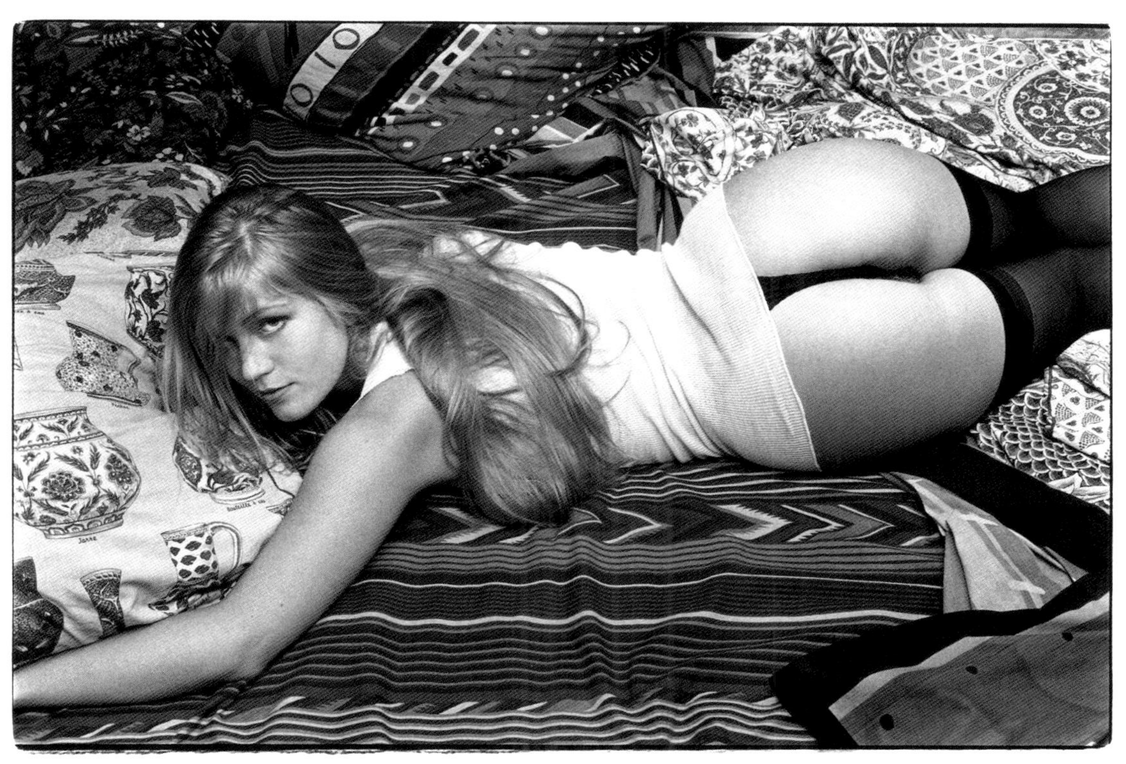

Sigrun 1993   87

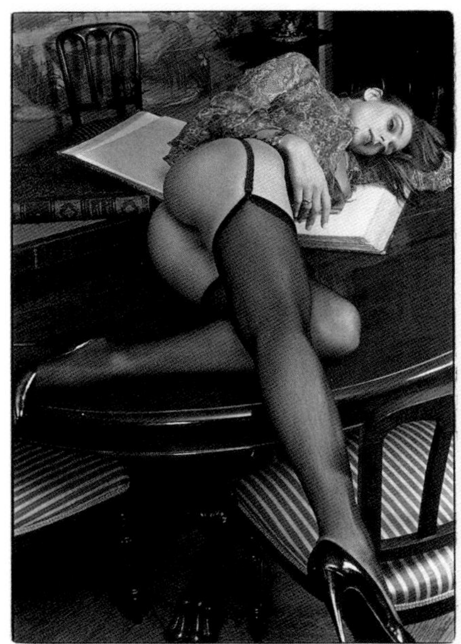

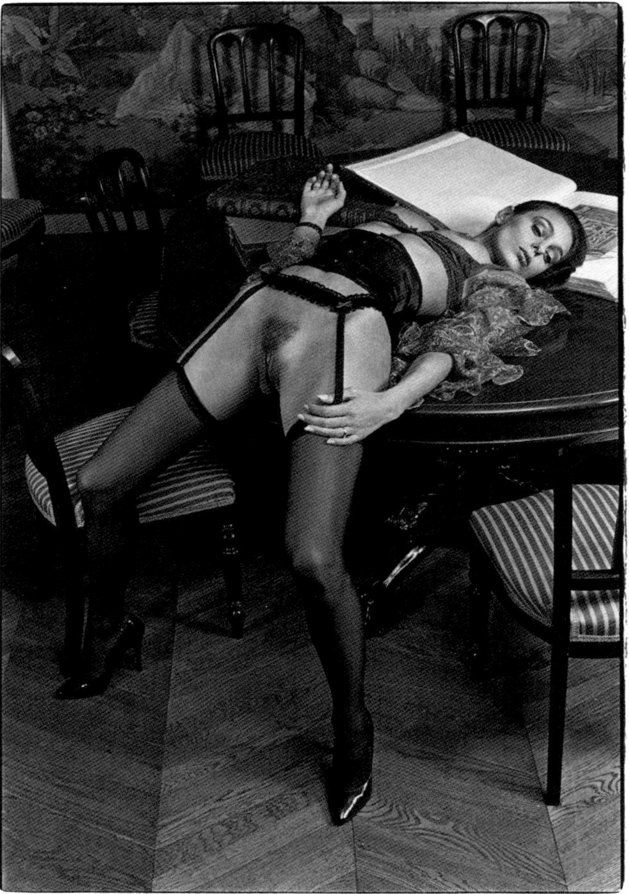

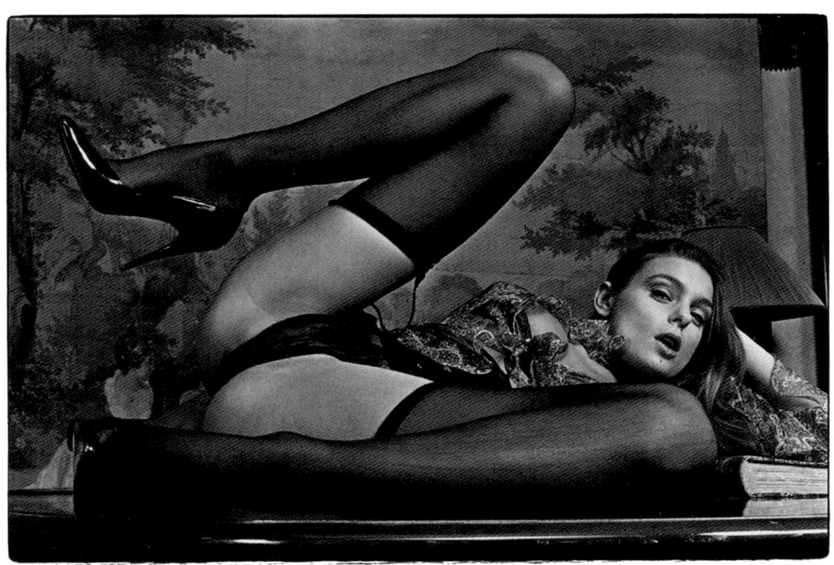

Zara 1995 →

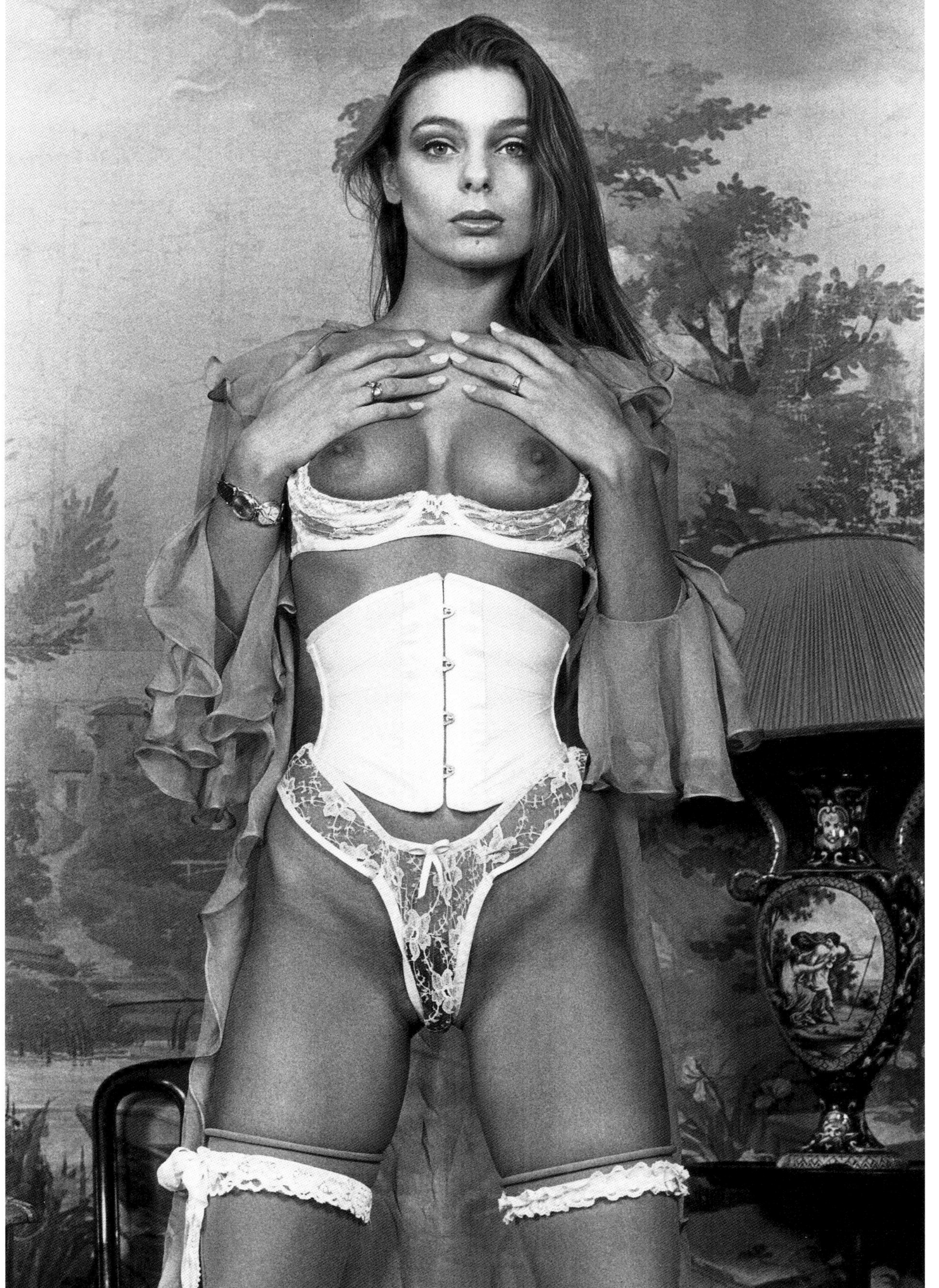

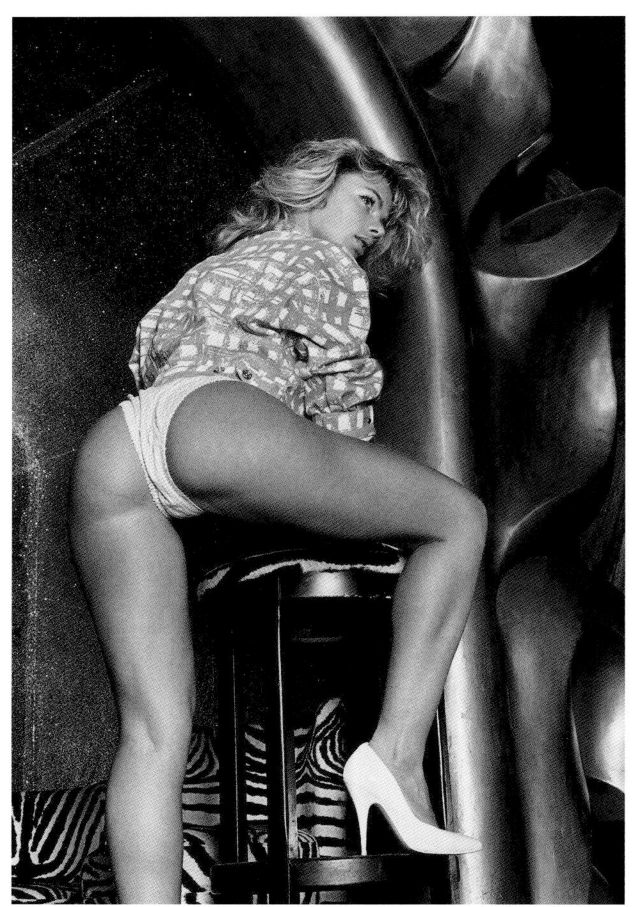

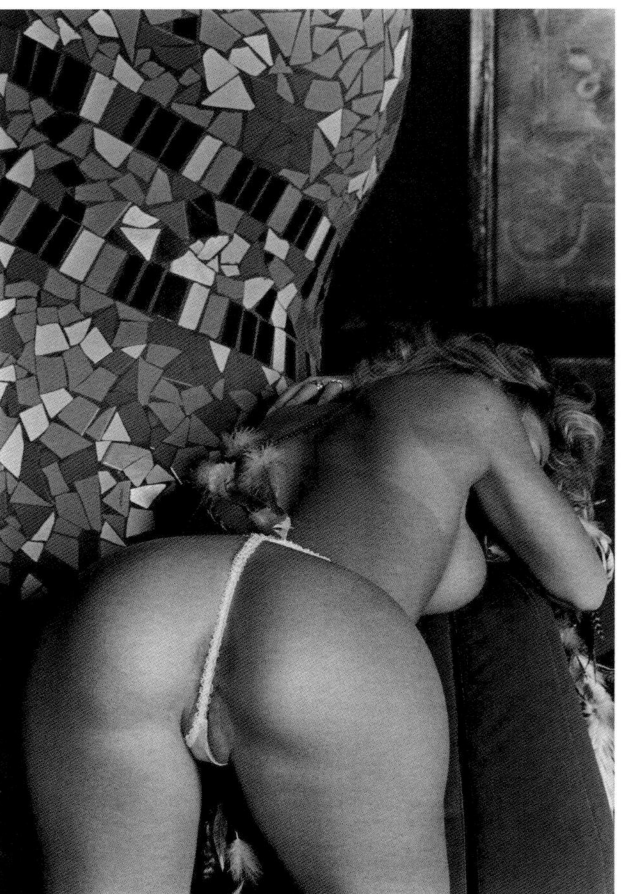

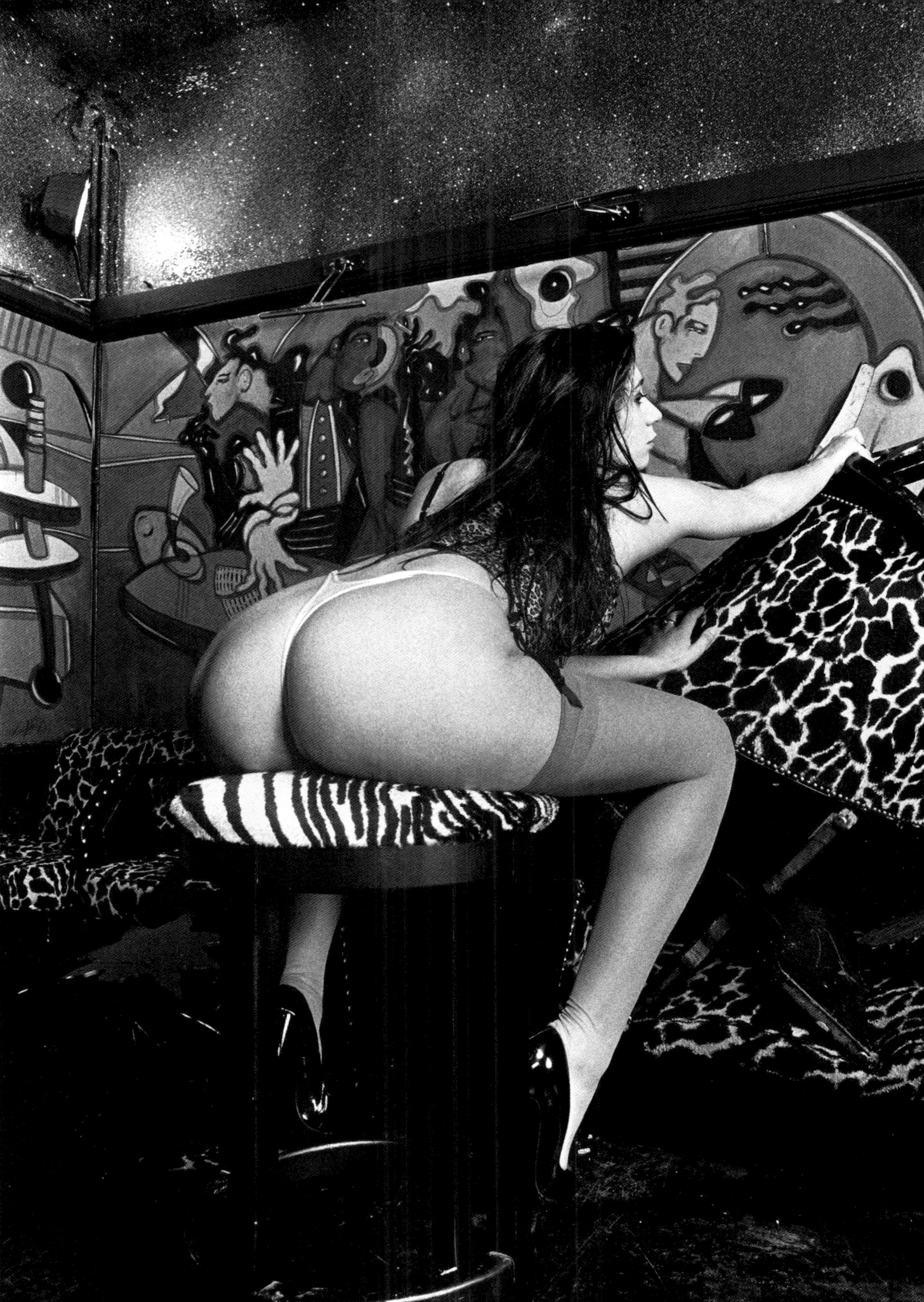

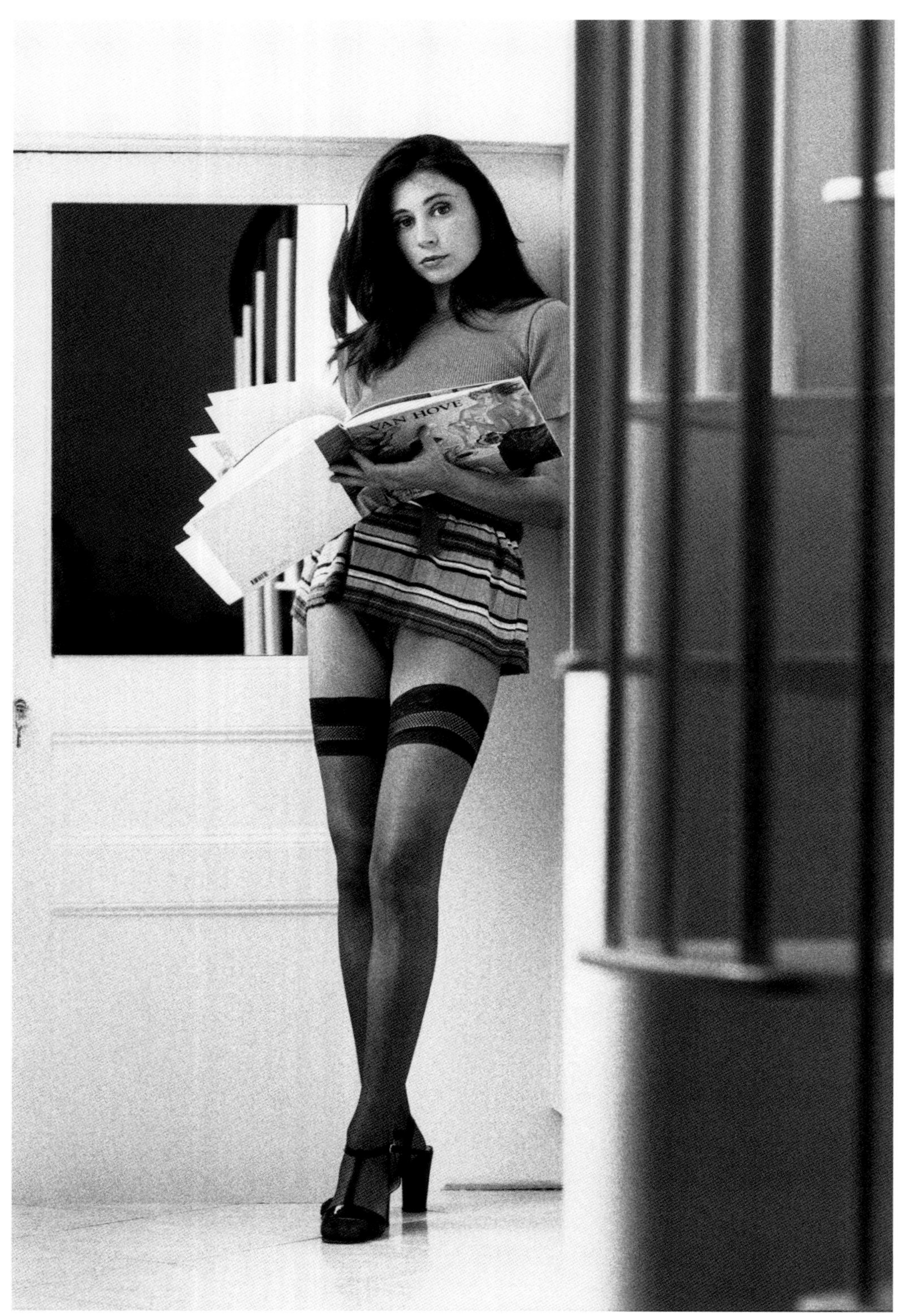

  Natacha 1996

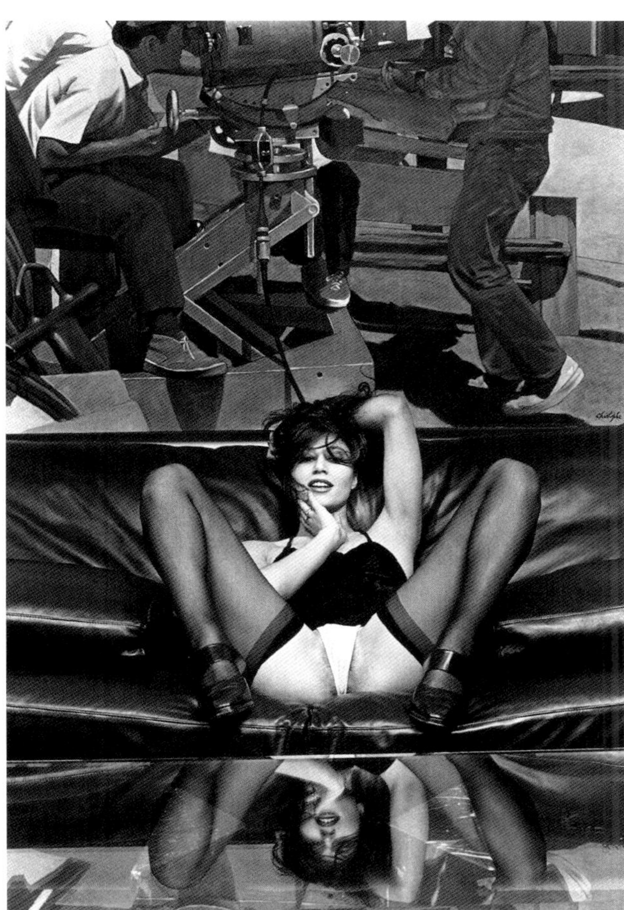

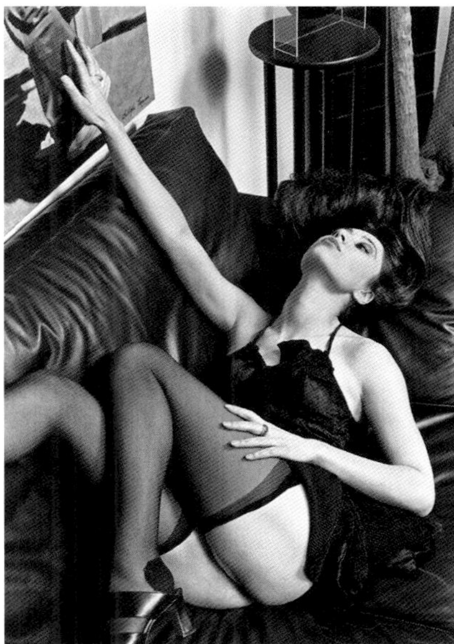

Natacha 1993

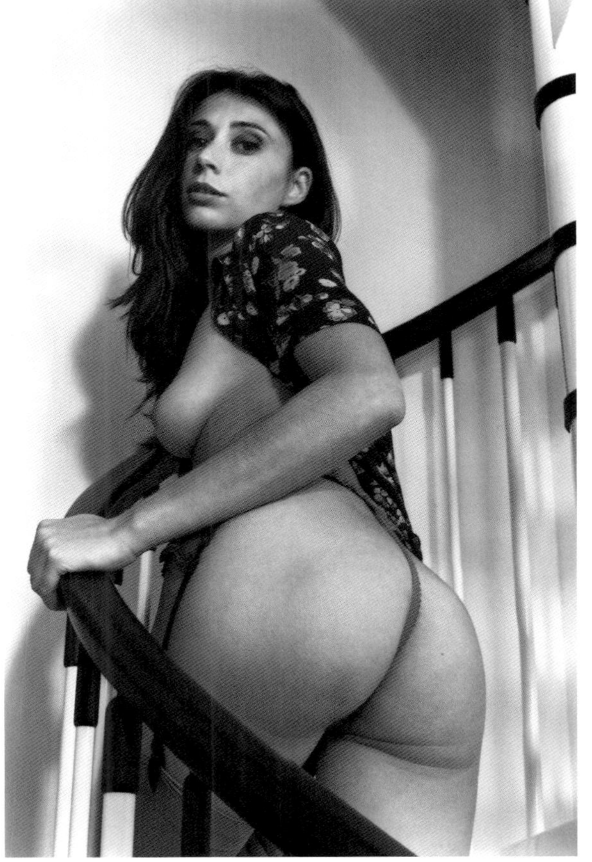

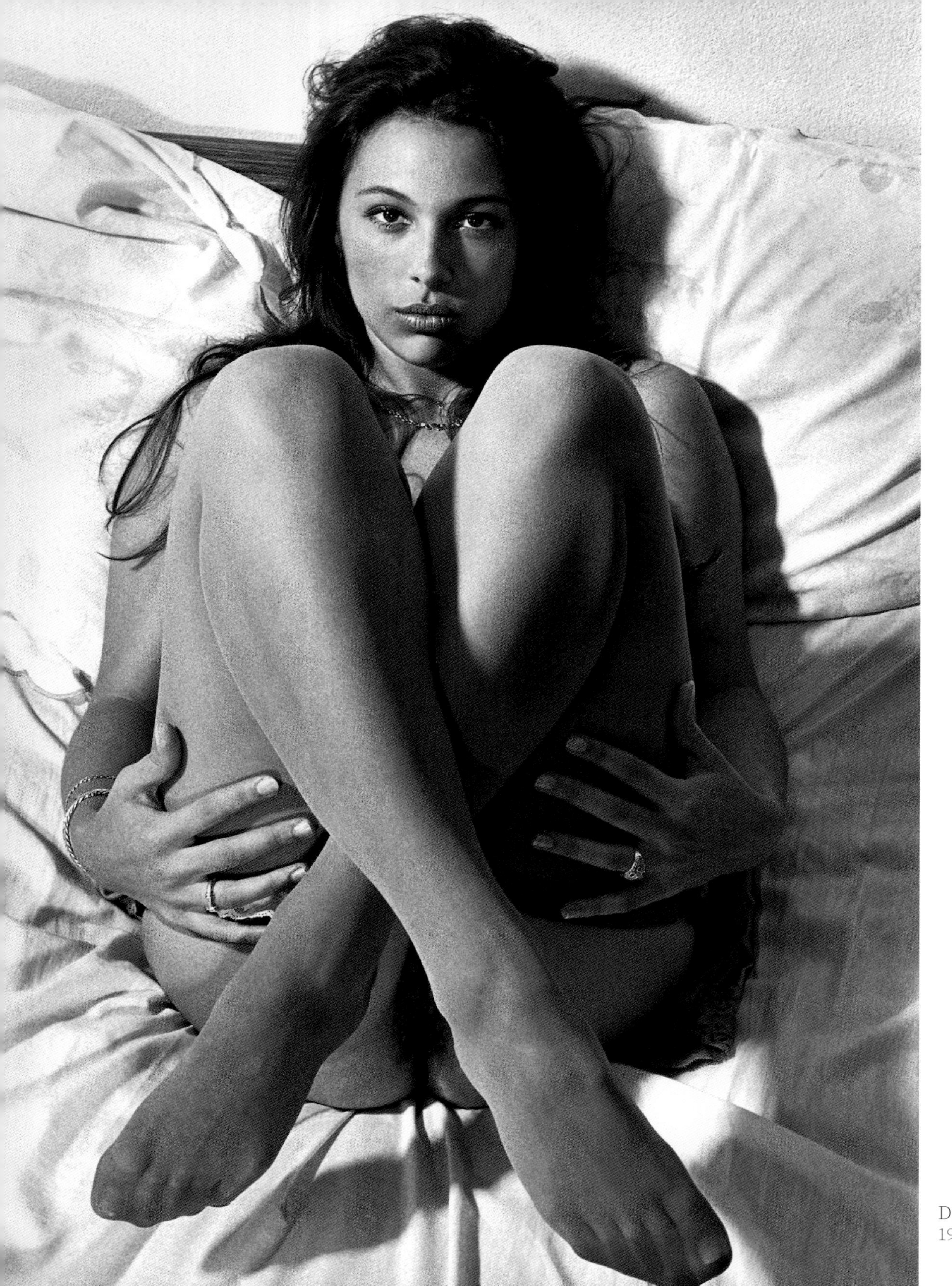

Diane
1993

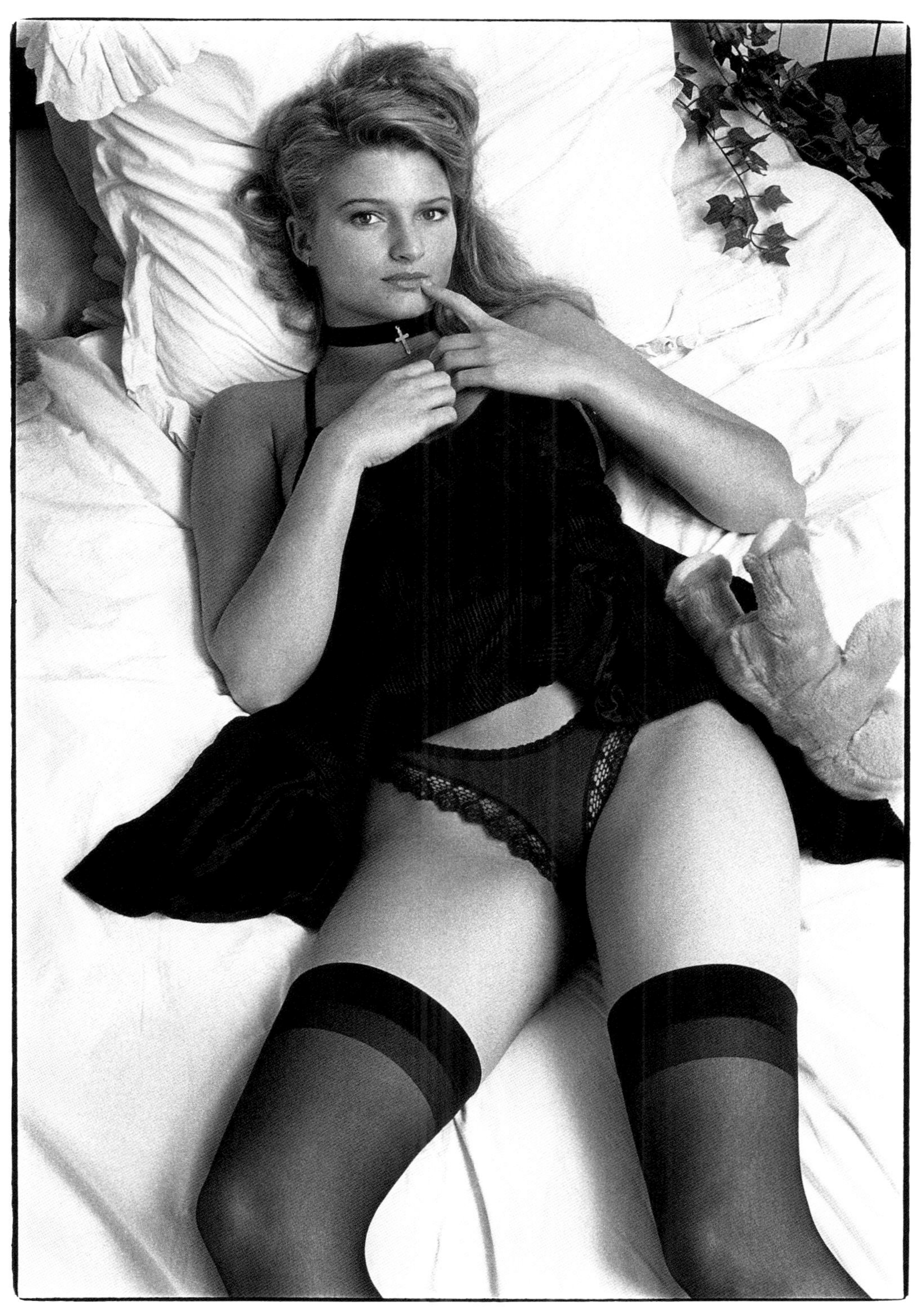

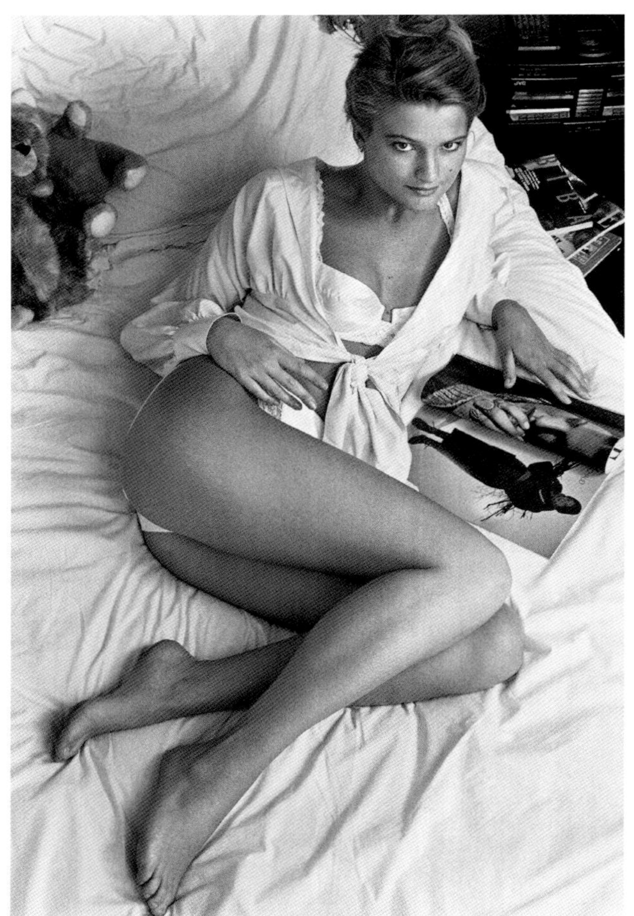

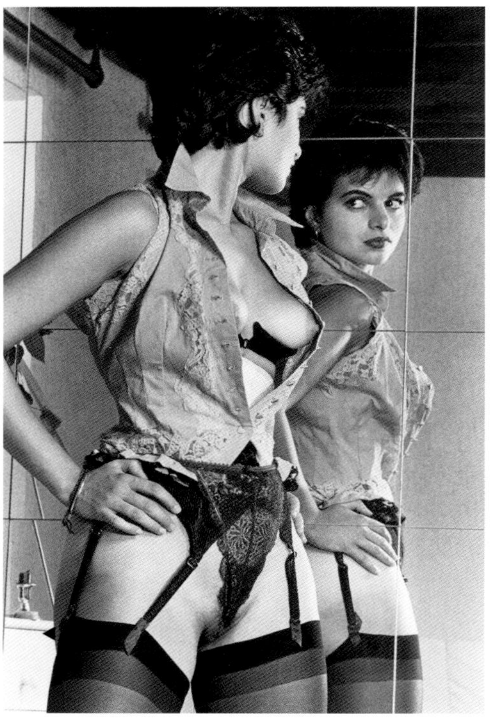

↓ Nina 1993

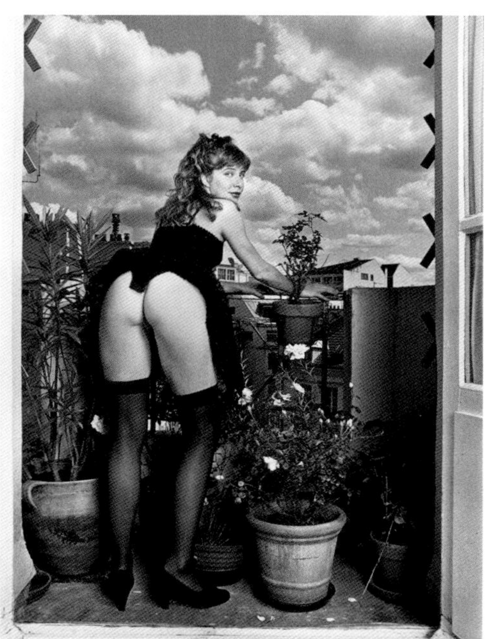

   Delphine 1993 ↑   Aline 1993

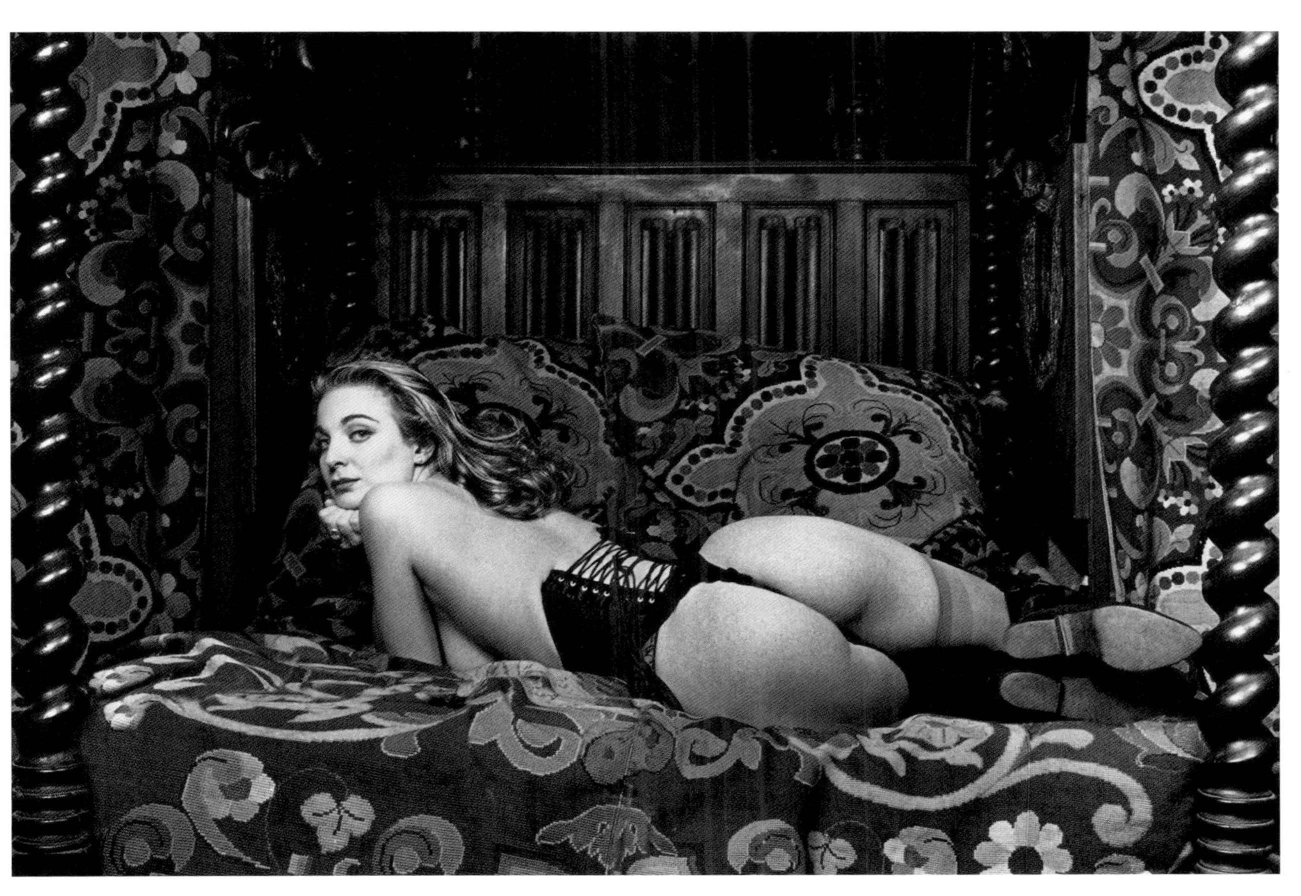

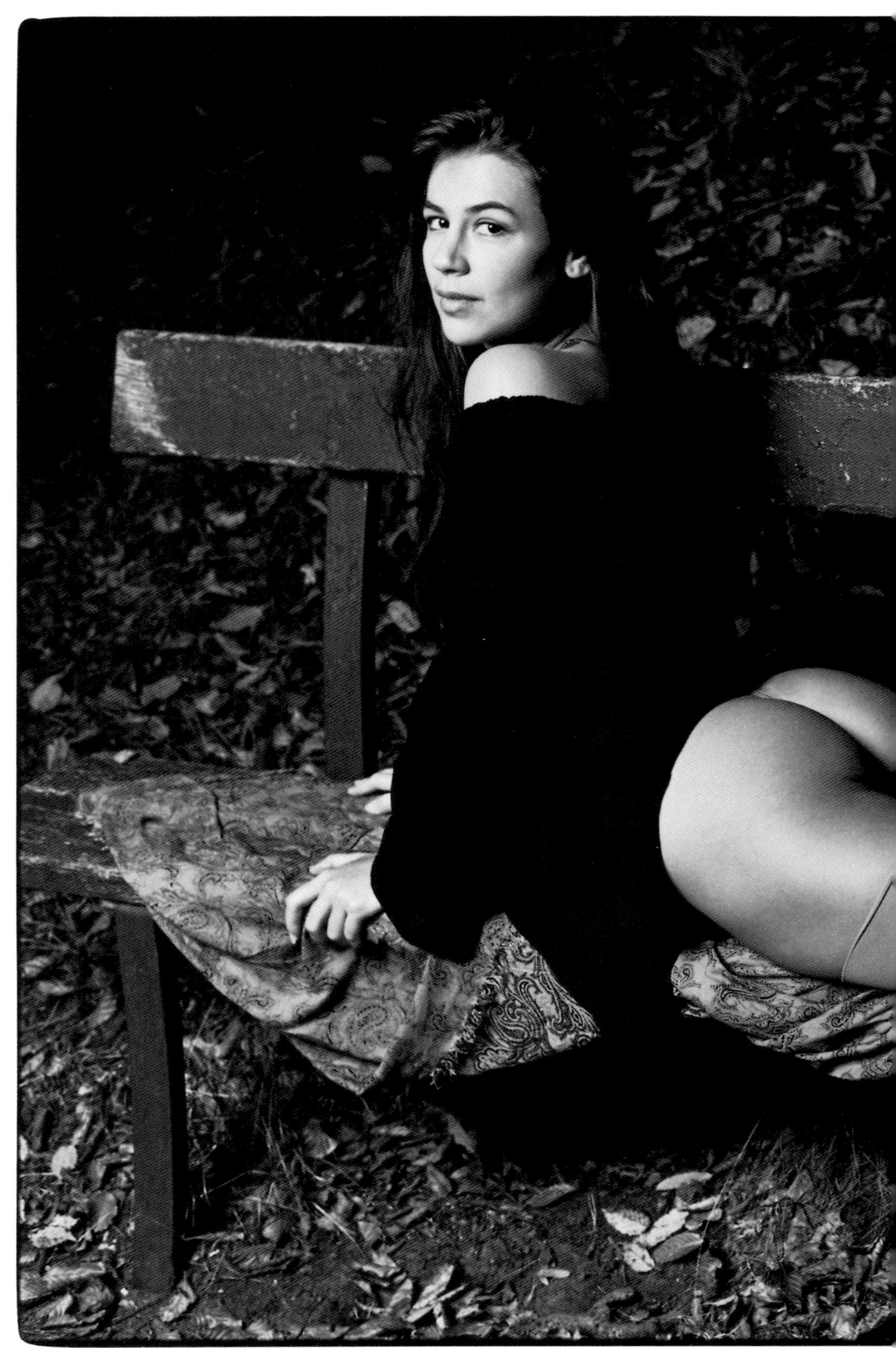

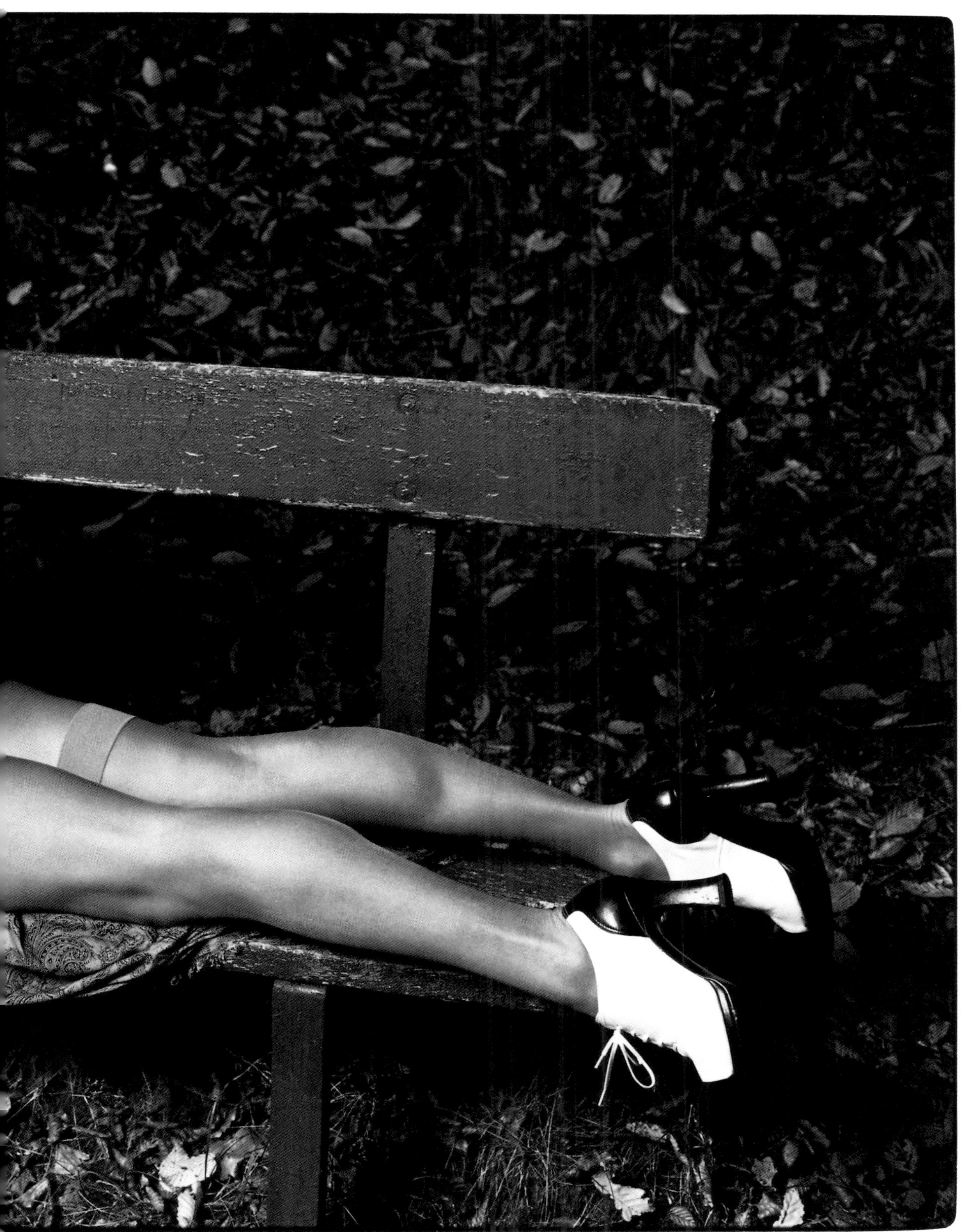

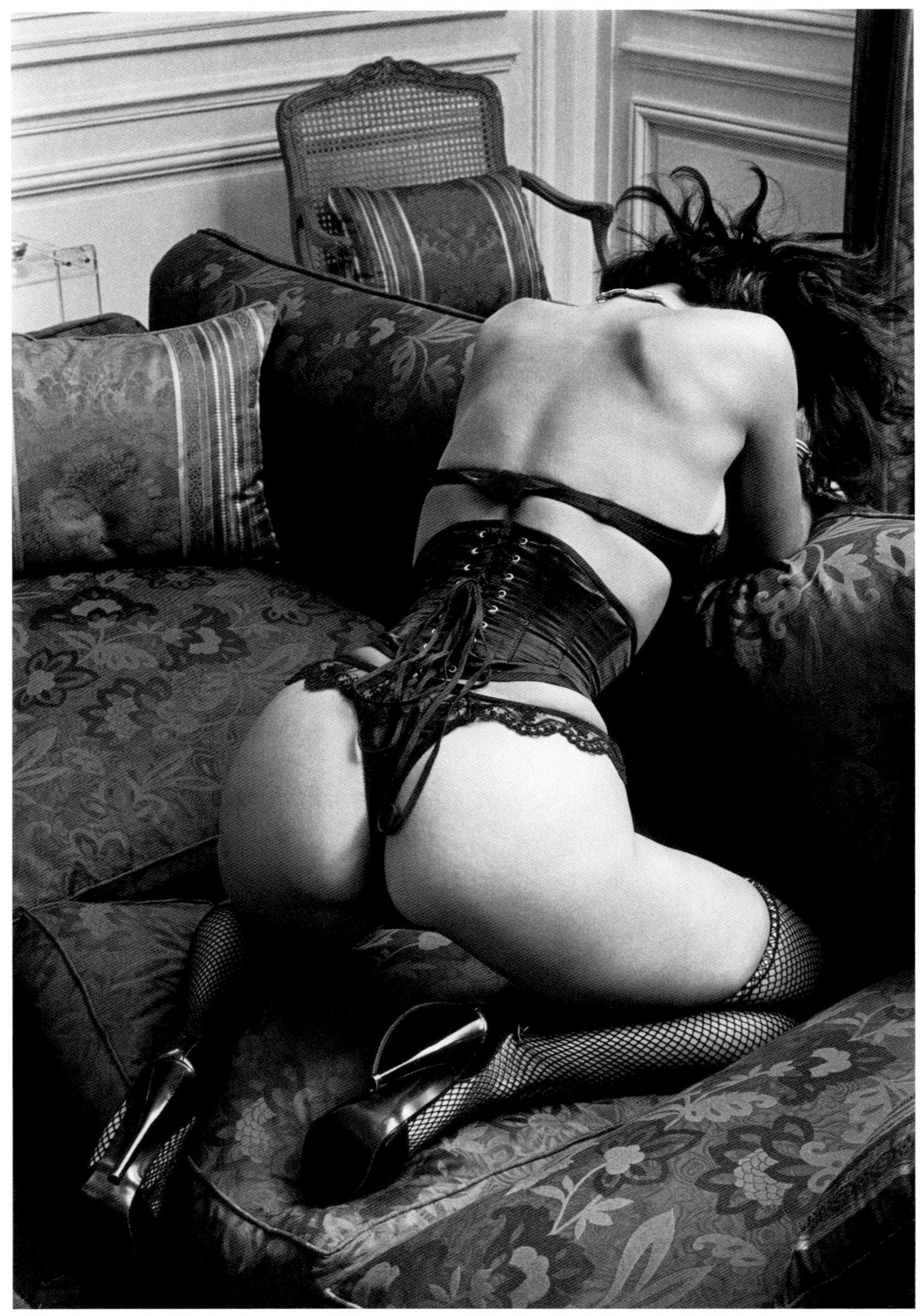

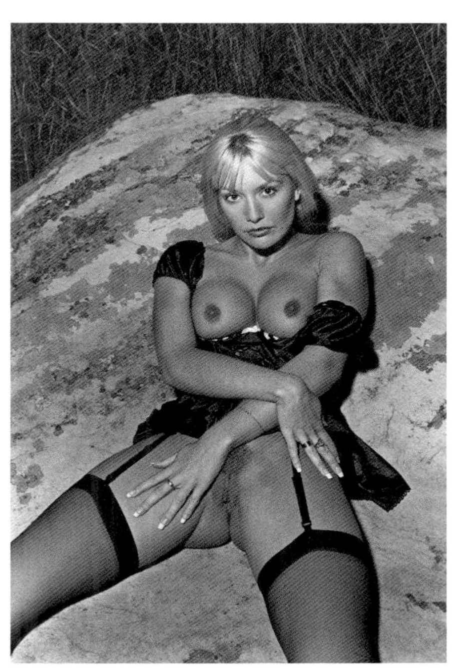

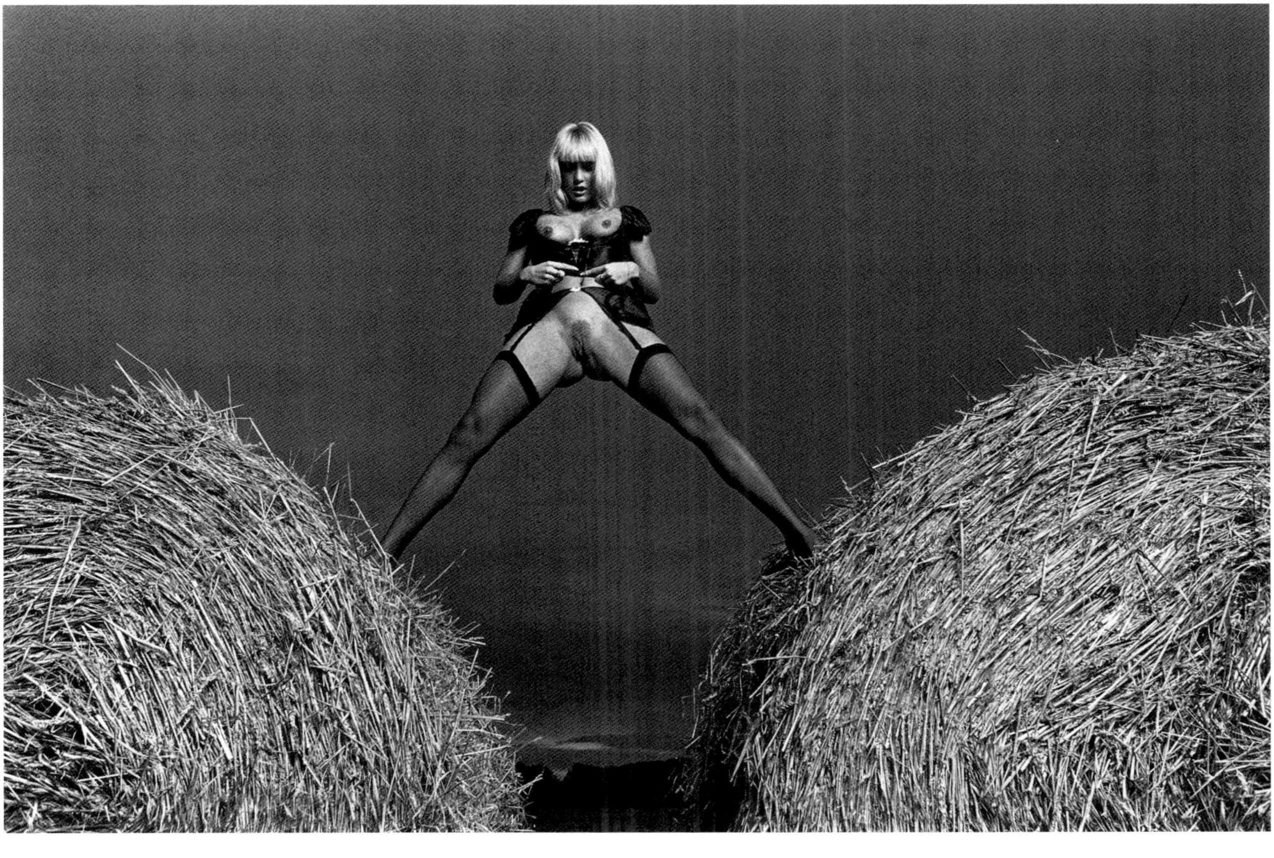

Sophie
1995

Leila
1996

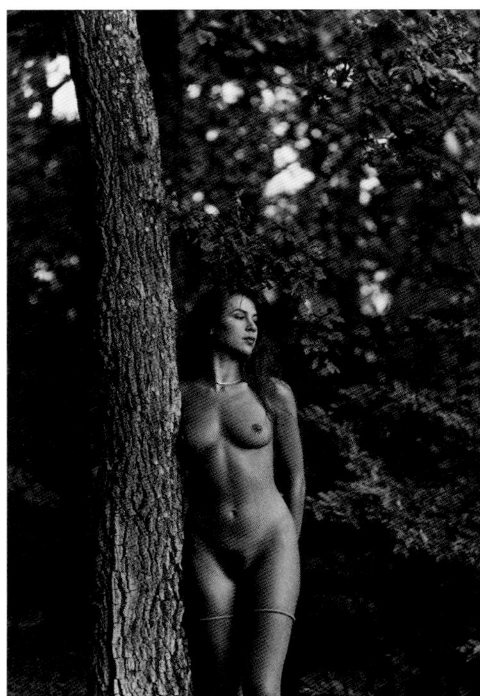

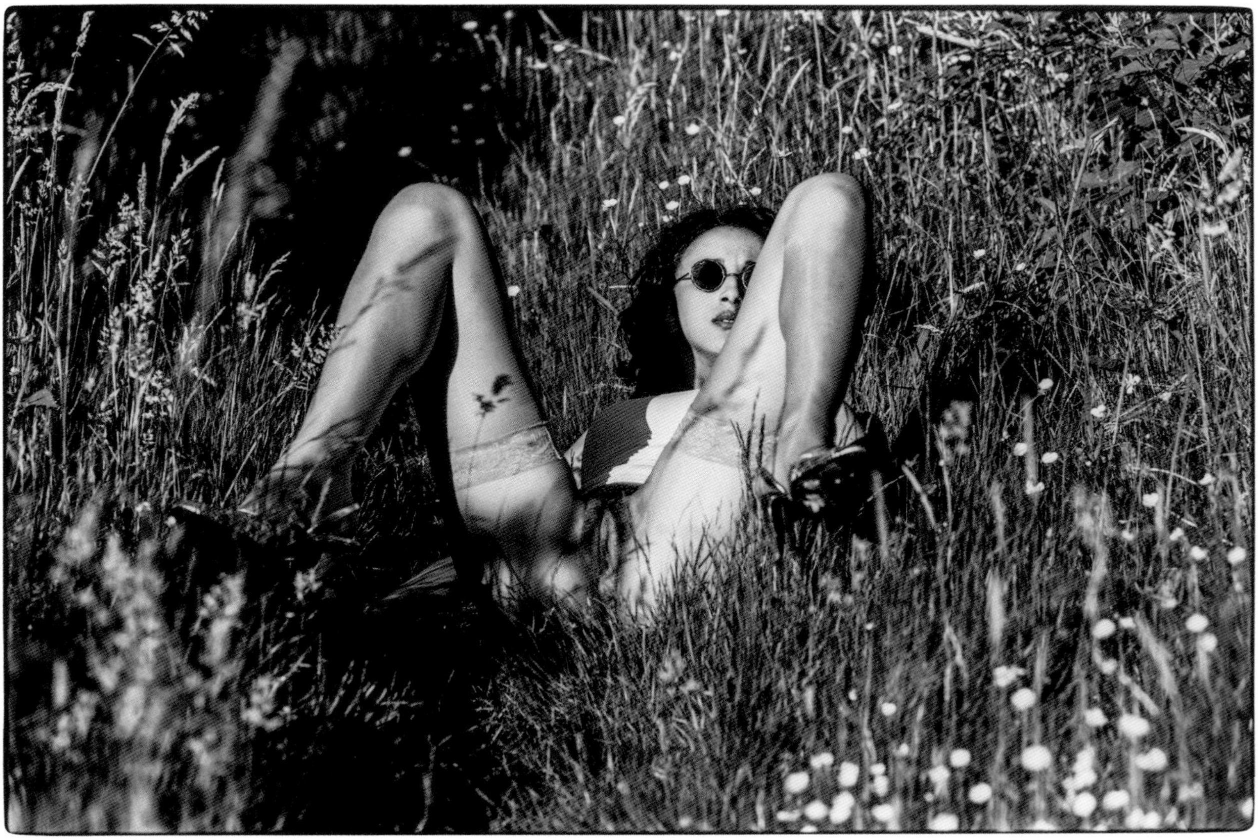

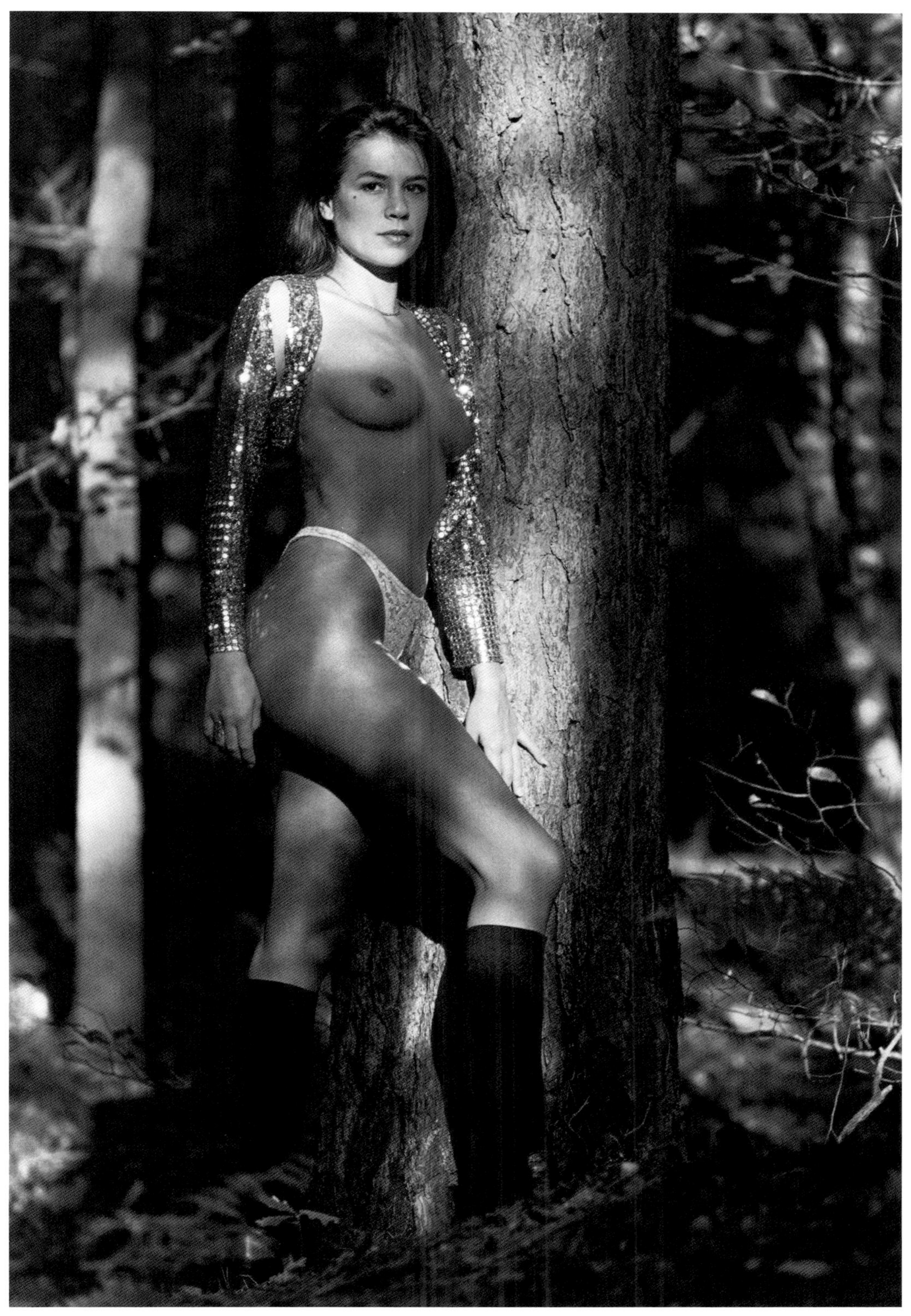

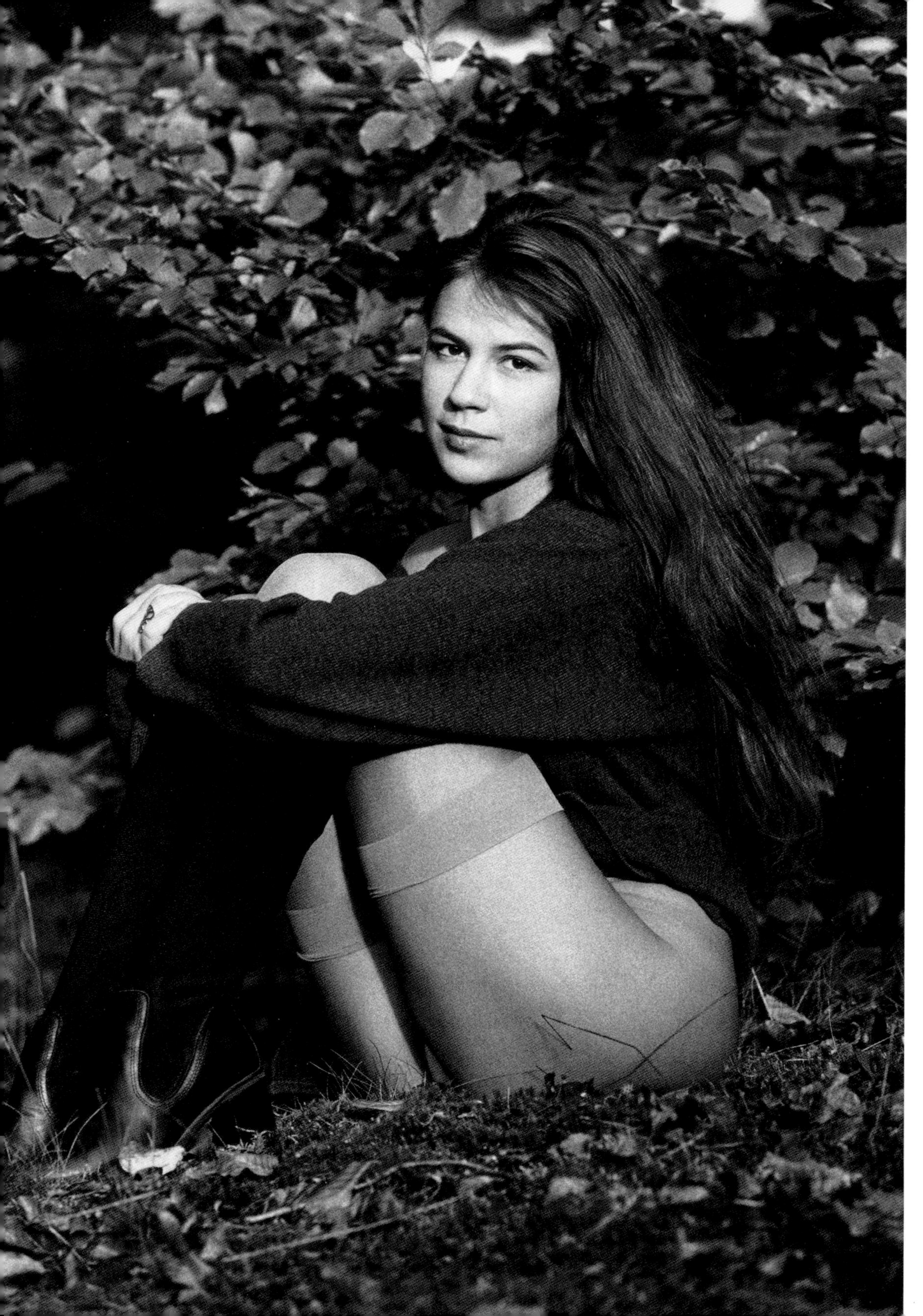

Sophie
1995

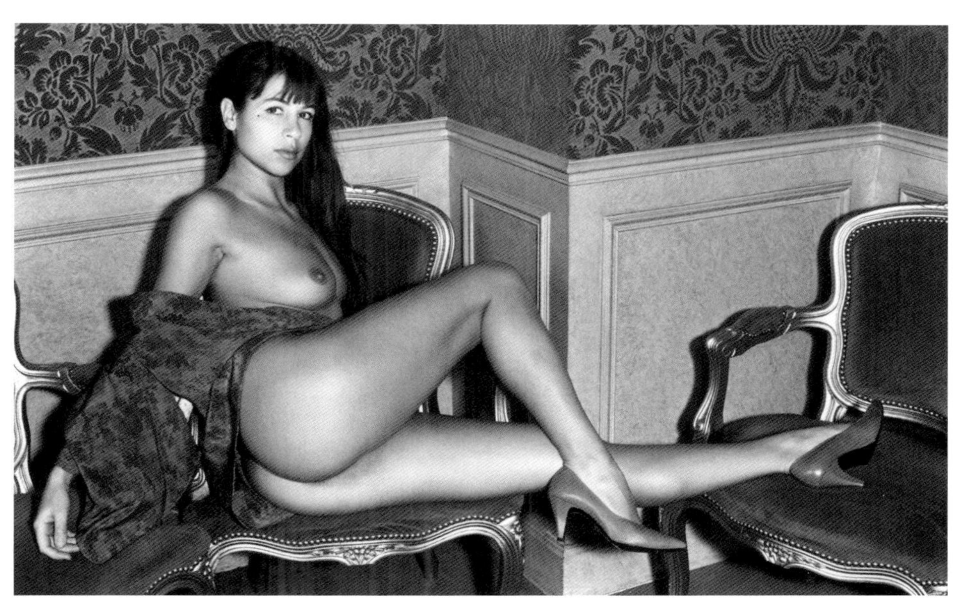

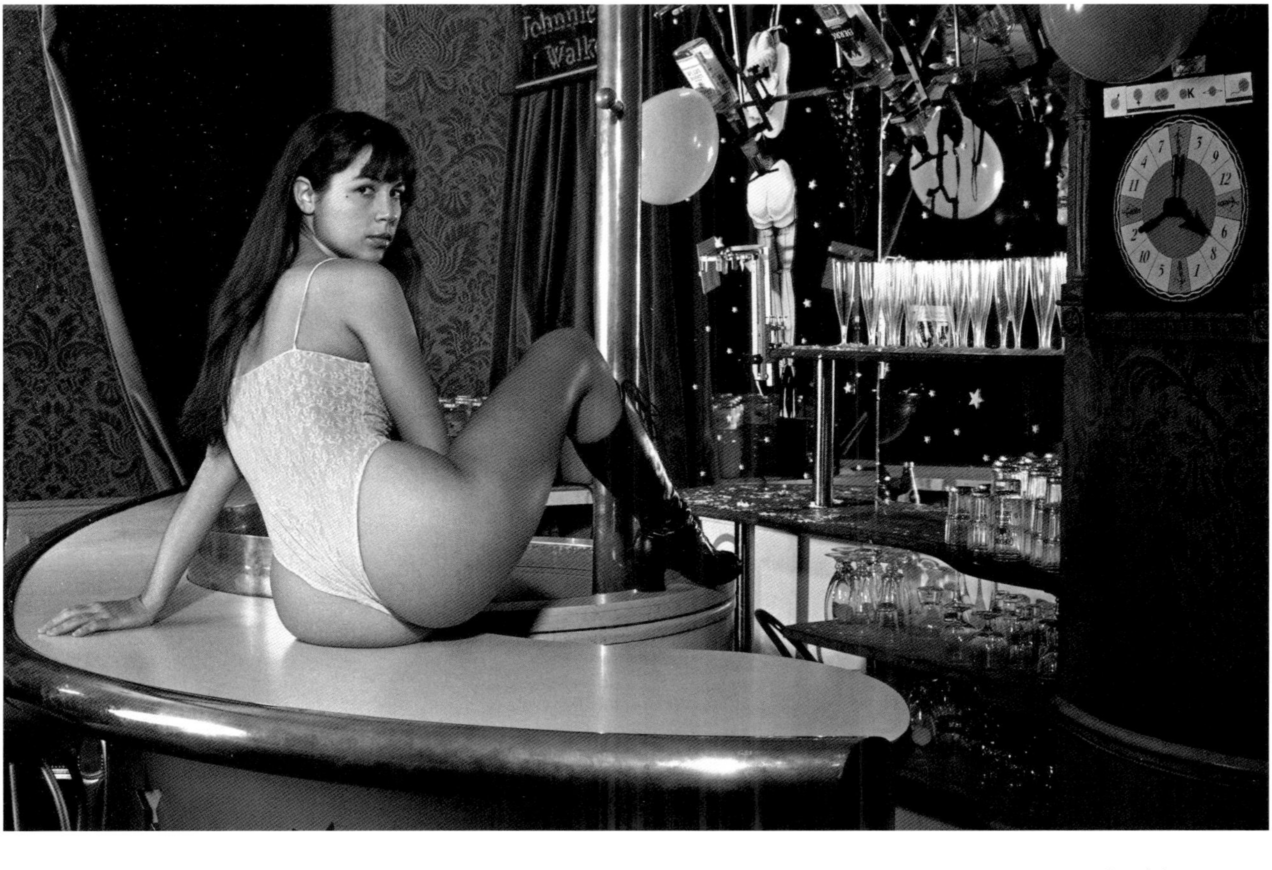

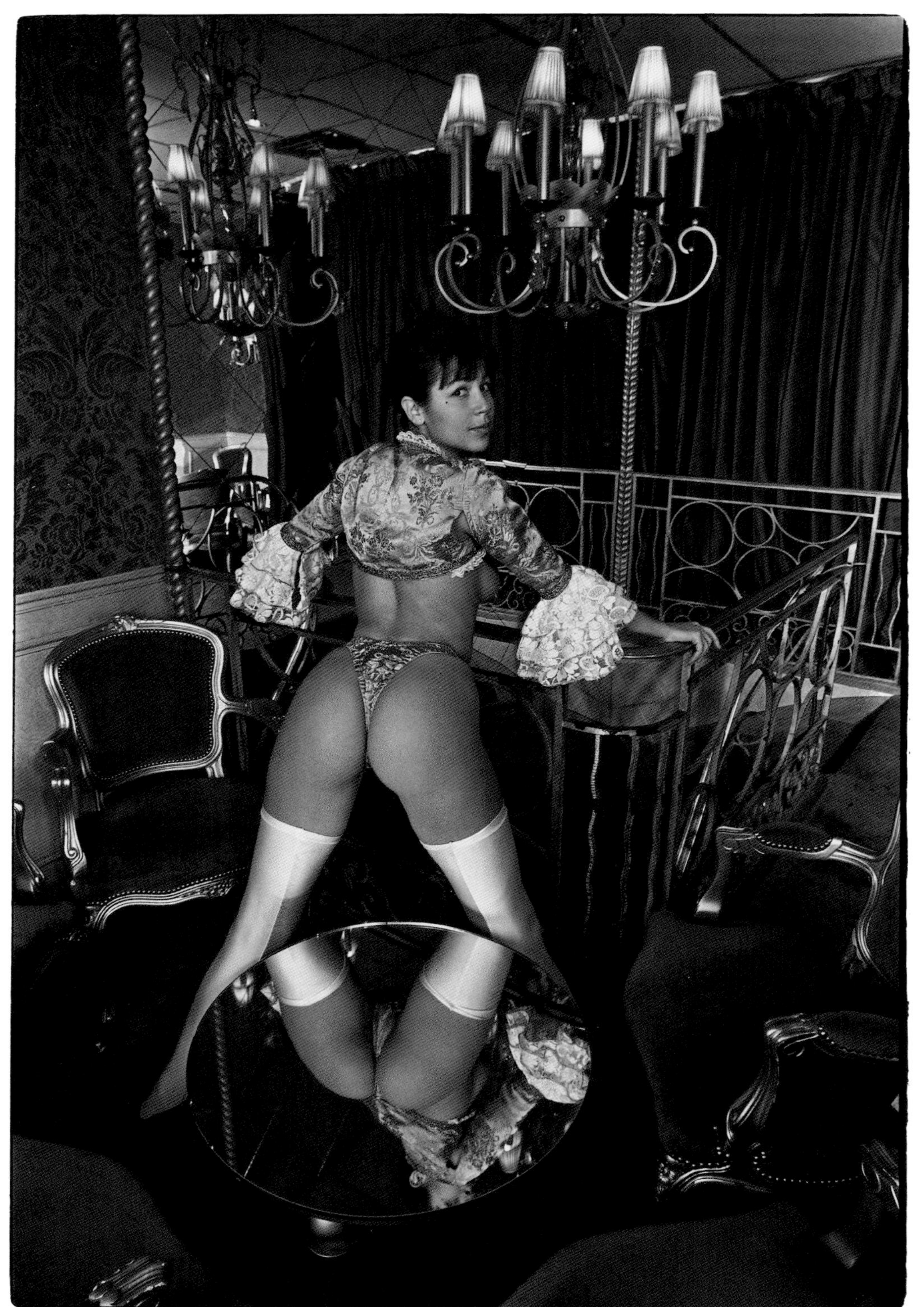

Tanya 1996 →

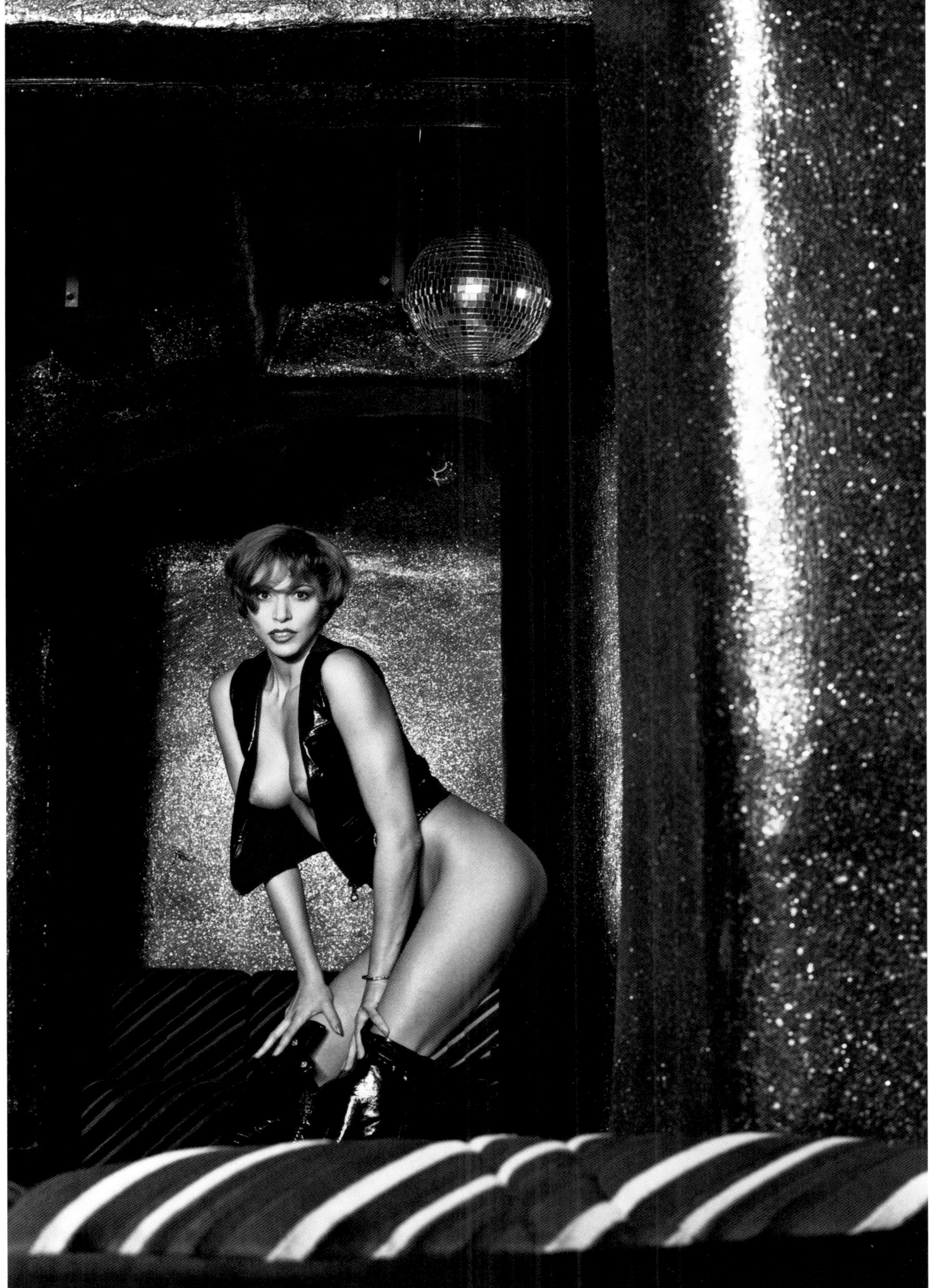

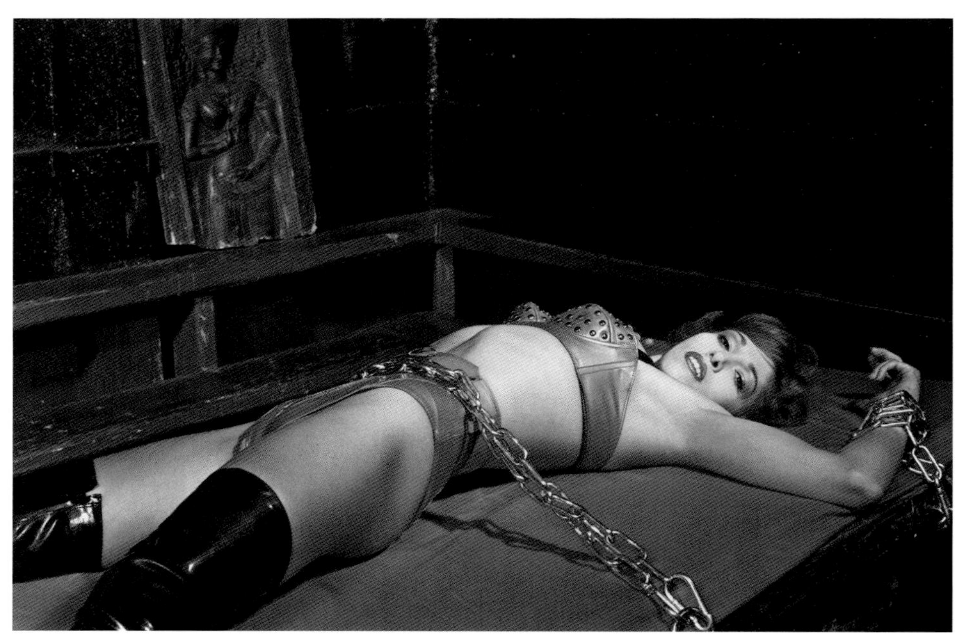

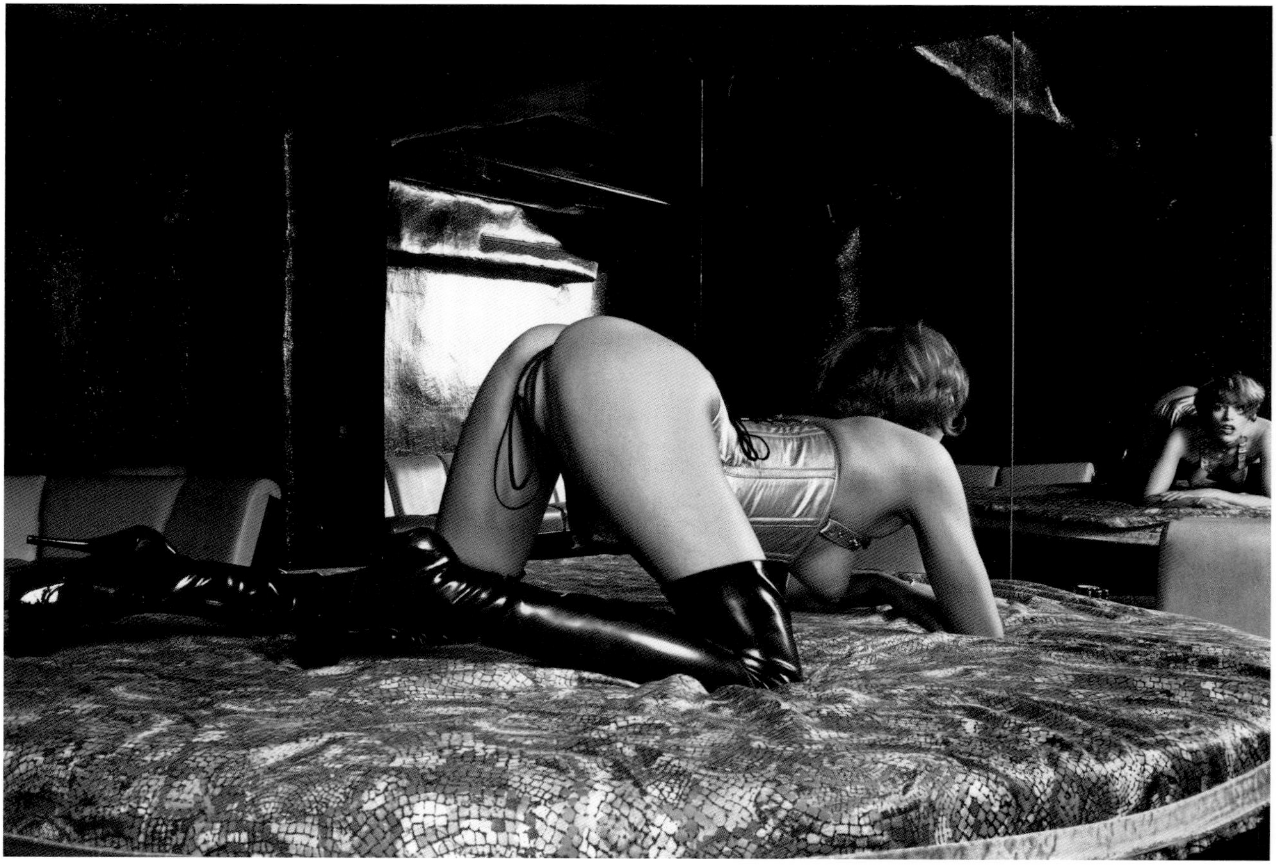

108   Tanya 1996

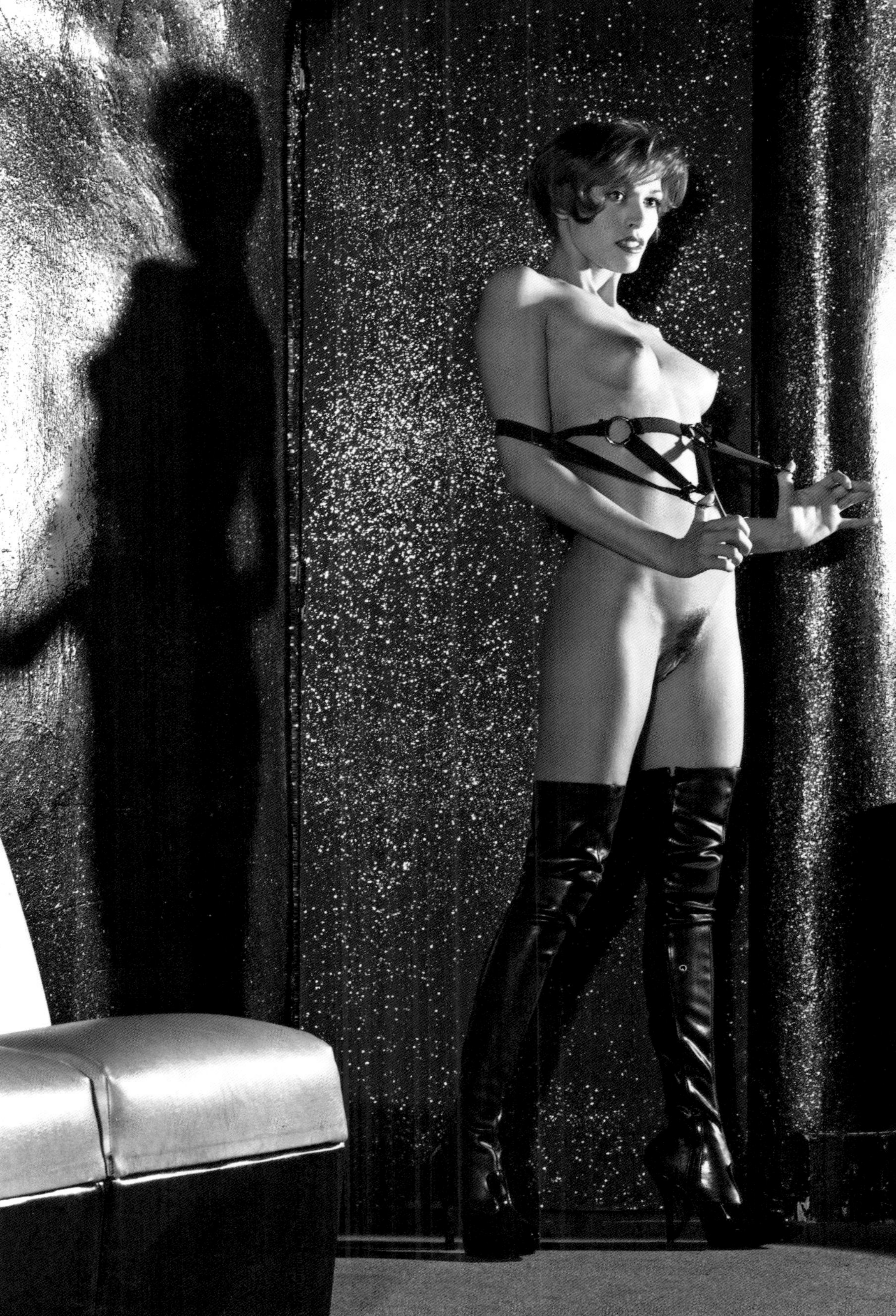

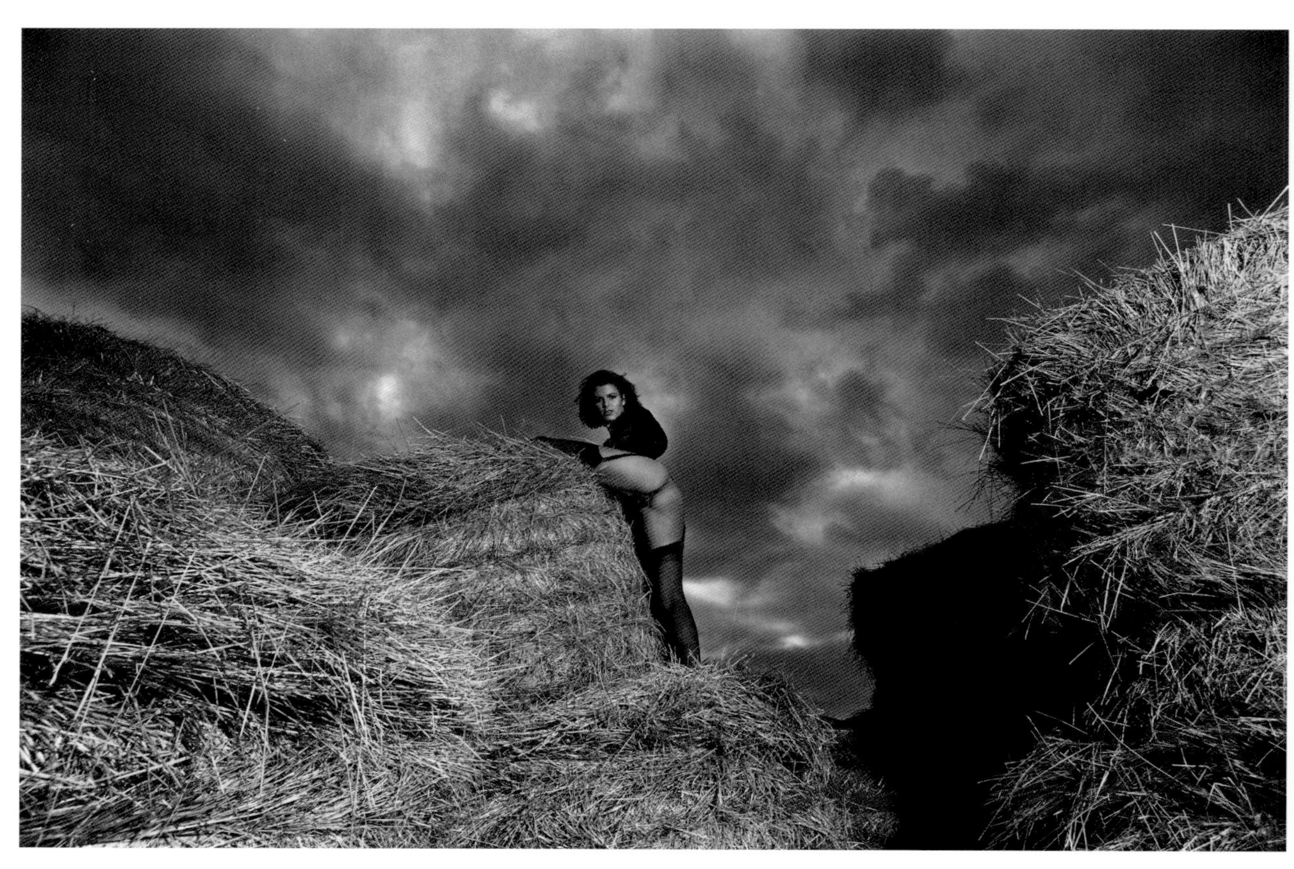

110 Nadine 1996

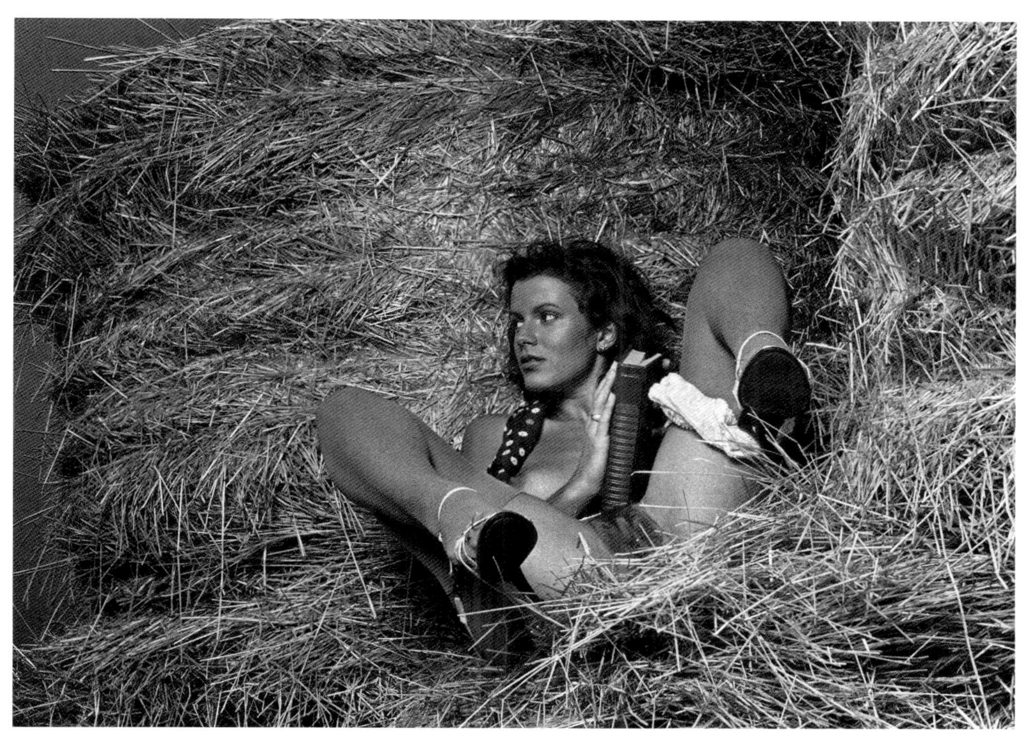

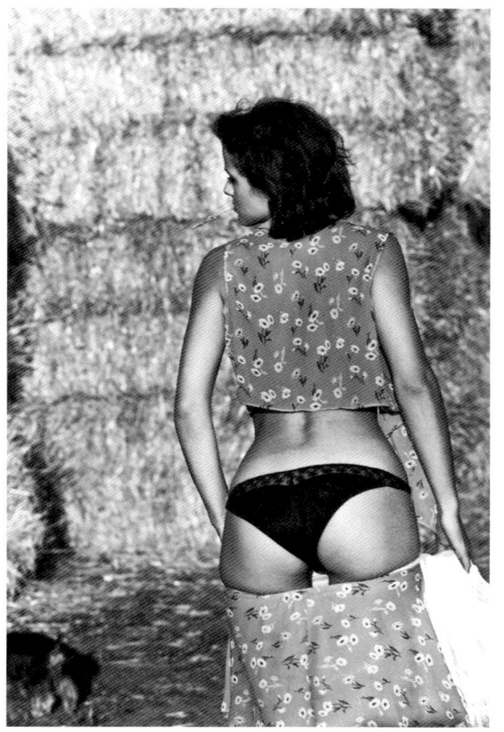

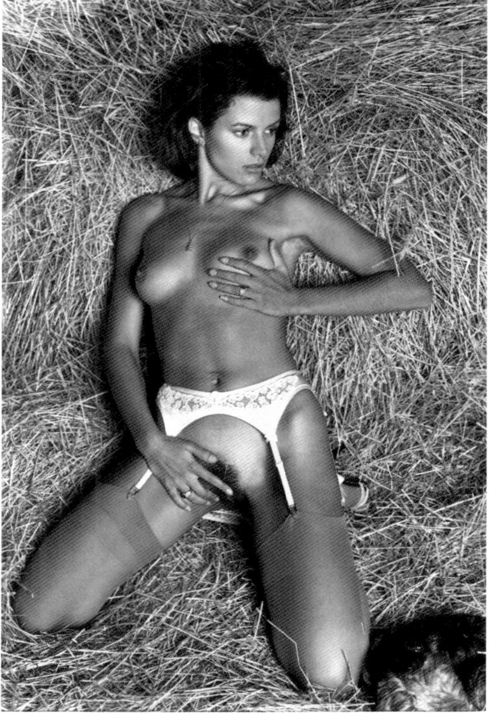

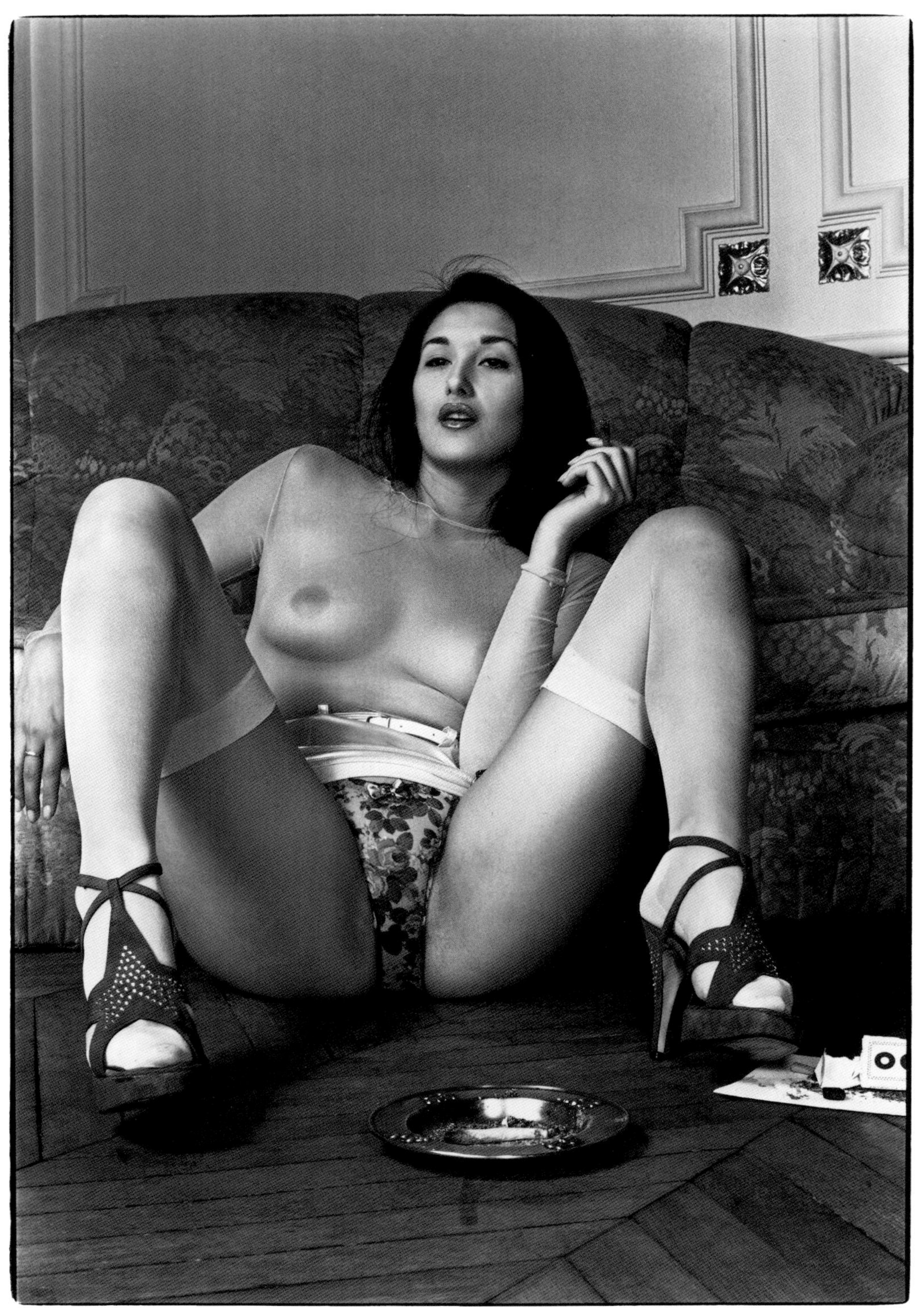

  Coralie 1996

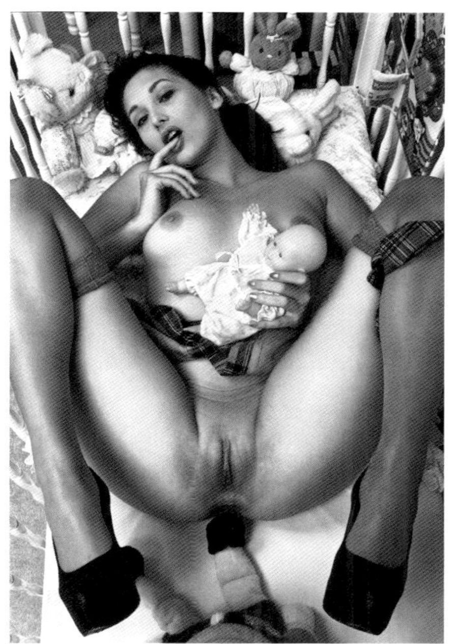

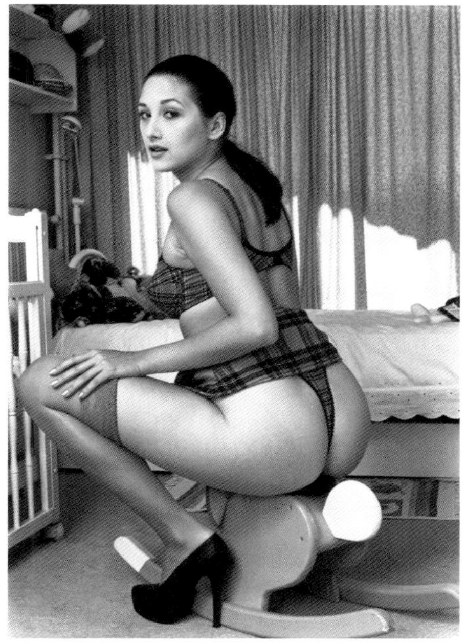

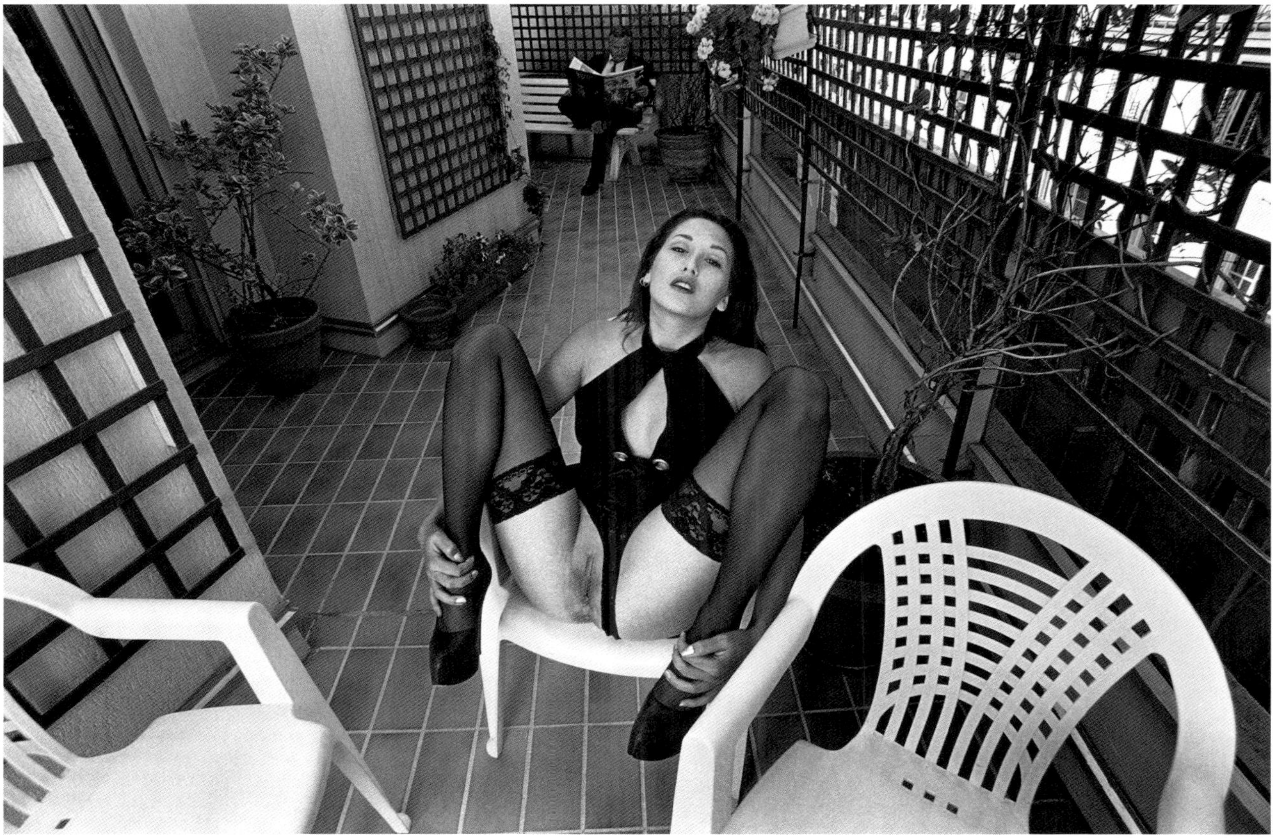

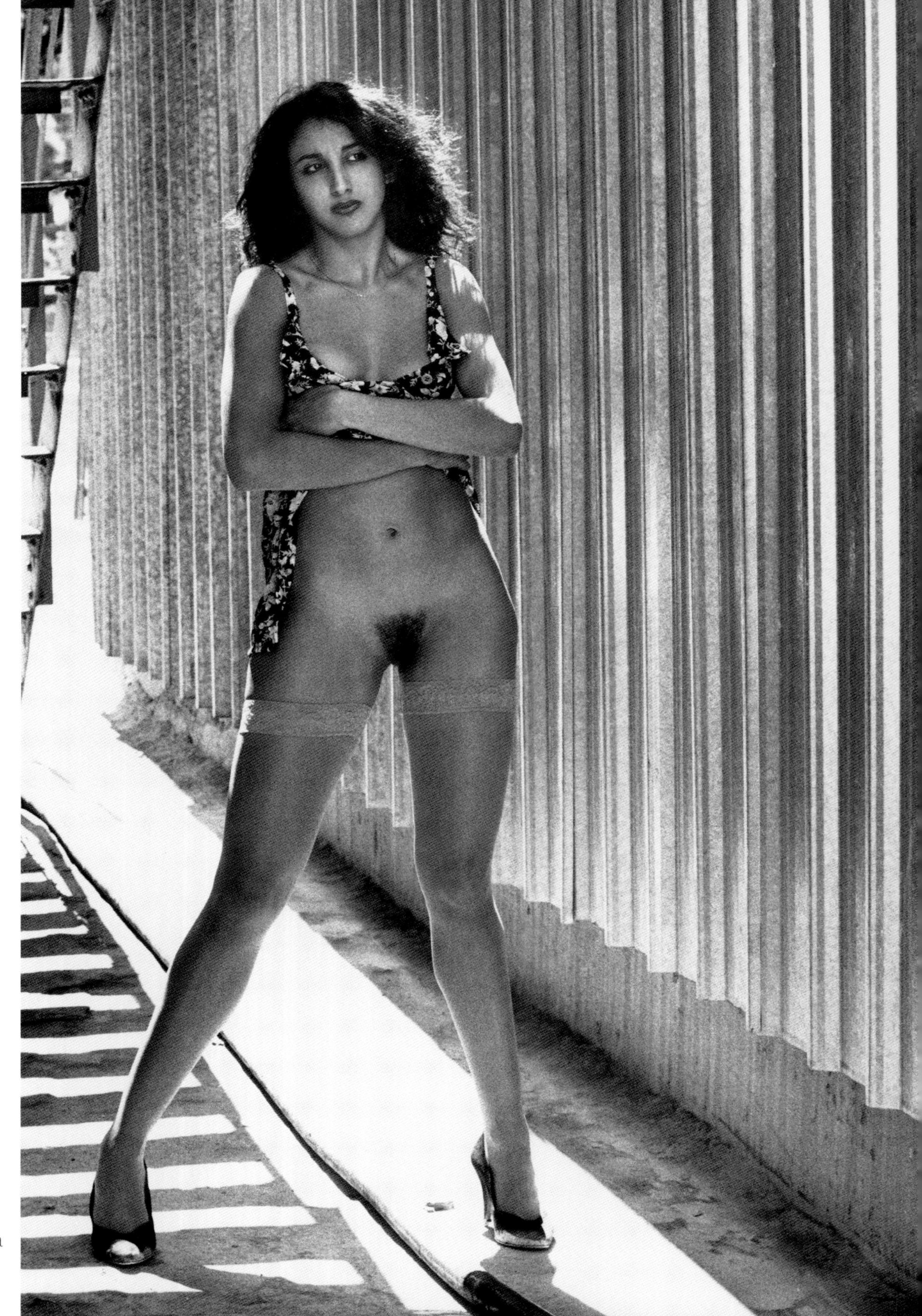

Leïla
114   1996

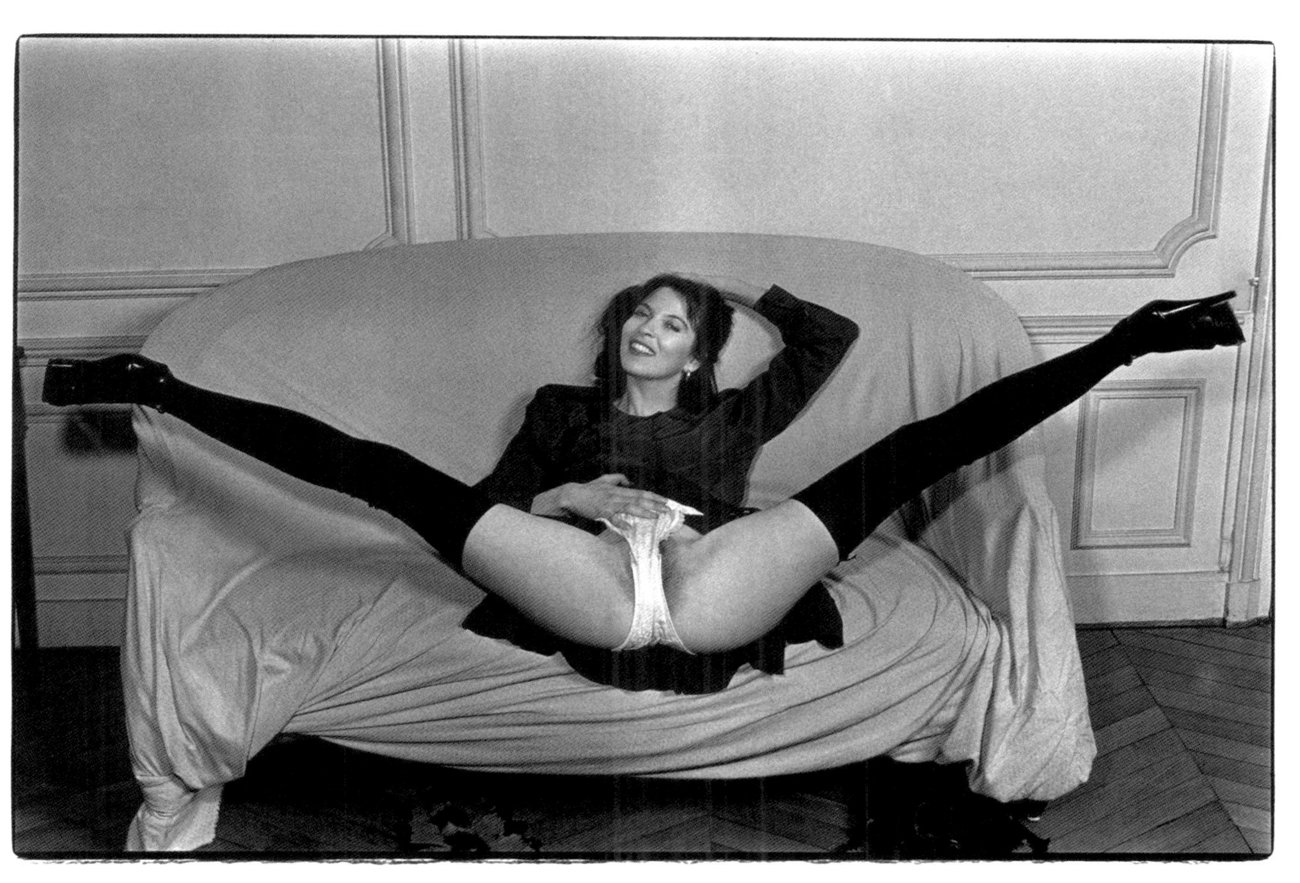

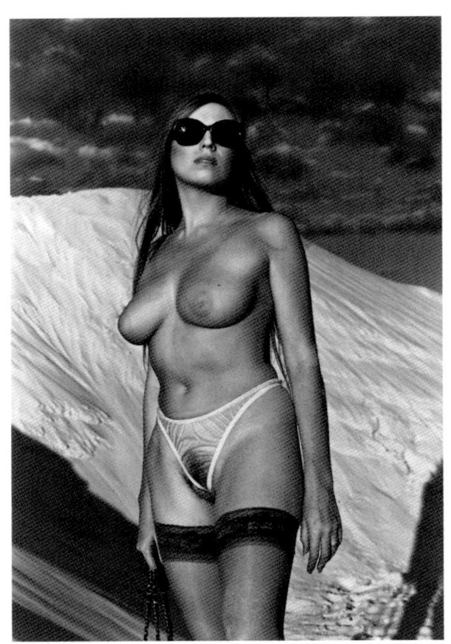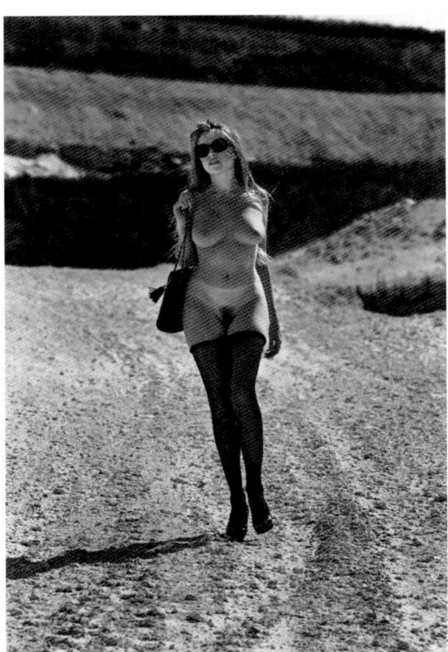

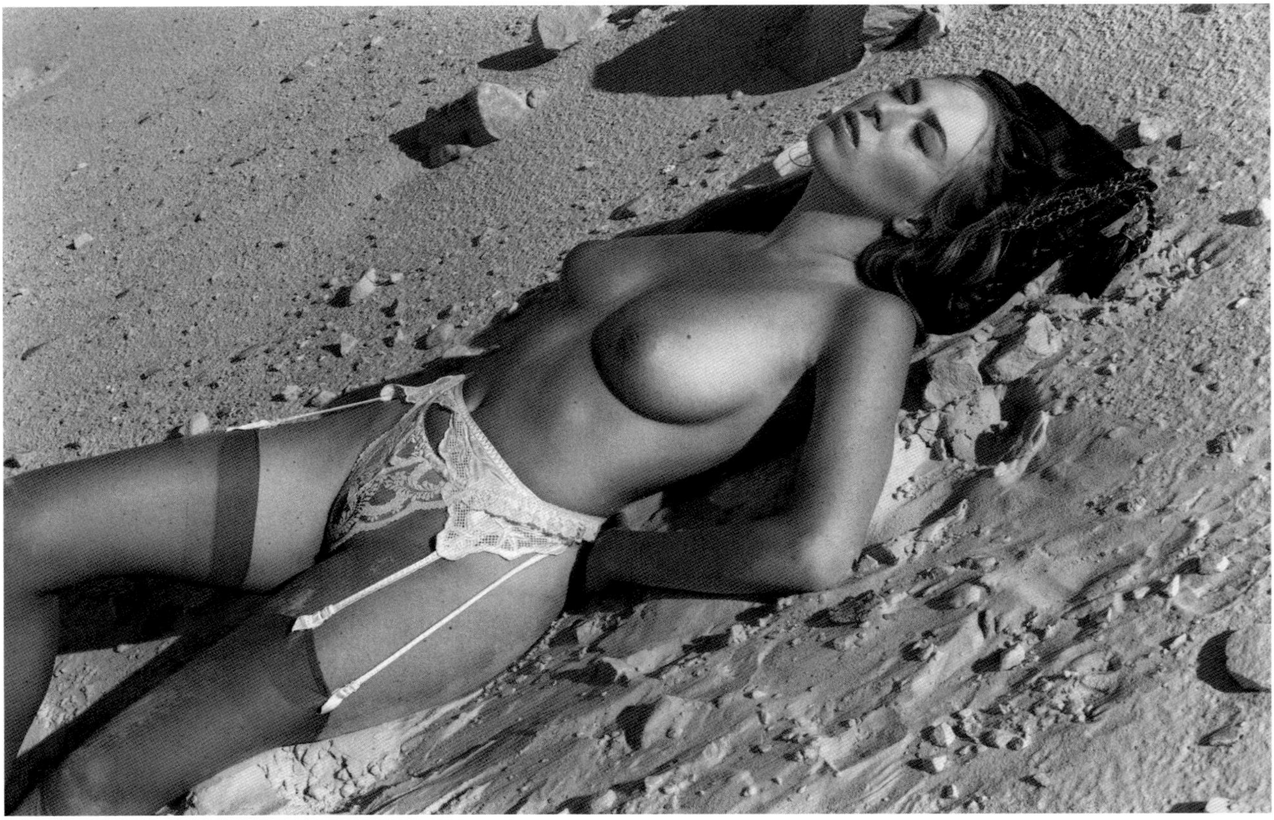

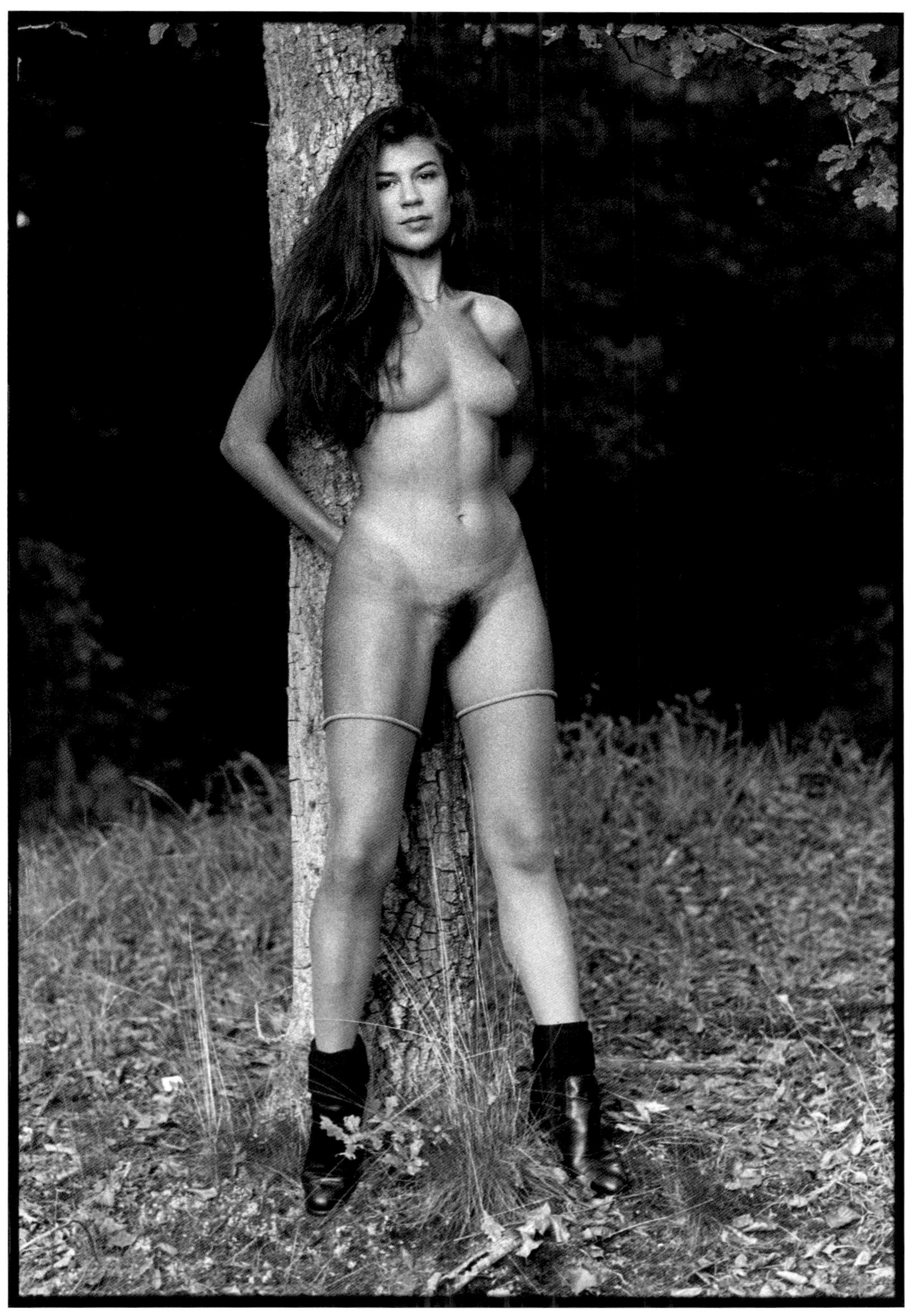

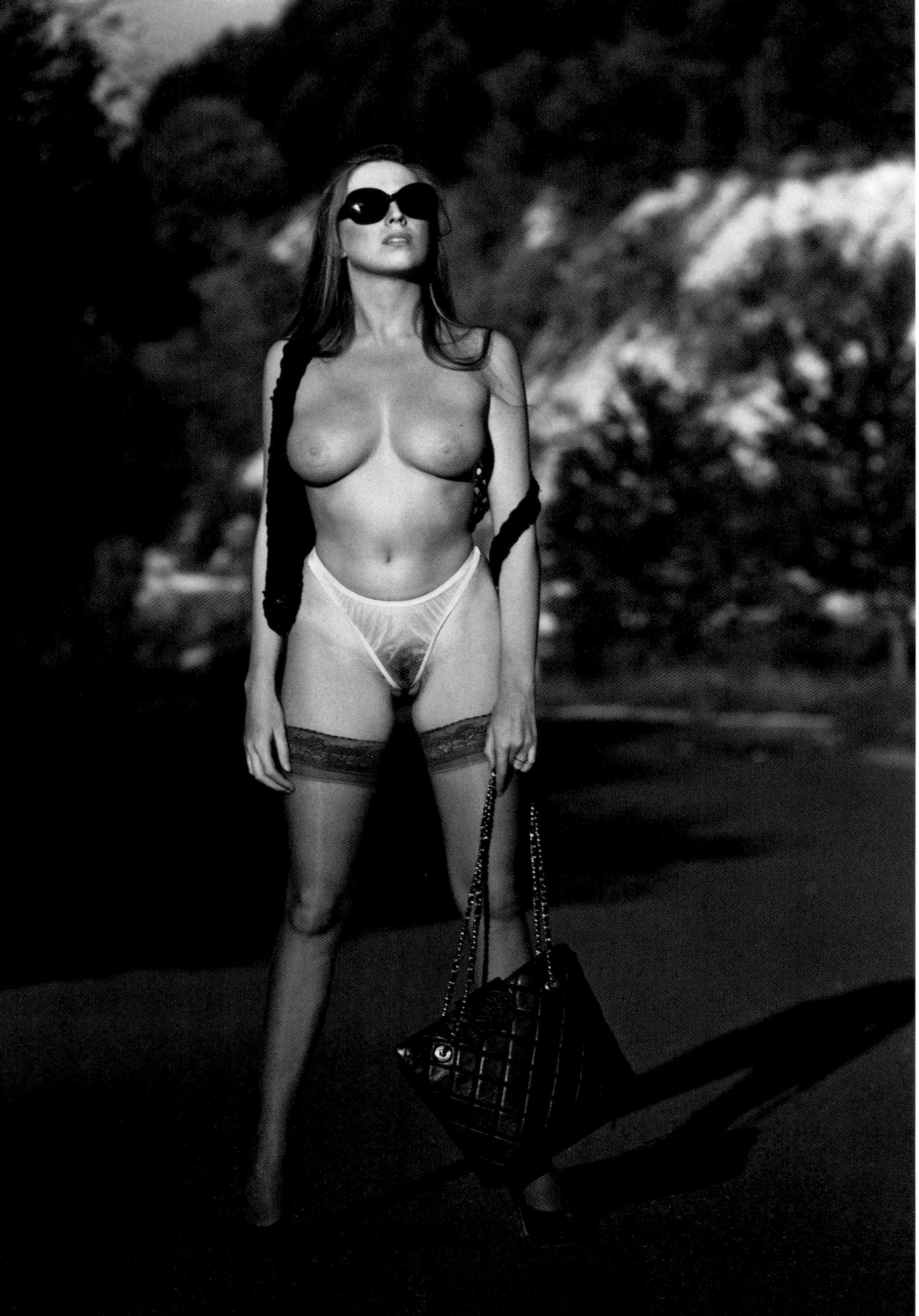

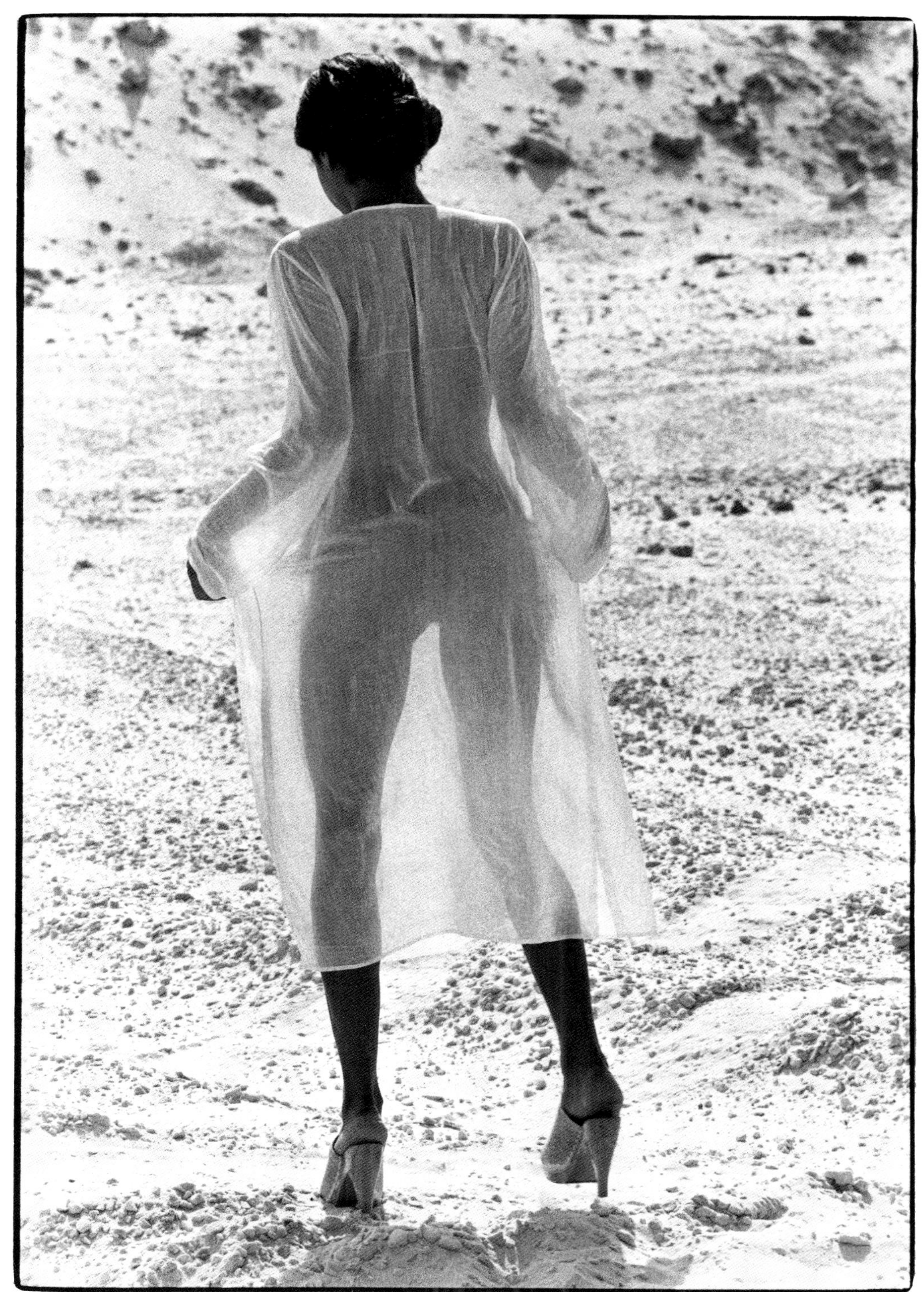

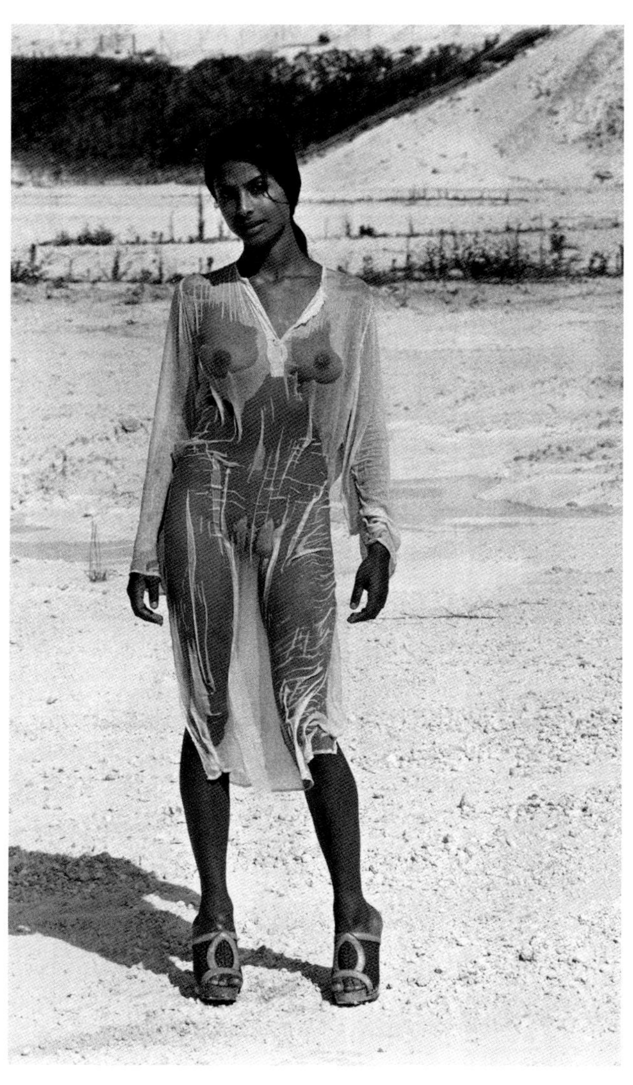

  Anne 1997

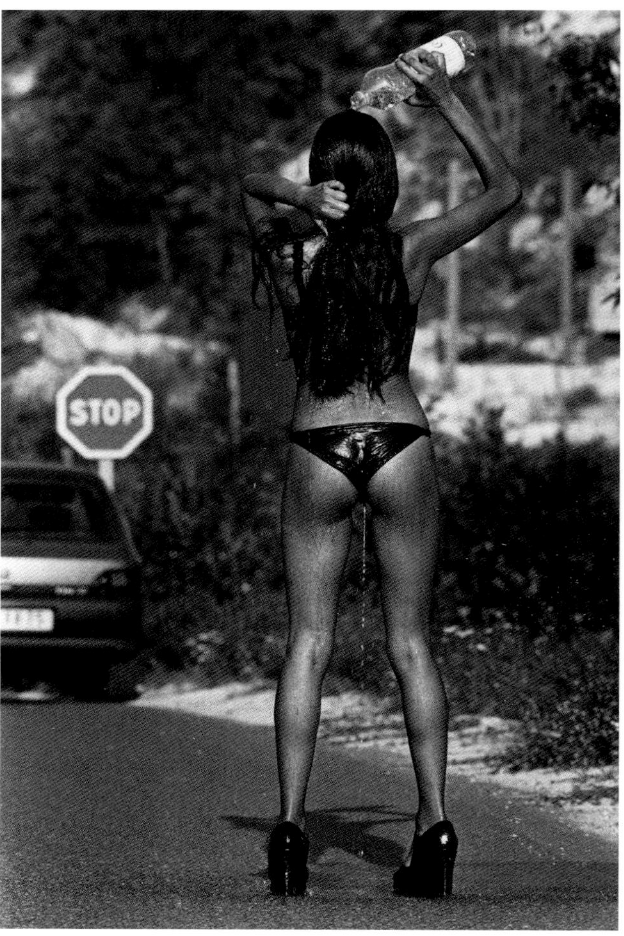

Anne 1999 →

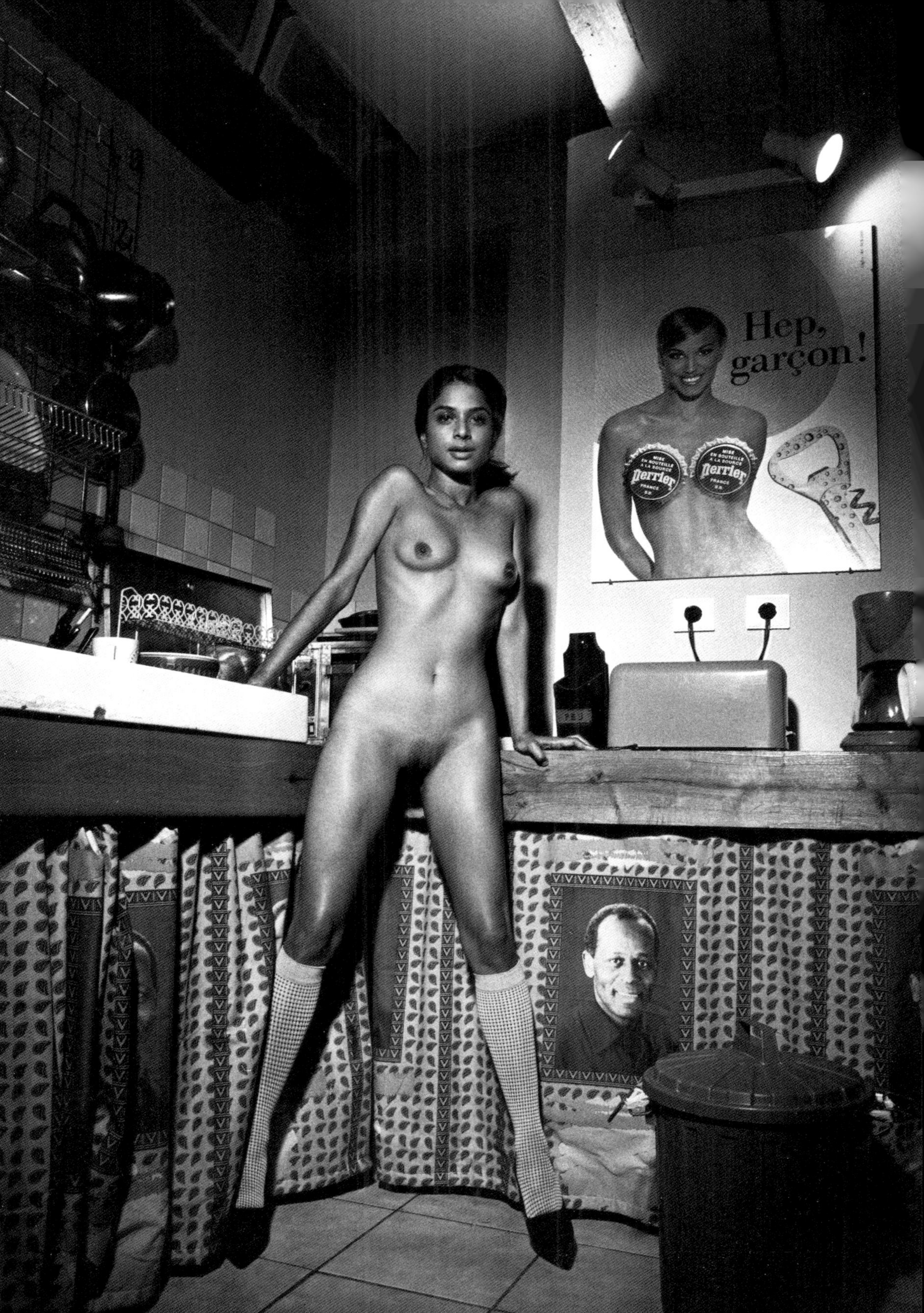

Hep,
garçon !
Perrier
Perrier

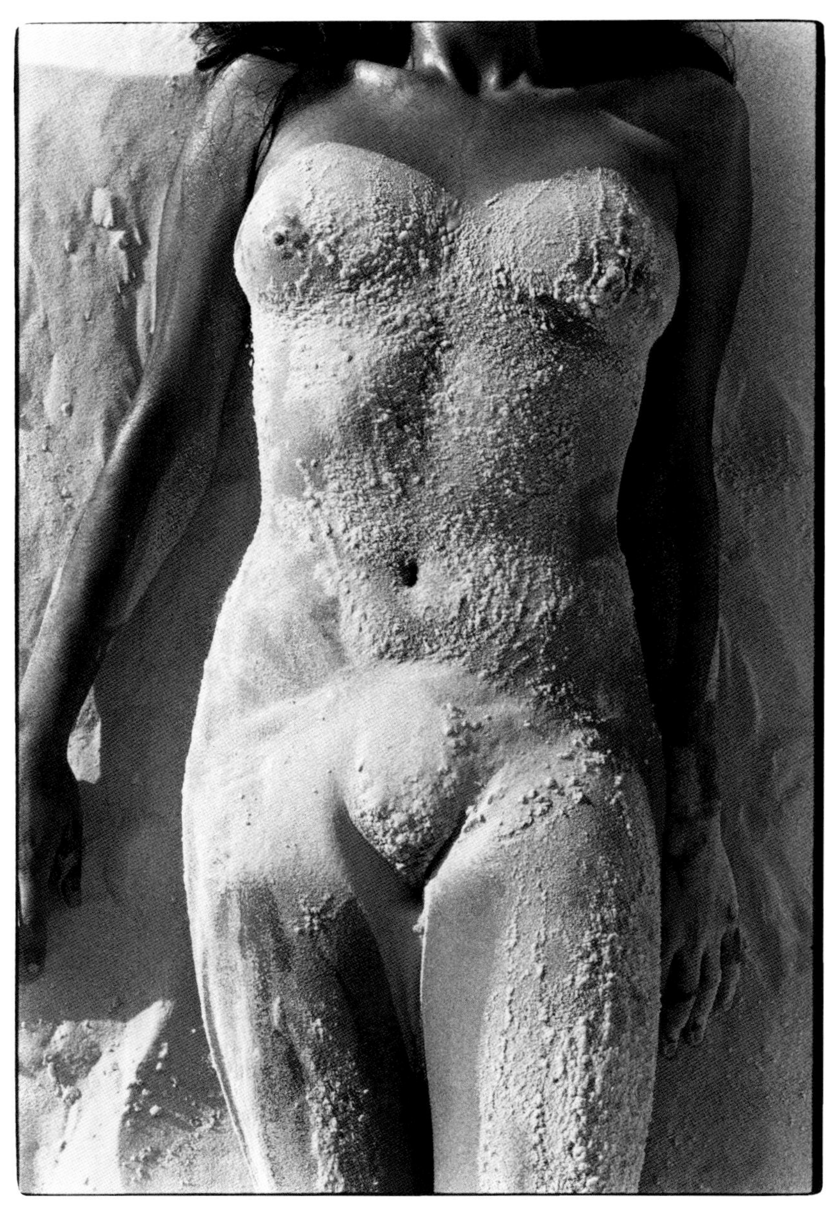

122 Anne 2002

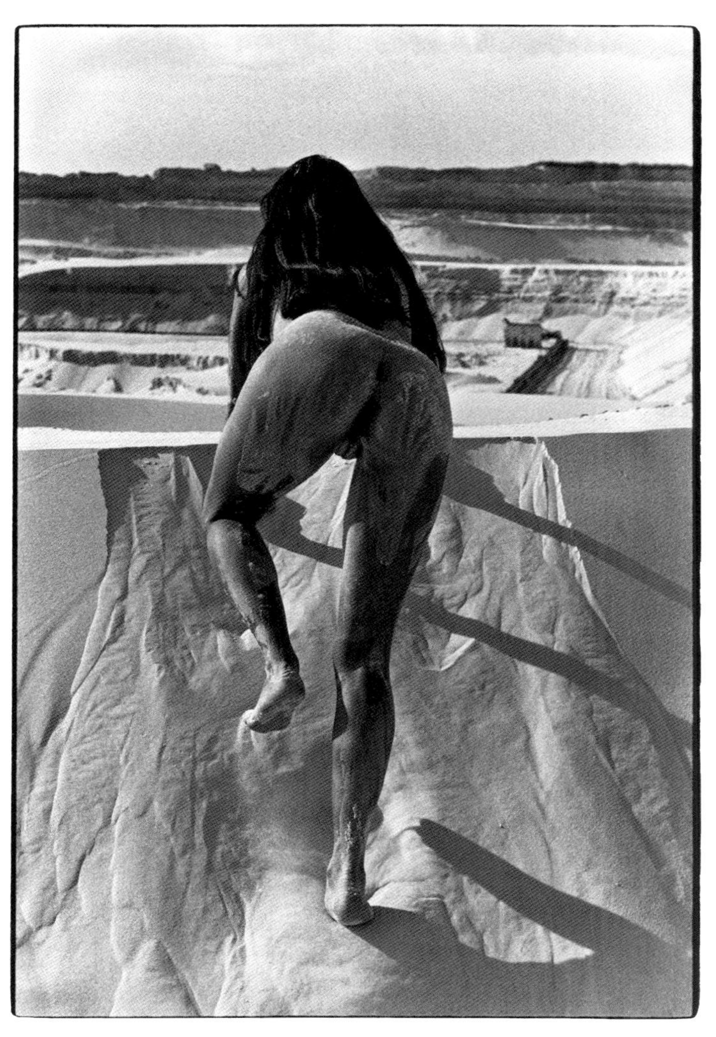
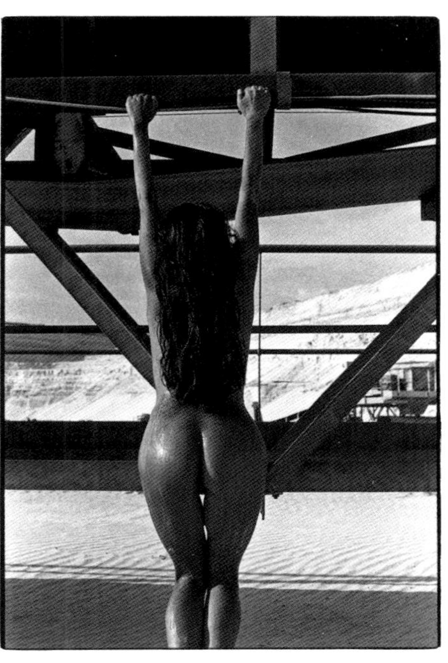

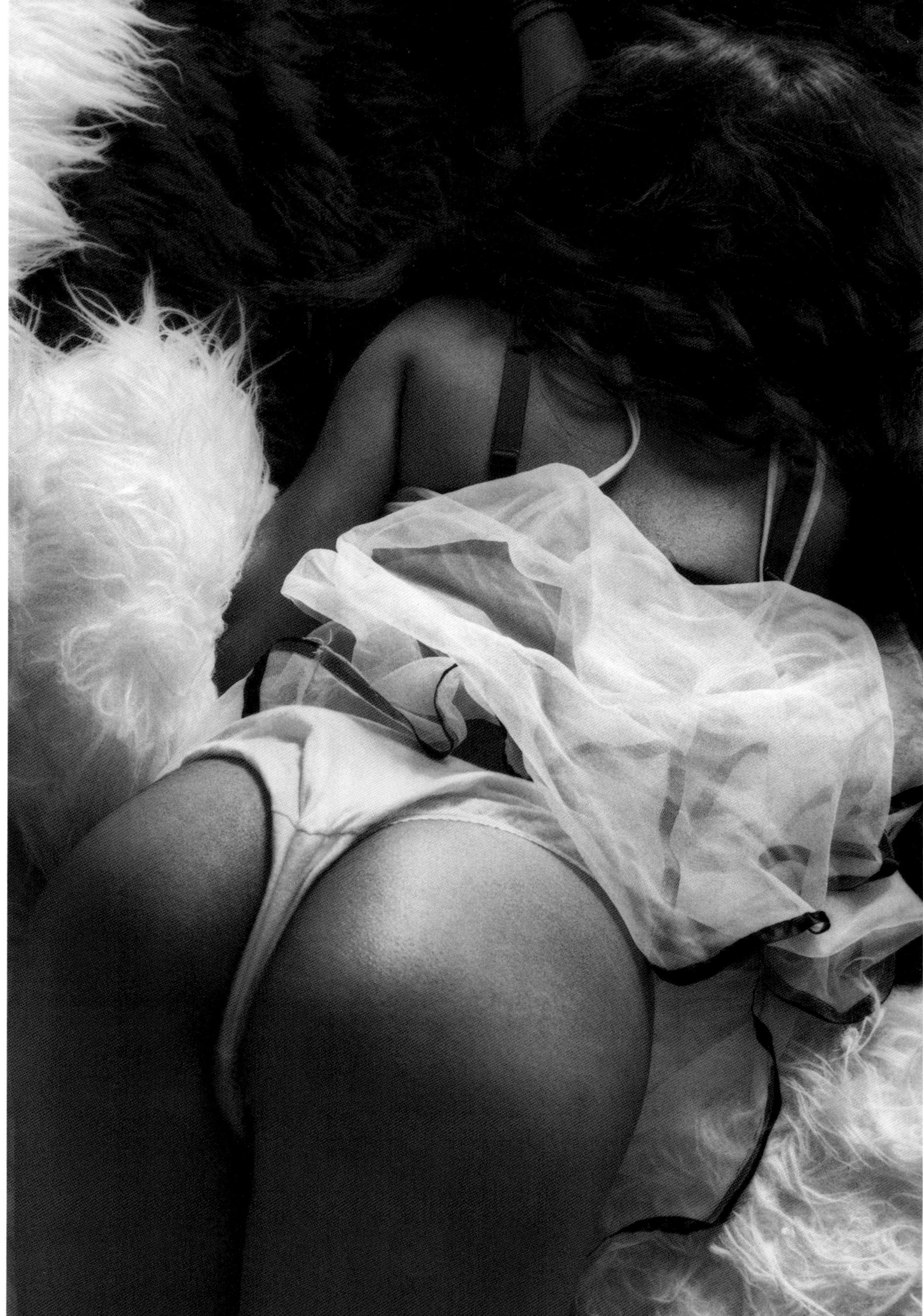

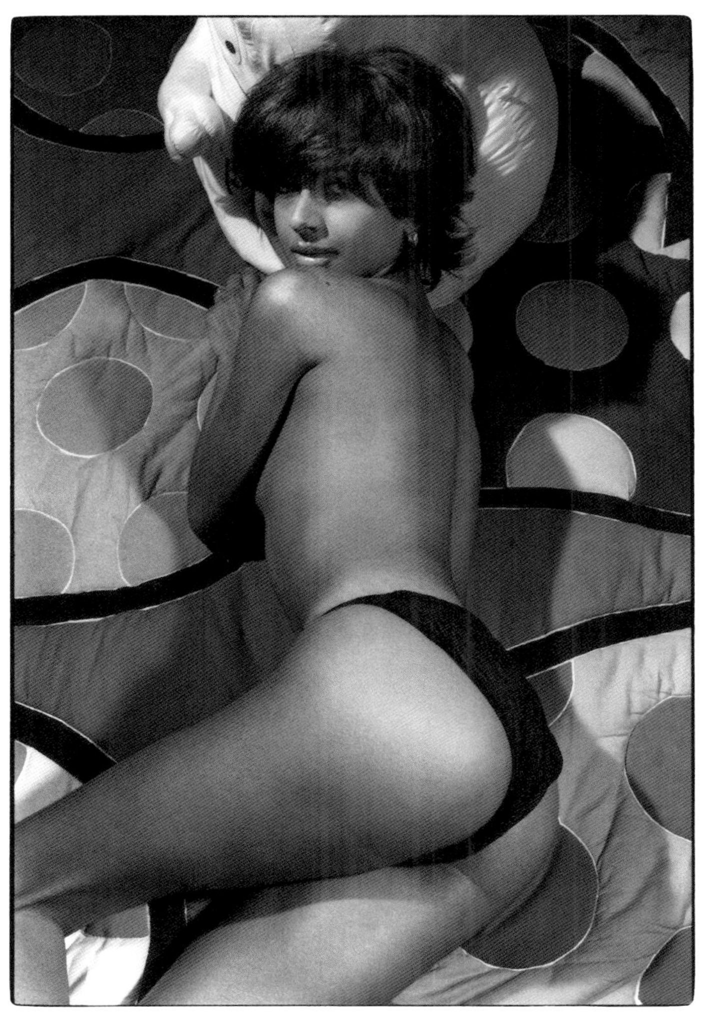

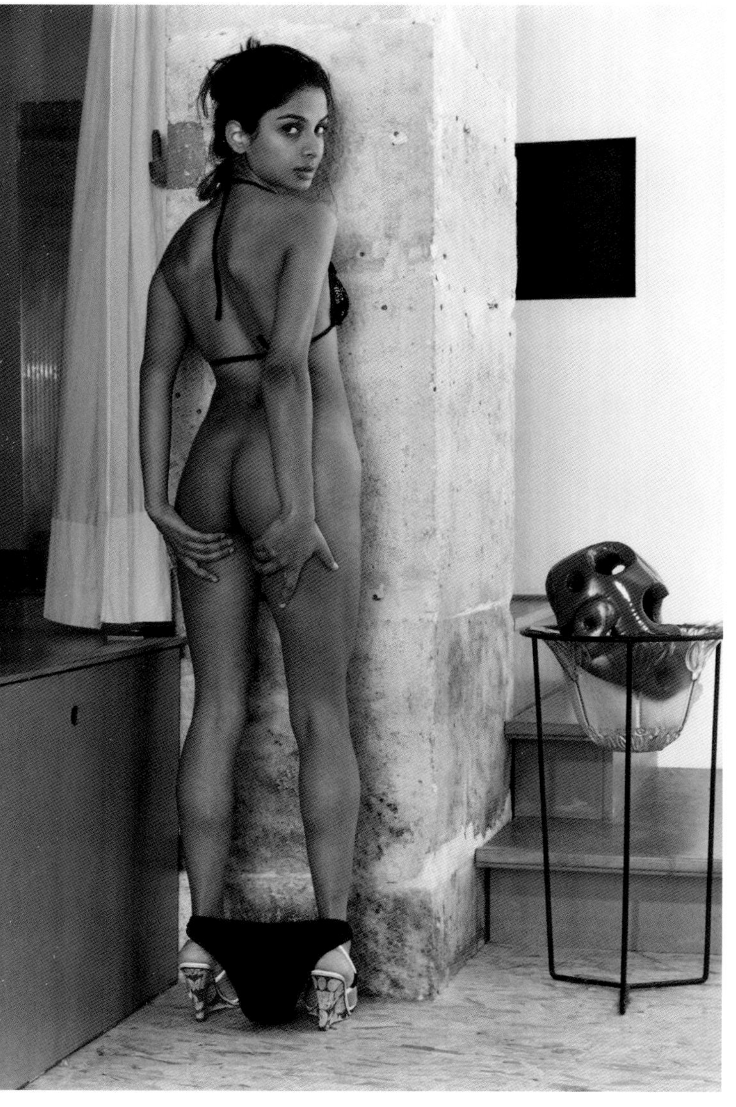

Anne & Valérie 1999 →

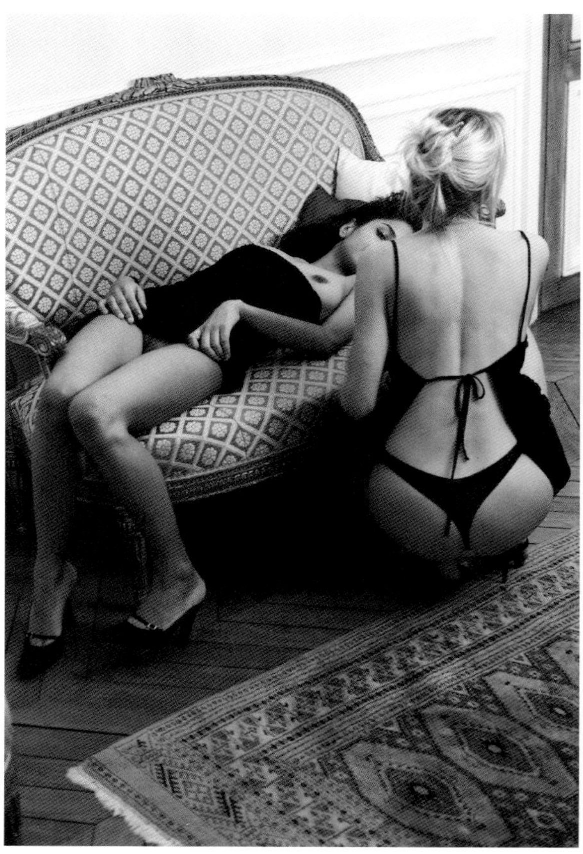

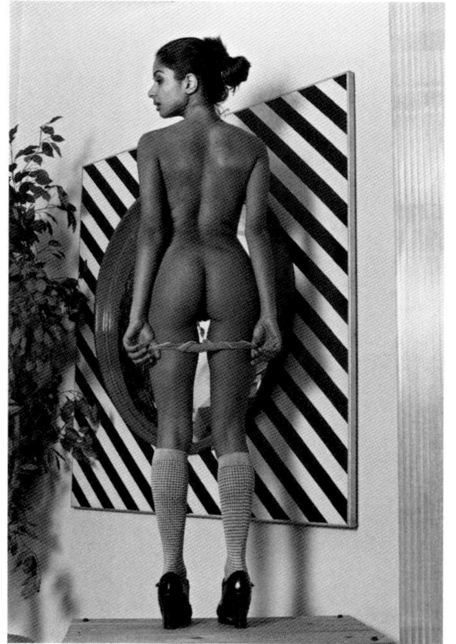

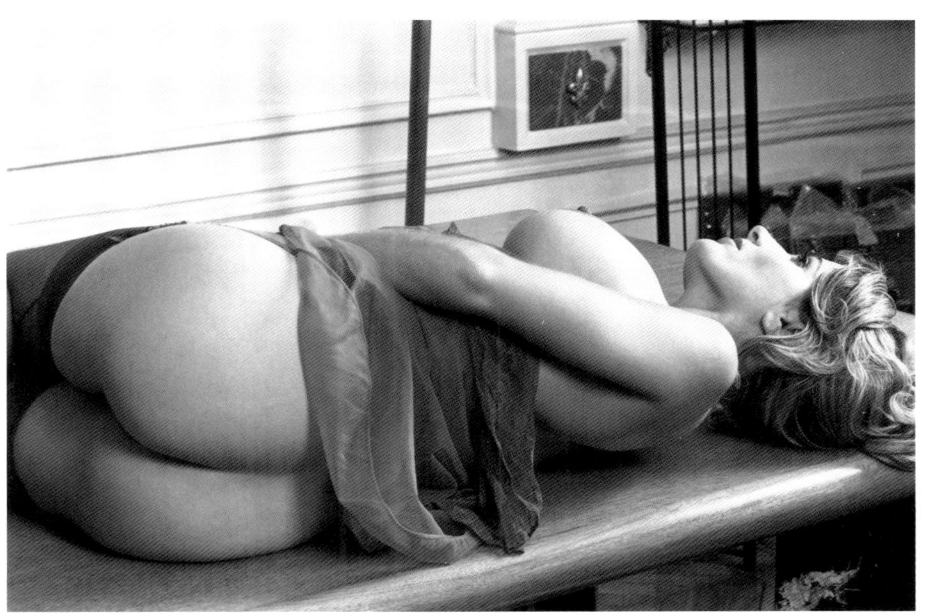

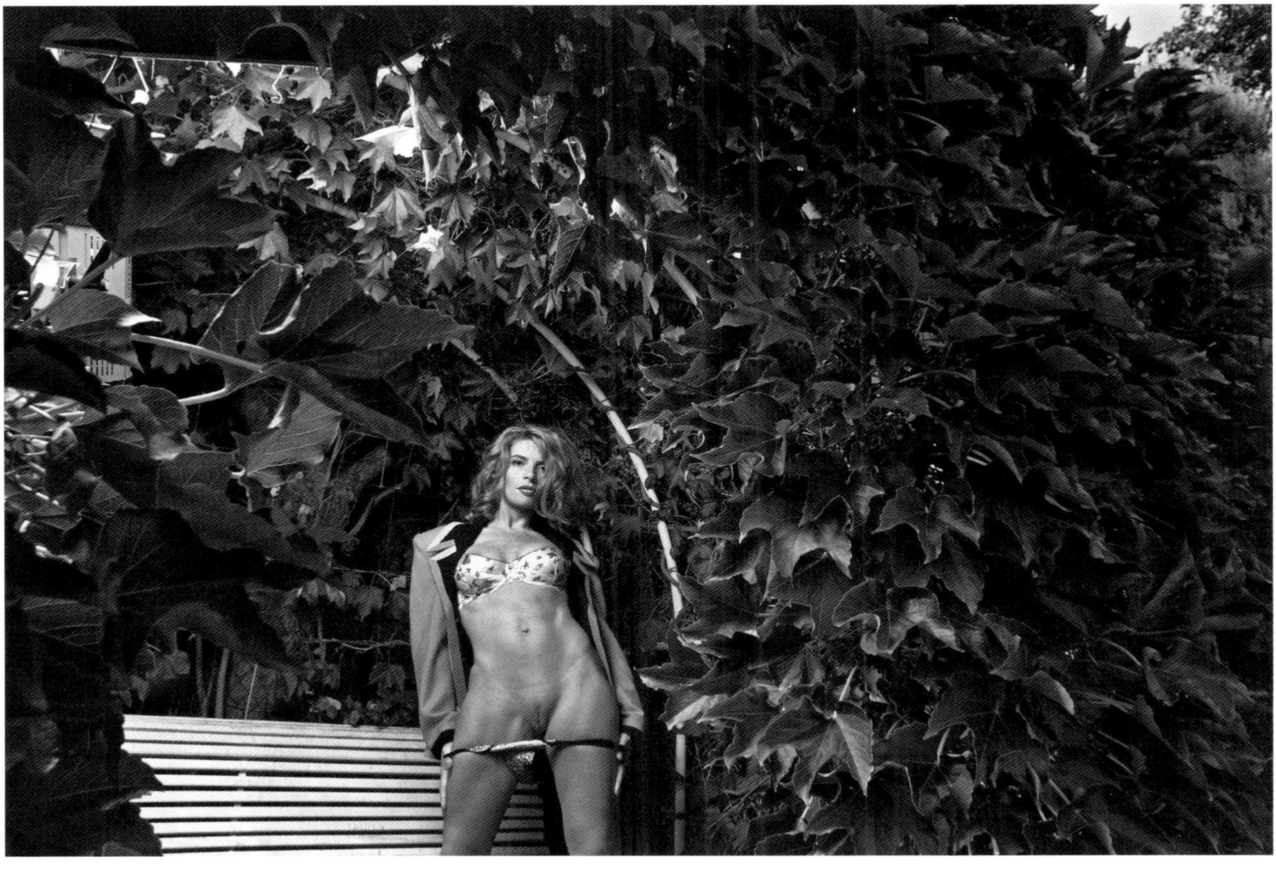

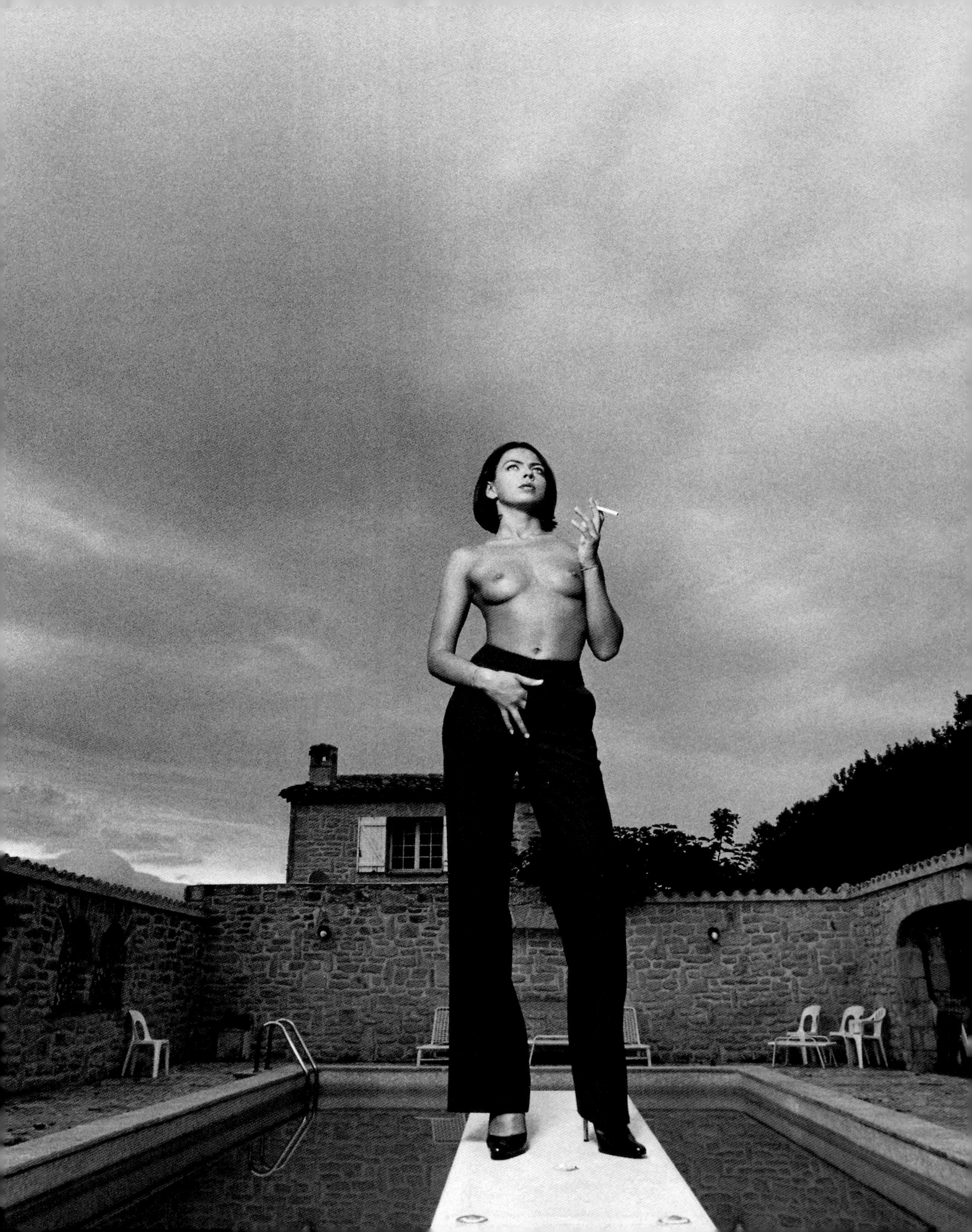

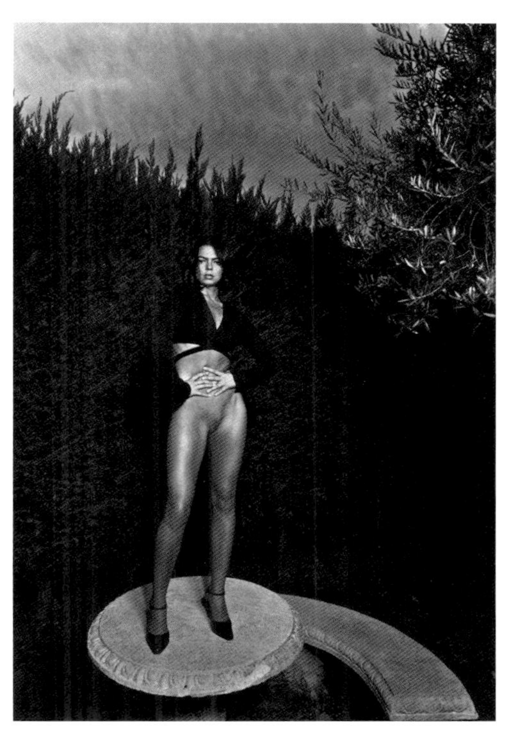

Jade 1997

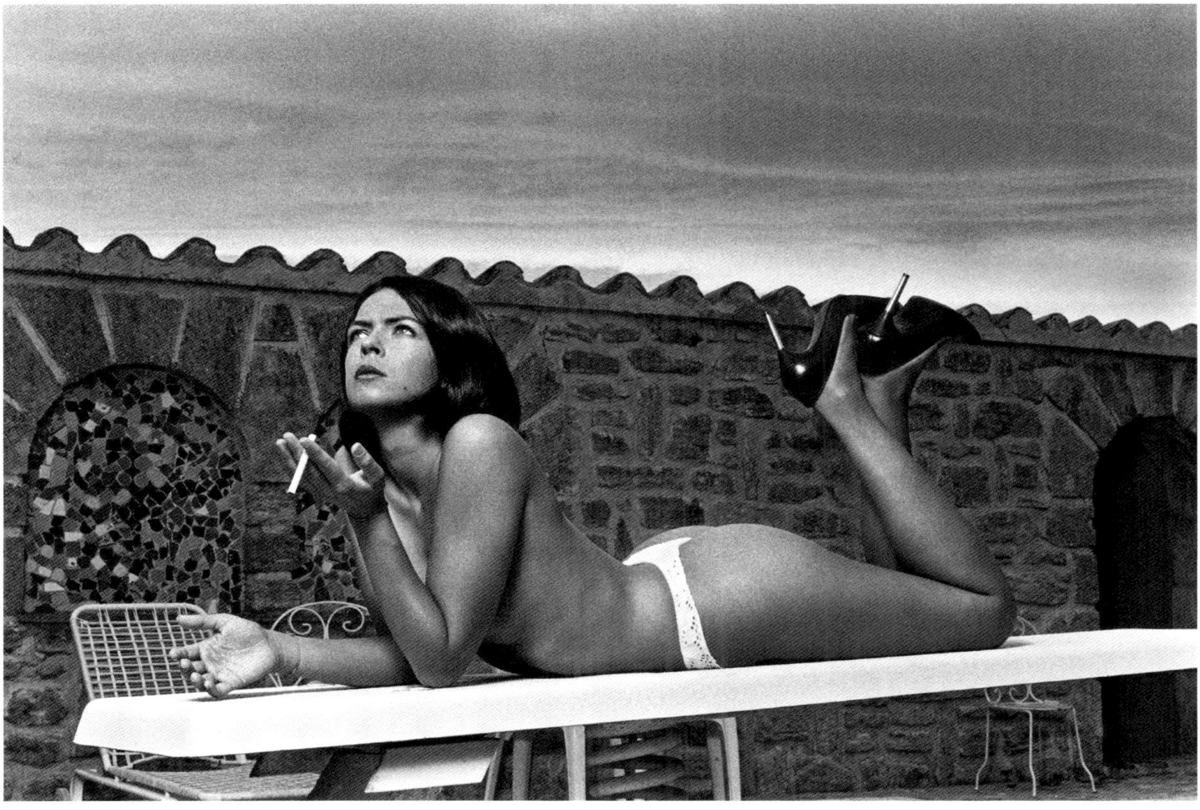

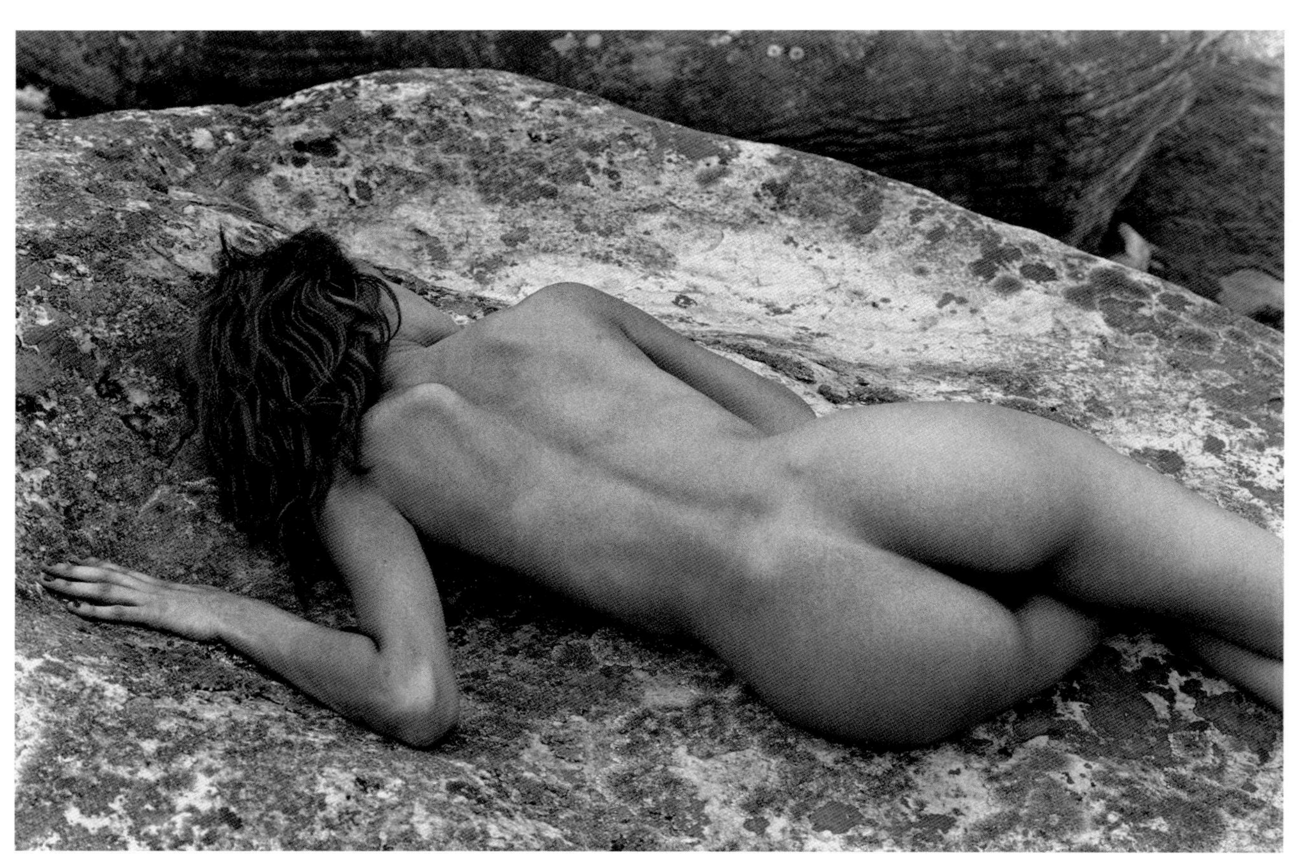

130 Farah 1997

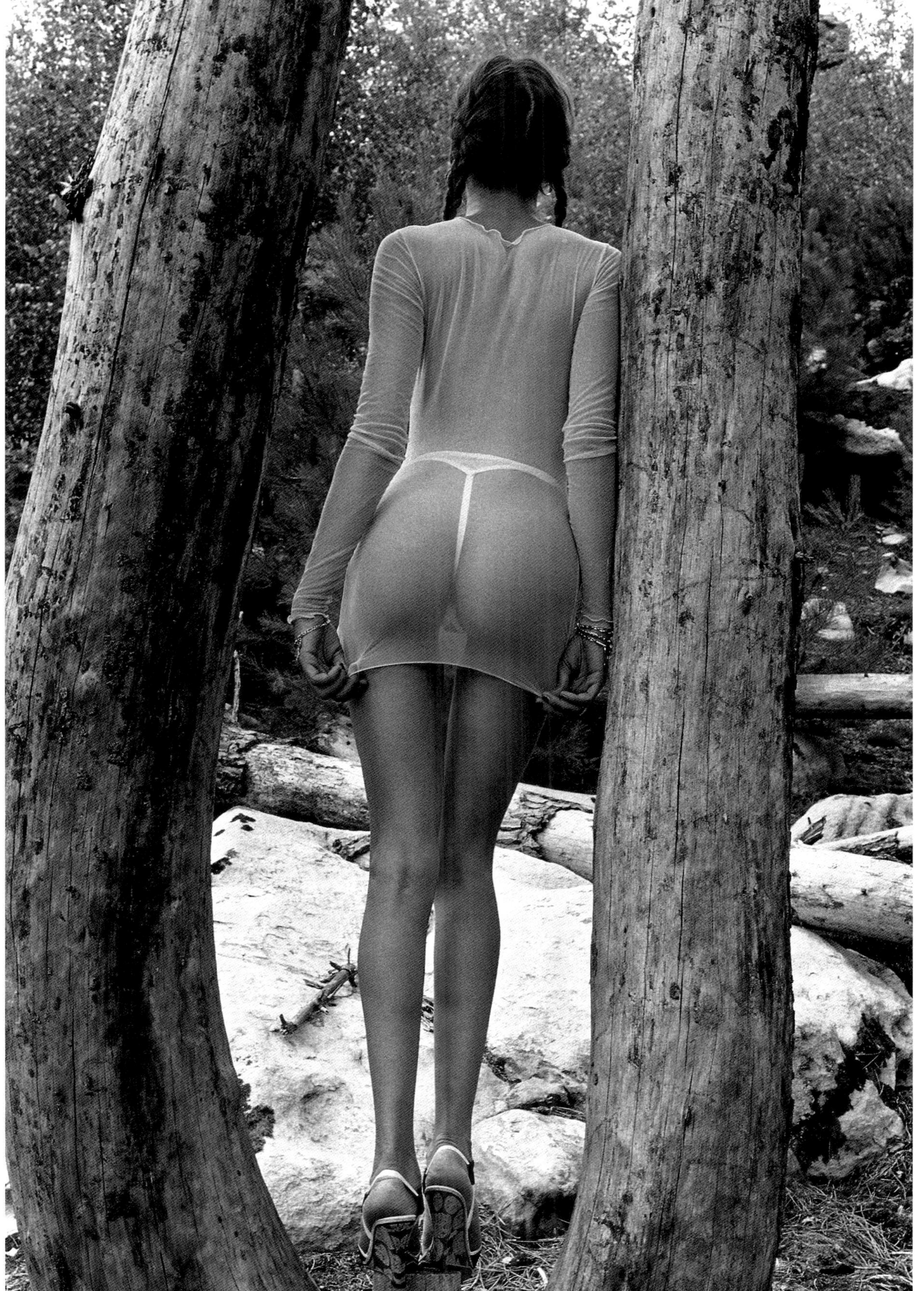

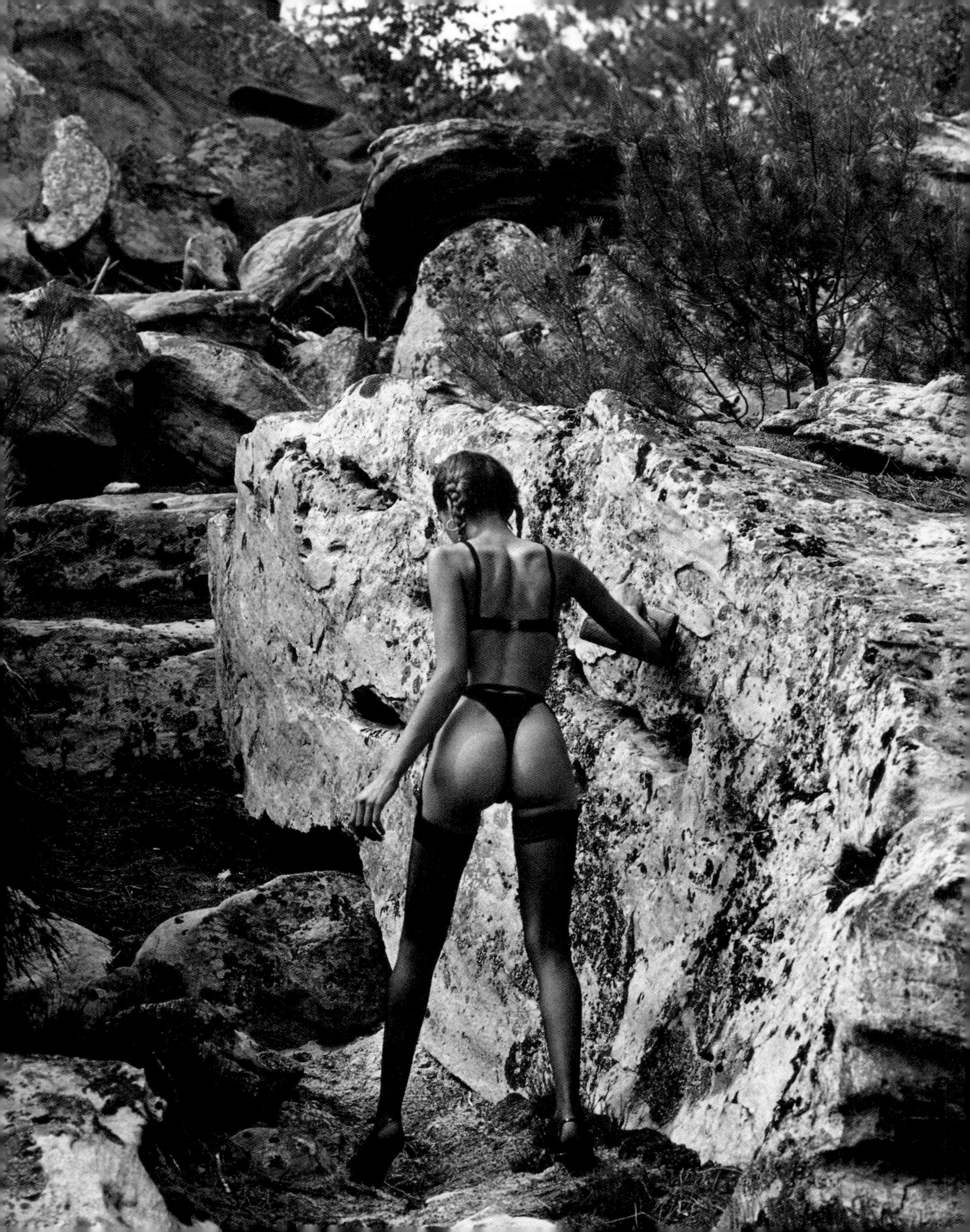

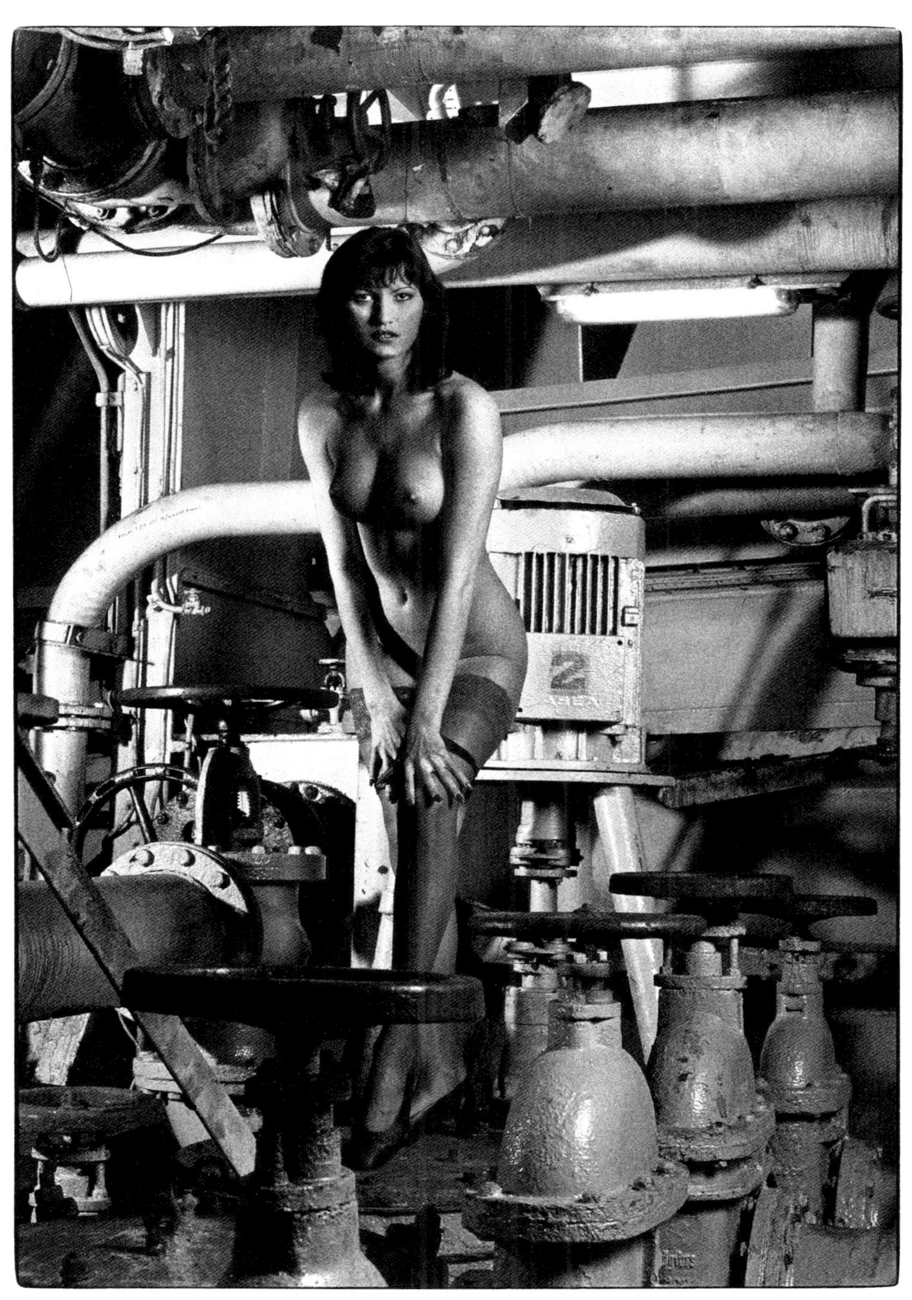

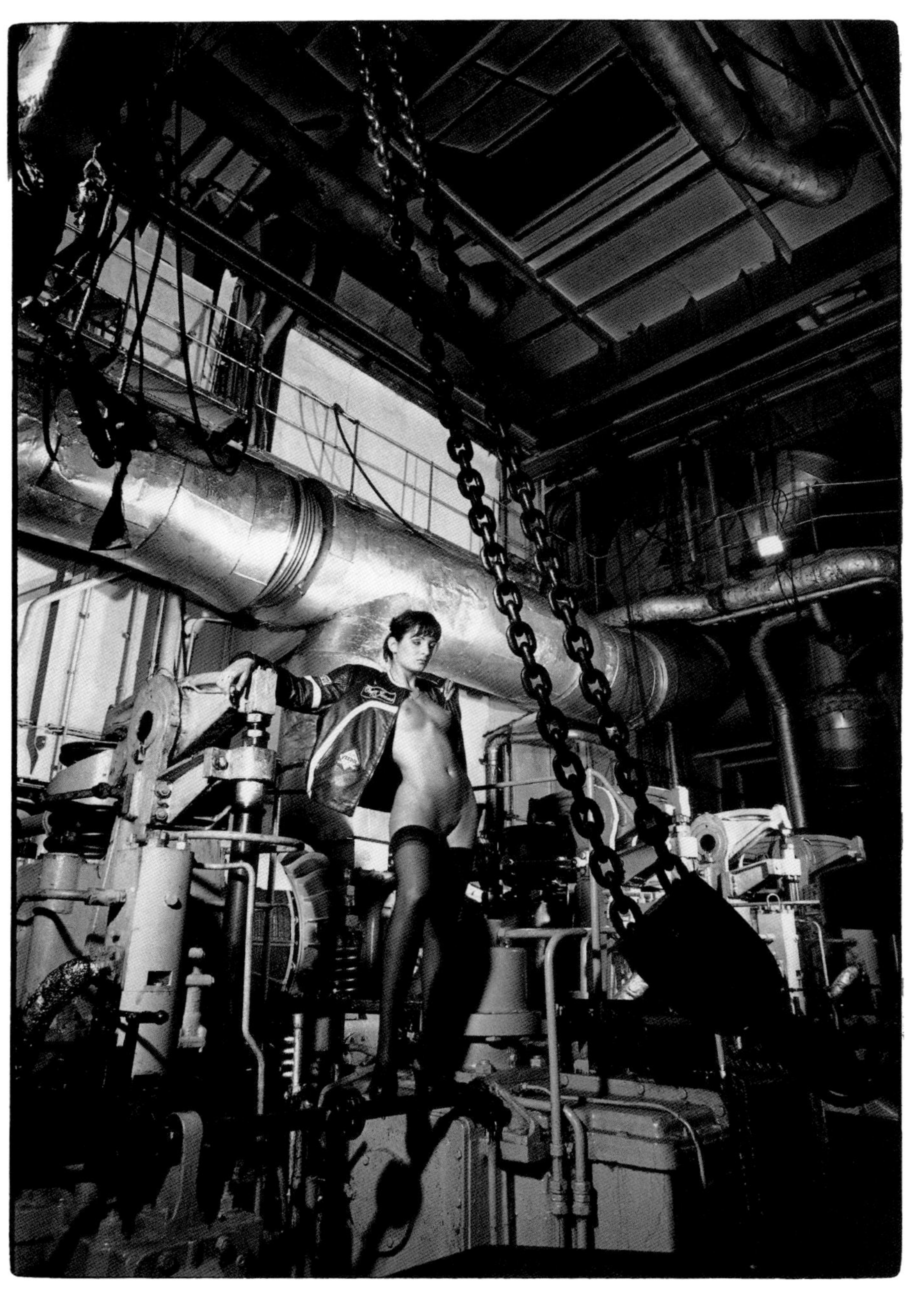

 Eva 1997

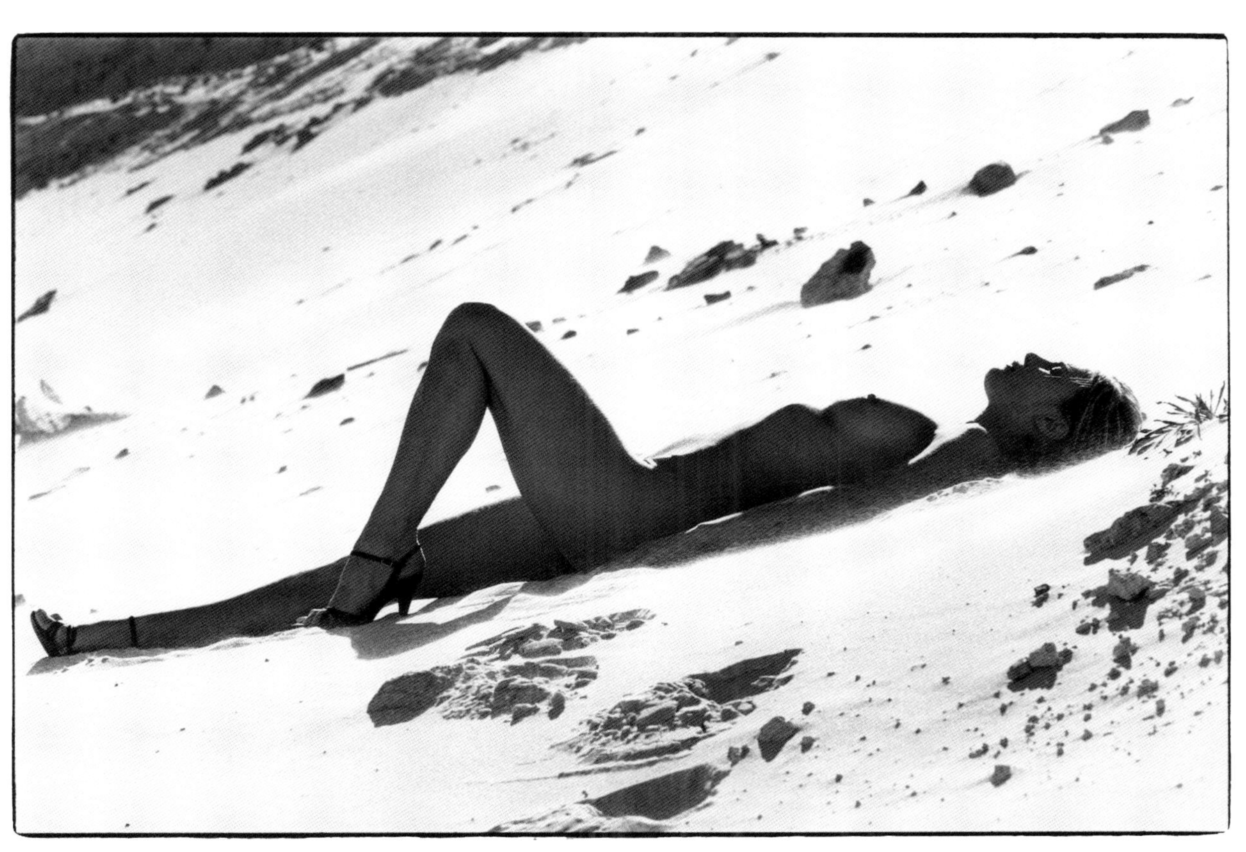

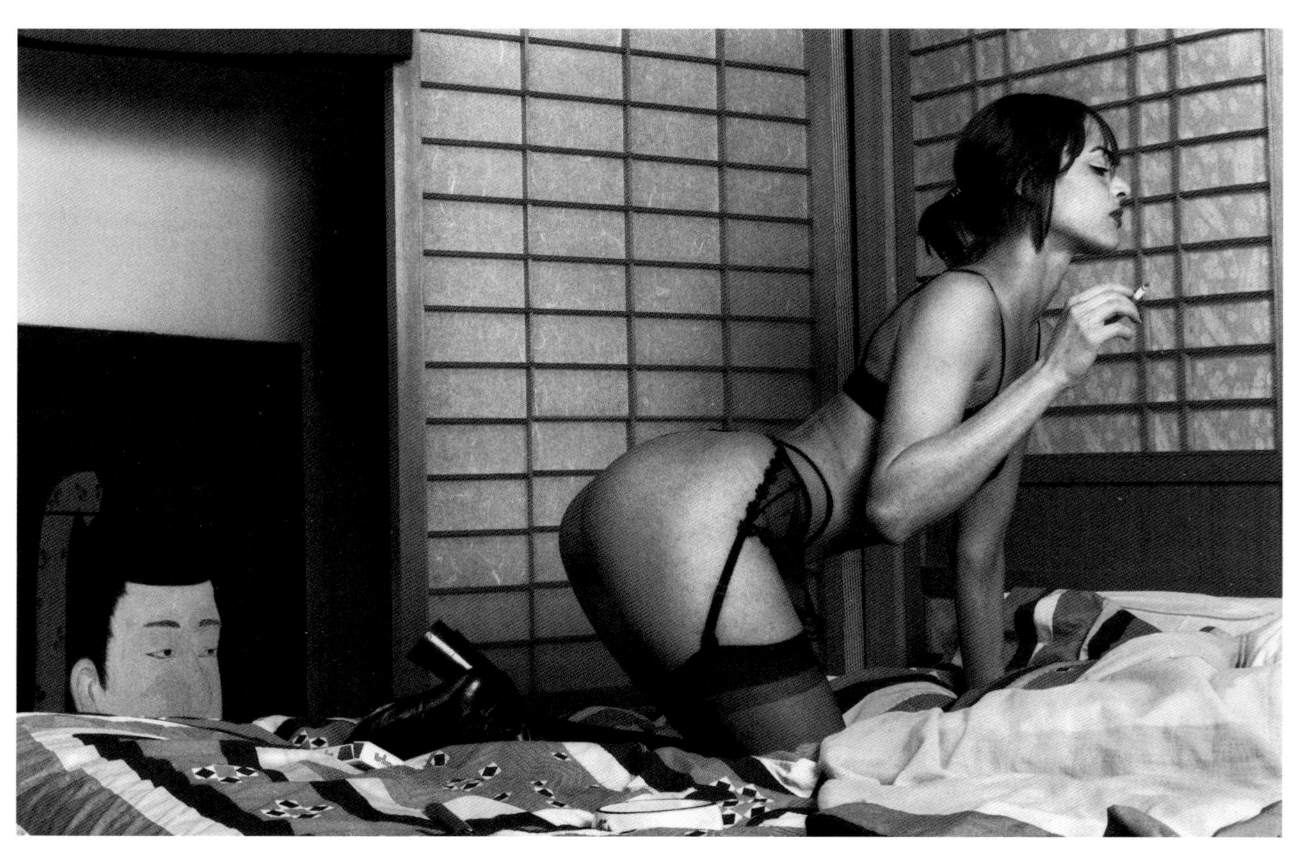

  Martina 1998

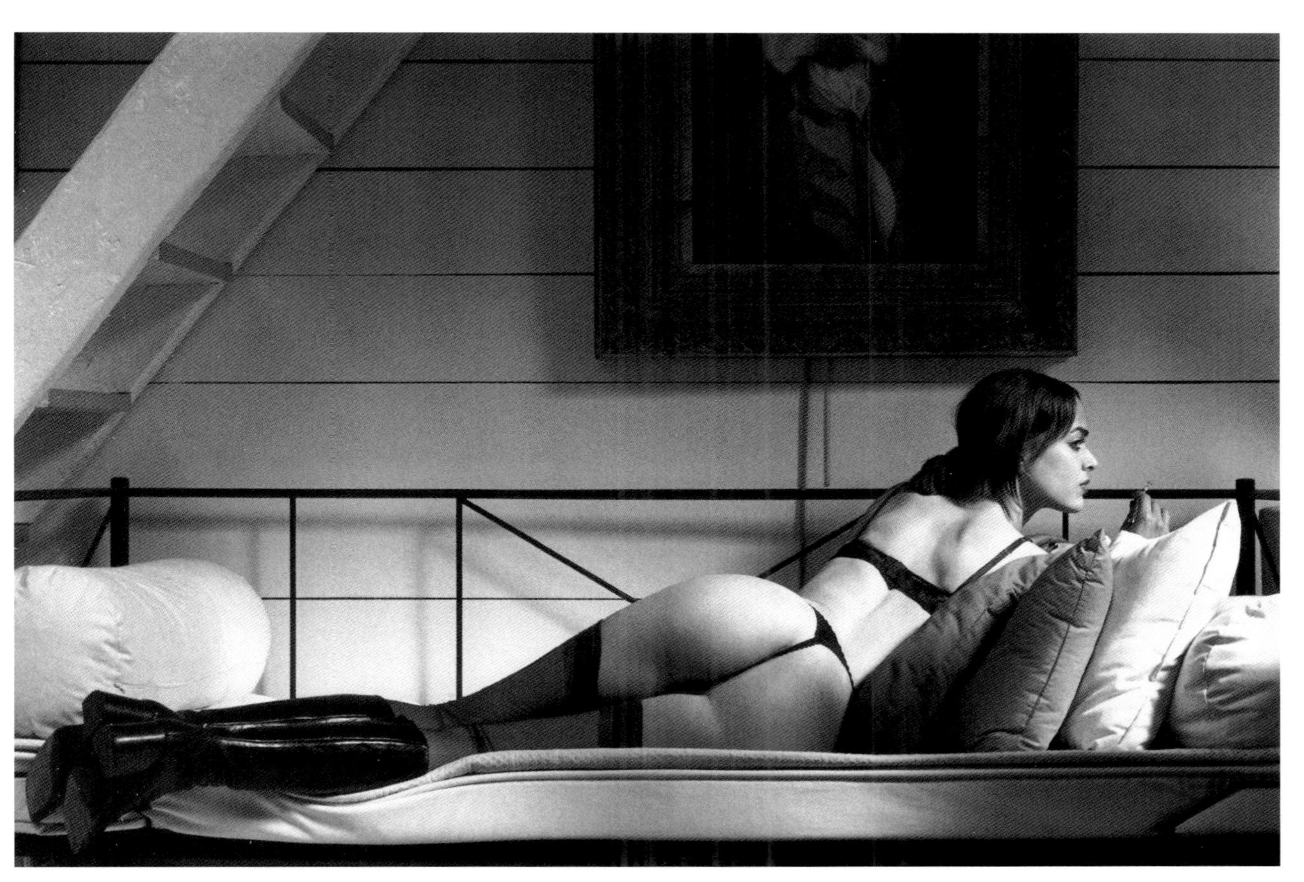

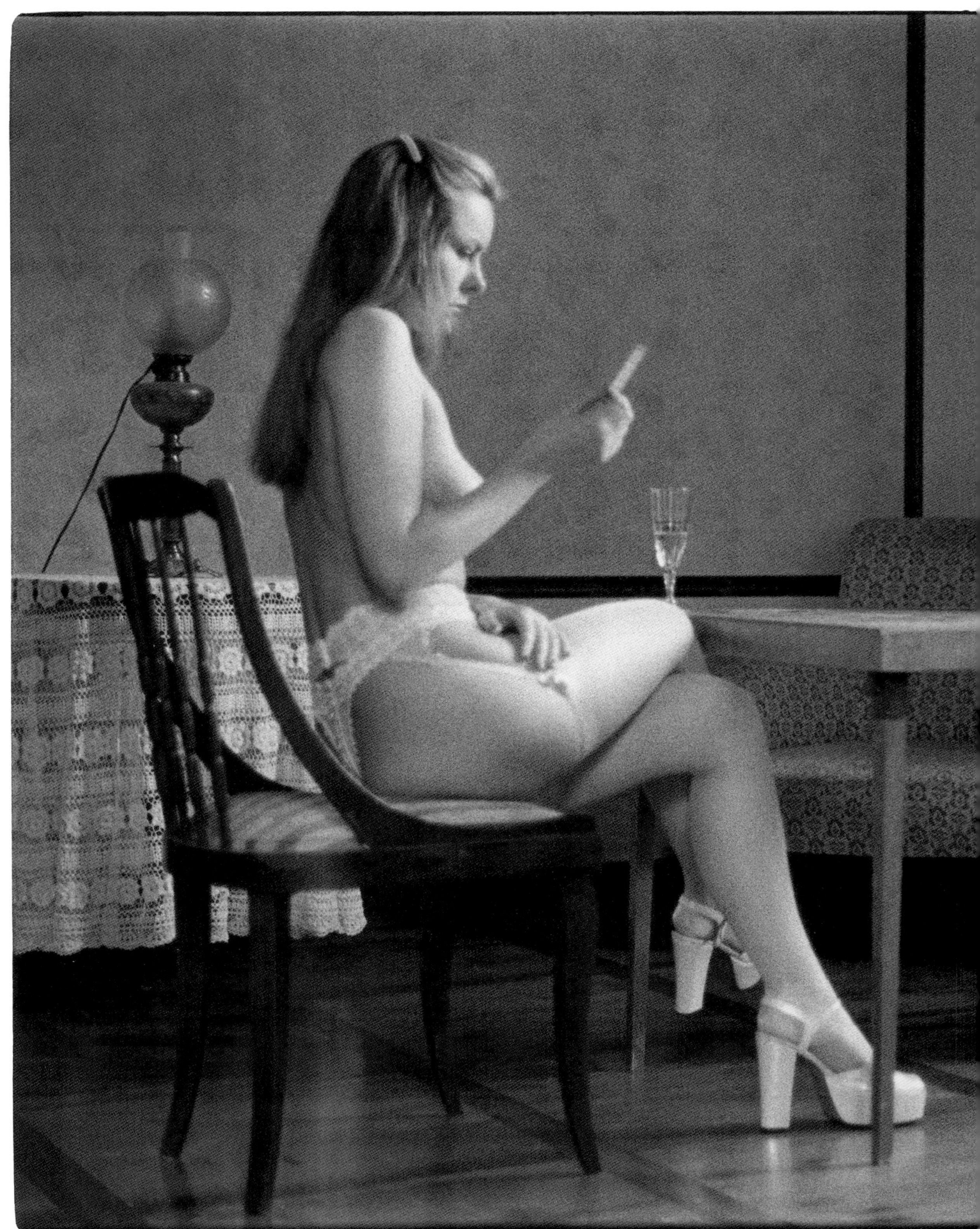

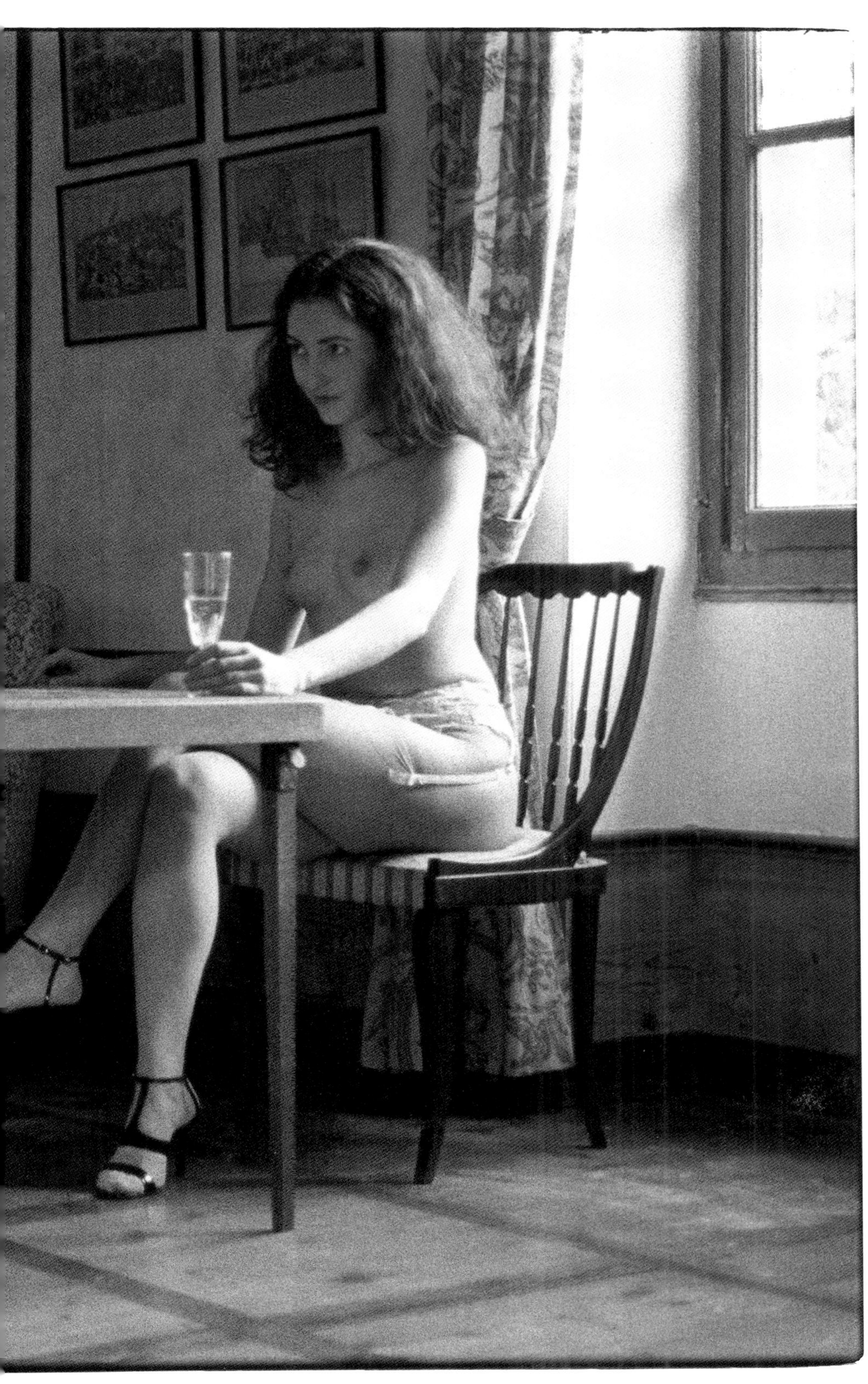

Julie & Johanna 1999

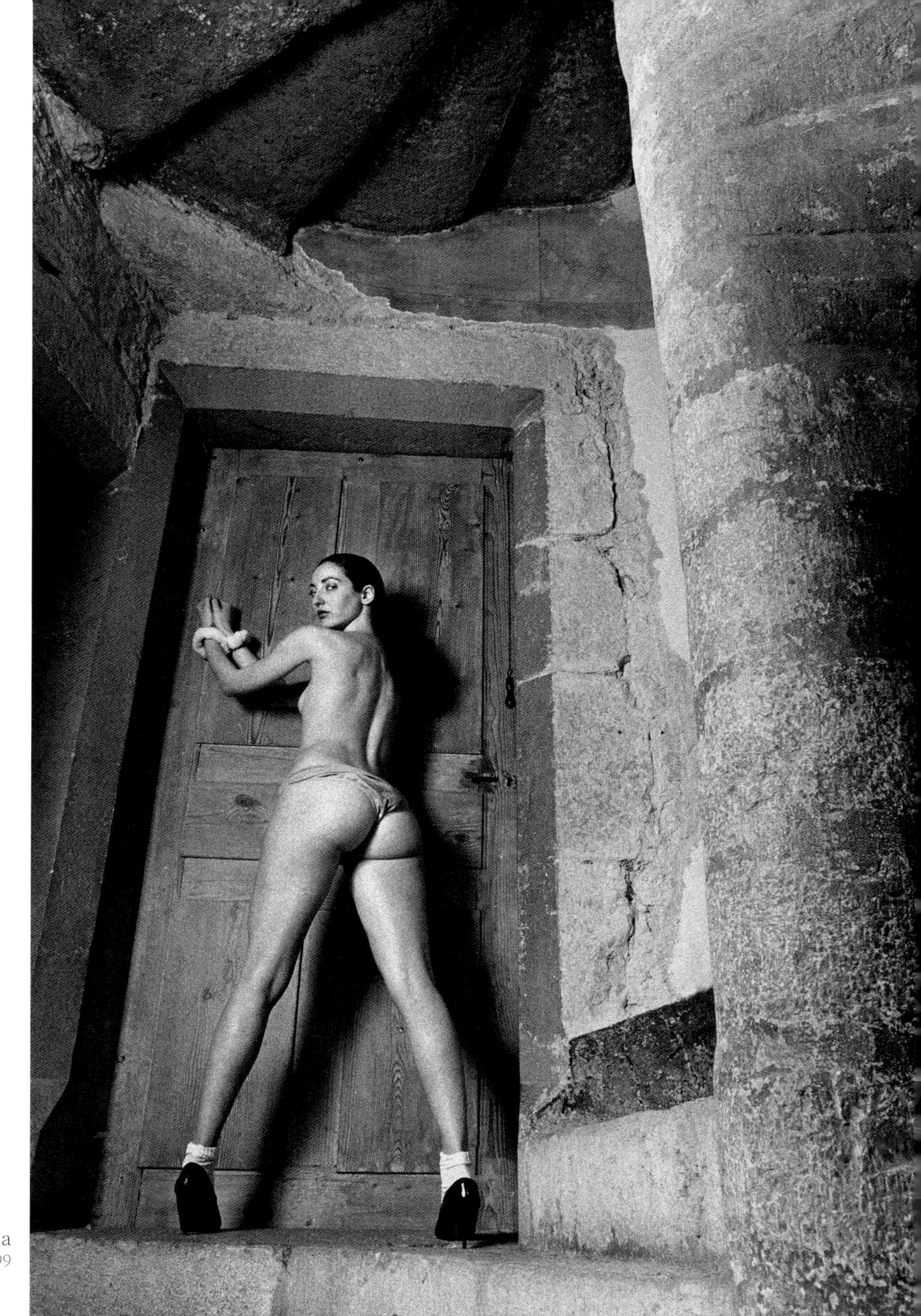

Johanna
140   1999

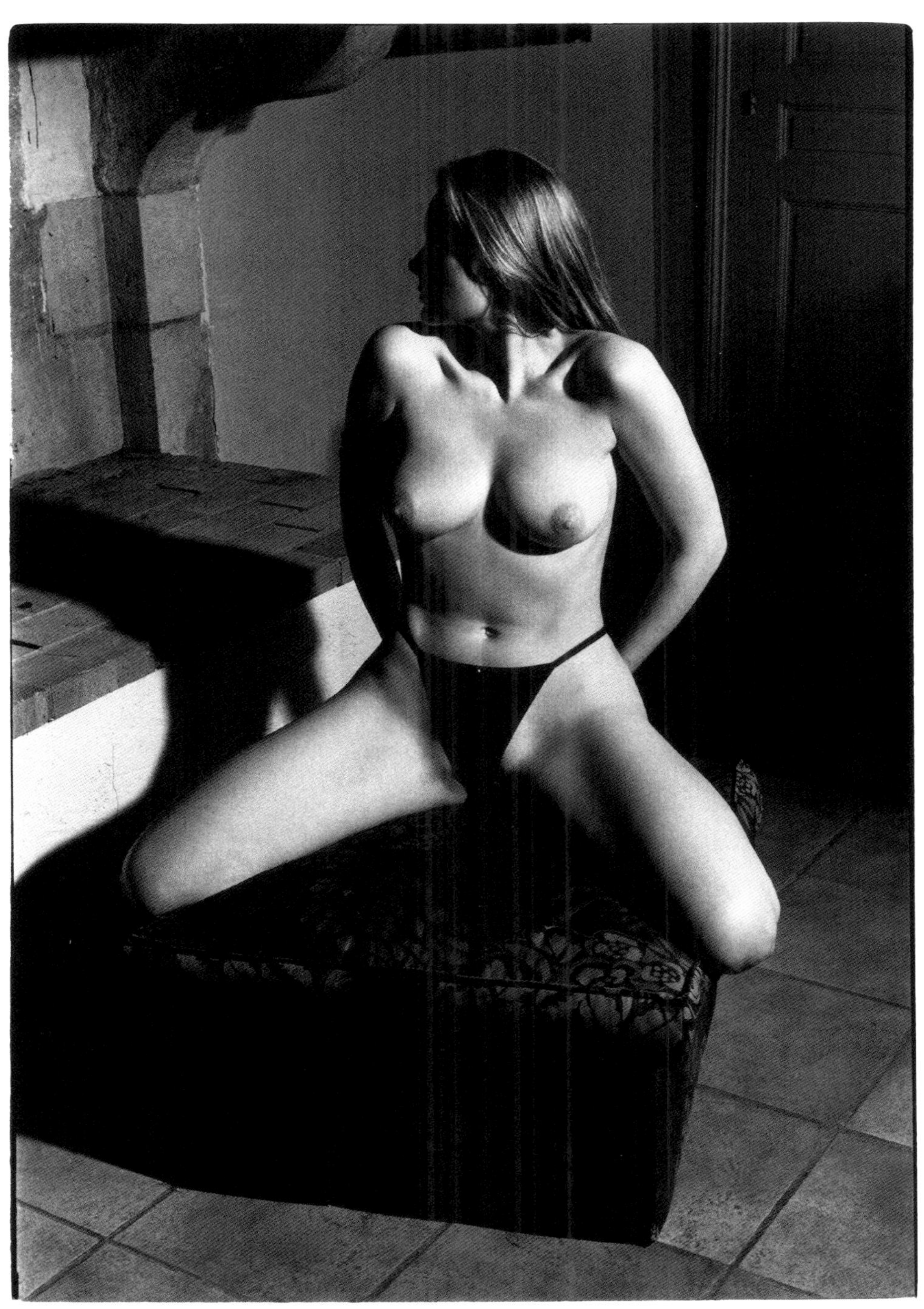

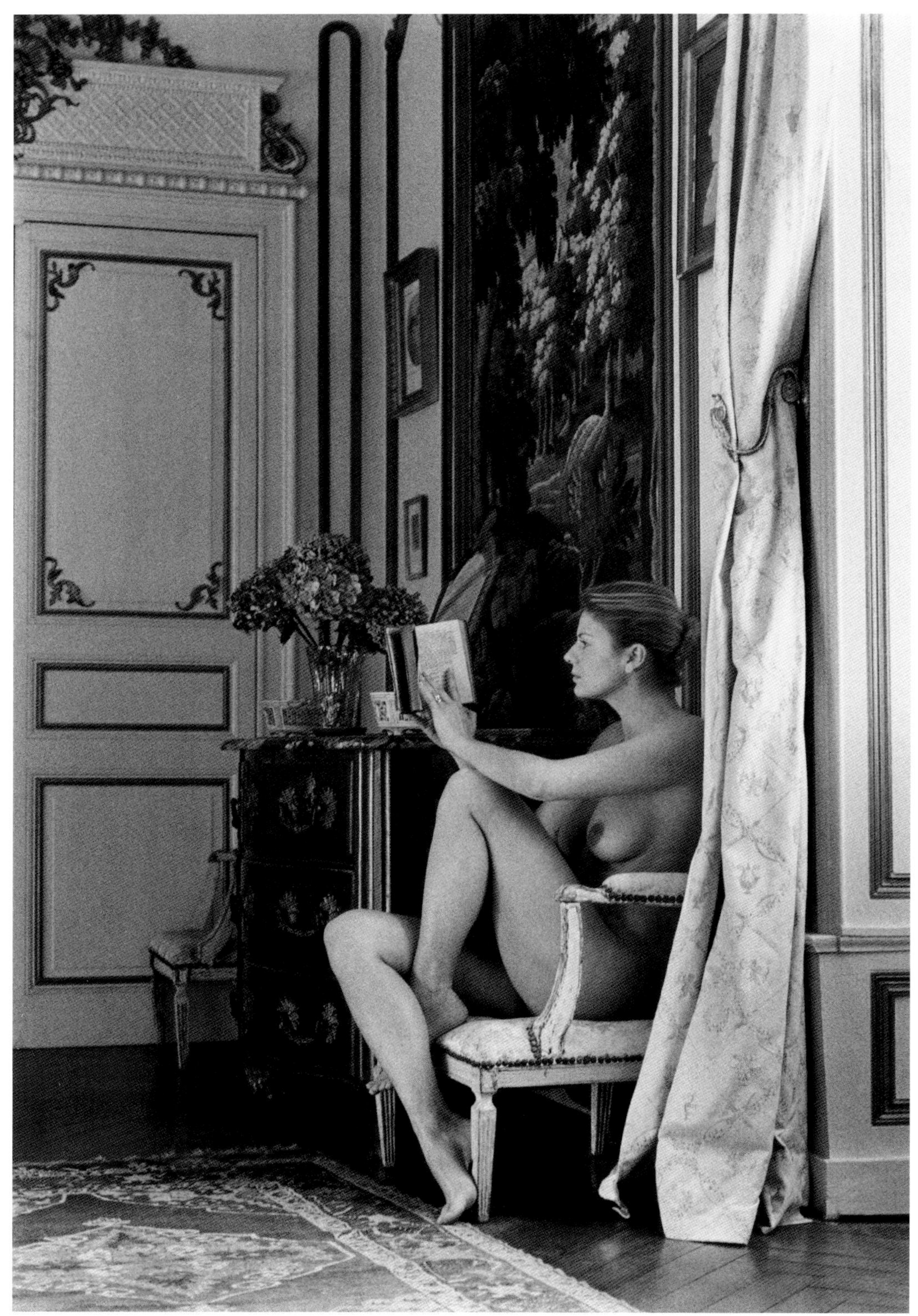

142   Juliette 1999

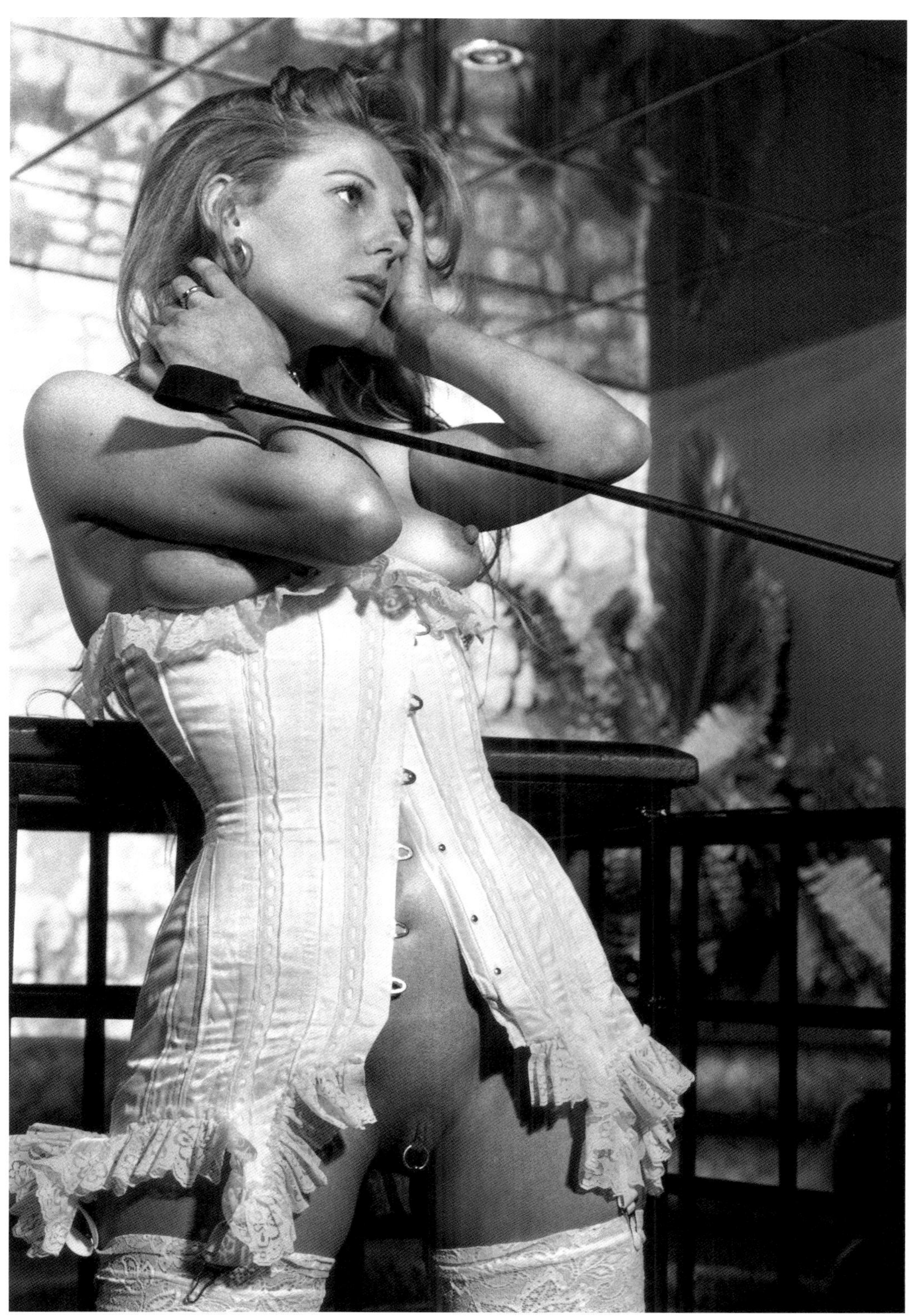

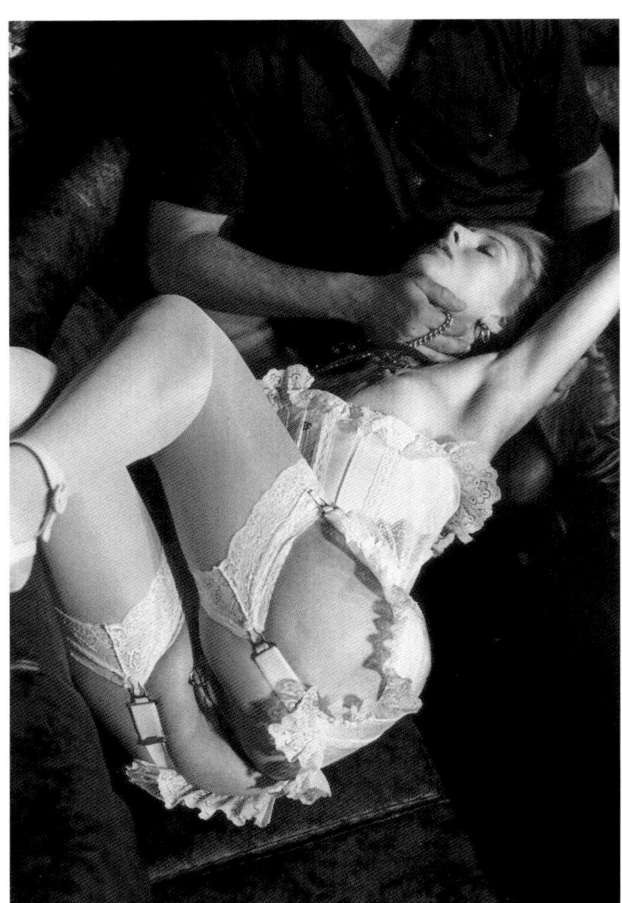

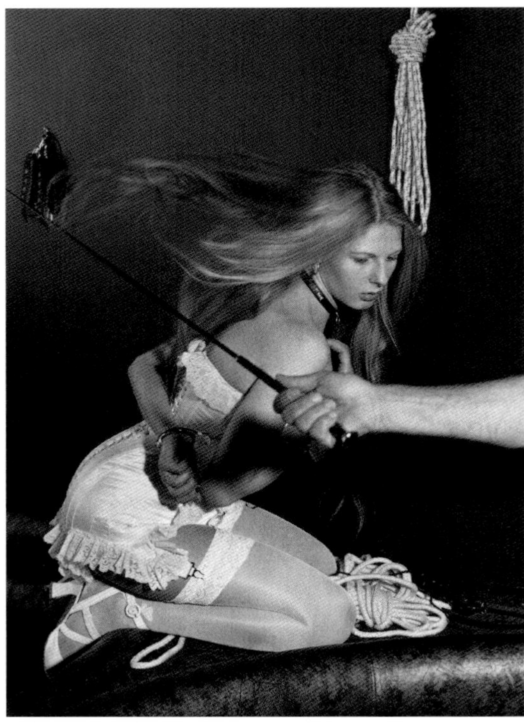

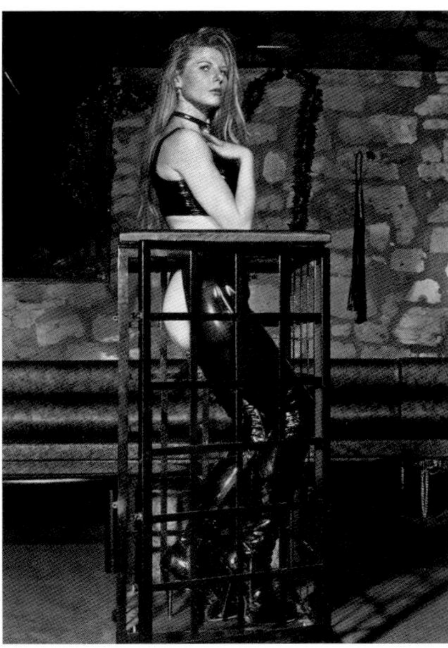

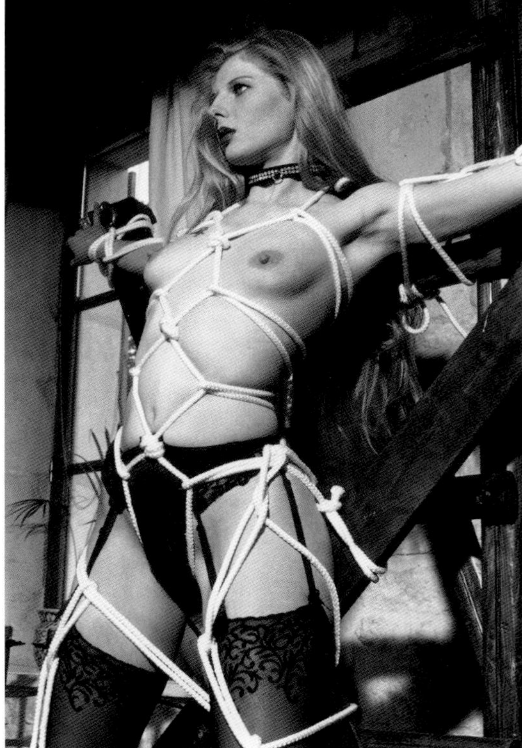

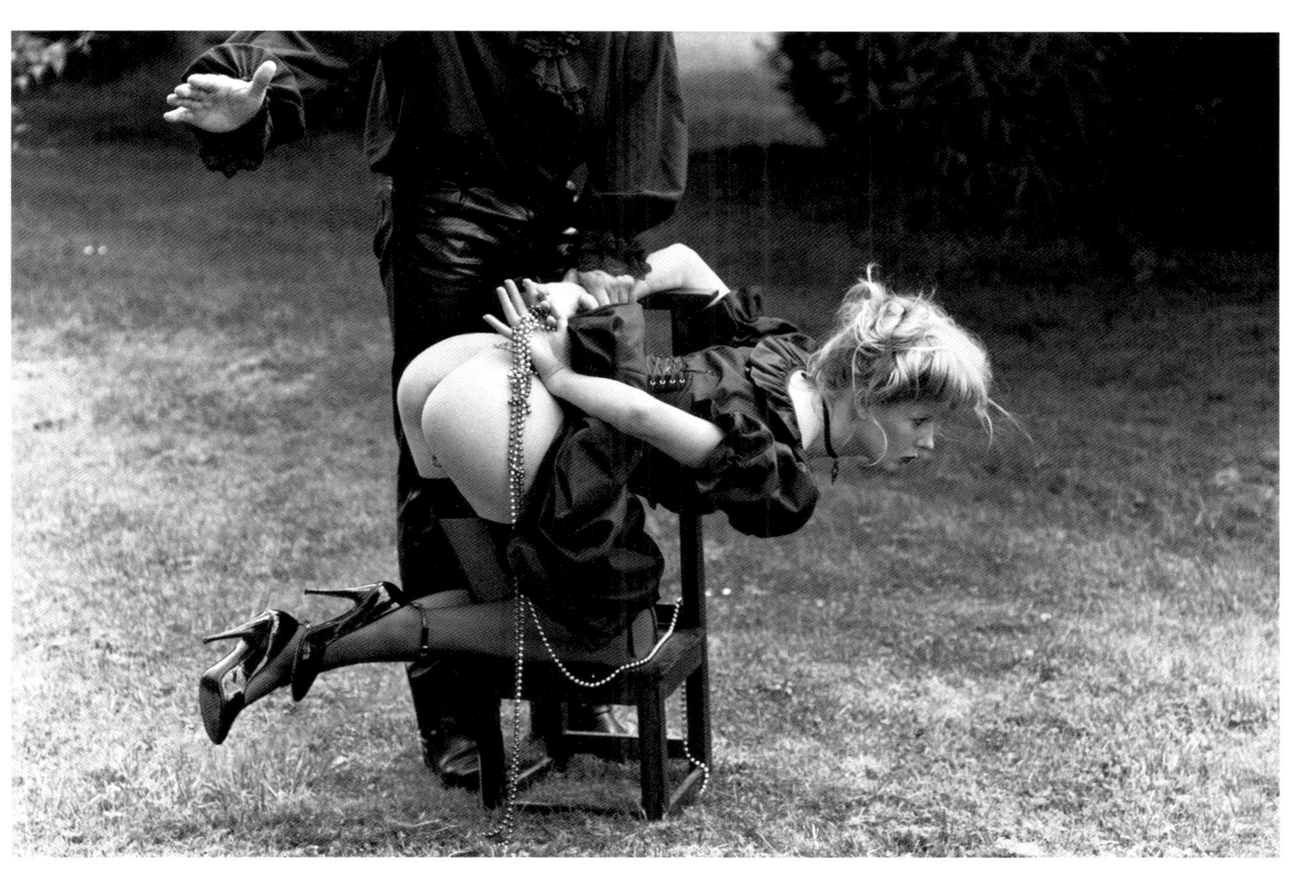

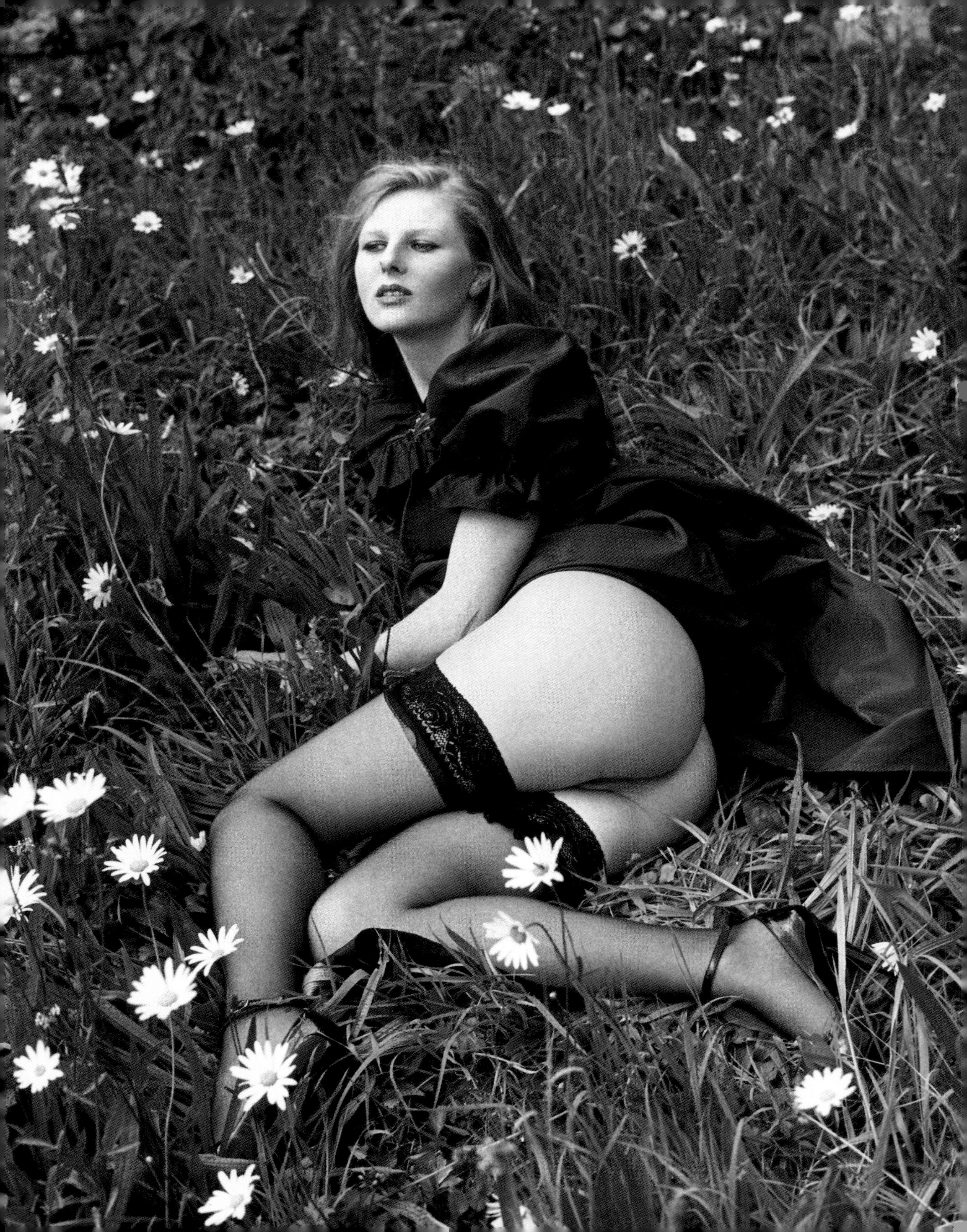

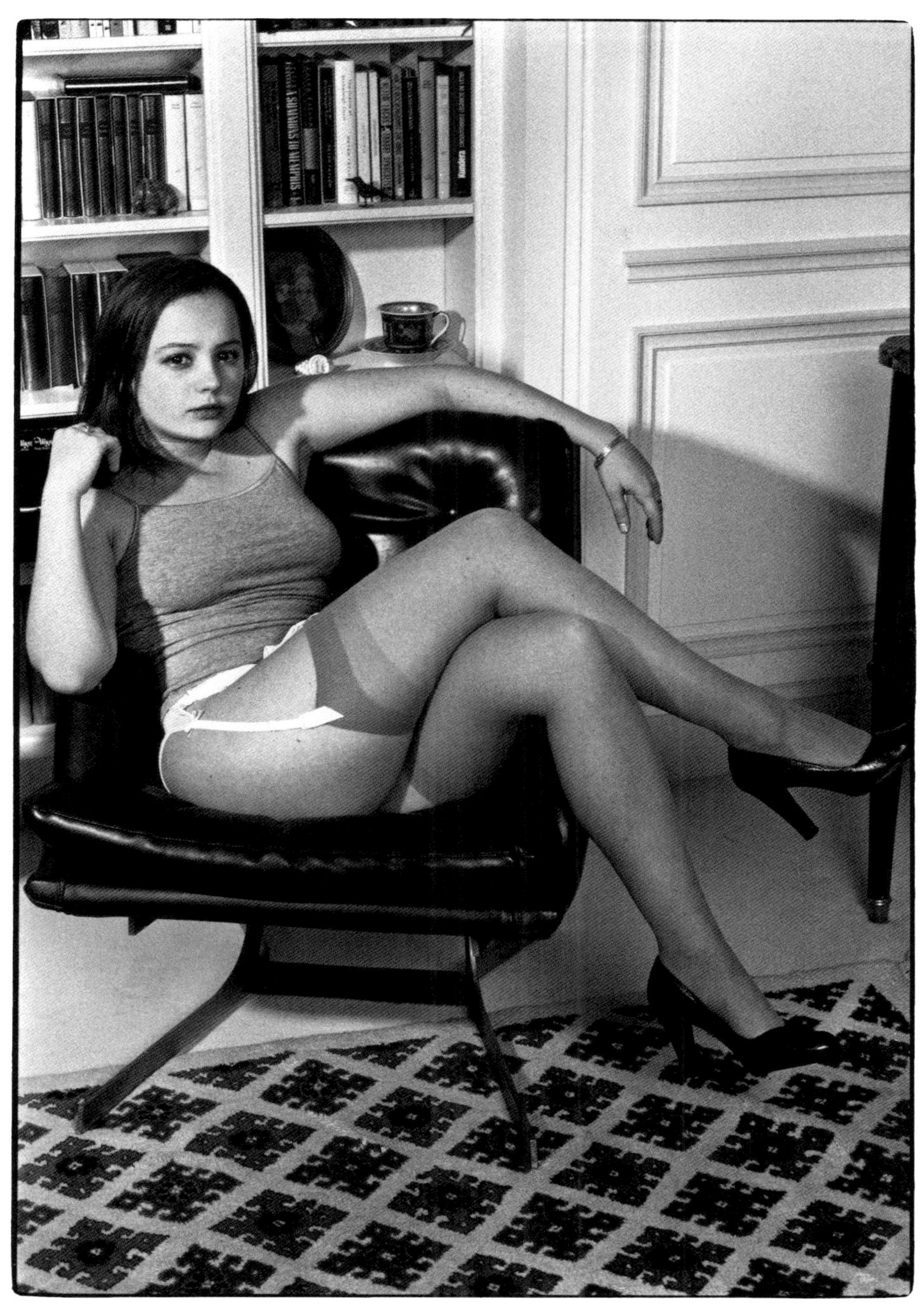

Daniela 1999   147

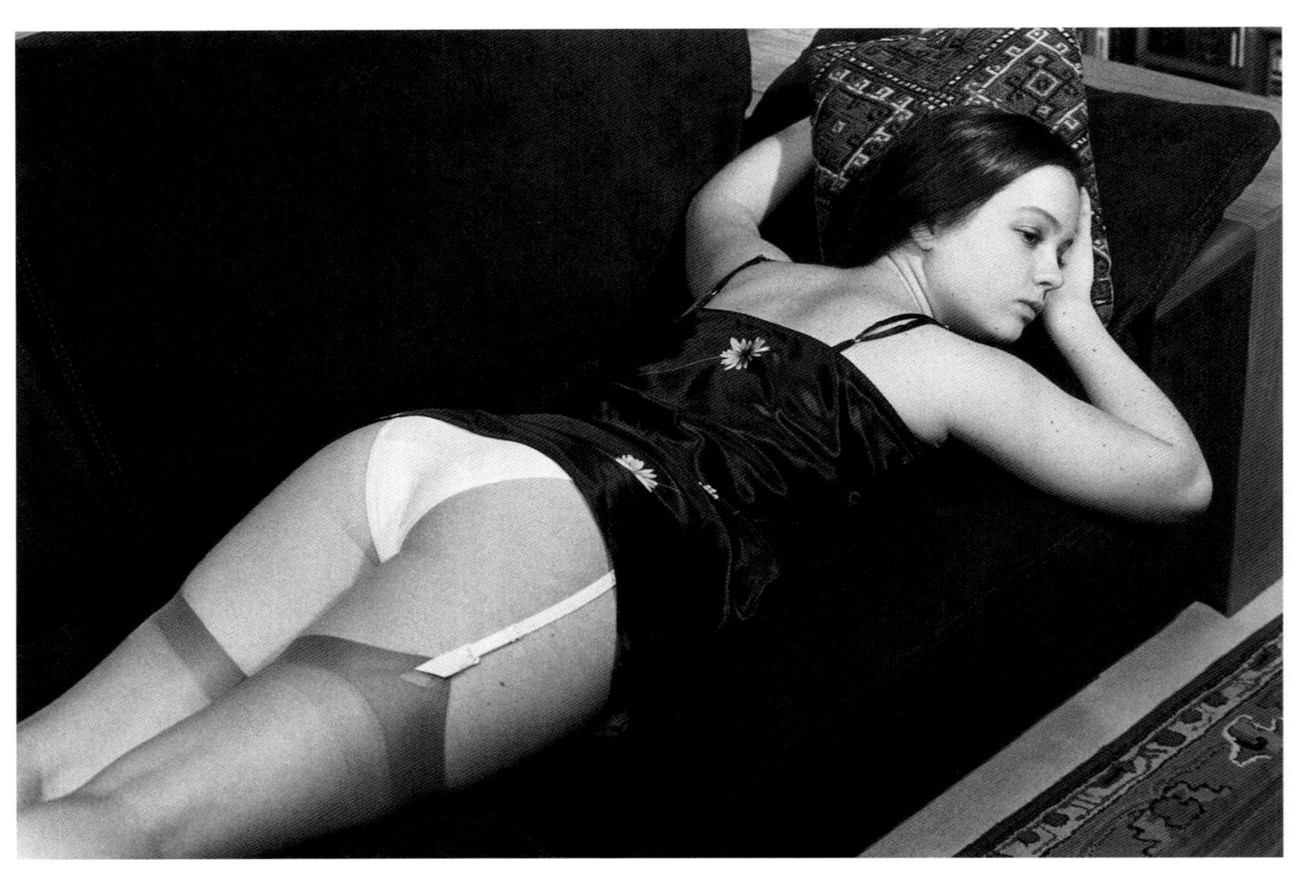

148   Daniela 1999

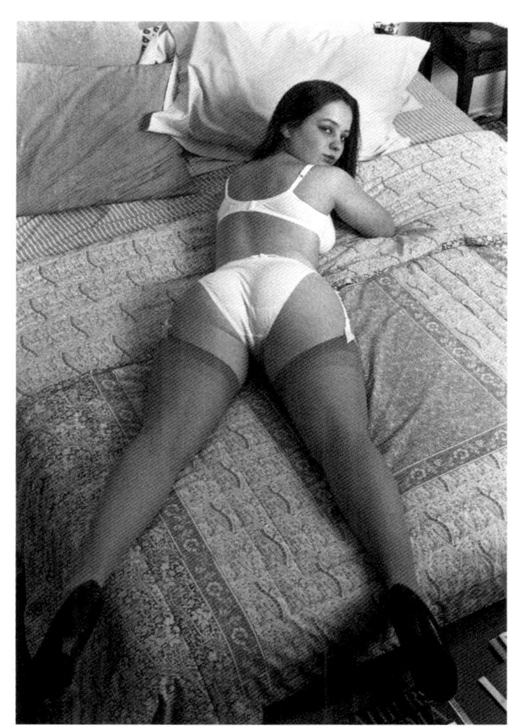

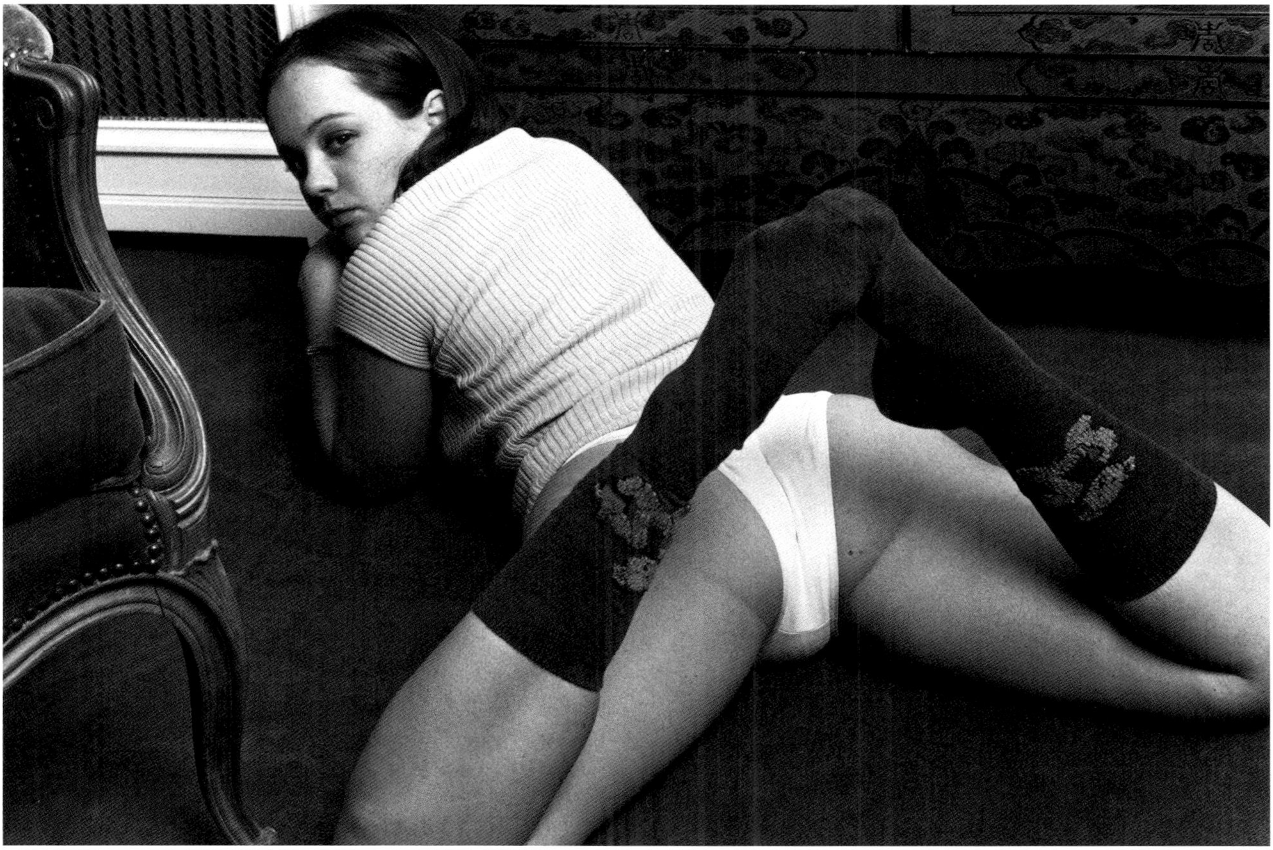

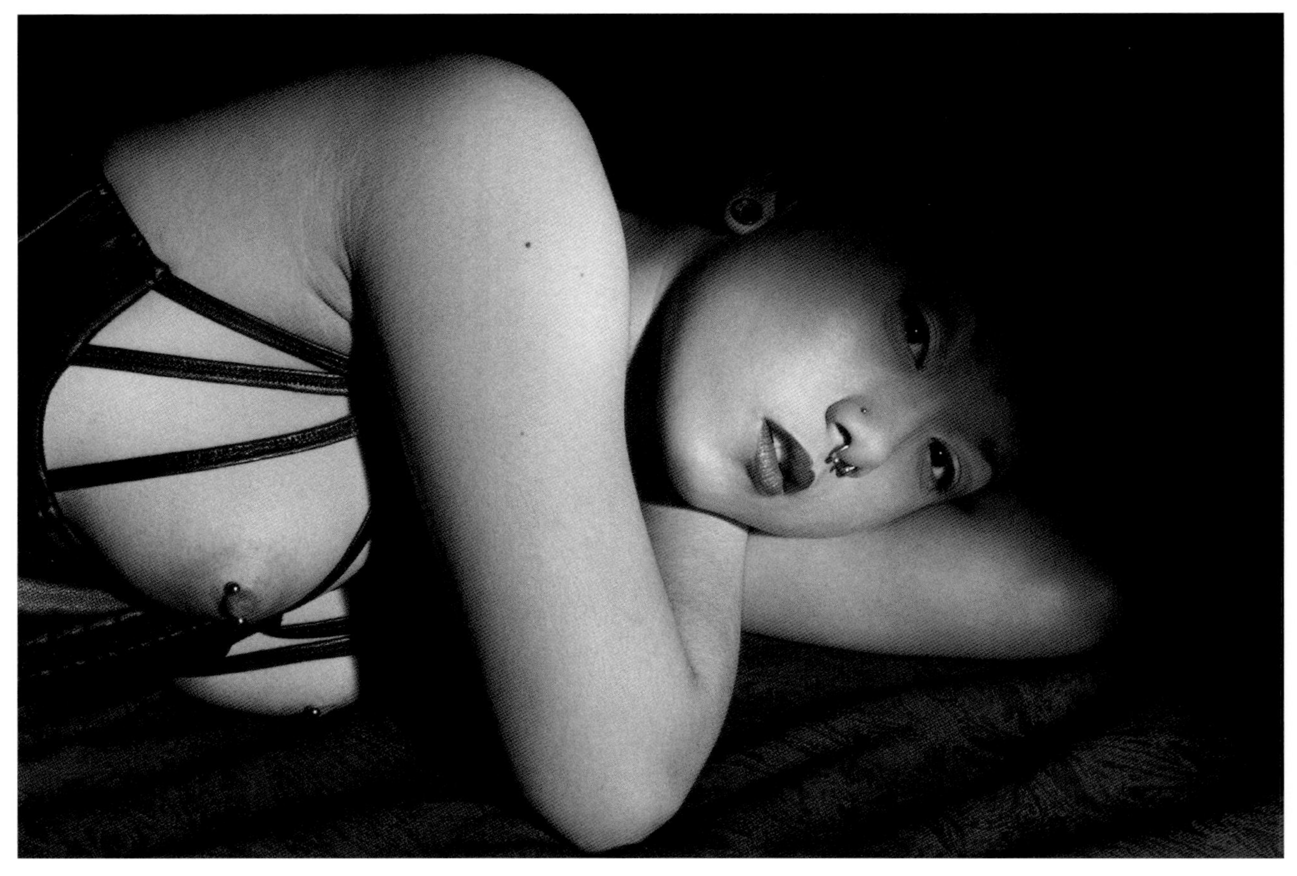

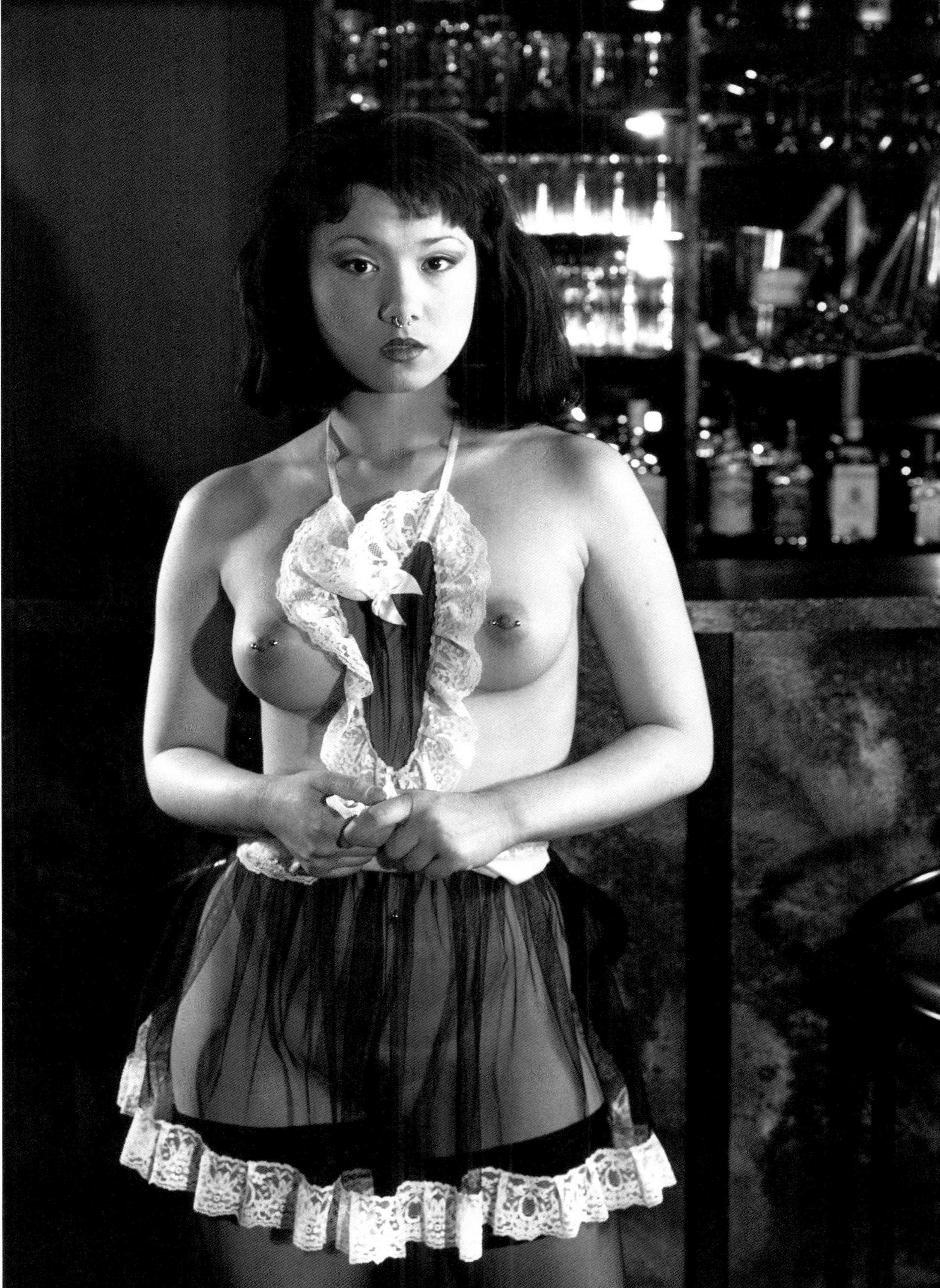

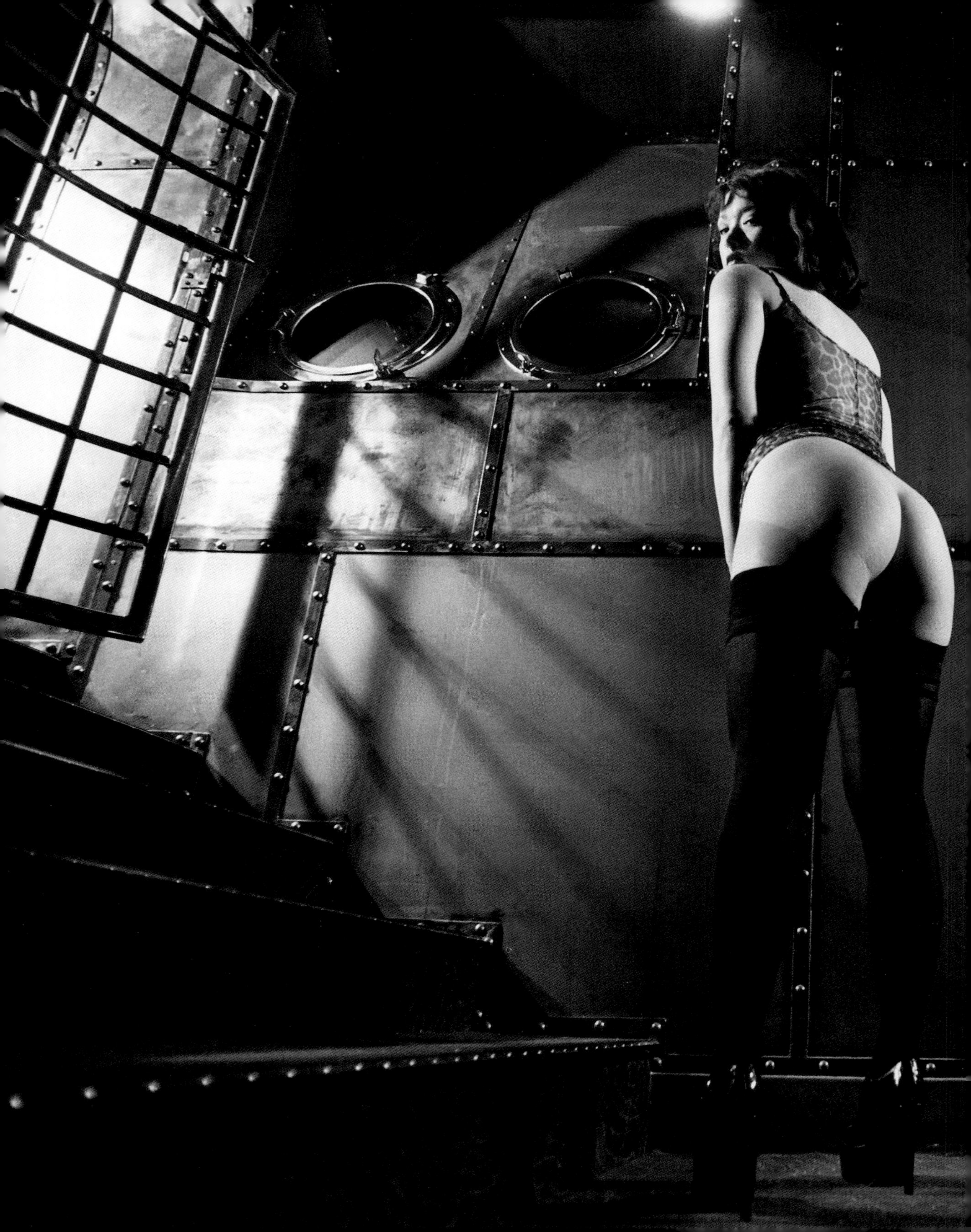

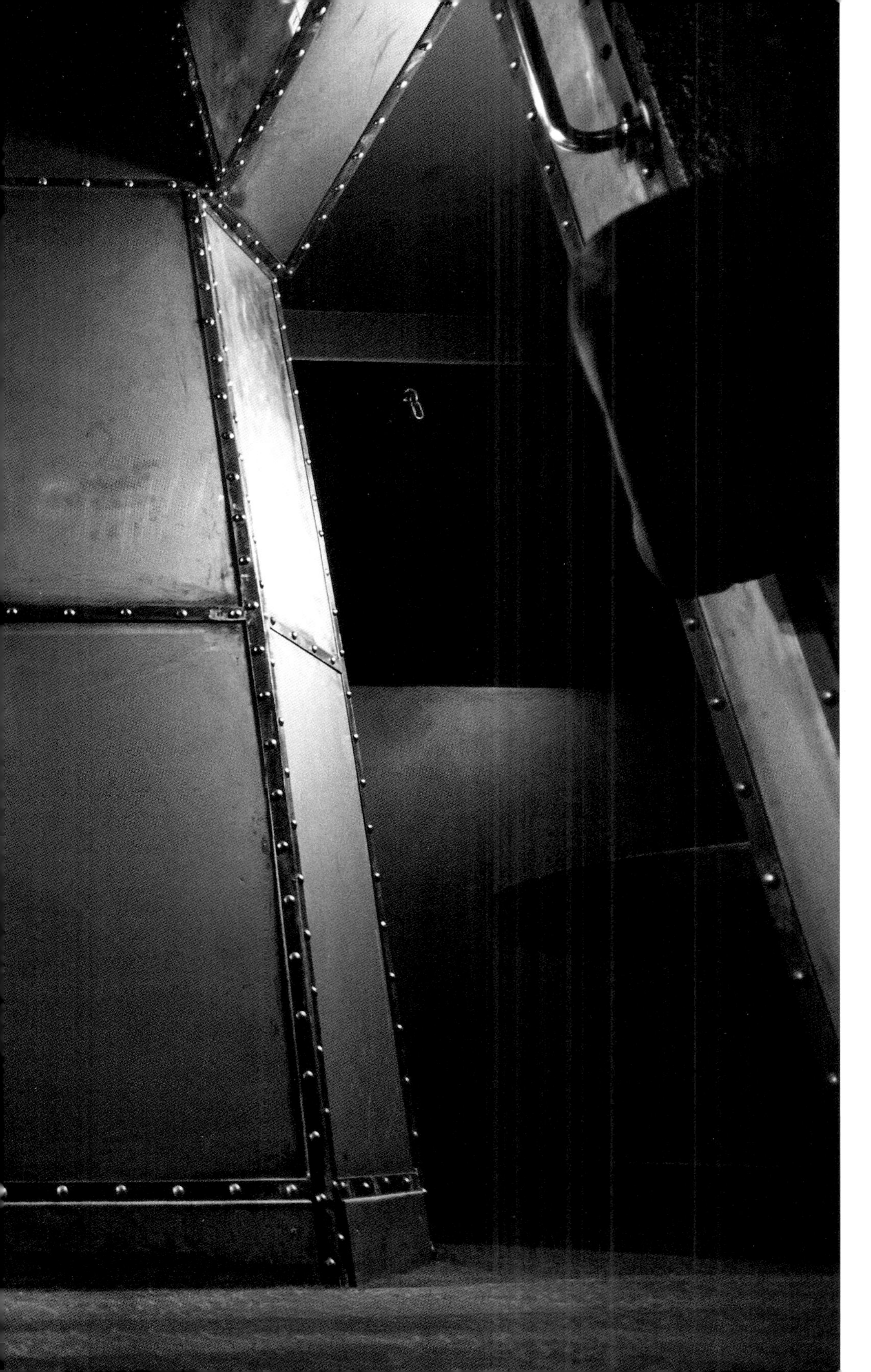

Sakura
1999   153

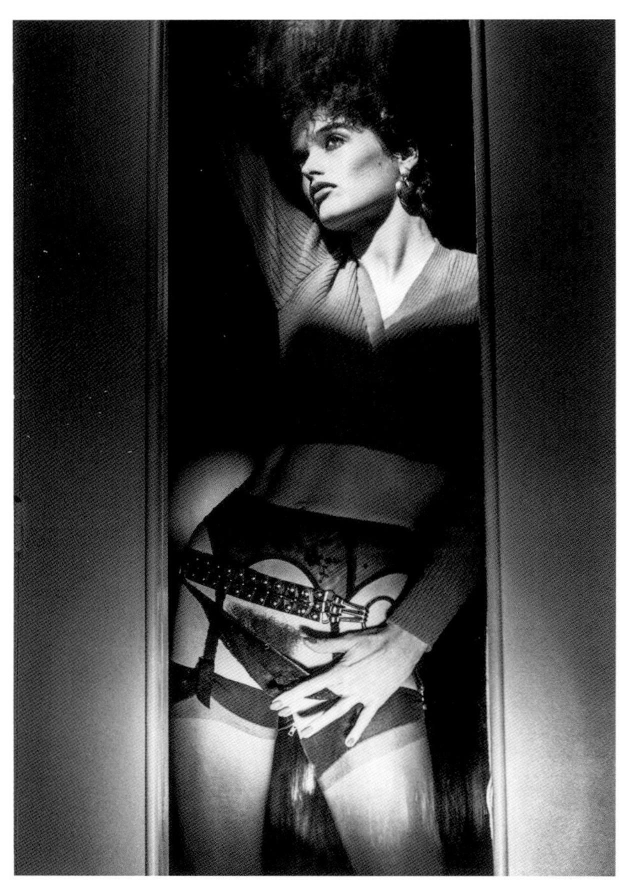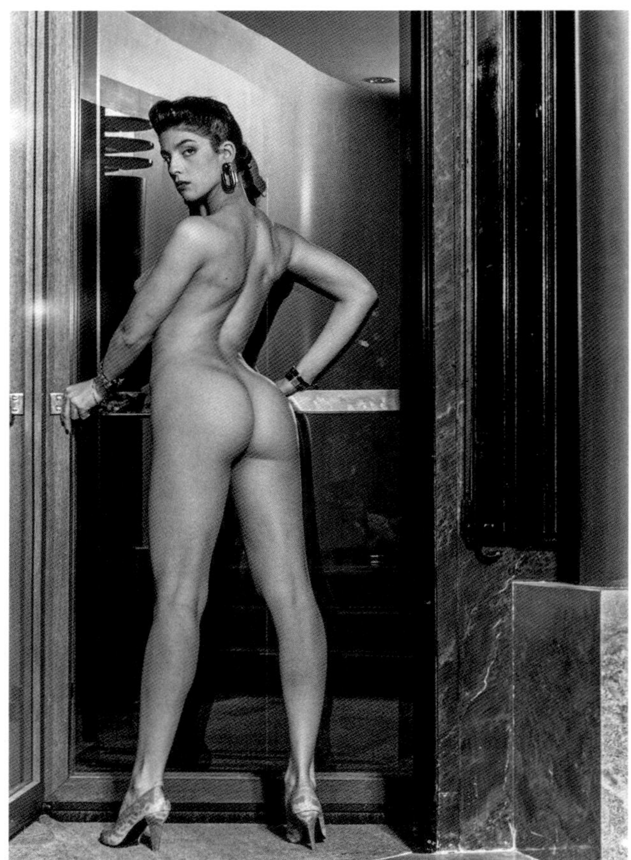

   Raphaëlle 1984   Coryne 1988   Pascale 1981 →

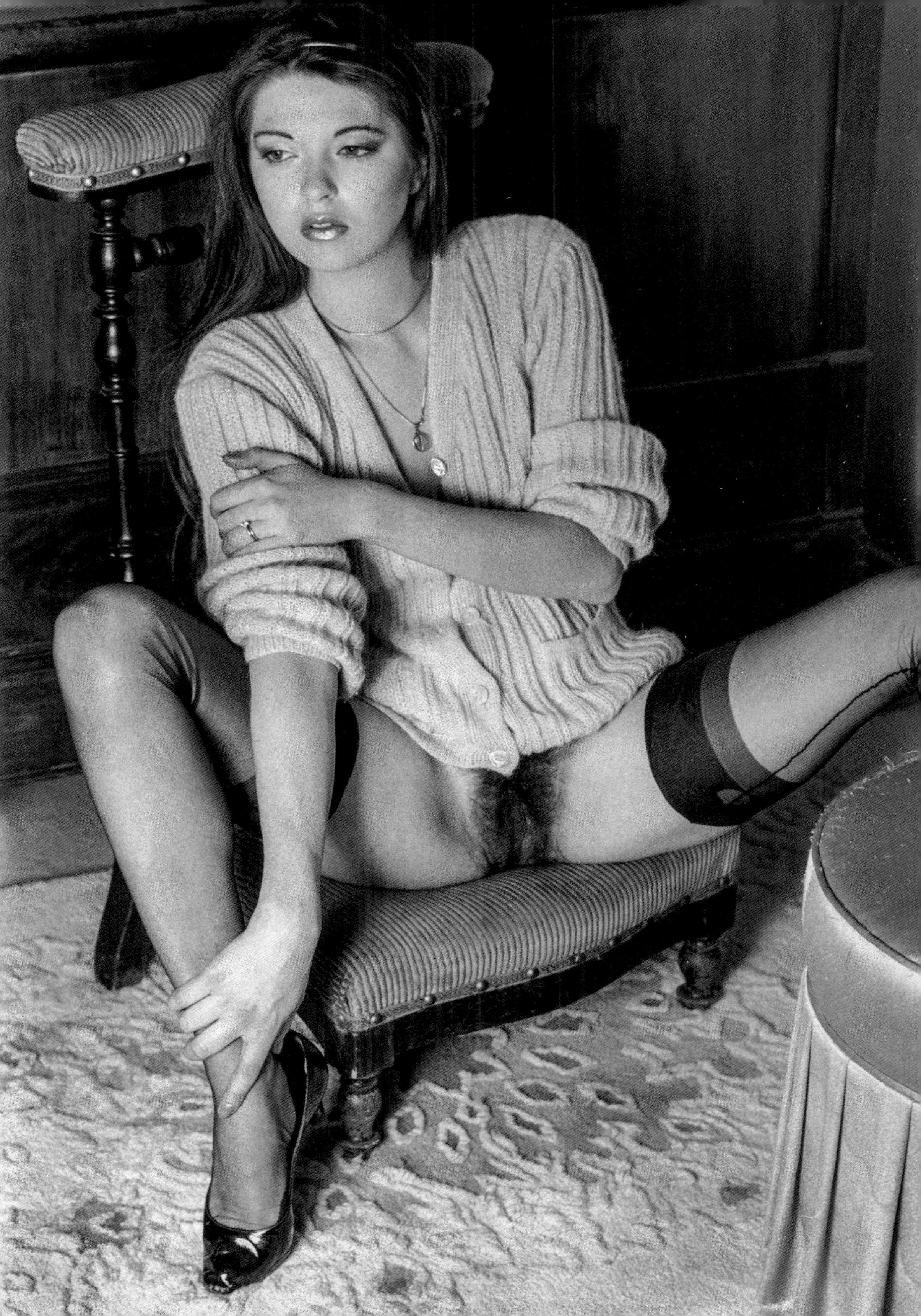

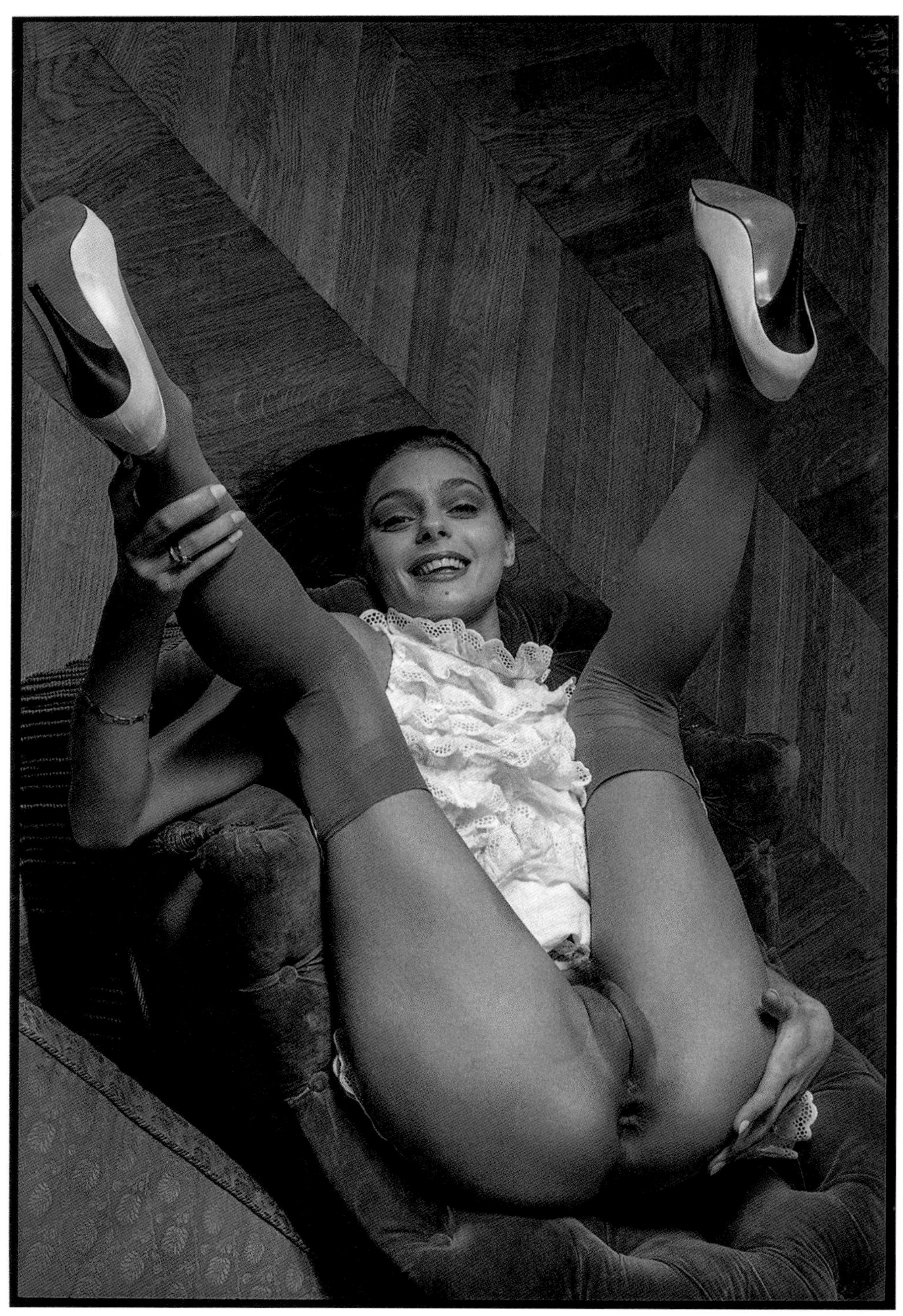

156   Zara 1995

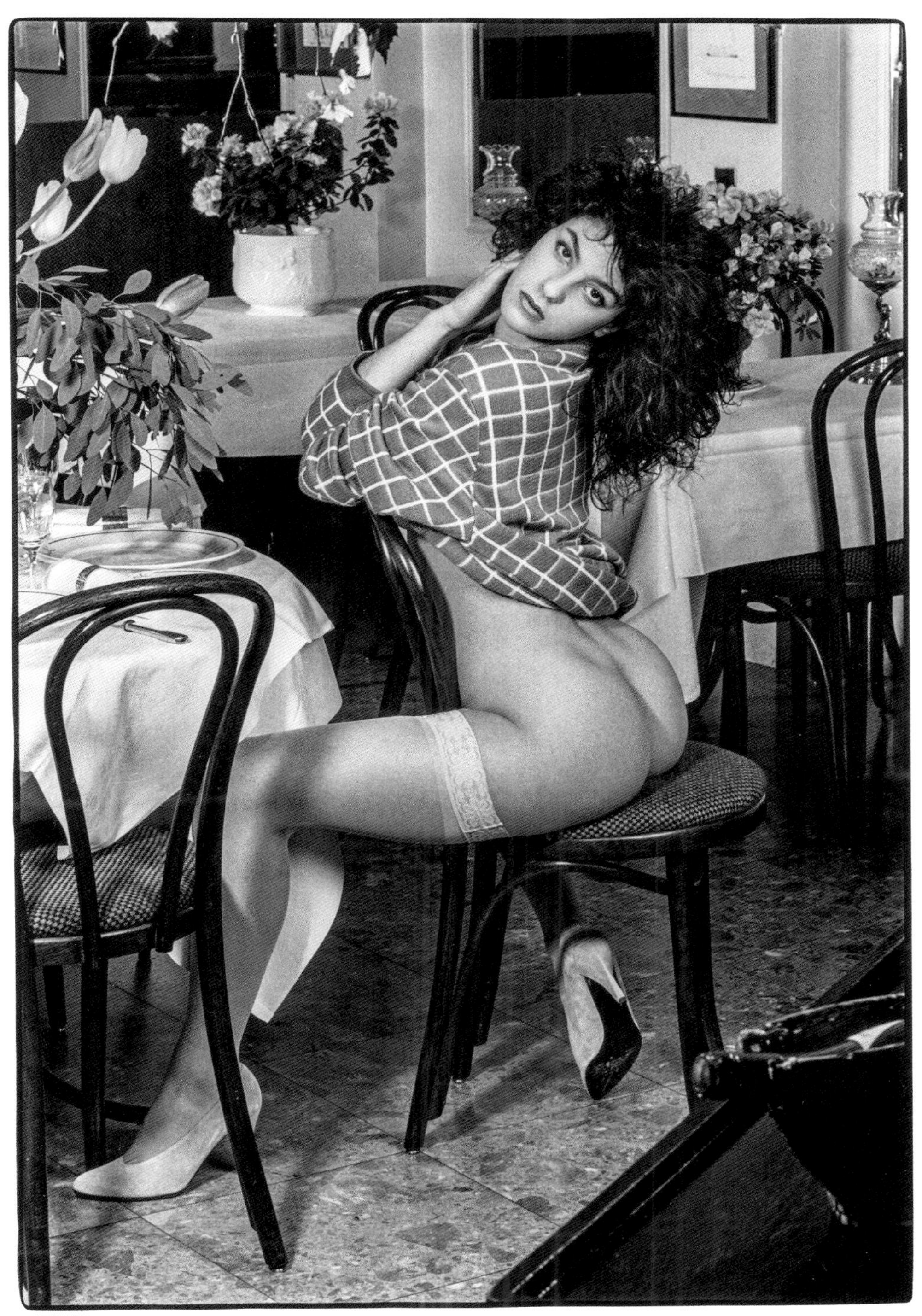

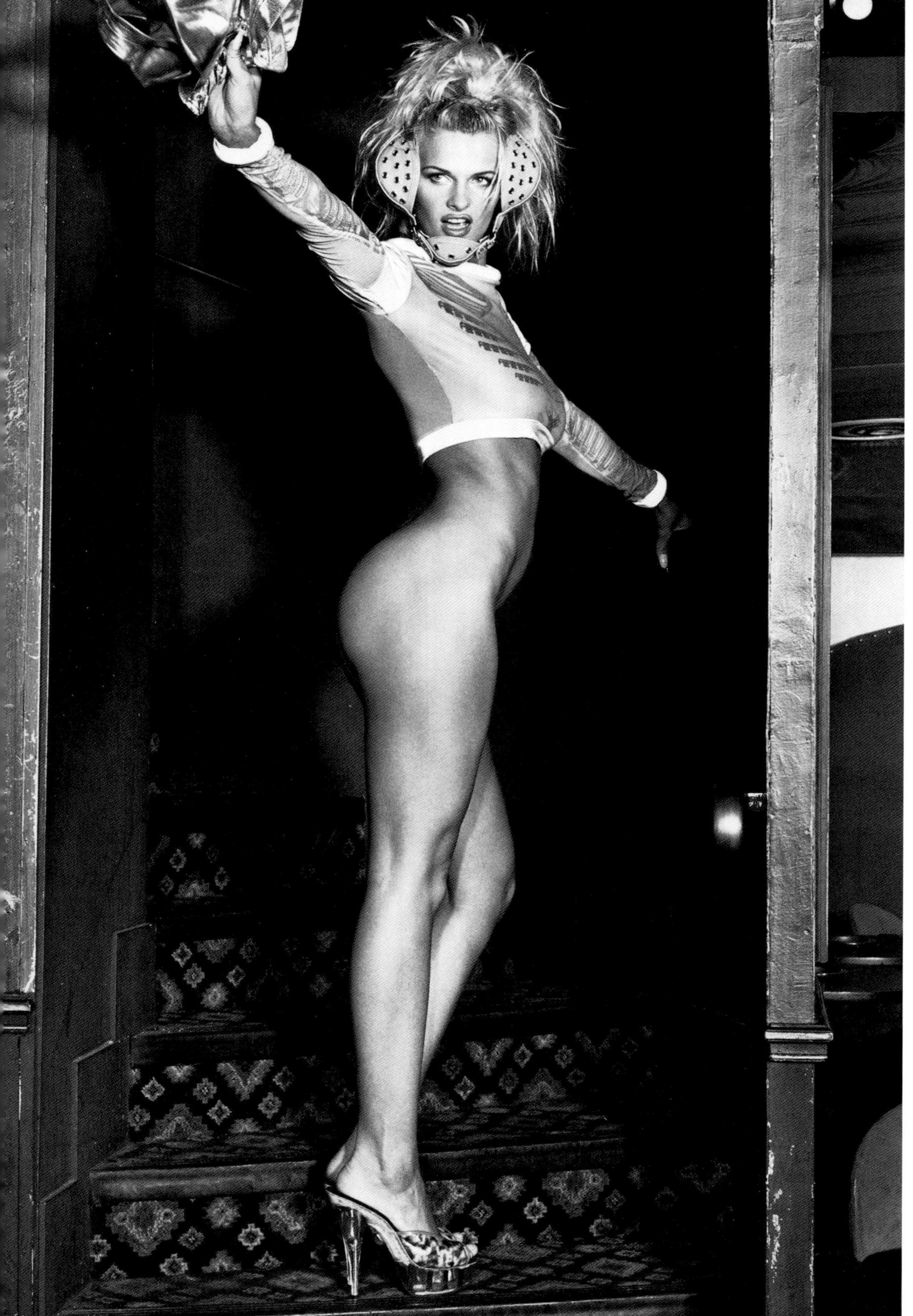

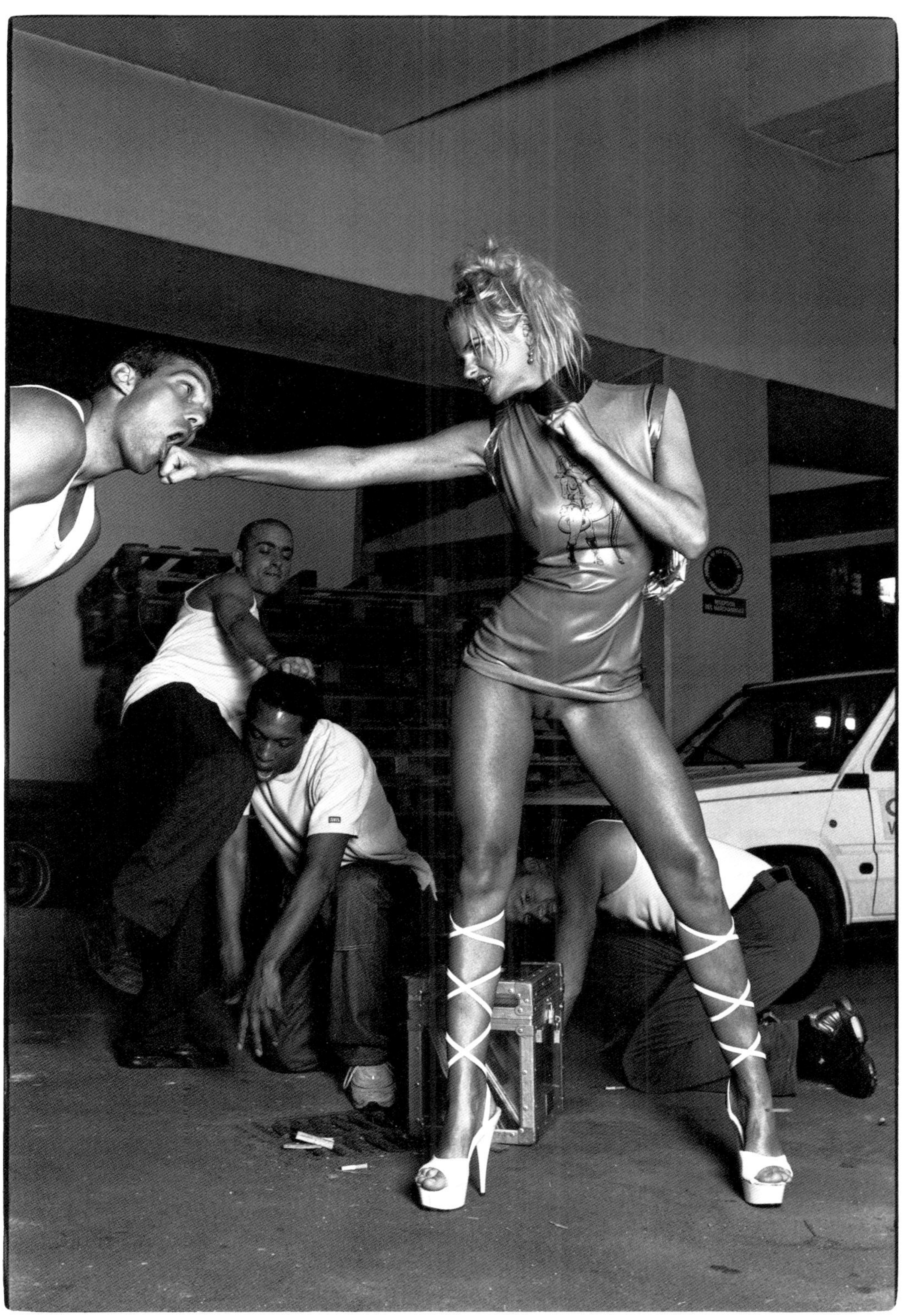

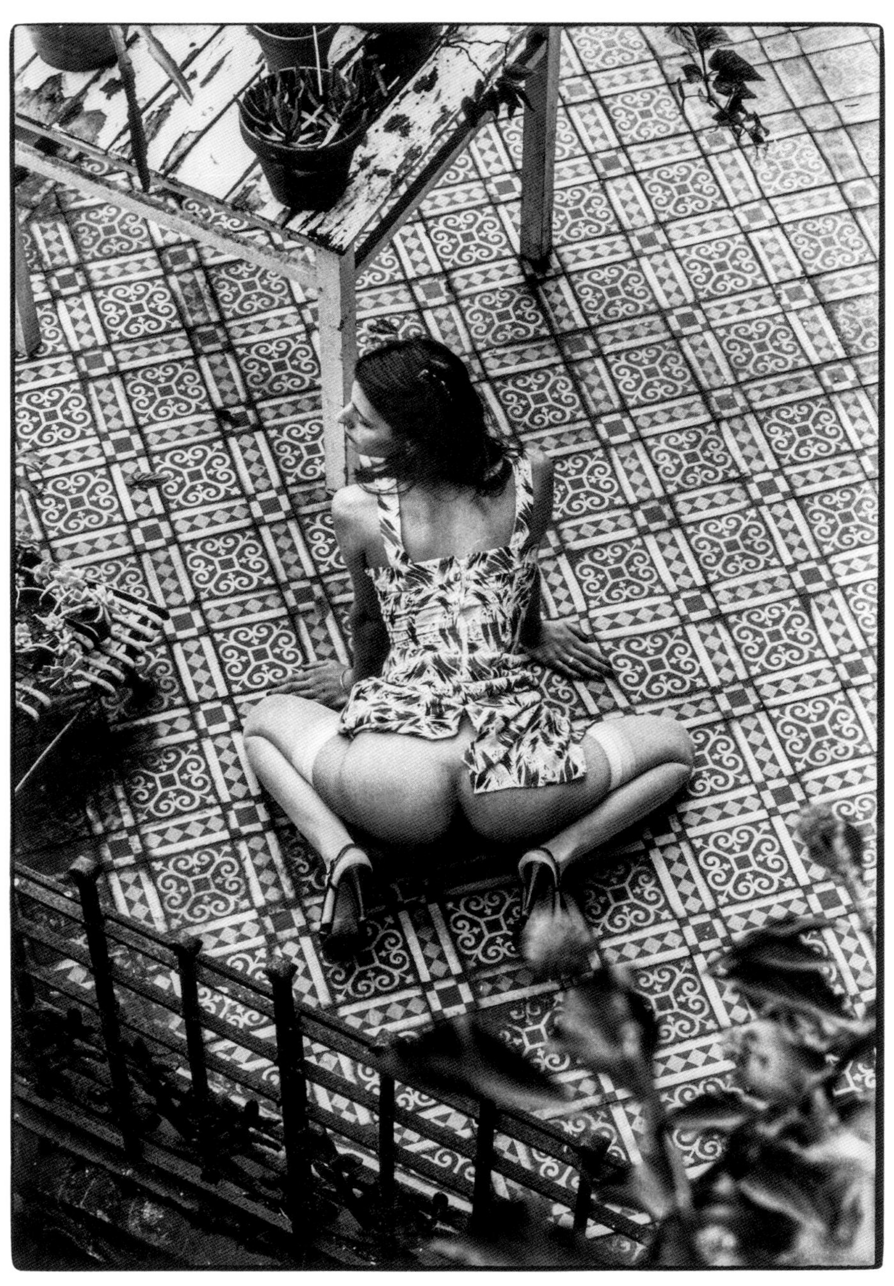

Violaine & Sakura 1999 →

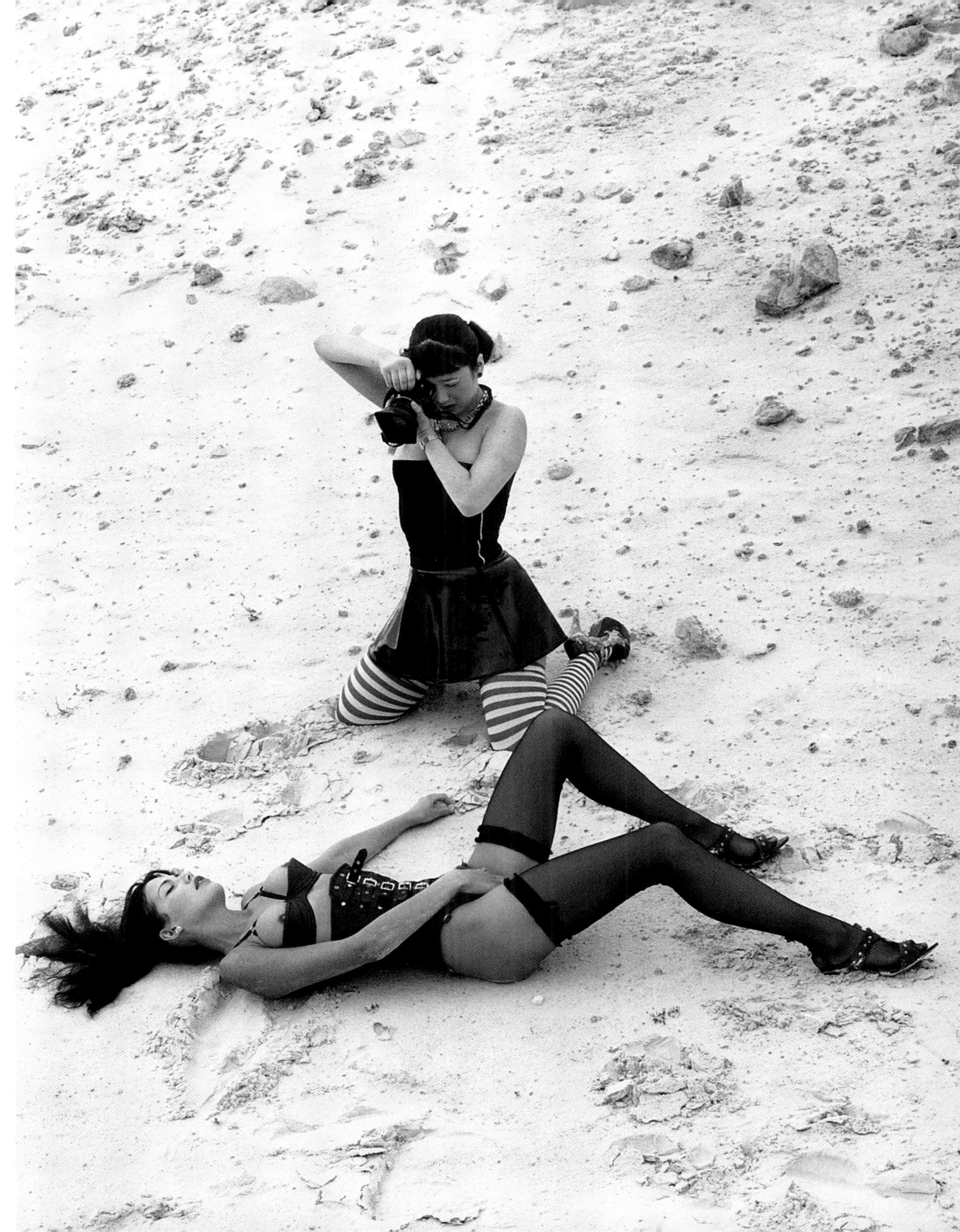

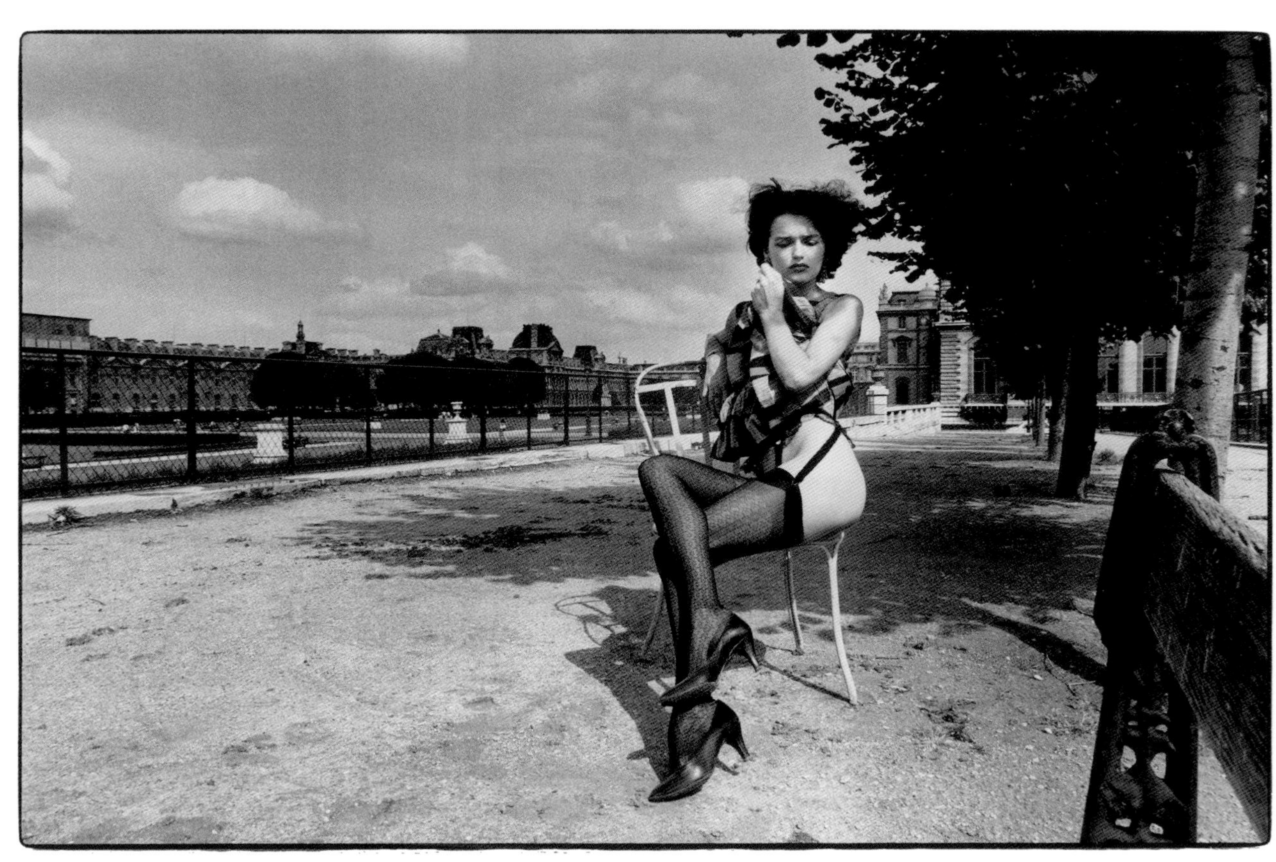

162   Raphaëlle 1982

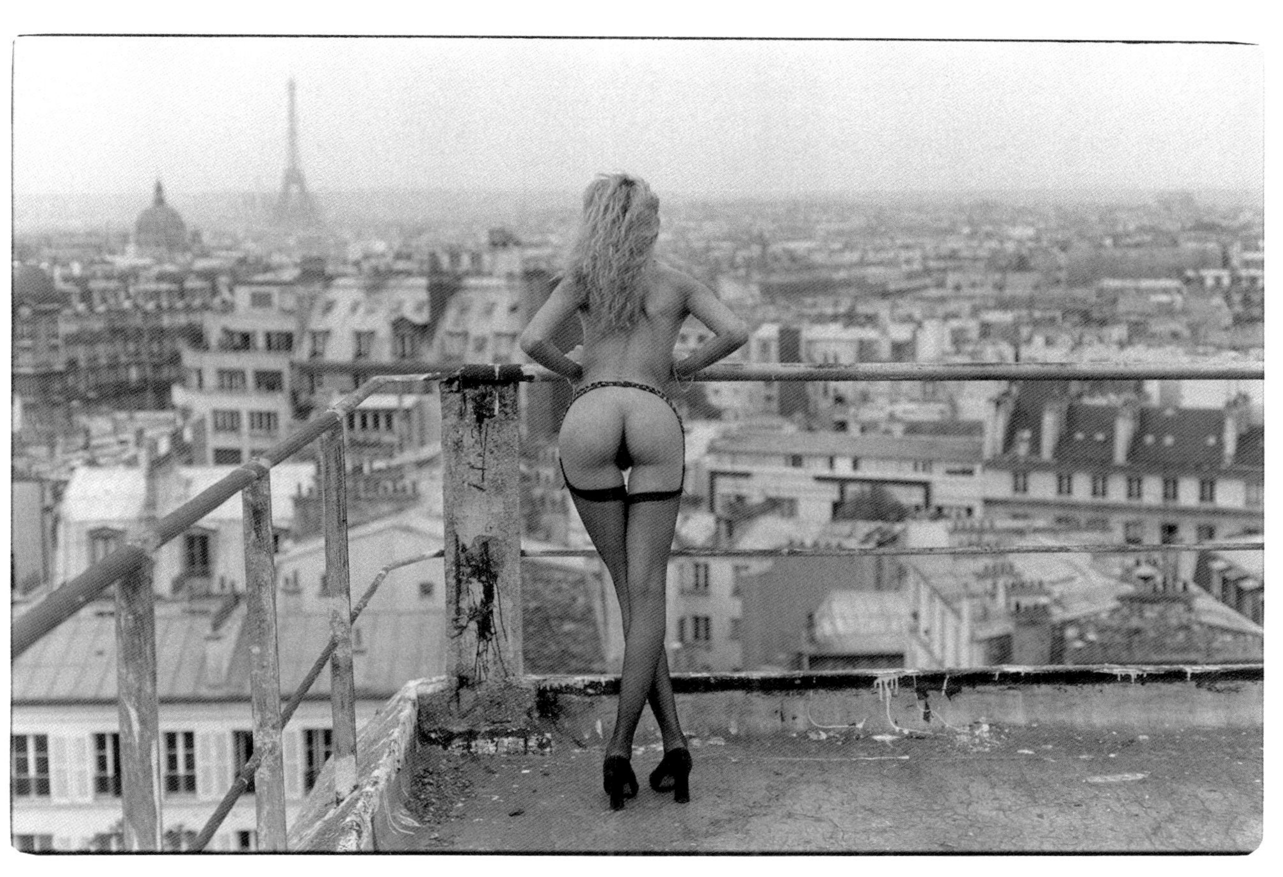

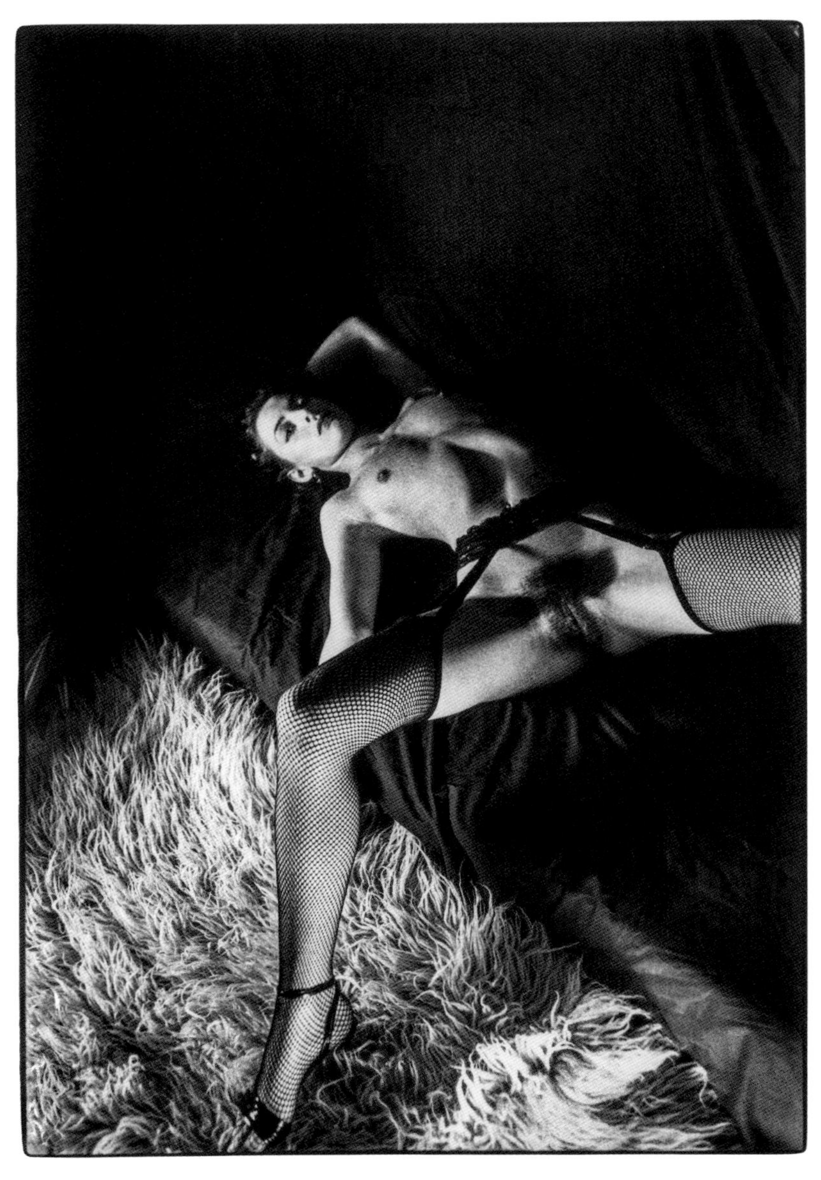

Raphaëlle 1983 →

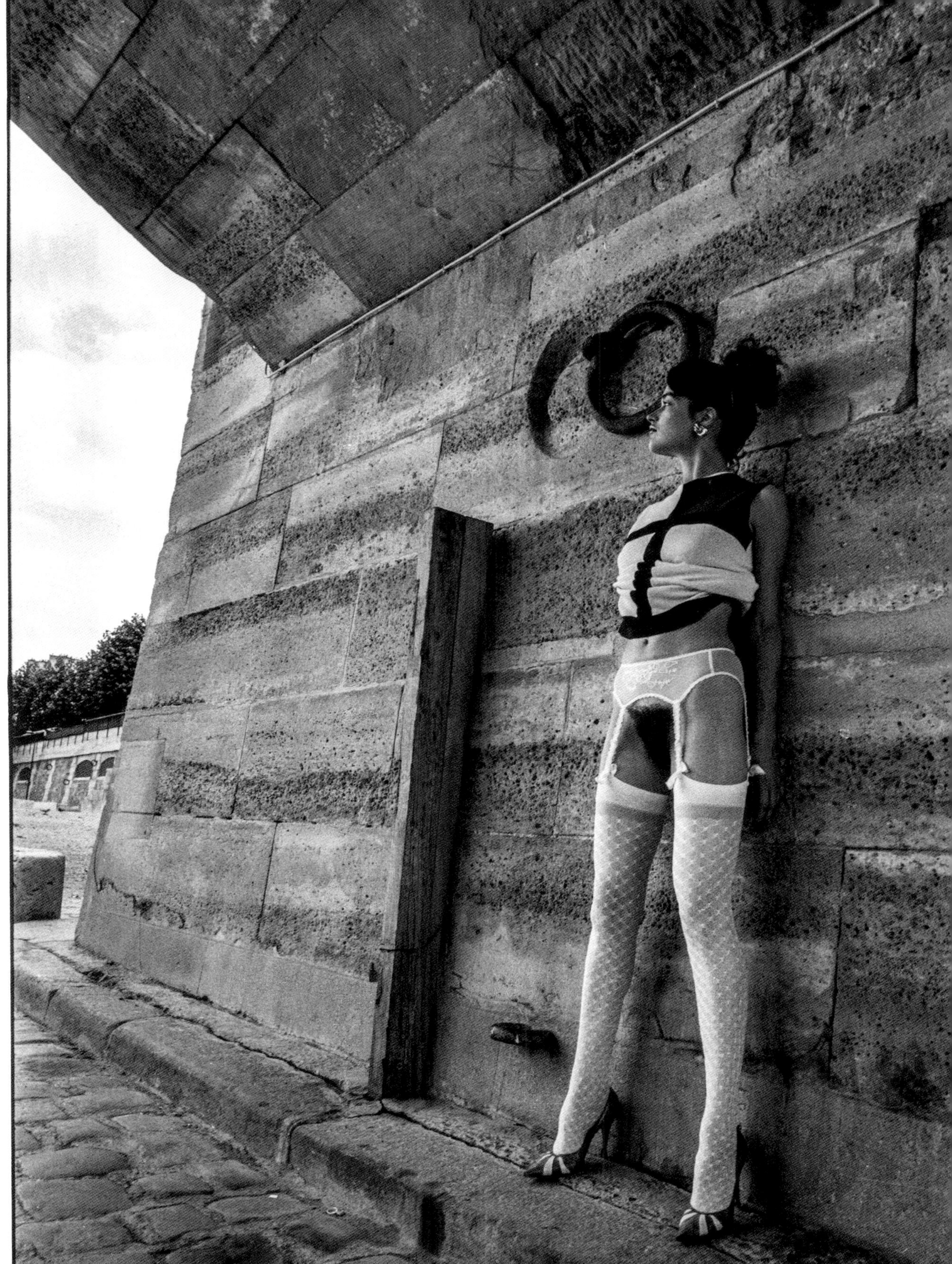

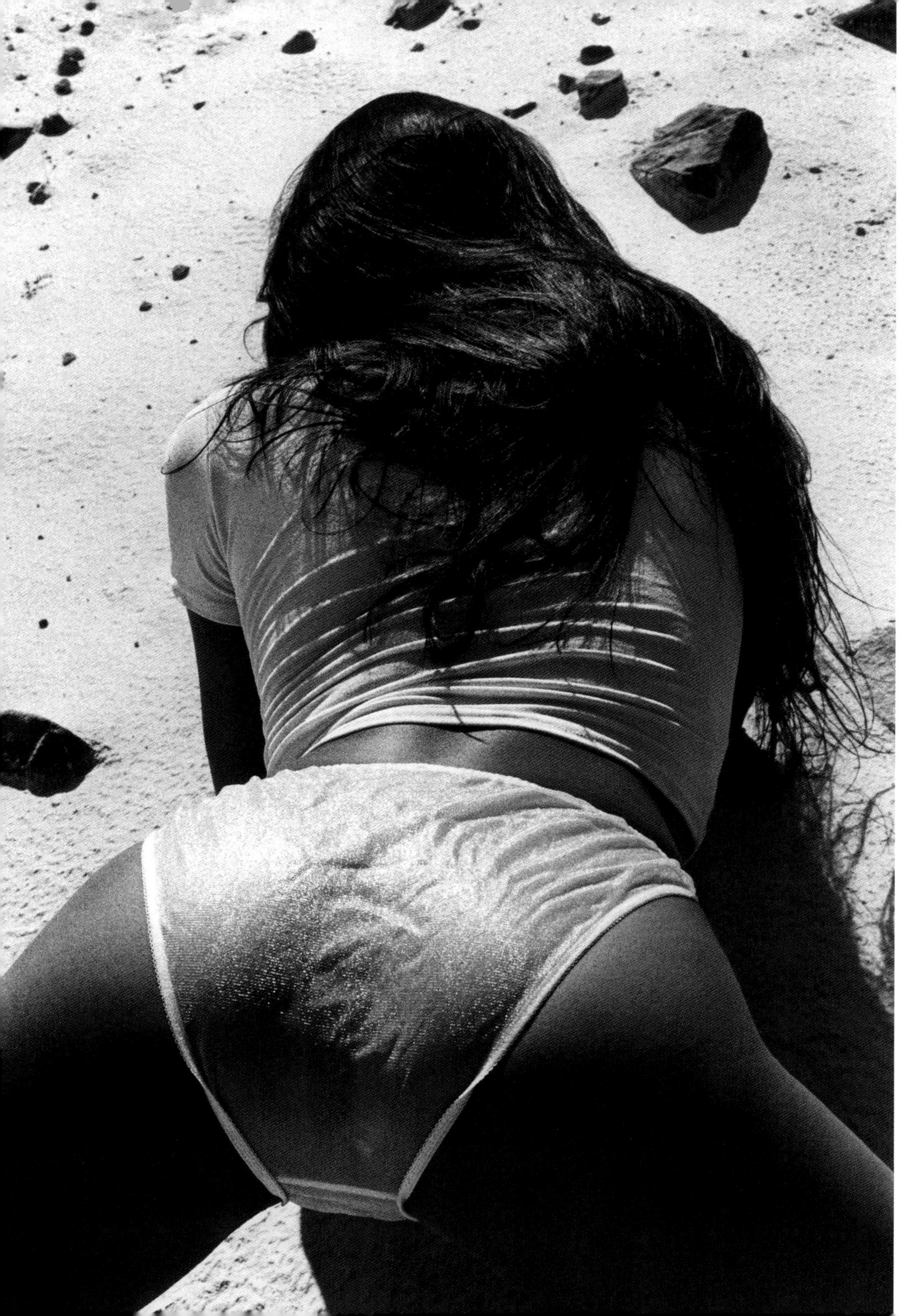

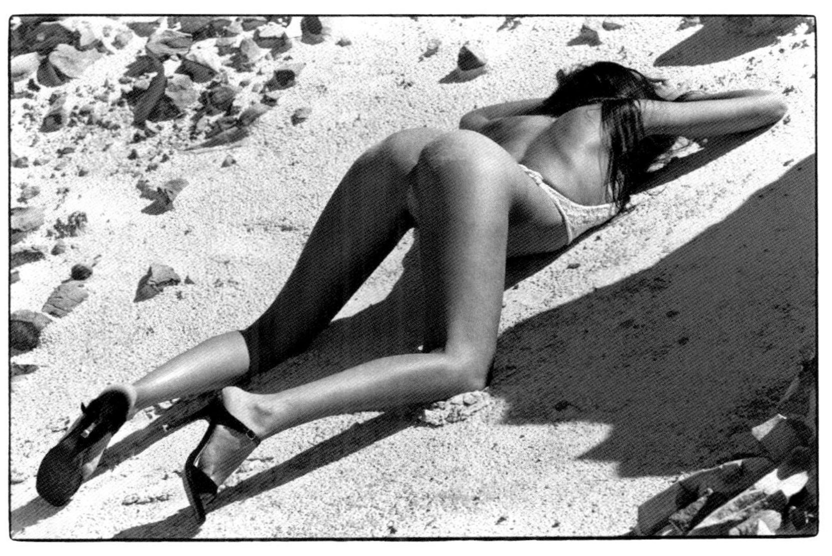

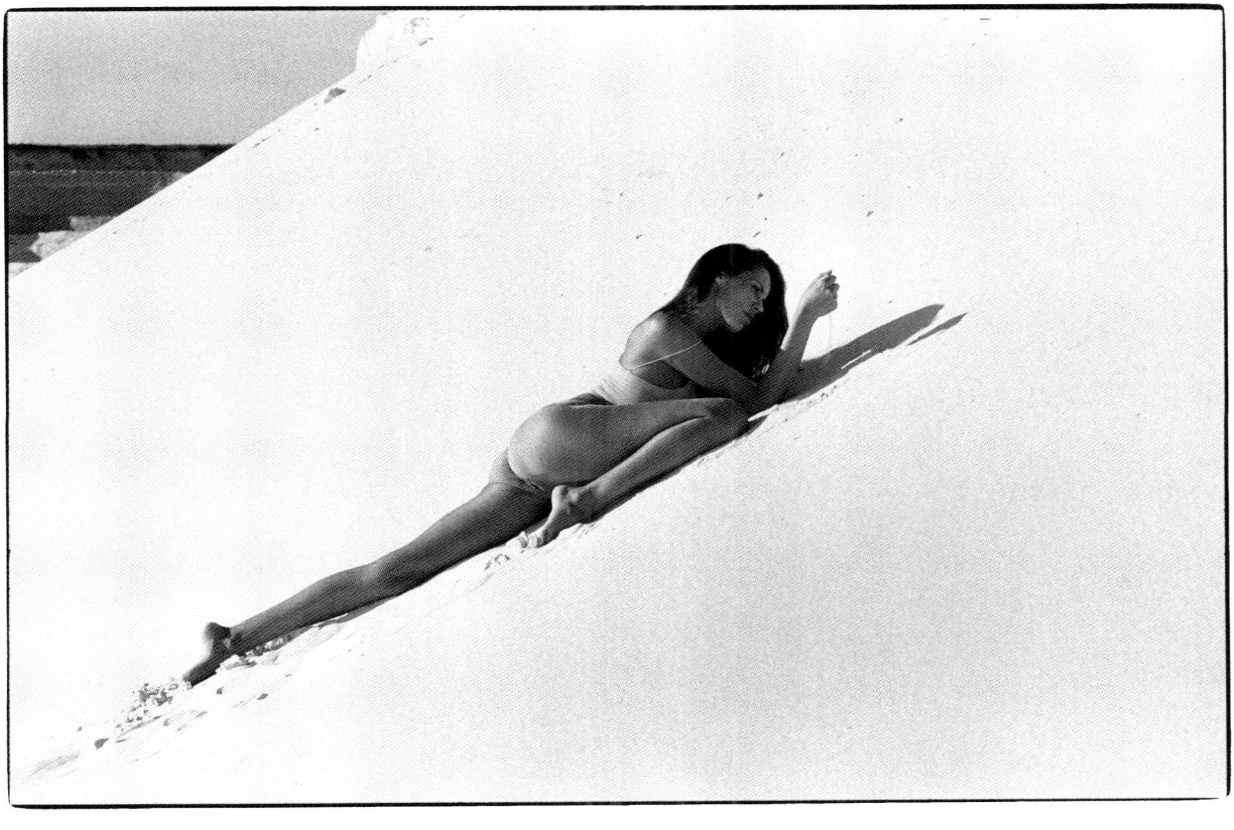

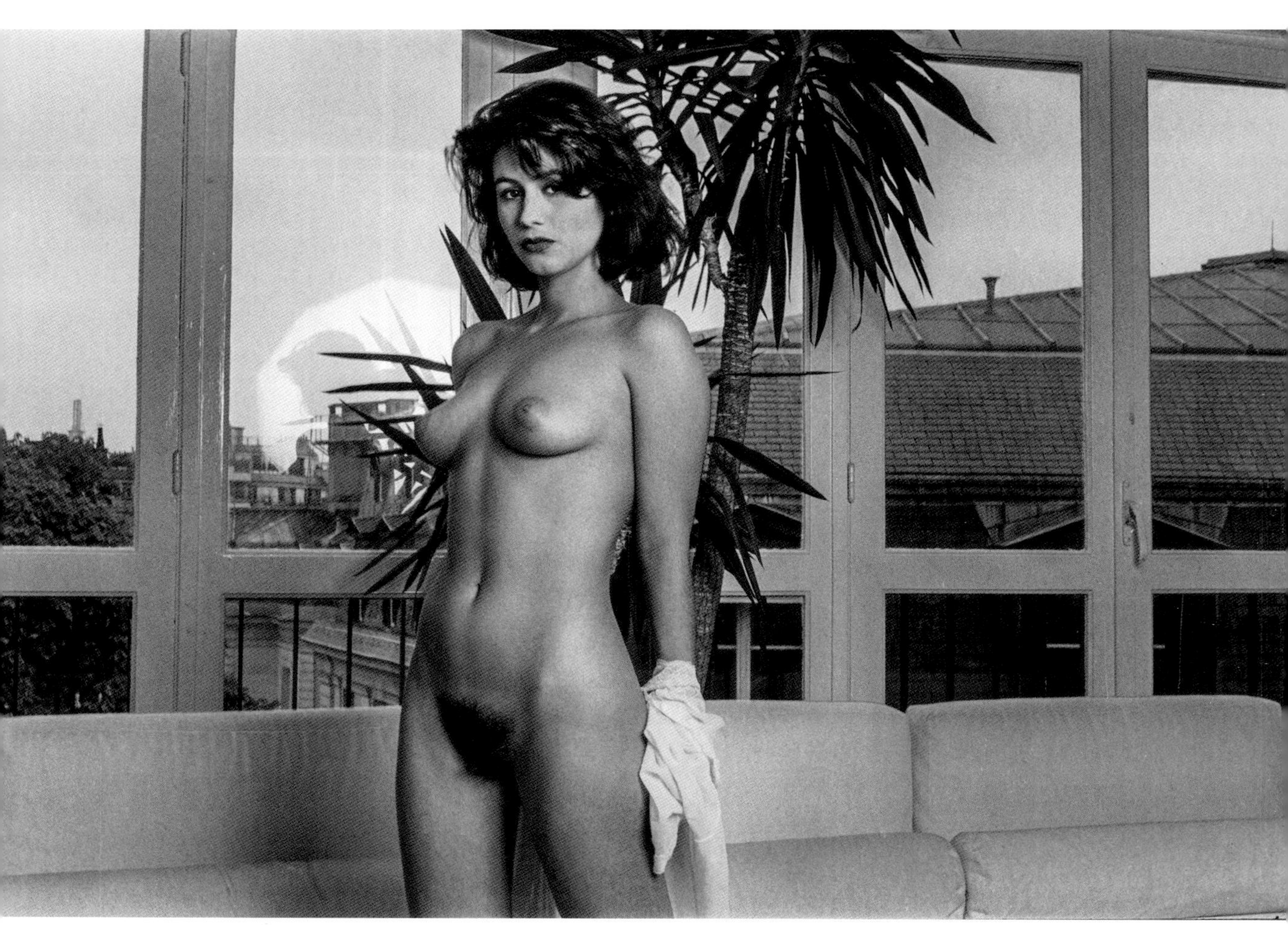

168 Toni 1985

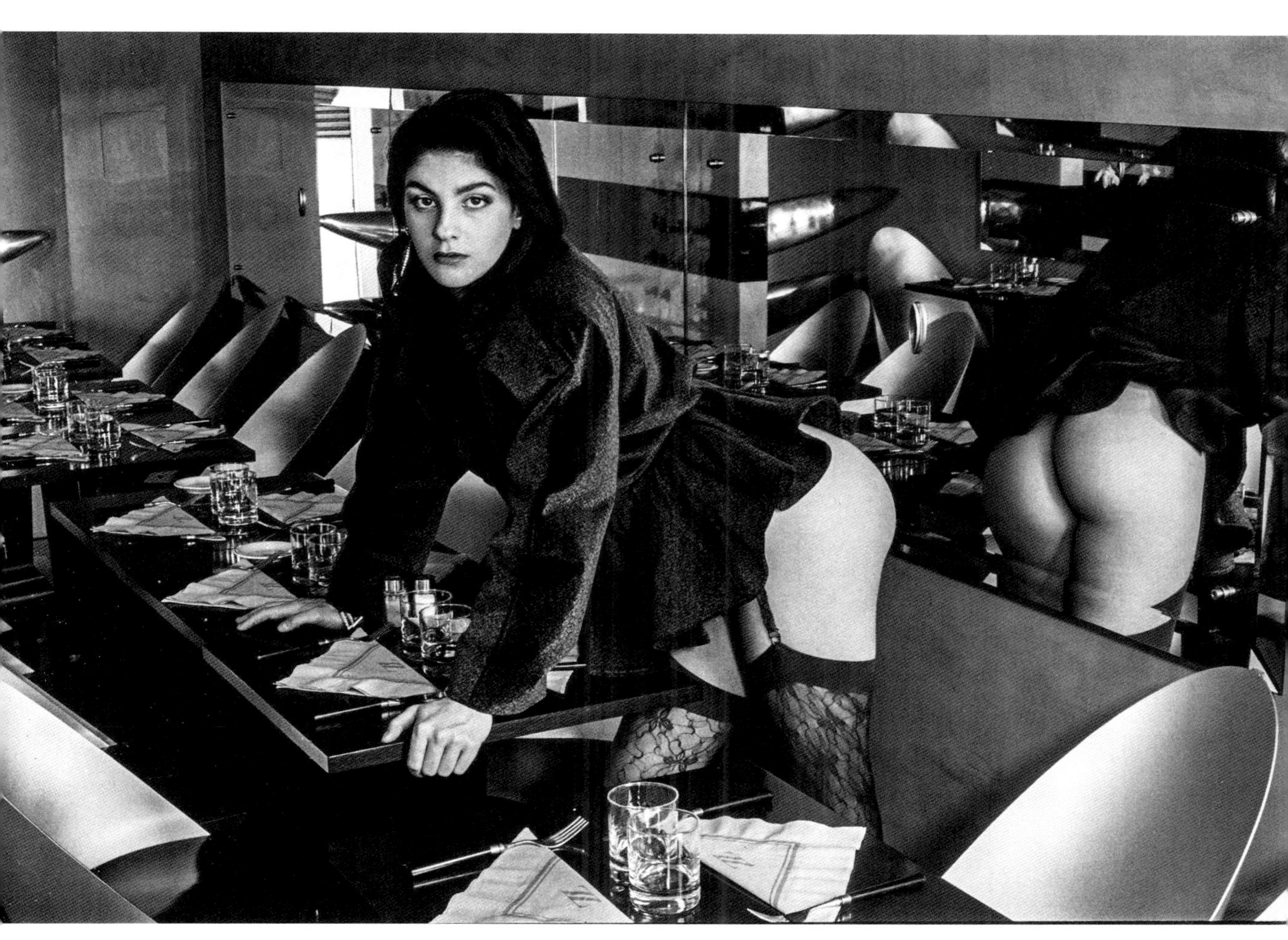

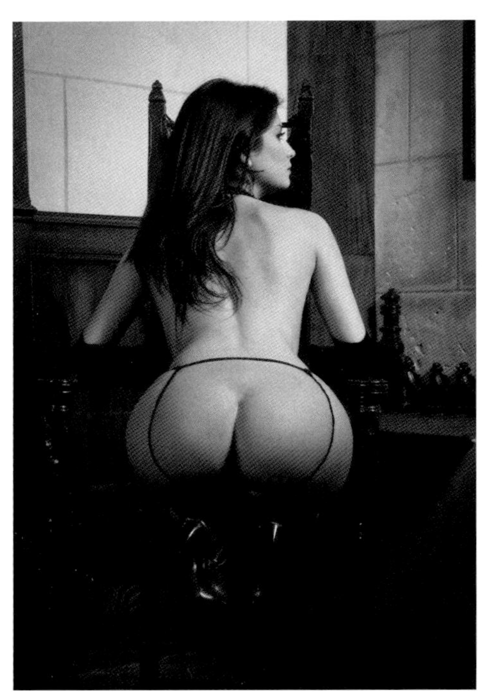

Amandine 2005

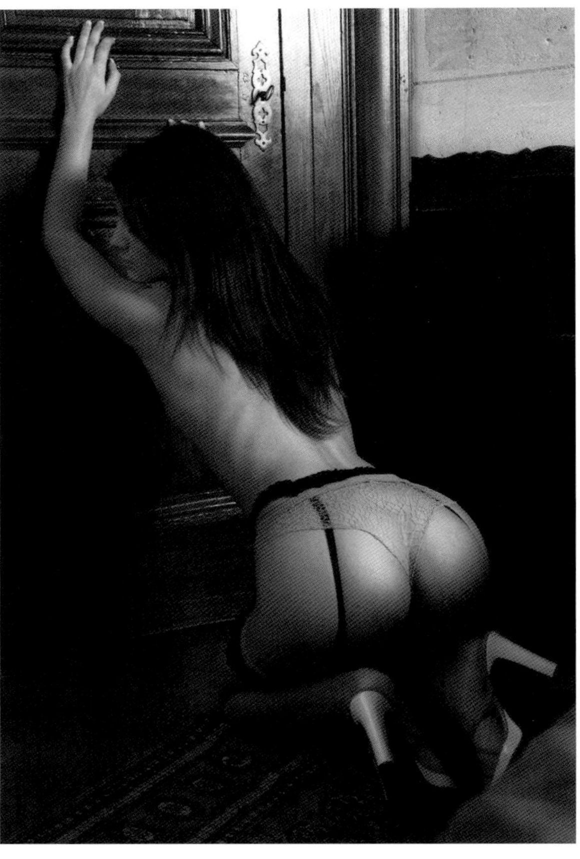

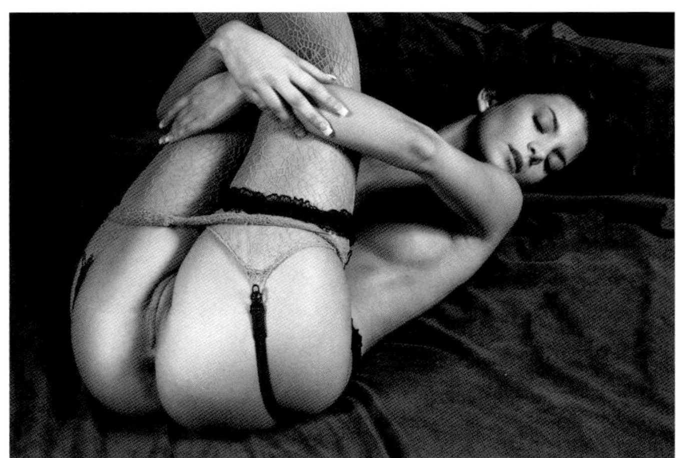

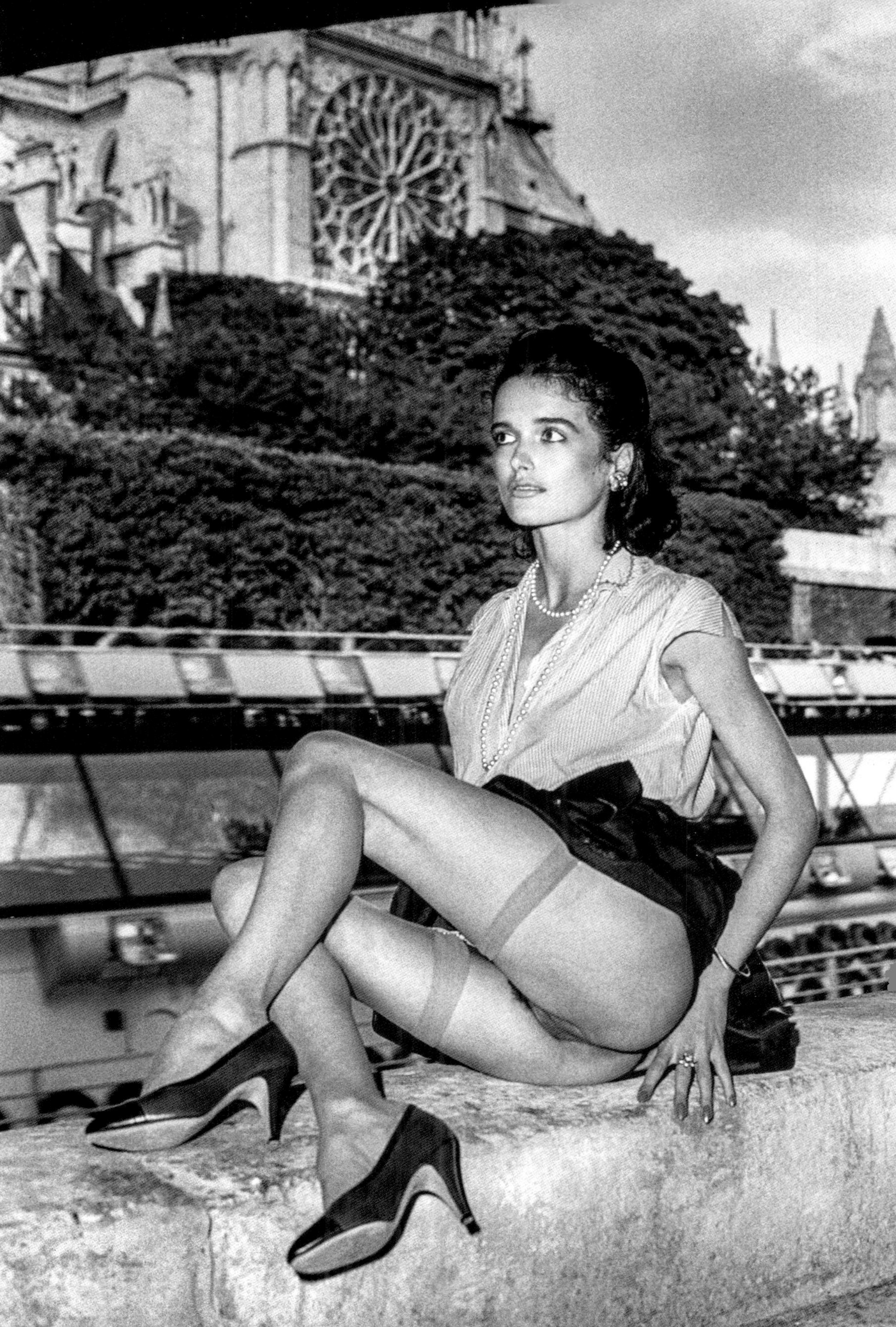

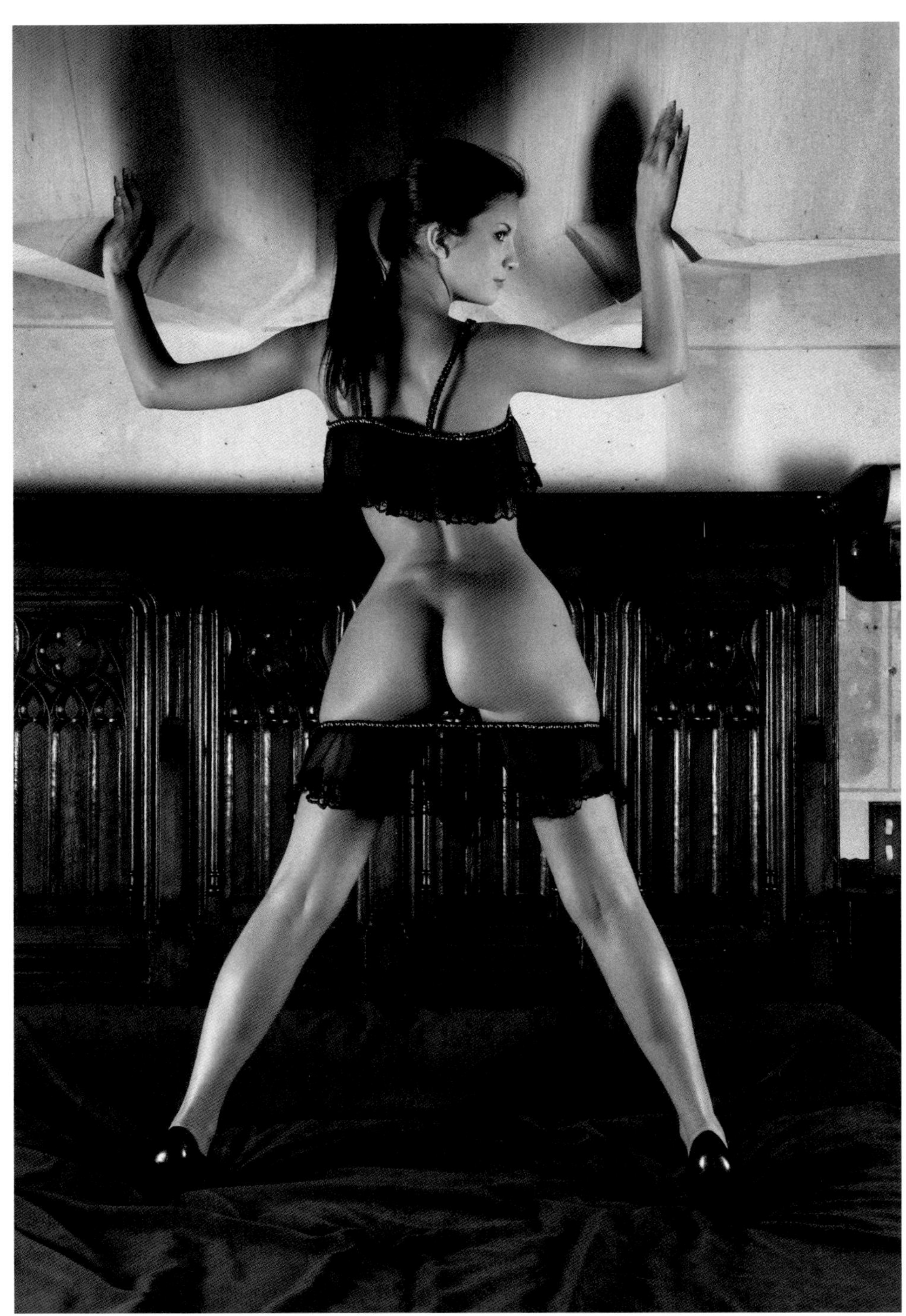

172   Amandine 2005

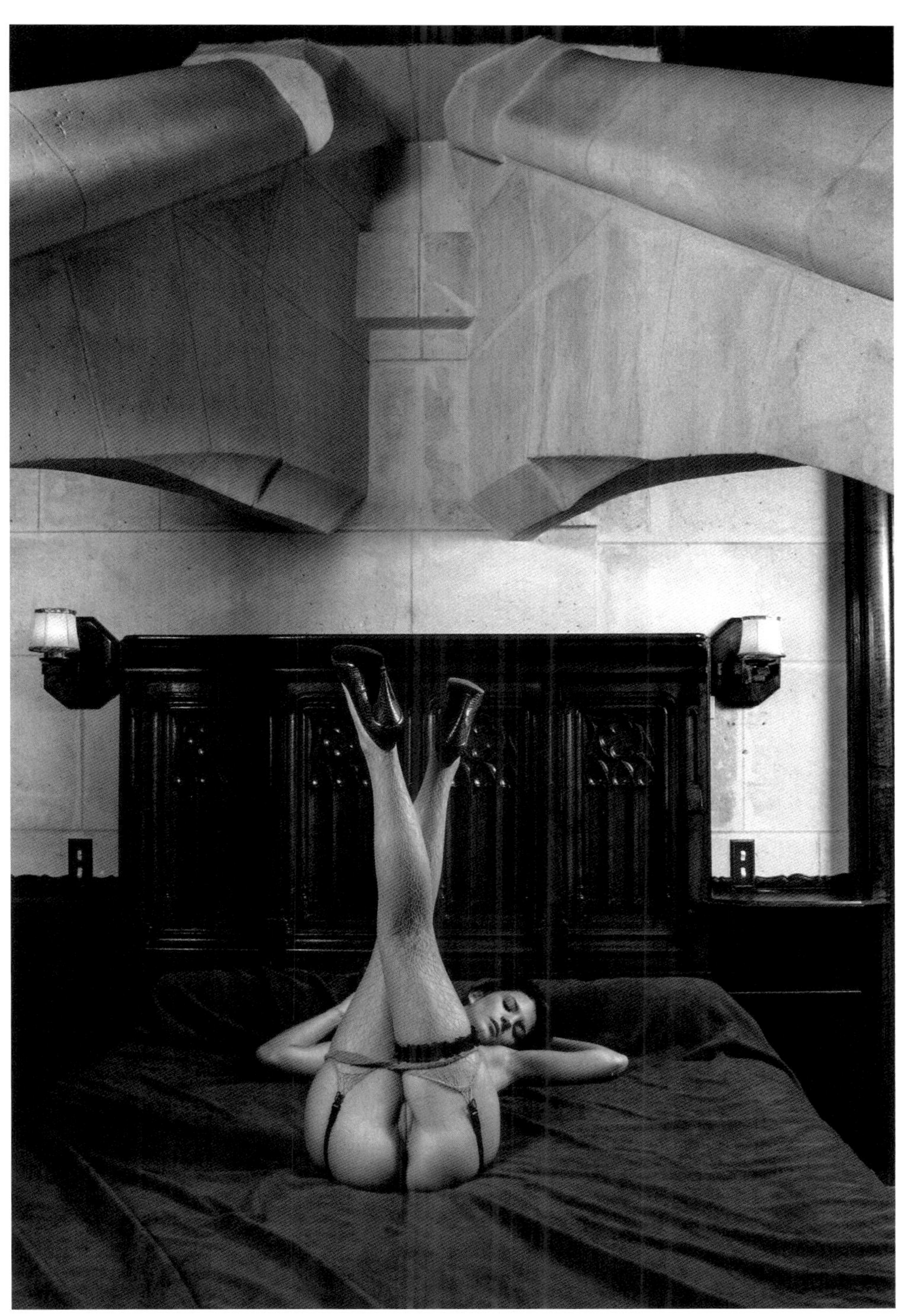

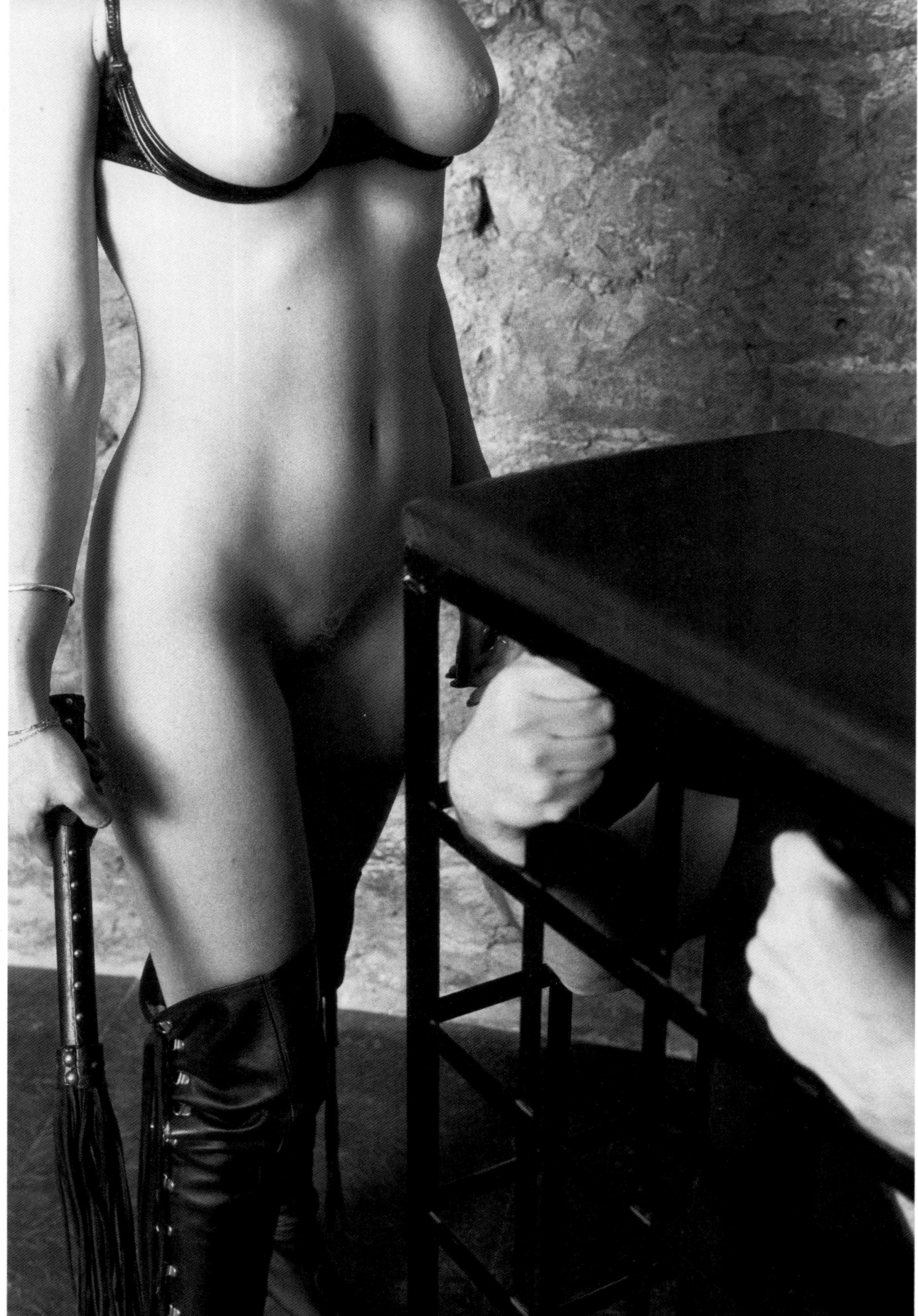

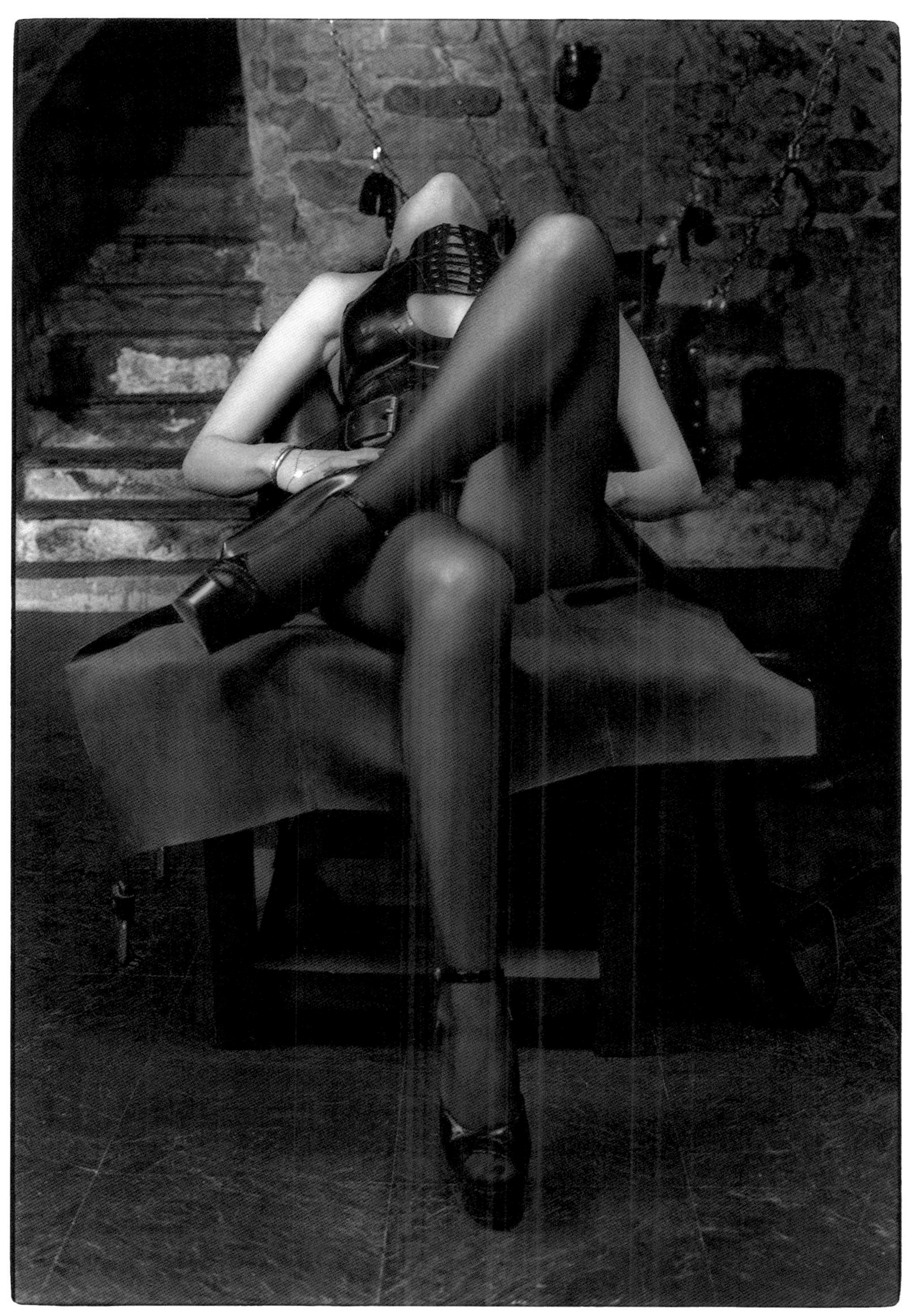

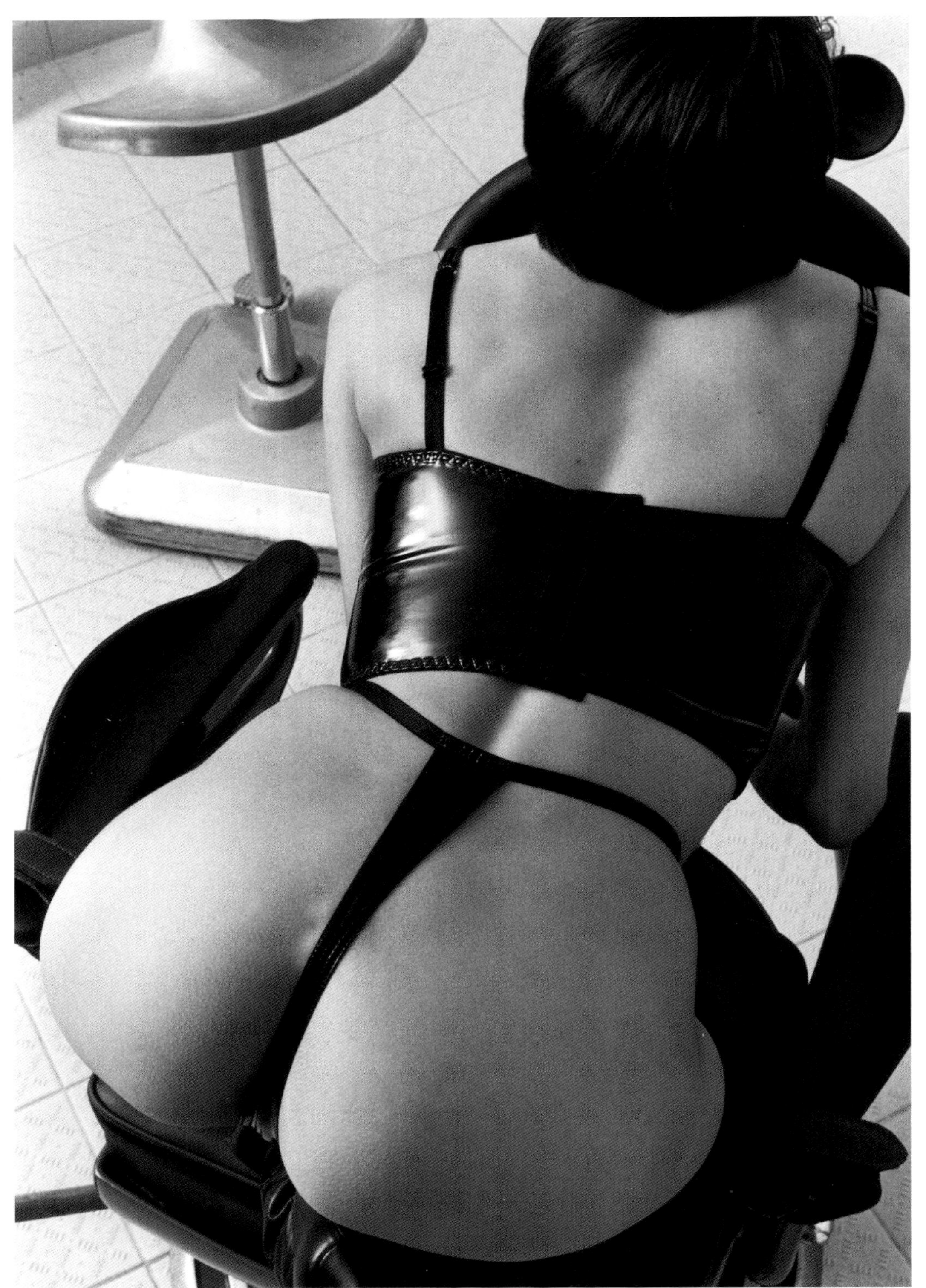

176   Julia 2000   Nicky 2000 →

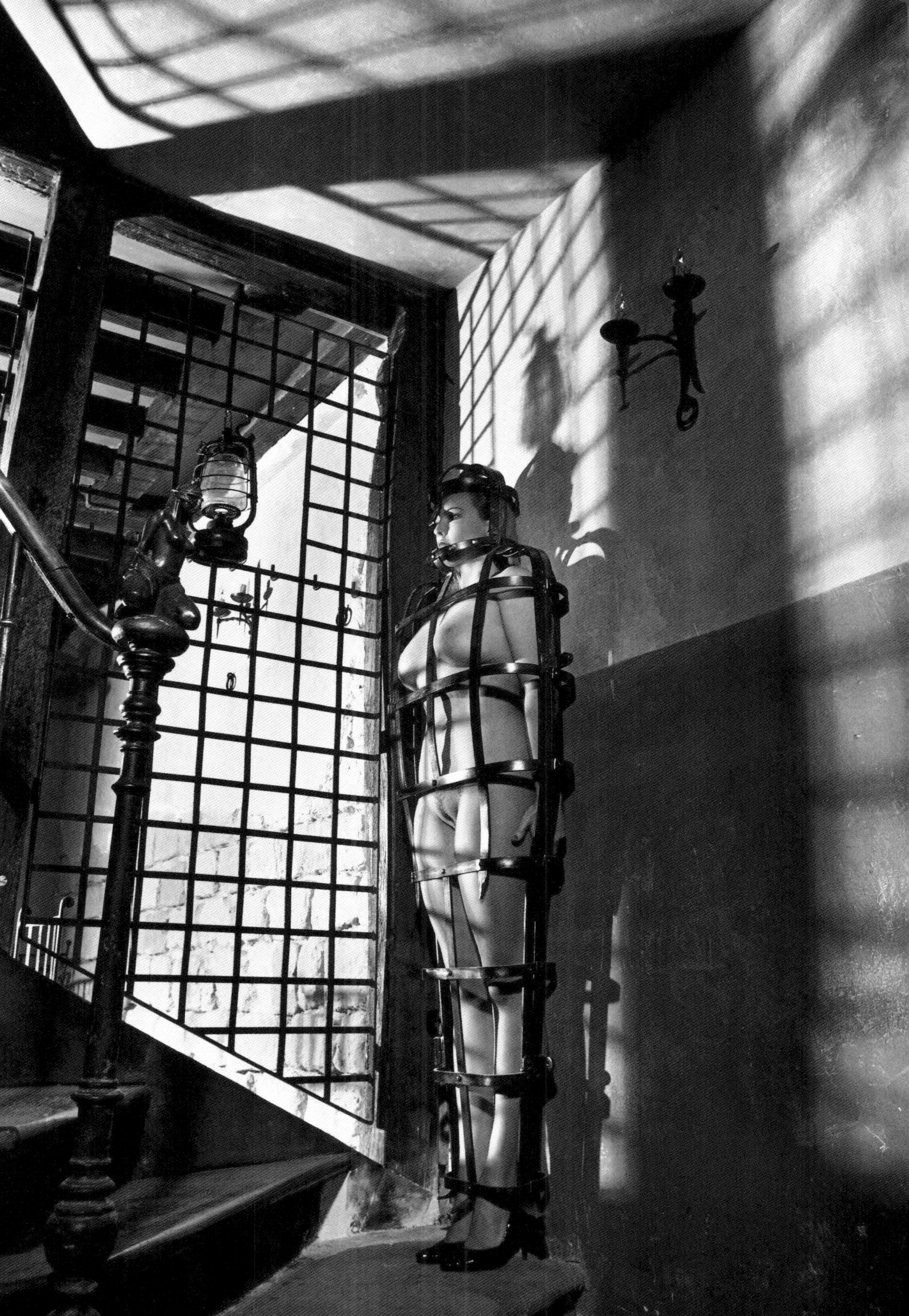

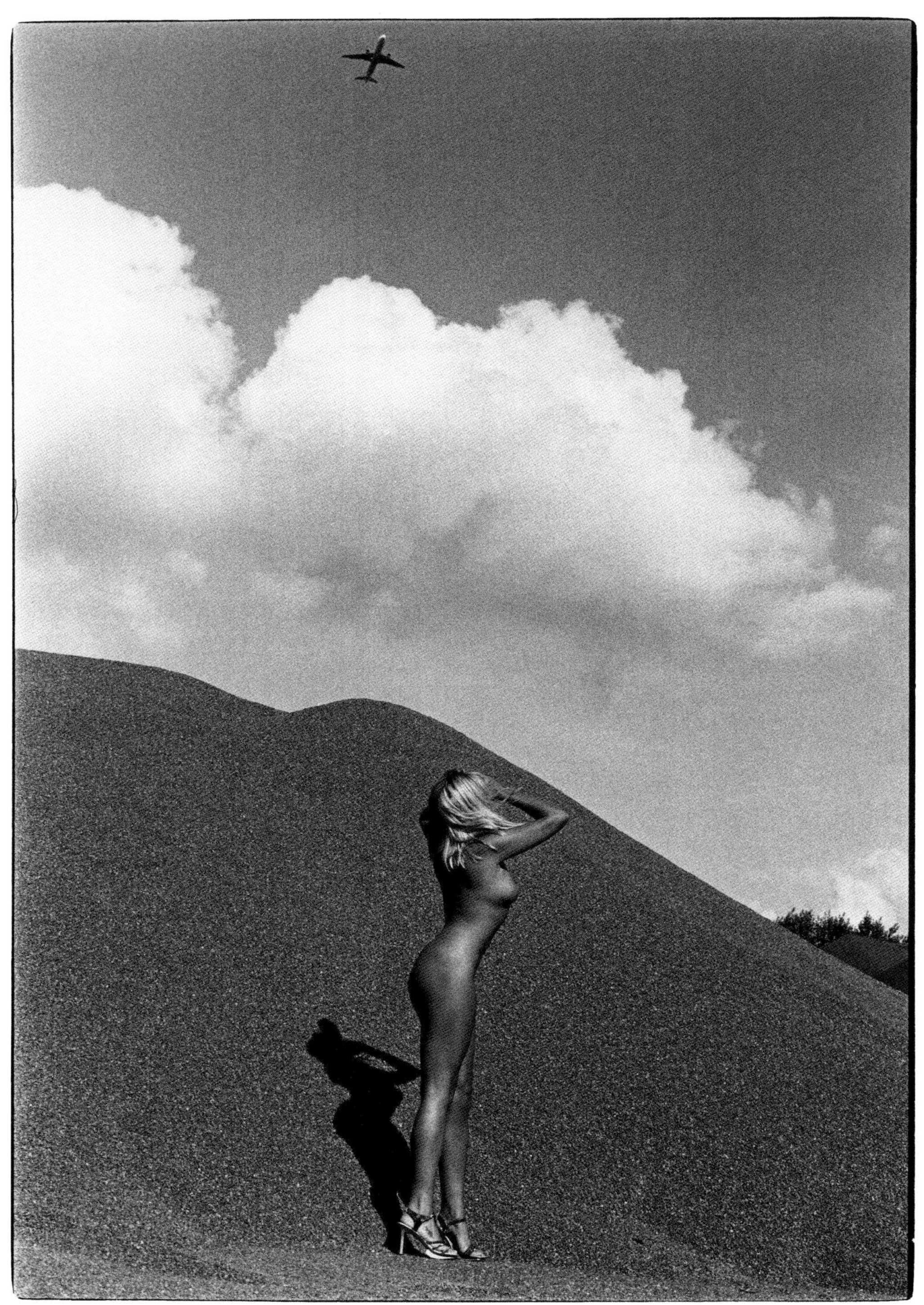

  Anne-Sophie 2000

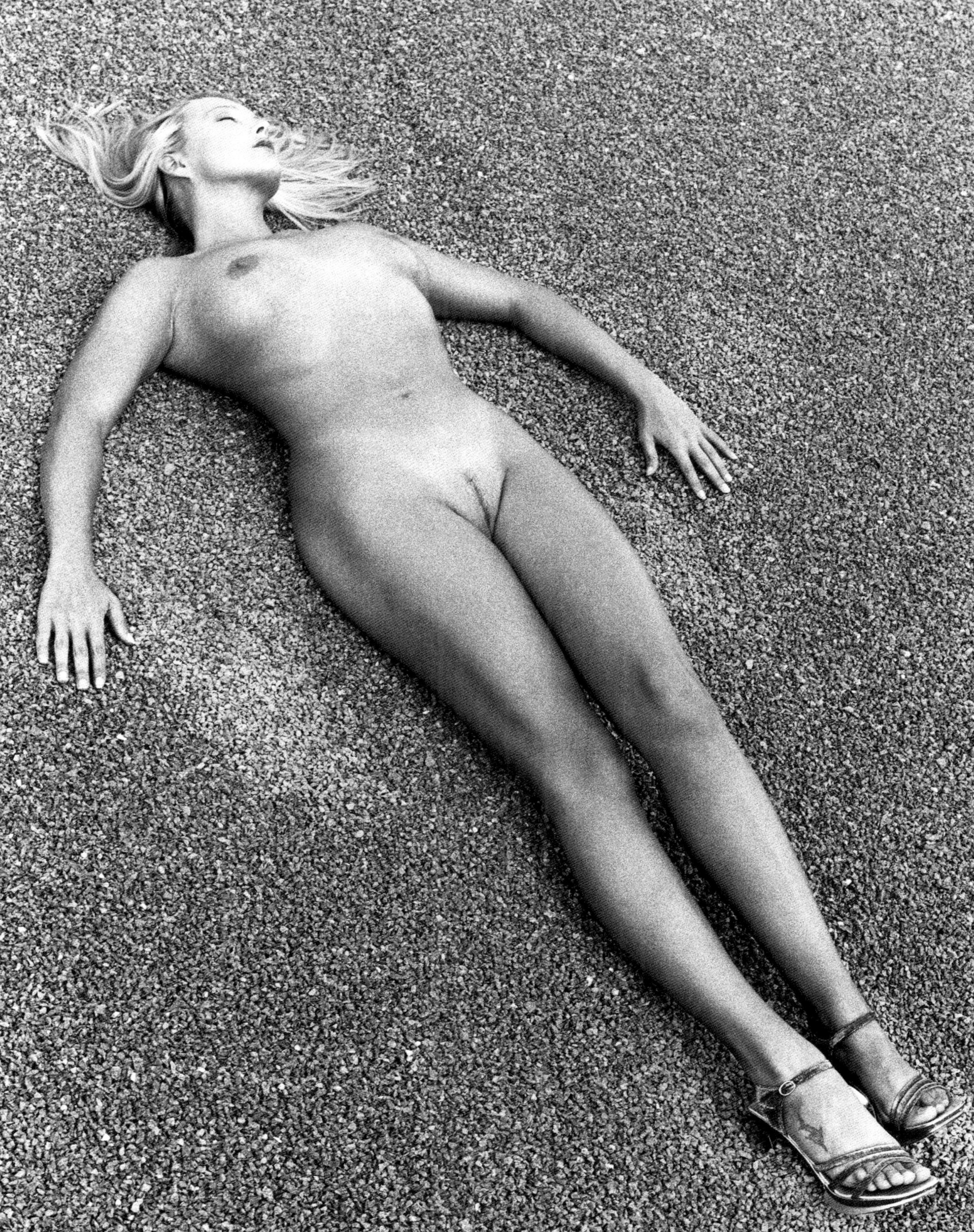

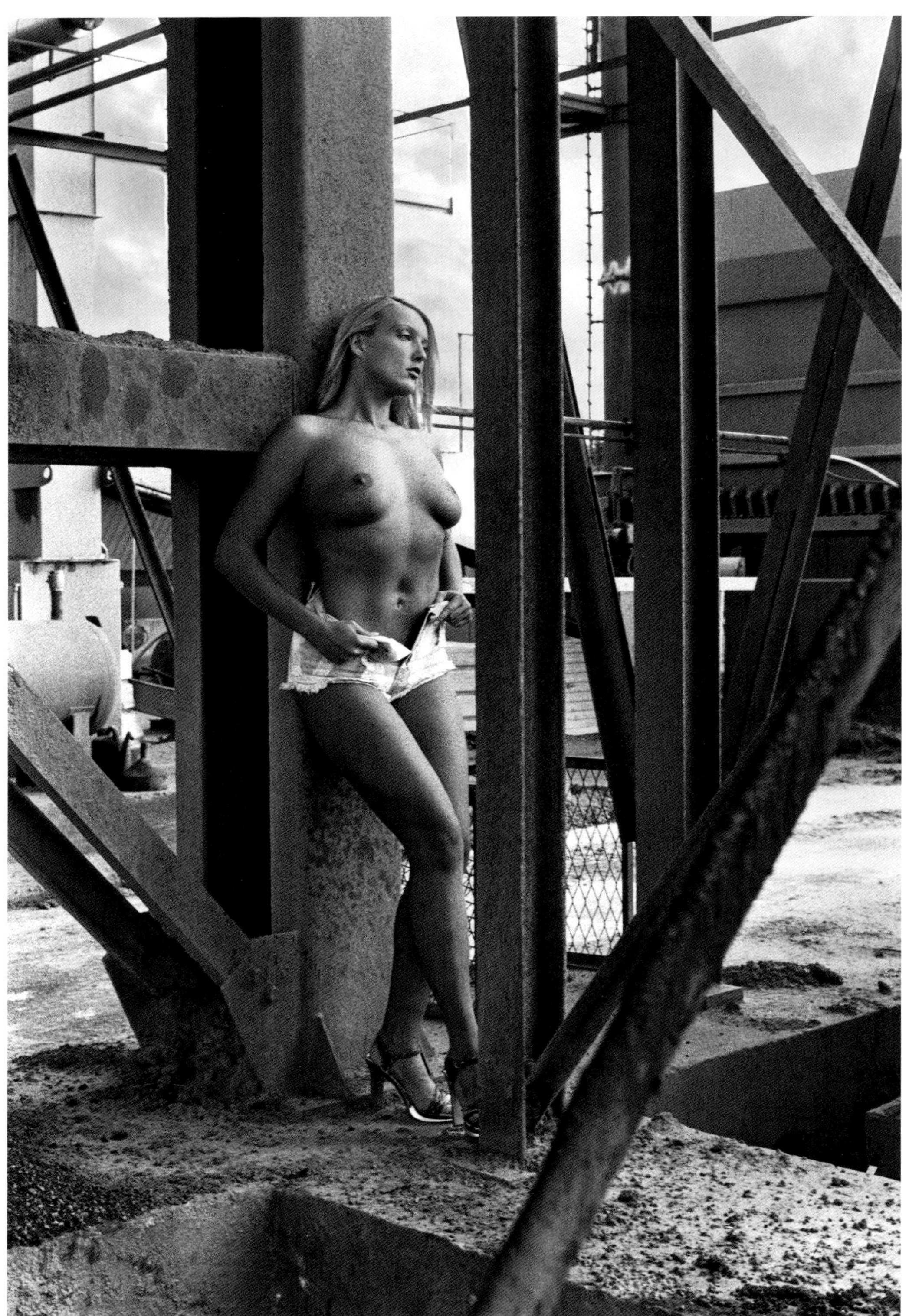

  Anne-Sophie 2000

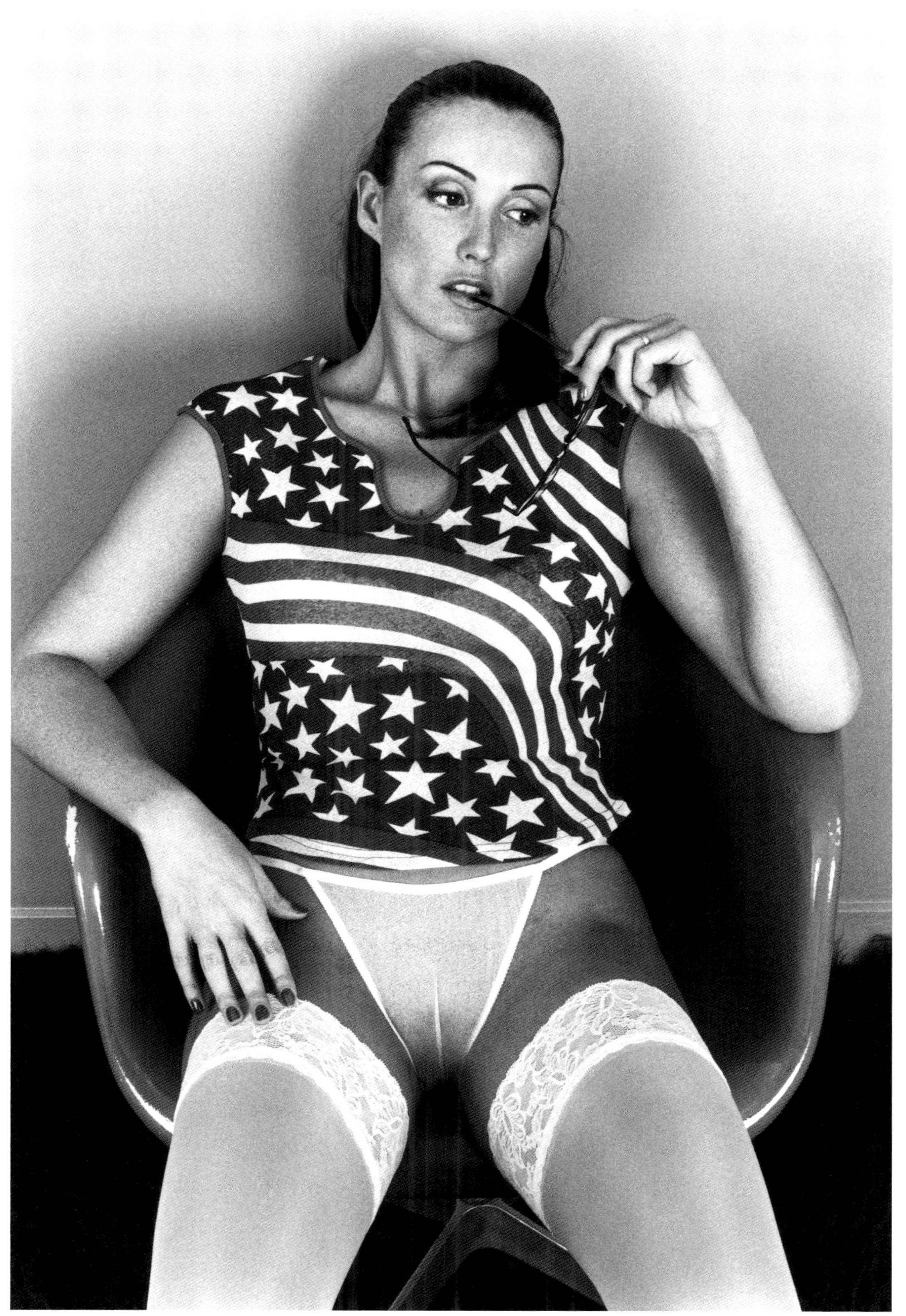

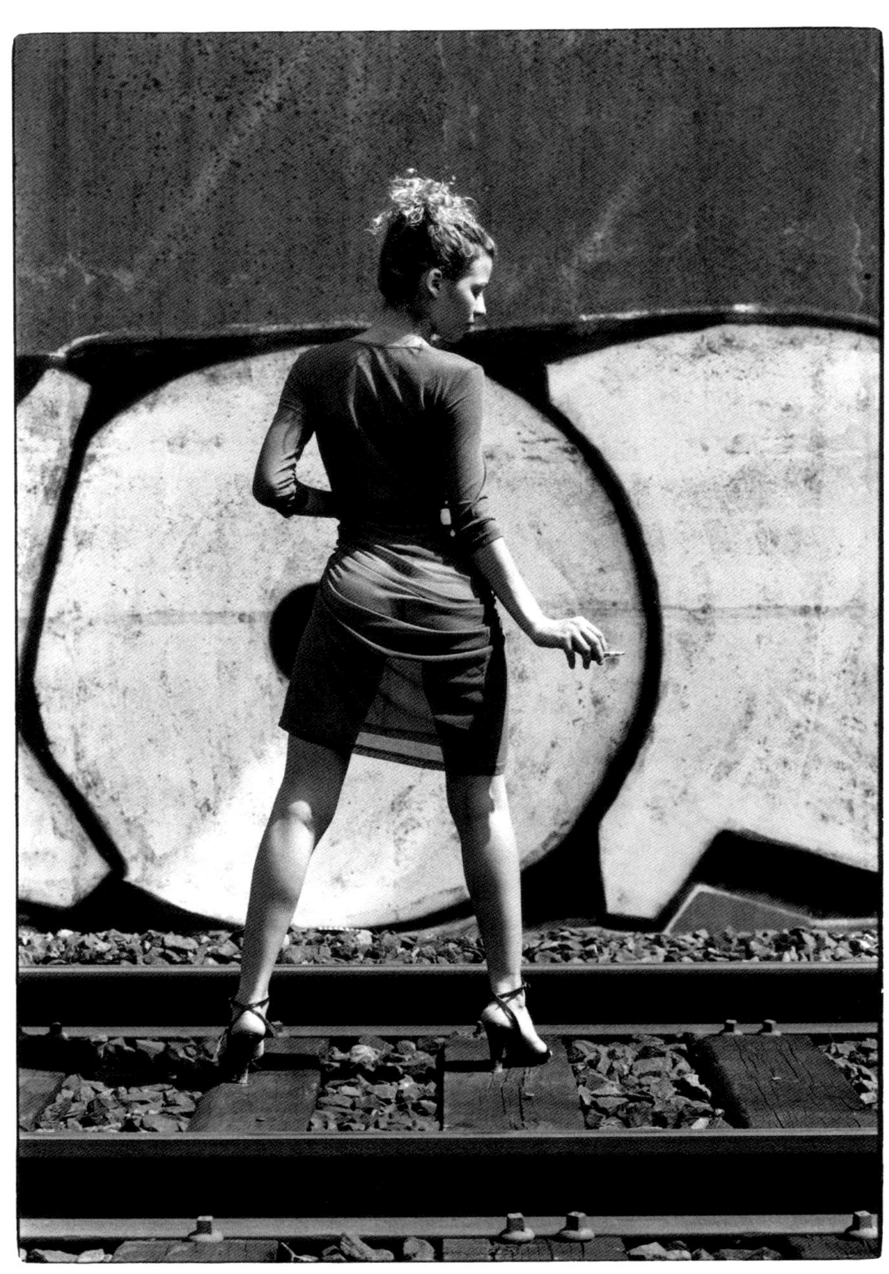

  Nawel 2000

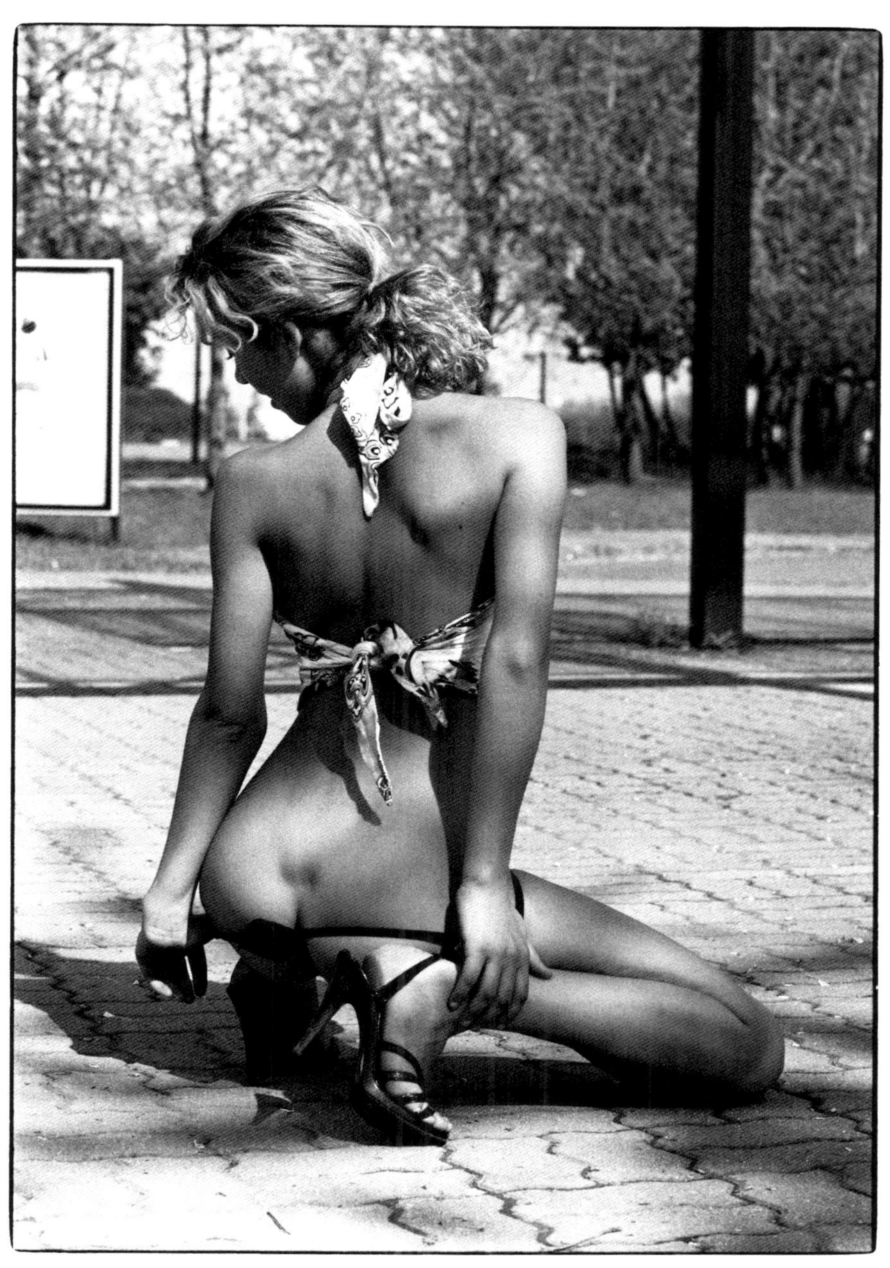

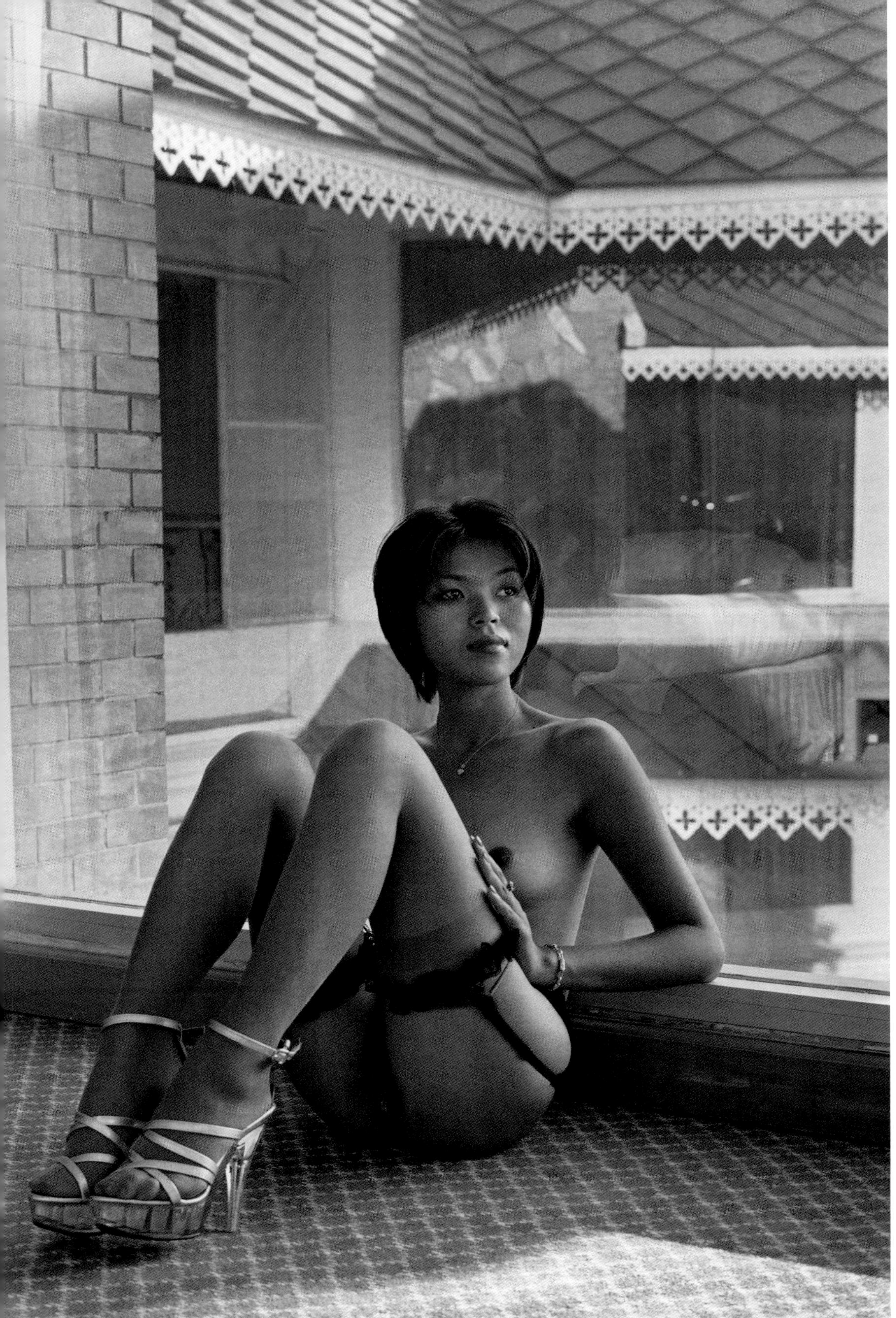

Kim
2000

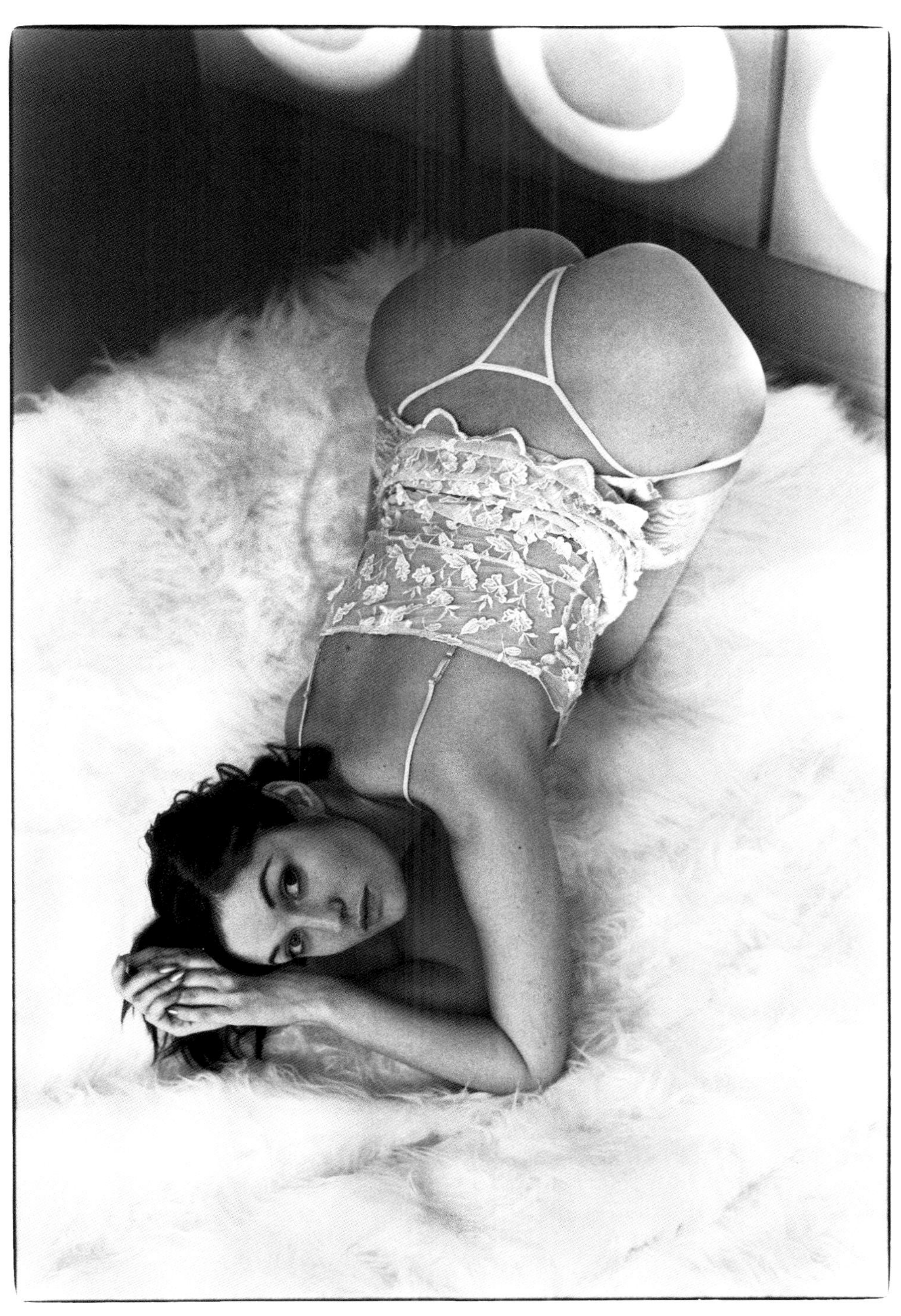

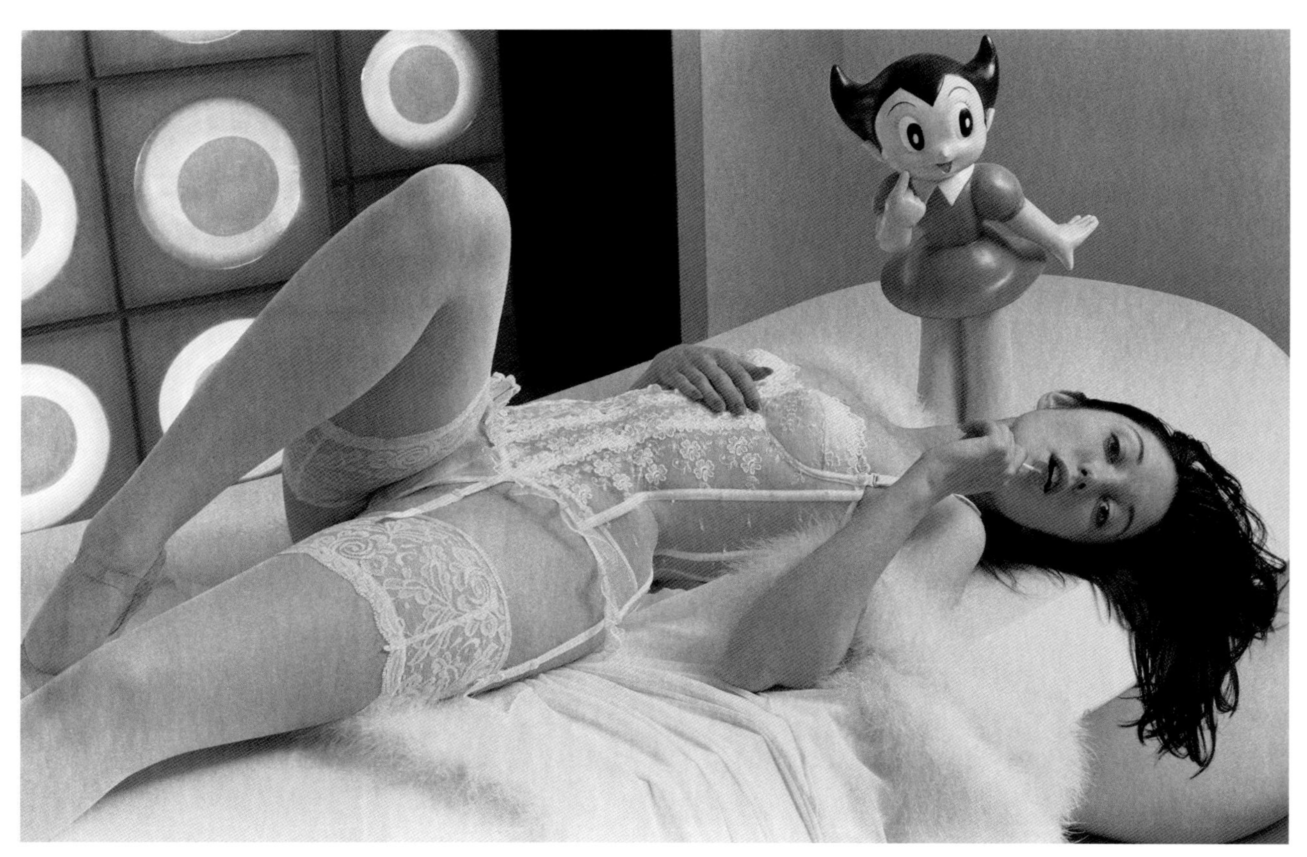

186   Sonrya 2001

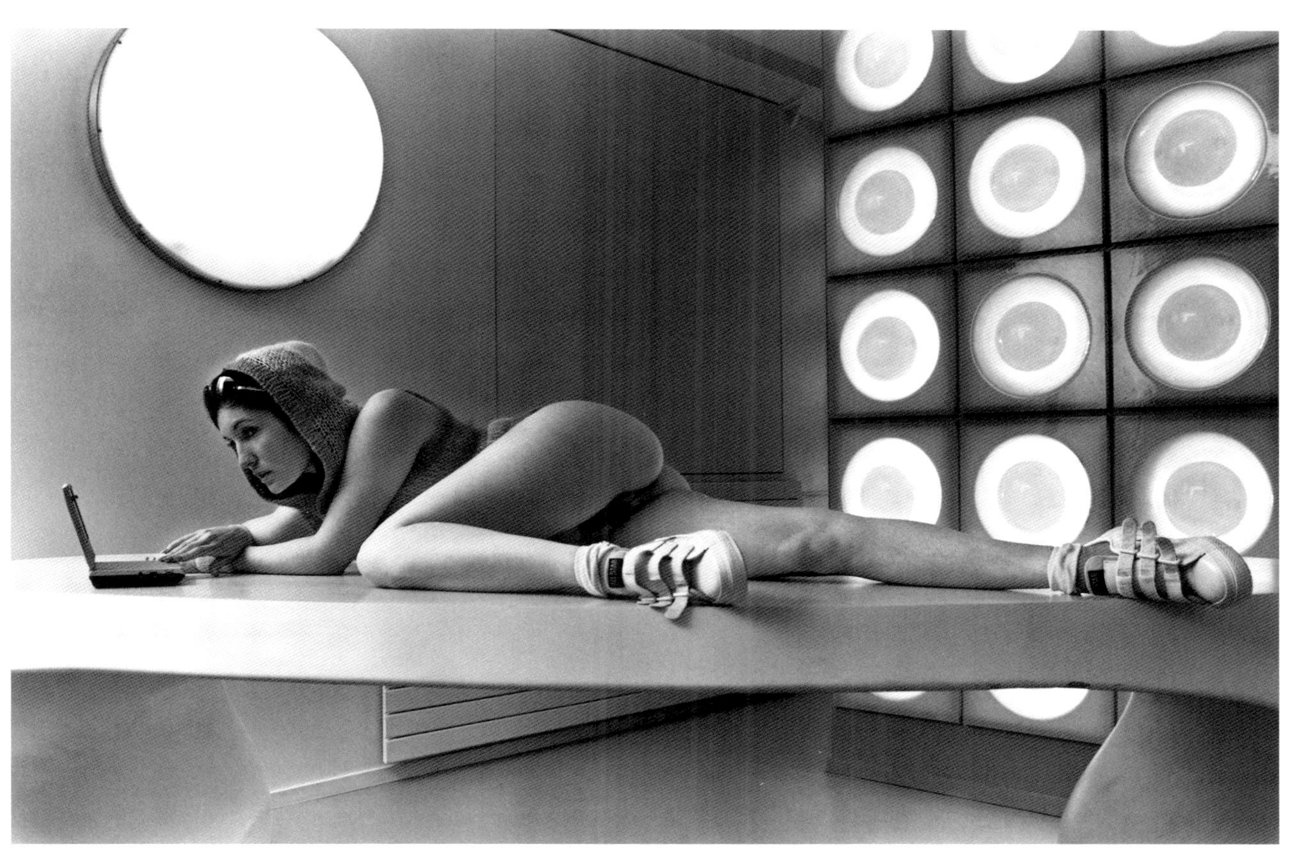

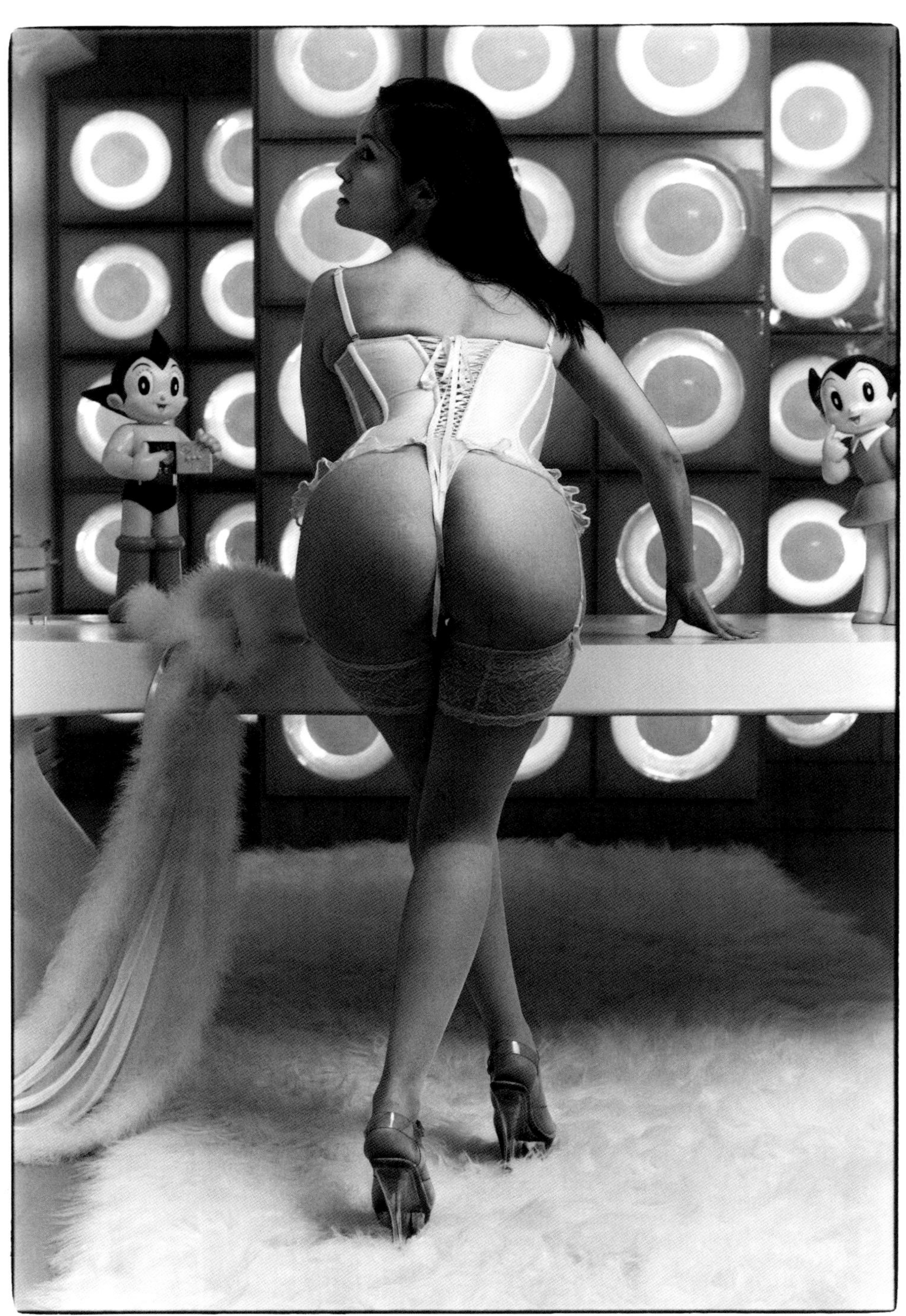

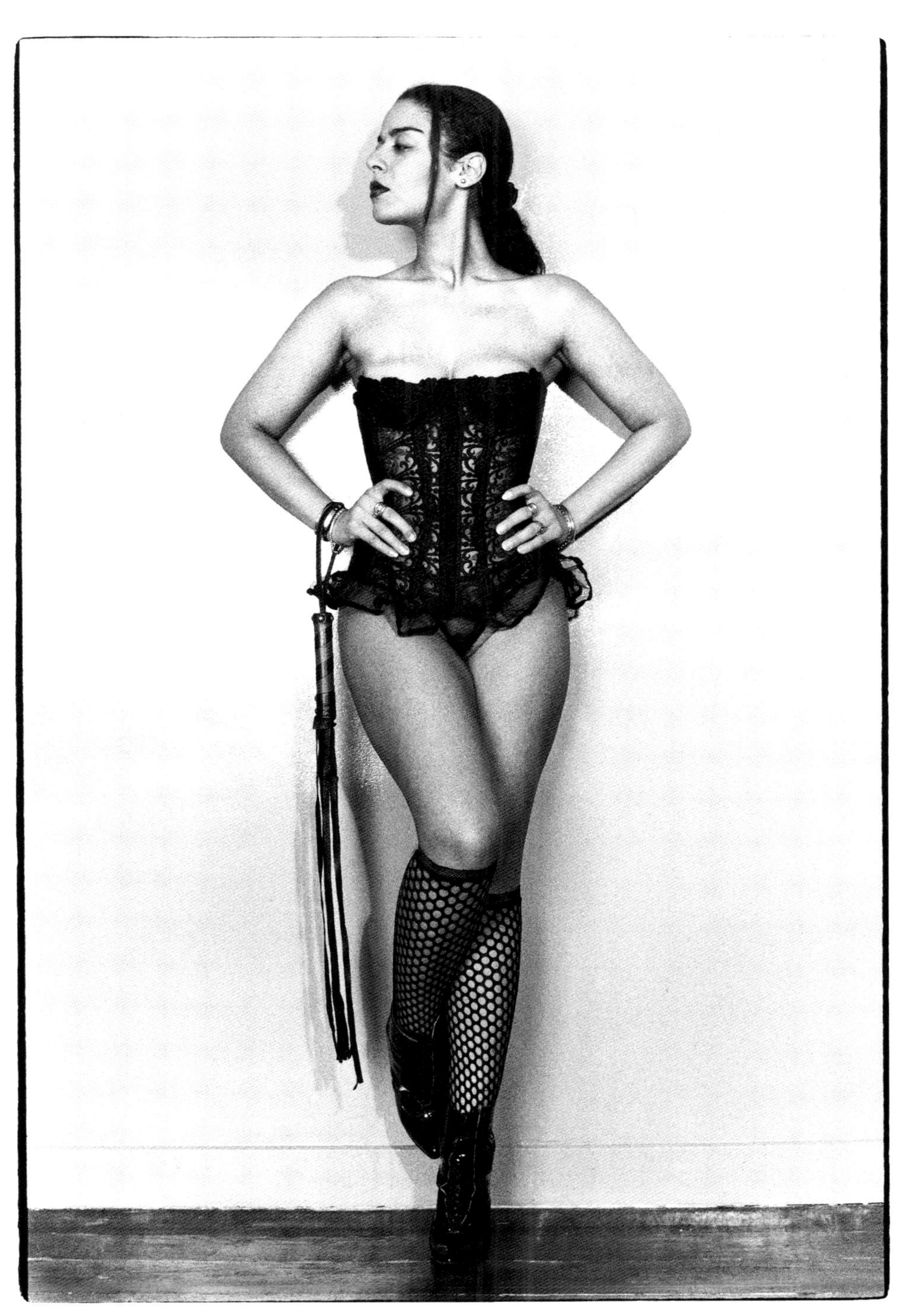

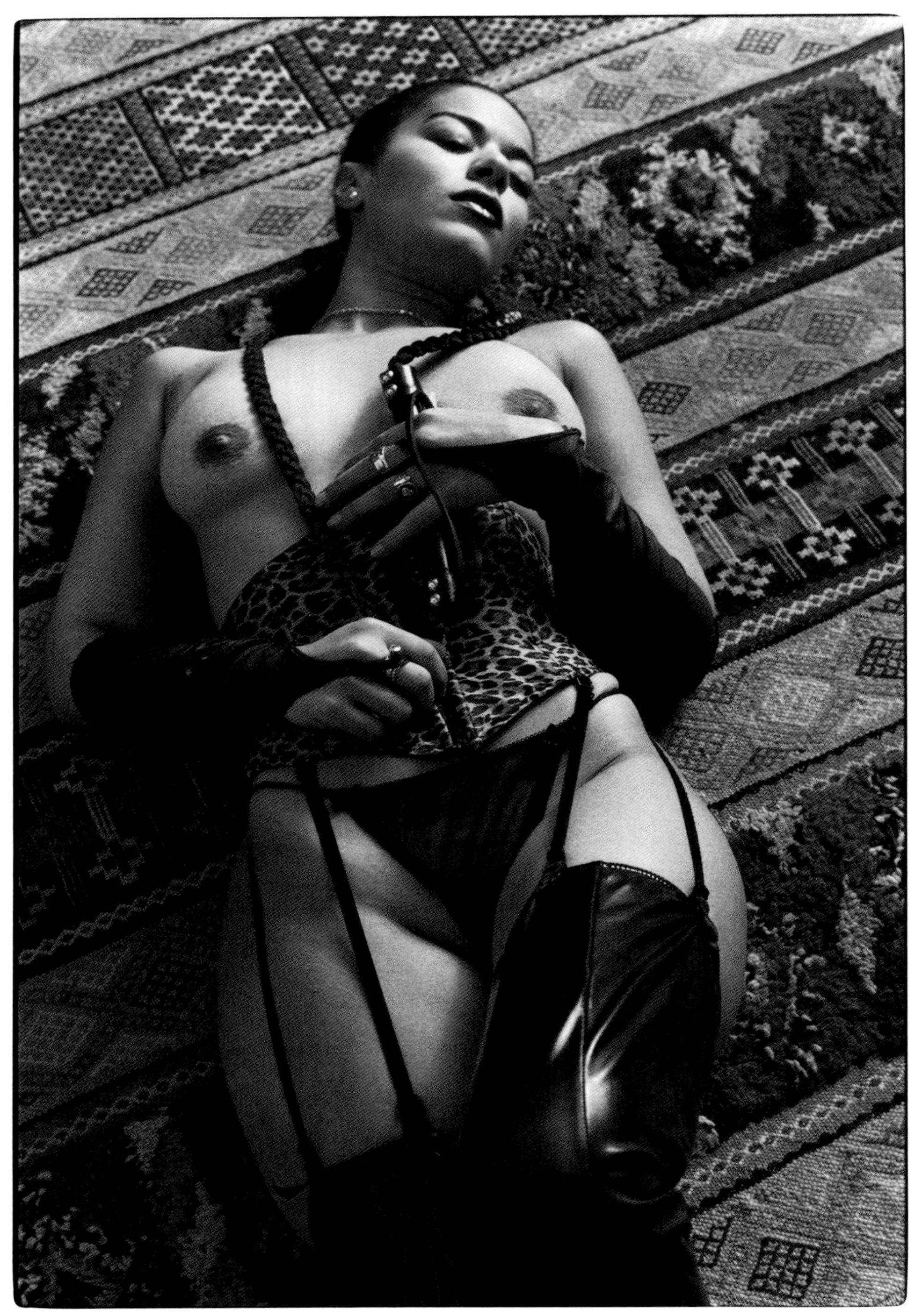

Alice 2001 →

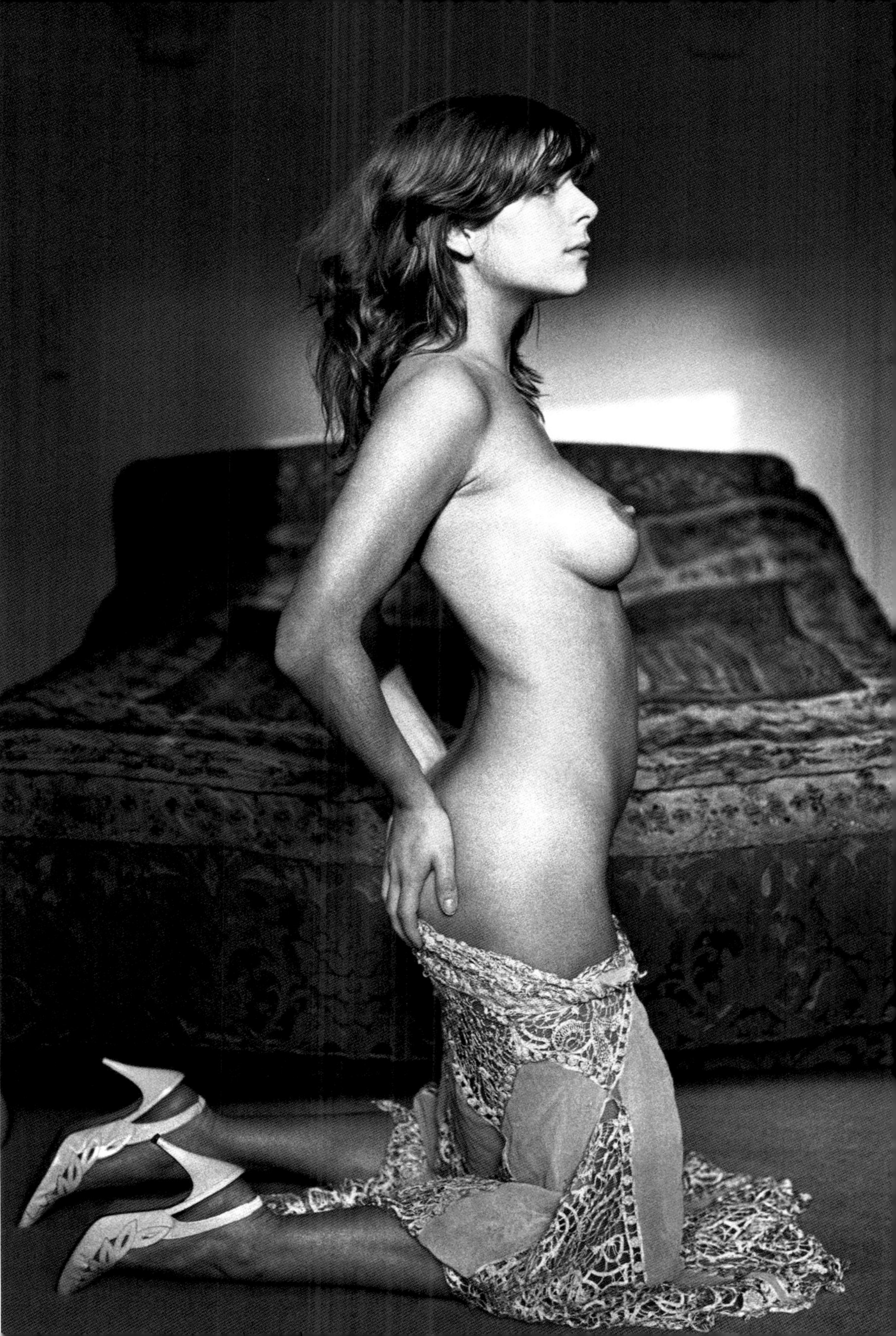

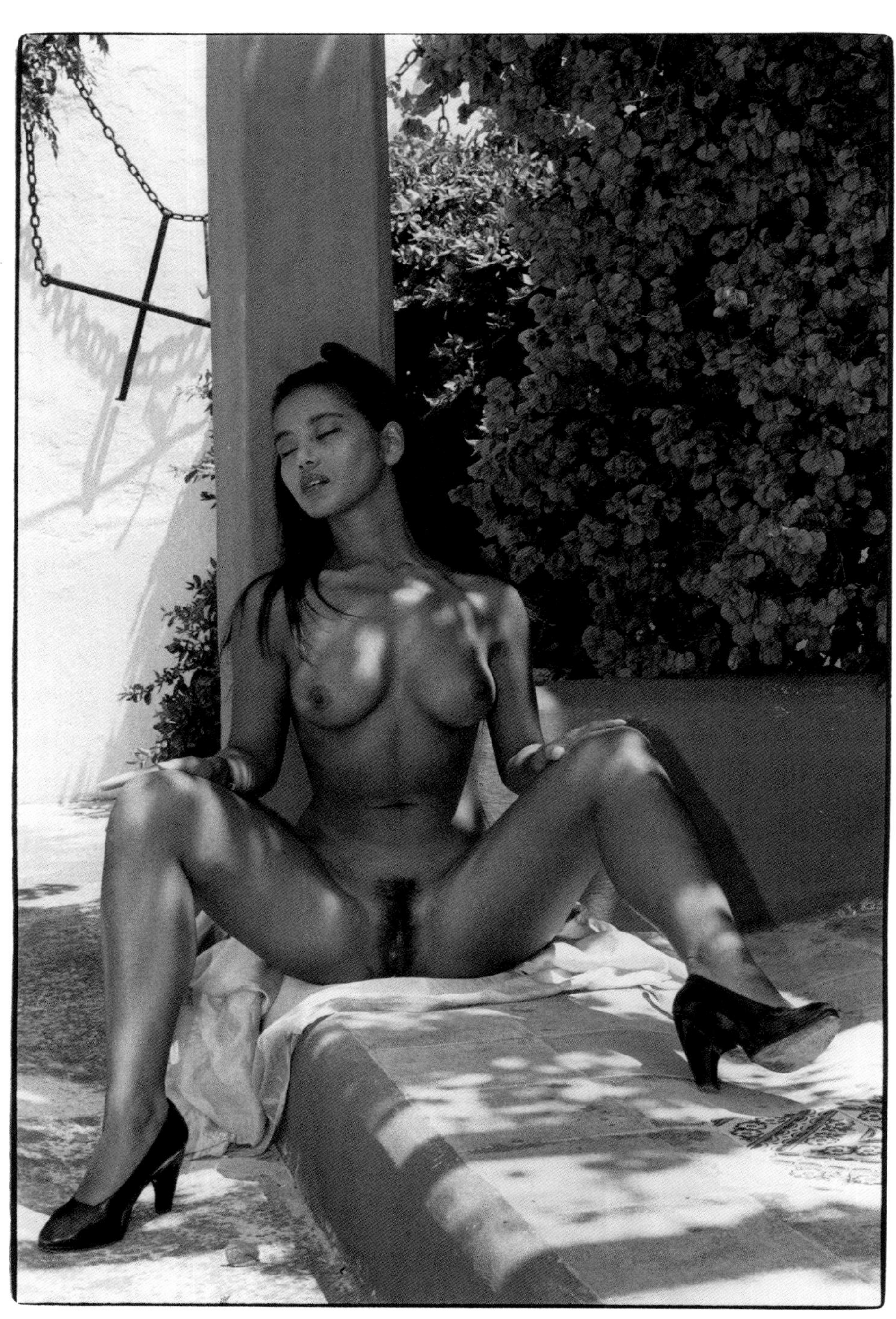

192   Laminah 1992

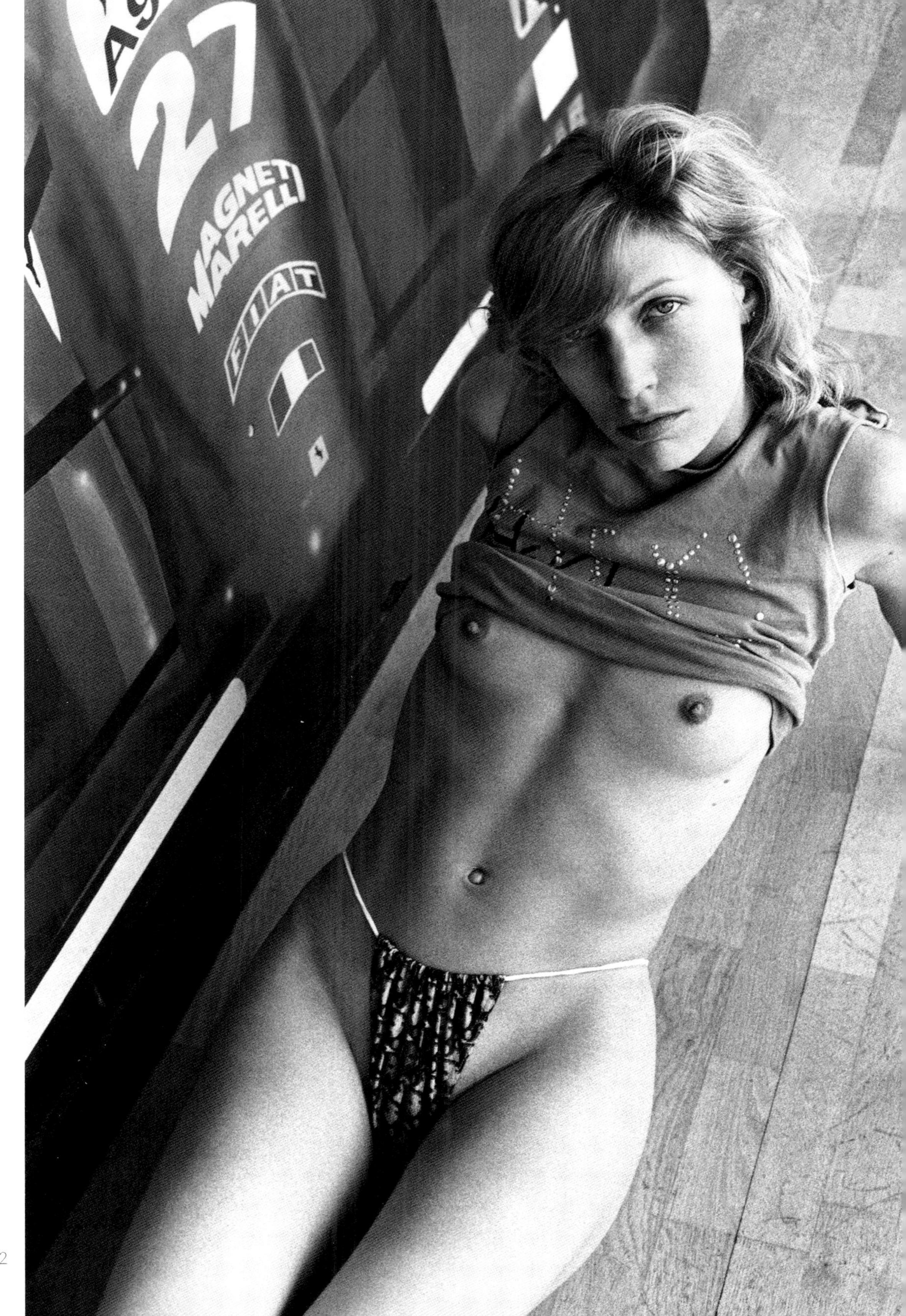

Juliette 2002

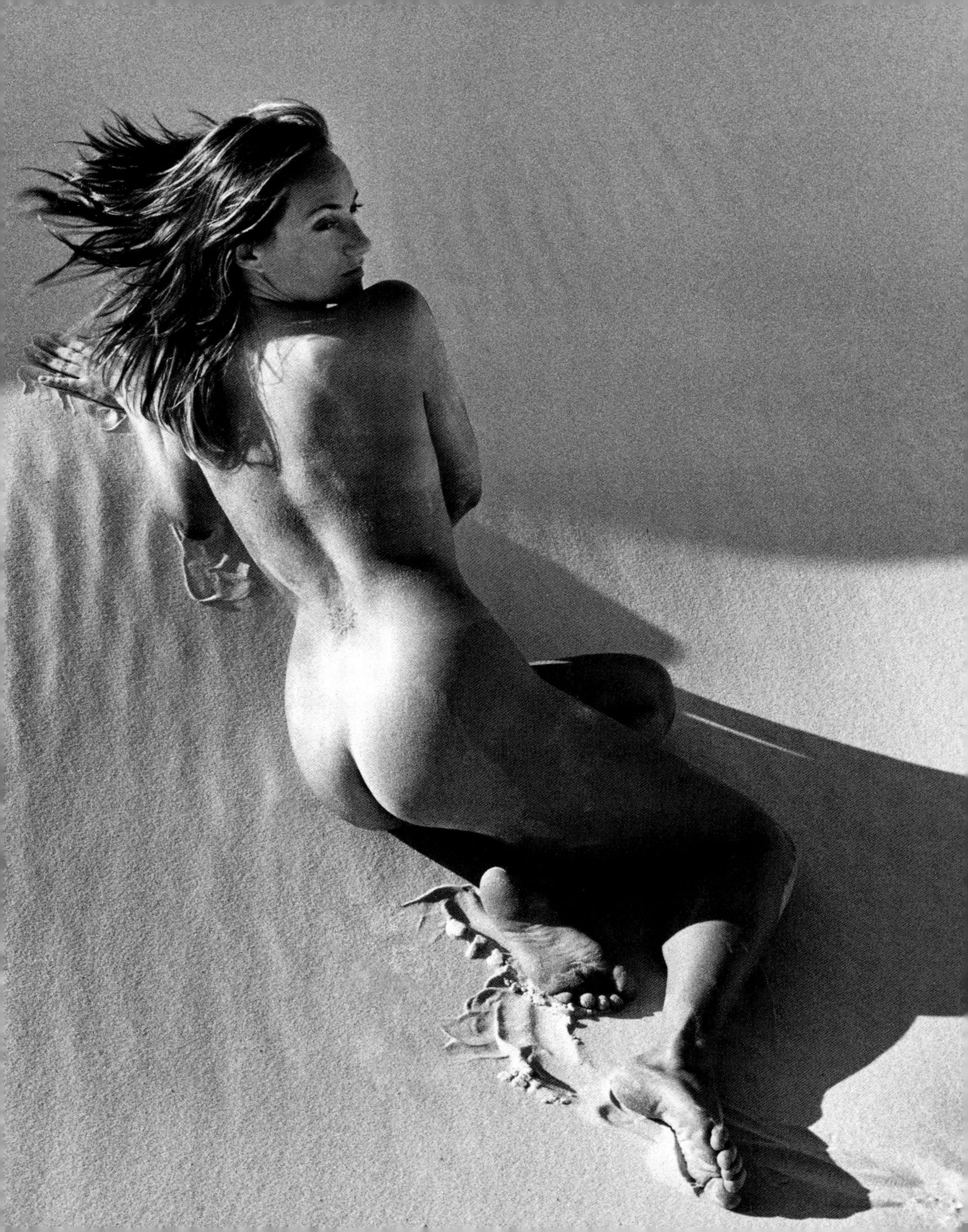

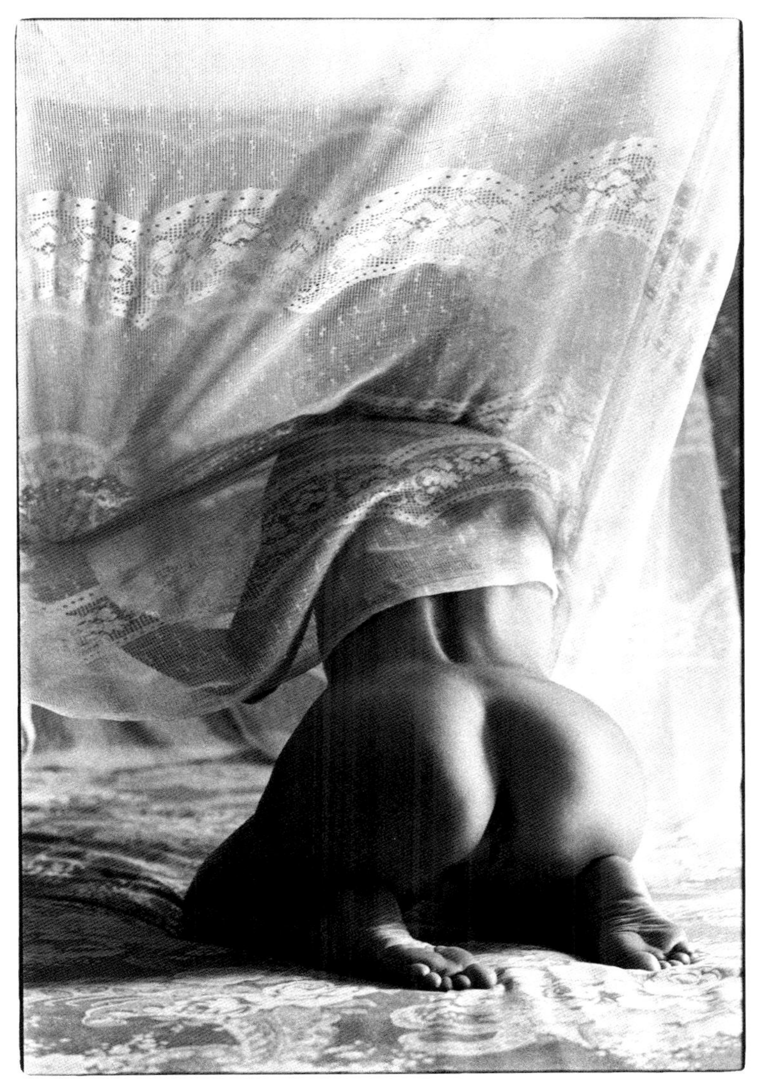

Victoire 2002   195

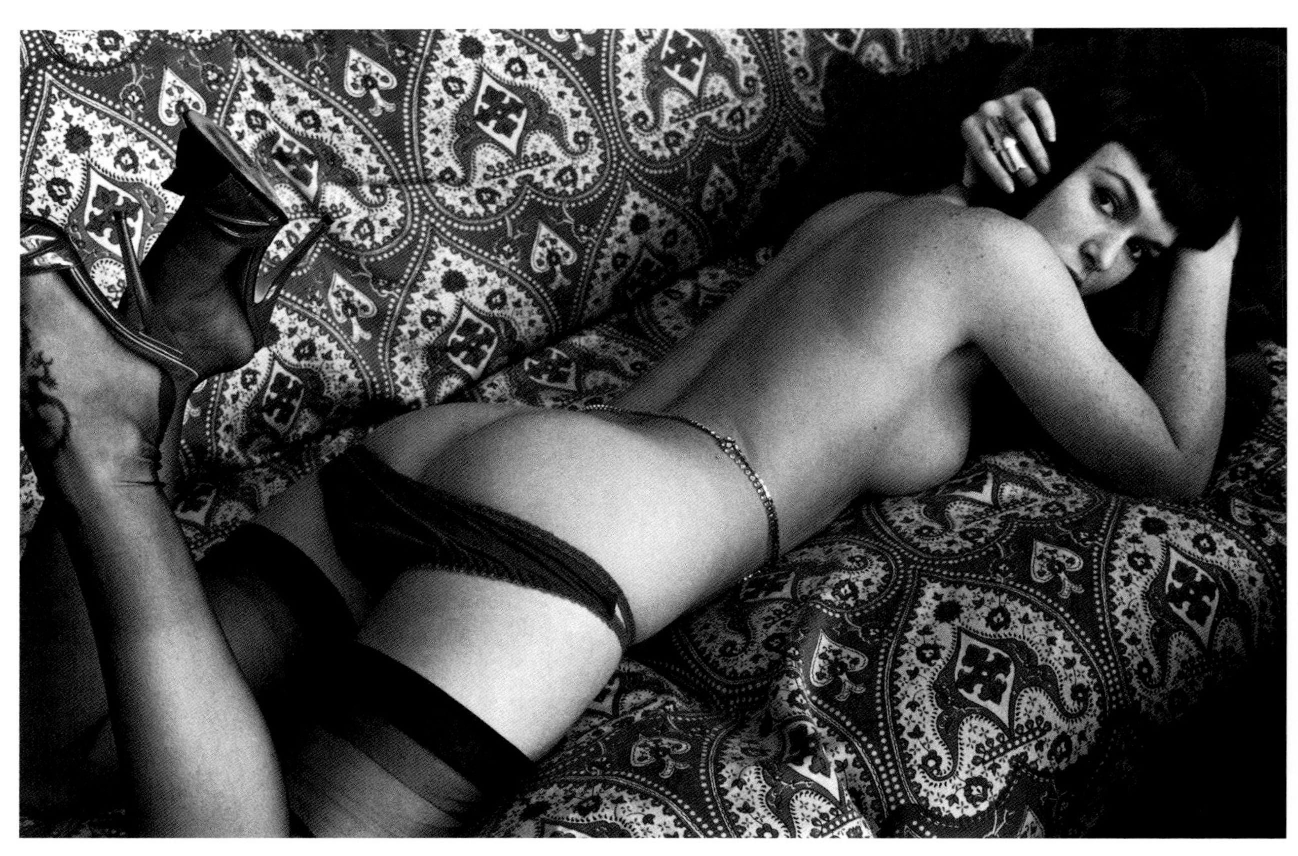

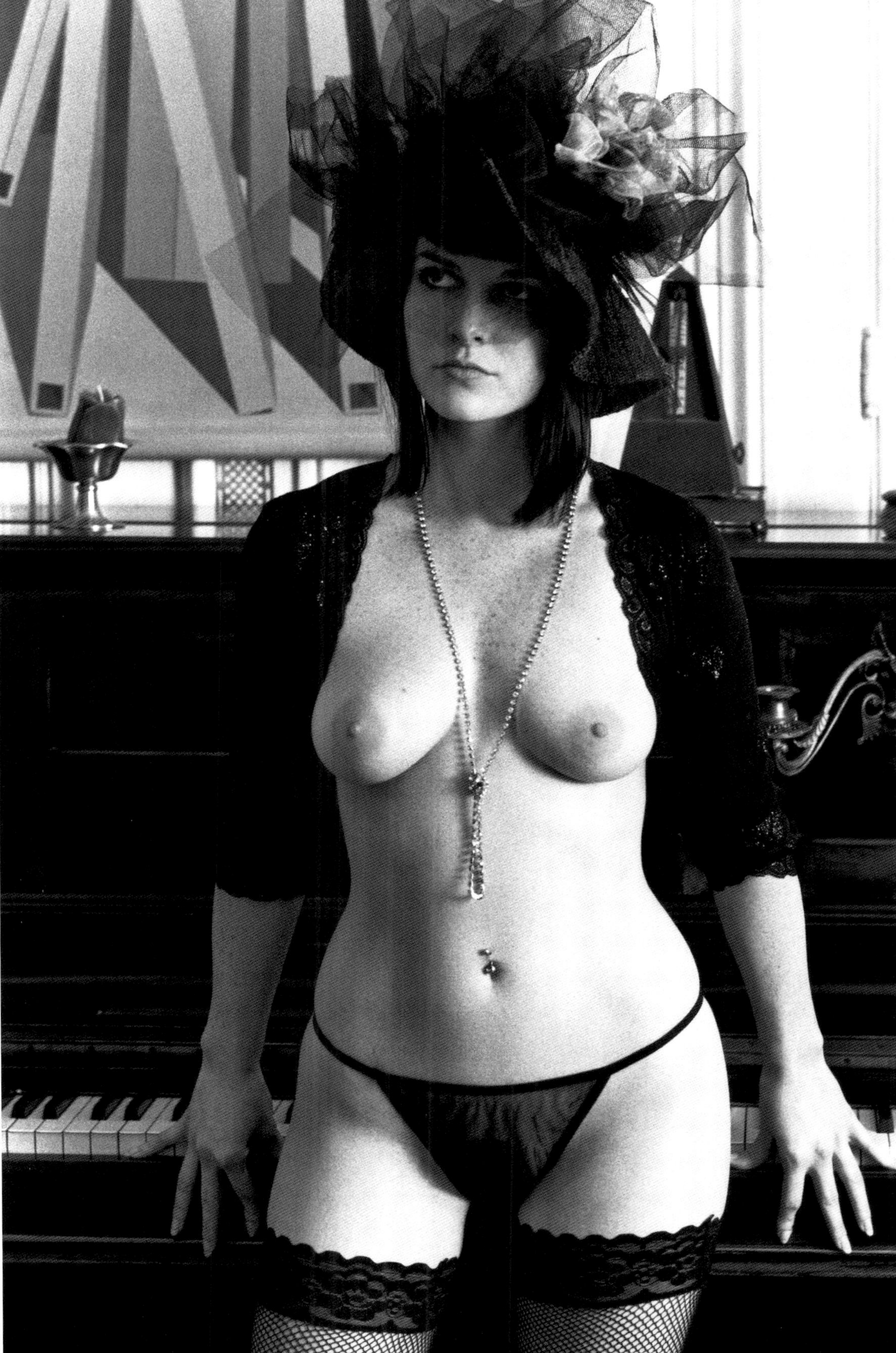

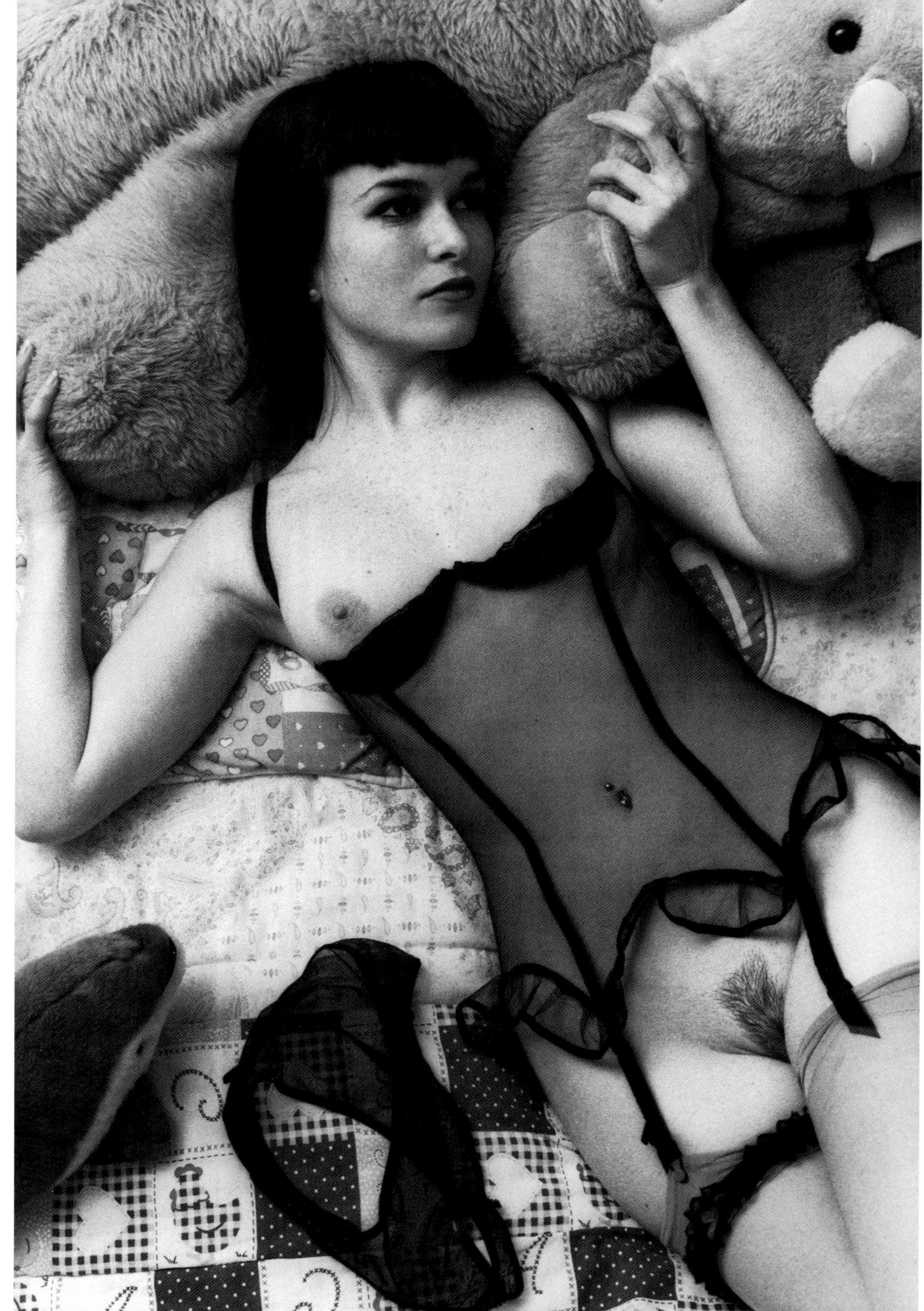

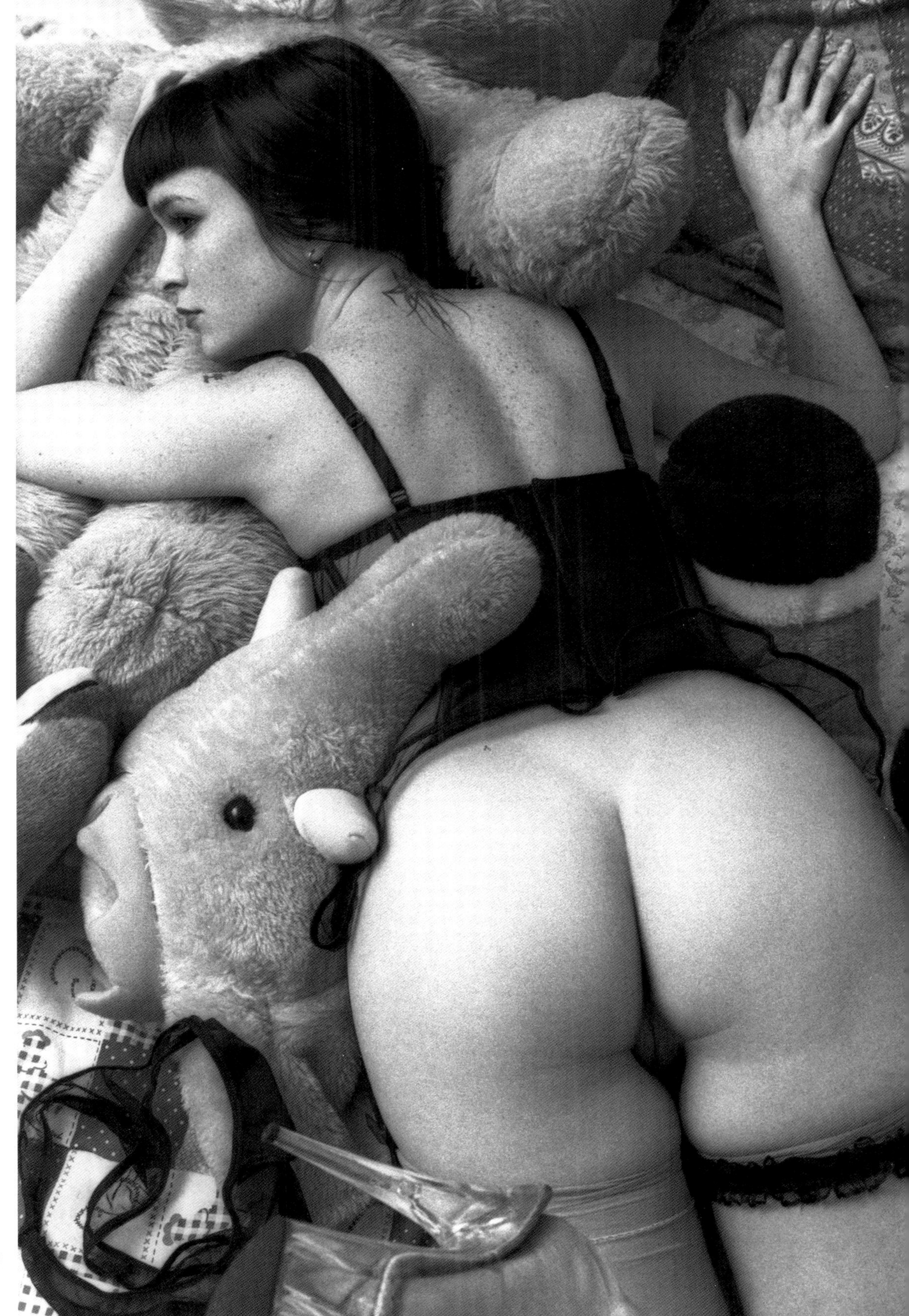

Marie 2002

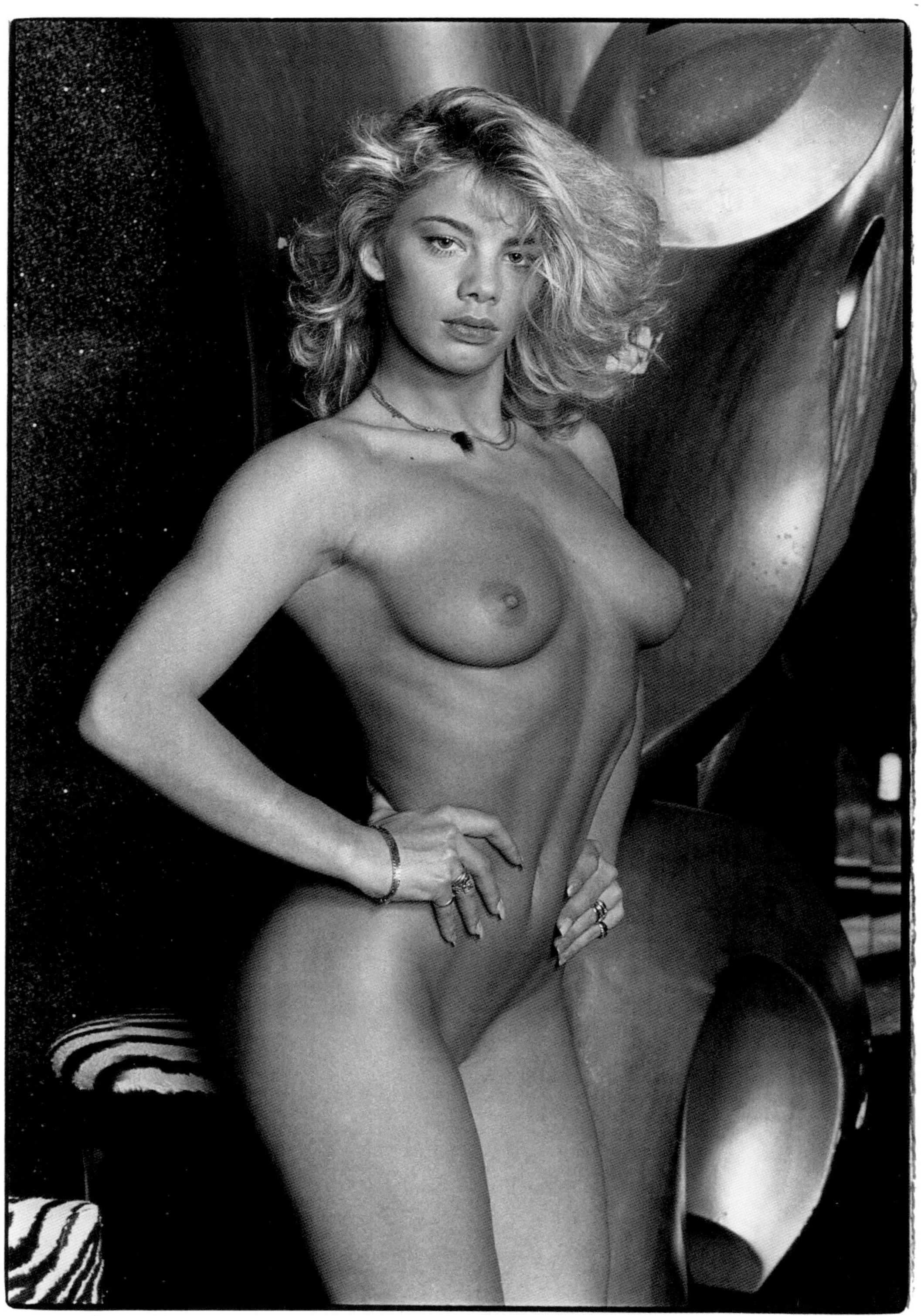